D0904051

REFERENCE DEPARTMENT

LIBRARY

WITHDRAWN

Manuscript Sources

in the

Library of Congress

for research on the

American Revolution

Compiled by

John R. Sellers, Gerard W. Gawalt, Paul H. Smith, and Patricia Molen van Ee

AMERICAN REVOLUTION BICENTENNIAL OFFICE

LIBRARY OF CONGRESS   WASHINGTON   1975

LIBRARY OF CONGRESS CATALOGING IN PUBLICATION DATA

United States. Library of Congress. American Revolution
    Bicentennial Office.
   Manuscript sources in the Library of Congress for
research on the American Revolution.

    Supt. of Docs. no.: LC 1.2: M31/3
    1. United States—History—Revolution, 1775–1783—
Sources—Bibliography. 2. United States. Library of
Congress. I. Sellers, John R. II. Title.
Z1238.U57 1975   016.9733   74–5404
ISBN 0–8444–0122–6

For sale by the Superintendent of Documents, U.S. Government Printing Office
Washington, D.C. 20402—Price $8.70
Stock Number 3003-0011

Z
1238
.U57
1975

Foreword

WELL BEFORE THE ENACTMENT on July 4, 1966, of Public Law 89-491, establishing a national American Revolution Bicentennial Commission, the Library of Congress began considering how it could contribute to the celebration of the Bicentennial of the American Revolution. In 1968 Congress approved the Library's plans for a phased Bicentennial program and subsequently authorized the addition to the Library's staff of several historians, all specialists in early American history.

The Bicentennial program took its theme "Liberty and Learning" from James Madison, who asked: "What spectacle can be more edifying or more seasonable, than that of Liberty & Learning, each leaning on the other for their mutual and surest support?" From the inception of the program, the Library placed the highest priority on the publication of a guide to its manuscripts of the Revolutionary period, a priority justified by its position as one of the world's principal repositories of original source material on the American Revolution. The present volume, prepared by the staff of the Library's American Revolution Bicentennial Office in cooperation with the staffs of the Manuscript Division and the Publications Office, discharges the task the Library set for itself. We hope that it will be useful to all students of the American Revolution.

We also hope that the publication of *Manuscript Sources* will encourage others to prepare similar guides to the Revolutionary period manuscripts in government and private repositories. So important did this objective seem to the 10 distinguished historians who then composed the Advisory Committee on the Library's American Revolution Bicentennial Program that they resolved on January 12, 1970, to urge the American Revolution Bicentennial Commission "to recommend the preparation in each of the several states of a comprehensive guide to manuscript materials in the libraries, historical societies, archives, and government offices of that state, to be compiled according to scholarly standards for identifying and describing such items and to be published in a standard format." This objective was endorsed by the American Revolution Bicentennial Commission when it approved the Library's plans for its commemoration of the Bicentennial of the American Revolution. There is still time for such guides to be undertaken.

This volume had its beginnings under Robert A. Rutland and was brought to completion under the direction of James H. Hutson, who succeeded him as Coordinator of the Library's American Revolution Bicentennial Program. It is also a pleasure to recognize the contribution of Prof. Carl Anthon of American University, who described the German-language materials.

Elizabeth Hamer Kegan
Assistant Librarian of Congress

YOUNGSTOWN STATE UNIVERSITY
LIBRARY
333517

YOUNGSTOWN STATE UNIVERSITY
LIBRARY

Contents

Introduction

REVOLUTIONS ARE RADICAL and pervasive changes in the social and political structure of society; it is impossible to determine when such changes begin and end, if, indeed, they ever end. There are those who claim that the American Revolution began with the landing of Englishmen at Jamestown and Plymouth and those who maintain that its effects are still being felt today. The present volume takes the view to which most historians, primarily as a matter of convenience, have long subscribed, that the period of the American Revolution covers the years from 1763 to 1789. The dates are admittedly arbitrary, but it should be kept in mind that 1763, the year that marked the end of the French empire in North America, is the year most authorities on the Revolution point to for the first tangible evidence of the developing Anglo-American conflict, while 1789 saw the end of experimentation in government with the inauguration of George Washington as President under the newly adopted Constitution.

In the preparation of this guide virtually every collection in the Library's Manuscript Division, Rare Book Division, and Law Library was surveyed for documents from the Revolutionary era. Initially, there was some question as to whether photostats, transcripts, enlargement prints, and microfilm would be included. The issue was decided in the affirmative, the justification being that since these materials are in the Library for the researcher to use, they should be described for him. In each instance, however, the institution holding the original documents has been cited. With regard to documents reproduced from foreign archives, the Library would have been negligent not to include such materials both because of their inaccessibility to the average researcher and because, in some cases, the Library of Congress is the only institution authorized to maintain these collections.

The format for the guide has been kept as simple as possible. Its two basic divisions, Domestic Collections and Foreign Reproductions, are arranged alphabetically. Within the Domestic Collections are the subdivisions Account Books, Journals and Diaries, Miscellaneous Manuscripts, and Orderly Books, each alphabetized independently. Individual collections appear by the name or title under which they are catalogued. Beneath the collection name the searcher will find the number of volumes, boxes, or folders that make up the collection, plus the outside dates of the material contained therein. On the same line is a brief explanation of the type of material when it is other than manuscript, i.e., microfilm, transcript, or photostat, and the name of the institution holding the originals. If a collection has been entered in the *National Union Catalog of Manuscript Collections*, the catalog number is provided.

Next is a biographical sketch of the principal figure or figures represented in each collection, including such information as birth and death dates, place of residence, occupation, and public or military service. This information is followed by a description of the relevant documents in the collection. In the description itself, no attempt has been made to list every item, although this is sometimes the result in unusually small collections; rather, emphasis is placed on topics covered by the material—society, politics, the economy, or the war. An effort has also been made to suggest areas of study in which the collection would be most useful.

Collections that are extremely large and uniform in content may receive more cursory treatment than smaller collections containing a variety of documents. Despite a collection's size, a consistent effort has been made to mention documents of an unusual nature or material explaining significant events, as well as items concerning prominent individuals. When a name appears in the body of an entry, it is omitted from the list of principal correspondents, which includes both prominent figures who may only be minimally represented in the collection and individuals whose papers compose the major part of the collection.

Collections for which there are printed calendars or indexes receive brief coverage. The same is true for such collections as the Papers of Thomas Jefferson and the Papers of James Madison, for which items from the Revolutionary era are available in published form. When materials have been printed, a citation is given, and published guides and calendars to both the Library's collections and its holdings of domestic and foreign reproductions are also noted.

The arrangement and description of collections from foreign archives in this guide reflect what obtained in the depositories at the period the material was reproduced, although it may since have been reorganized. This approach has resulted in several geographical anachronisms, particularly with regard to German archives, which were surveyed before World War I. But throughout the Foreign Reproductions section, the researcher need only be aware that the collections are arranged according to their historical context.

In addition to the information provided in this guide, searchers are encouraged to consult a variety of research aids in the Manuscript Division. Available in the division's reading room, for example, are a dictionary catalog of printed cards; a catalog of collections; a master record of collections; a general index containing entries for individual manuscripts, registers and calendars of individual collections; and an inventory, arranged by country, repository, and archival file, of the collection of foreign reproductions. The dictionary catalog, which is made up largely of cards prepared for publication in the *National Union Catalog of Manuscript Collections*, often provides crucial data on the provenance, restrictions, and literary property rights of the collections. The master record of manuscript collections provides chiefly quantitative information and should be used in conjunction with the registers and calendars where they exist. These items often contain biographical information on the person or family represented, partial or complete indexes to correspondence, and in most instances a series description and container list. A card index identifies the collections for which registers are available.

Finally, prospective readers are cautioned that they may occasionally encounter restrictions that donors of certain collections have made as a condition of gift and would be well advised to write to the Manuscript Division before visiting the Library.

Two indexes, both keyed to entry rather than page numbers, are supplied. One lists all repositories from which manuscripts or photoreproductions were obtained; the other is a conventional proper name and subject index. A boldface number indicates the entry which describes the principal collection of an individual's or firm's papers.

Domestic Collections

JAMES ABEEL LETTERBOOK
1 vol., 1778–80.   *NUCMC* 62–4586
1   Abeel (1733–1825): Capt., John Lasher's regiment, New York Militia, 1776; deputy quartermaster general, 1778.
   Contains about 165 letters Abeel wrote to various Revolutionary officers, chiefly concerning the acquisition and distribution of supplies and provisions. Also includes photostats of five letters from Gen. Nathanael Greene, quartermaster general, concerning the business of the department and the disposition of the Army.

Account Books
Business and Personal Accounts

ANONYMOUS
1 vol., 1788   Force manuscripts
2   Accounts of a Philadelphia clerk of court, consisting of a record of fees he received, Mar.—Oct. 1788, for searching legal records. Copies of judgments, deeds, docket entries, various lists, and supplied references.

ALEXANDER BALMAIN
1 Vol., 1782–1821.   Photostats.
3   Balmain: Rector of Augusta Parish, Va., before the Revolution and of Frederick Parish during the postwar period; chaplain in the Virginia Line.
   About half of this material comprises Balmain's accounts for nearly two decades after the Revolution. Much of the remainder consists of registers of marriages, 1783–93, lists of subscribers for the support of the church at Winchester, and letters reflecting the adverse economic impact of the war on Episcopal ministers in Virginia. A few letters deal with Balmain's efforts after the war to collect his back pay as chaplain and to obtain title to land due for military service. Also includes letters, apparently copied from newspapers, on the founding of Washington College, Chester, Md., on Robert Morris' superintendency, and on the Huddy-Lippincott-Asgill affair, 1782.

NATHAN BASSETT
1 vol., 1753–1828.
4   Bassett (1715–91): Sandwich, Mass., blacksmith.
   Consists of three parts: Bassett's accounts, 1753–83, accounts of Lemuel Barlow, 1799–1811, and accounts of a third person, maintained in the hand of Seth Barlow, 1812–28. Bassett's detailed accounts, 100 pages in length, are for "Sundrys of Smith work" performed during the years 1753–72. Entries after 1772 relate chiefly to settling accounts due

7

YOUNGSTOWN STATE UNIVERSITY
LIBRARY

333517

Bassett. His records provide comprehensive information on the work of a New England blacksmith and the wage and price levels of the period. Includes genealogical data on the Bassett and Barlow families, 1685–1838.

BOINOD & GAILLARD
2 vols., 1784–85.

5   Boinod & Gaillard: Philadelphia booksellers; editors, *Courier de l'Amérique*, 1784.

A company ledger, May 1784—Aug. 1785, and a volume of accounts, June 1784—Jan. 1785, pertaining to *Courier de l'Amérique*, the first French newspaper published in the United States. Includes a list of subscribers to the *Courier* and the entries concerning the distribution of the paper. The ledger contains accounts current with several firms and persons with whom Boinod & Gaillard conducted their business, including Charles Cist, printer of the *Courier*.

PHINEAS BROWN
1 vol., 1785–1818.

6   Brown (1747–1819): Addison County, Vt., farmer and storekeeper.

During the 1780's Brown used this volume as a daybook to record his business transactions at New Haven (later at Vergennes and Waltham), Vt. Contains an index and genealogical data pertaining to the Phineas Brown family.

BUSH TOWN STORE
2 vols., 1747–68.

7   Bush Town Store: Bush River, Baltimore County, Md.

Accounts of the Bush Town Store, Mar. 1765—Dec. 1768. One volume contains a full record of wheat purchased and flour milled during the fall and winter of 1766–67. The second volume contains a copy of an indenture executed by John Hall, Isaac Webster, and Jacob Giles in 1747, forming as partners the "Bush Town Iron Works." An inventory of company property is appended which lists the assets of the ironworks: 2,874 acres land, eight servants and 16 slaves, one schooner, gristmill, sawmill, oxen, horses, tools, equipment, provisions, etc. Contains no records of the operation of the ironworks, which was located "on the Head of Bush River."

WILLIAM CHAMBERLAYNE
1 vol., 1786–1812.   Photostats.

8   Chamberlayne (1764–1836): New Kent County, Va., planter.

Fragmentary accounts recording Chamberlayne's gaming activities and transactions bearing upon the management of his estate.

MARTIN COCKBURN
3 vols., 1765–1818.

9   Cockburn (1742–ca. 1818): Fairfax County, Va., planter.

Two volumes comprise a journal and ledger of a prosperous Chesapeake planter who shipped and imported merchandise for the accommodation of several of his neighbors. The third volume is an index, prepared in 1893, to names recorded in the account books. Contains two significant items concerning Truro Parish: "Articles of Agreement" drawn up Apr. 1769 for construction of a new church, and three pages of detailed building specifications for the structure, witnessed by George Washington and other vestrymen of the parish.

JOSEPH COGGESHALL–SILAS CASEY LEDGER
1 vol., 1771–86.

10   Casey: Rhode Island merchant.

Although this ledger apparently was used by Joseph Coggeshall when it was opened in

1771, the early entries were closed out within a few months. The ledger was subsequently used by Silas Casey to maintain his accounts with ships he outfitted and provisioned. In 1774–75, and later in 1783–86, the accounts are with captains embarking on fishing voyages. During the war years Casey's accounts are chiefly with privateers operating from Rhode Island. The ledger is in the papers of Silas Casey (1841–1913), American naval officer and descendent of the Silas Casey of the Revolutionary era.

CRENSHAW & CO.
1 vol., Jan.—Aug. 1770.
11   Crenshaw & Co.: Petersburg, Va.
Detailed record of the company's transactions with over 600 customers (fully indexed) spread across 14 southern Virginia counties south of the James and Appomattox Rivers and a portion of northern North Carolina. The company operated through several principal agents and paid wages to four employees who operated stores in Amelia and Pittsylvania Counties as well as in Petersburg. A wide range of articles were sold by the company to the planters of southern Virginia, most of whom marketed small quantities of tobacco and corn, and even smaller amounts of wheat, tallow, peas, and beeswax.

JOHN DAVIDSON
1 vol., 1780–87.
12   Davidson: Annapolis, Md., storekeeper.
Large ledger of accounts which, in addition to routine information on Davidson's business, contains entries on his transactions with many Maryland leaders of the Revolution and with several members of the national Congress when the government was convened at Annapolis in 1784.

SILAS DEANE
2 vols., 1775–81.
13   Deane (1737–89): Member. Continental Congress, 1774–76; agent to France, 1776–78.
Chiefly receipts, vouchers, bills, and invoices, 1776–77, together with additional accounts compiled by Deane in 1781, pertaining to his activities in France before his recall. Includes a letter to Deane from Thomas Morris, May 1777, and a folio of facsimiles of documents in the Papers of the Continental Congress related to his mission to France.
See also Silas Deane Letterbooks, entry no. 236.

EDWARD DIXON
37 vols., 1743–1801.
14   Dixon: Port Royal, Va., merchant and storekeeper.
Mercantile records, most of which relate to the operation of Dixon's store on the Rappahannock at Port Royal and contain detailed information on imports and exports handled by Dixon, price levels, and exchange rates. The collection includes 12 ledgers and journals from the Revolutionary era, plus an invoice and inventory book, two blacksmith ledgers (in which Dixon carefully calculated annual expenses for materials and for the support of four to six Negroes employed in smith work), an exercise book containing mathematical rules and tables of weights and measures, and a small volume of receipts, bills, and miscellaneous papers.

EDWARD DORSEY, JOURNAL OF ACCOUNTS AND SCRAPBOOK
1 vol., 1747–84.   Force manuscripts.
15   Dorsey (fl. 1750): Merchant and legislator of Annapolis and Elk Ridge, Md.
The portion relating to the Revolutionary era consists of a daybook kept at Annapolis by an unidentified person settling the estate of Edward Dorsey. The journal entries—keyed to "Ledgers of the Estate of Edward Dorsey in Private Accounts" (Nos. 1499 and 1500), Maryland Hall of Records, Annapolis—cover the period Mar. 1761—Dec. 1765.

FAIRFAX ESTATE EXECUTORS
2 vols., 1781–98.

16   Thomas Lord Fairfax (1693–1781): Sixth Lord Fairfax; proprietor of Virginia's Northern Neck.

   The first book of accounts kept by the executors of the Fairfax estate consists of detailed entries of sums collected and paid out for the estate during the period 1781–86. The second book duplicates, in abbreviated form, the entries through 1786 and continues similar entries until 1798. Accounts were balanced in 1798 "at Col. Martin's Death." According to Fairfax's will, the executors were Thomas Bryan Martin and Gabriel Jones.

   See also Fairfax Family Papers, entry no. 262.

LEWIS GINNEDO
1 vol., 1755–1815.

17   Ginnedo (d. 1801): Newport, R.I., merchant.

   Although this book contains sporadic entries for the years 1755–56, 1765–69, and 1796–1800, the most important part comprises Ginnedo's accounts for the years 1769–75, fully one-third of which are with Aaron Lopez, 1769–70. In addition to the records for several vessels, full accounts for an "Oil Work," 1769–70, are included. Entries for the period 1801–15 were made by Ginnedo's son Daniel.

ISAAC GRUBB
1 vol., 1773–88.

18   Grubb: Delaware farmer; located at Brandywine Hundred, New Castle County.

   Grubb's accounts with various neighbors and several men periodically employed by him are fullest for the years 1774–78 and 1782–87 and provide considerable information on the economic and social condition of a Delaware farmer of moderate means. The record of wages and prices pertains almost entirely to agricultural labor and farm produce. Grubb commonly sold beef, mutton, hogs, sheep, tallow, butter, cider, and corn and rented land. His workmen received payments for such jobs as harrowing, sowing, reaping, mowing, cording, hauling, and making staves.

ELIHU HALL, SR.
1 vol., 1777–95.

19   Hall (1726–90): Baltimore, Md., merchant.

   Mercantile account book pertaining to Chesapeake economic life during the years 1777–95, from the collected ledgers of his son, Washington Hall.

MARK HARDIN
1 vol., 1779–1828.

20   Hardin (d. 1815): Farmer, Fauquier County, Va., and Washington County, Ky.

   Includes a few accounts of debts owed Hardin and records of payments for stud service, 1779–86. Also records of births and deaths of Hardin's 12 children.

RICHARD HARRISON & CO. LEDGER
1 vol., 1779–83.

21   Harrison (1750–1841): Alexandria, Va., merchant; agent for Virginia at Martinique; merchant and unofficial consul at Cádiz, 1780–86; auditor, U.S. Treasury, 1791–1836.

   Accounts maintained at the firm's Alexandria office and at its store at Port Tobacco and warehouse and wharf on Point Lubley. Harrison did business with the governments of Virginia and Maryland, the Continental Congress, and numerous individuals. His accounts reflect fluctuations in the economy and the depreciation of Virginia currency during the years 1780 and 1781.

JONATHAN HOBBS
1 vol., 1781–99.

22   Hobbs (1717–85): Farmer [Falmouth, Maine?].

Chiefly accounts of Hobbs' estate kept by his son, Josiah Hobbs. Includes records of the children of Jonathan and Josiah Hobbs.

SAMUEL HOLTEN
3 vols., 1757–74.   Force manuscripts.

23   Holten (1738–1816): Danvers, Mass., physician.

Accounts pertaining to Holten's practice, with cryptic notes concerning his patients' illnesses, accidents, and deaths and the remedies he prescribed. Includes records of payments received and defaulted accounts.

See also Samuel Holten Papers, entry no. 340.

JAMES HUNT
1 vol., 1779–1820.

24   Hunt: Halifax and Pittsylvania Counties, Va.

This book belonged to Lt. William Pointer of Capt. John Mark's company of the 10th Virginia Regiment in 1779, when Pointer began a clothing account for the company (fragmentary notations appear on a few pages). It was apparently taken home after the war by a member of the Hunt family, four of whom were in Mark's company, and was used successively by James Hunt and one of his children. It contains copies of several indentures to which one of the Hunts was a party; miscellaneous accounts with neighbors, 1780–91; lumber accounts and building records for the Gilbert Hunt house; an estimate of expenses to maintain a minister in "Straitstone Church" and subscribers' pledges; and a scale of depreciation of Virginia currency showing monthly changes, Jan. 1777—Dec. 1781.

MATTHEW IRWIN
1 vol., 1769–84.

25   Irwin: Pennsylvania merchant.

Journal of accounts concerning Irwin's commercial affairs. Contains information on Pennsylvania price levels and the diversity of goods available during the war, as well as the names of firms and persons transacting business with Irwin.

LANCASTER COUNTY, PENNSYLVANIA, STOREKEEPER'S LEDGER

Accounts of a substantial general store located in Lancaster County, Oct. 1787—Dec.

26   1 vol., 1787–1801.
1801.

MANUFACTURING SOCIETY OF PHILADELPHIA
1 vol., 1788–90.

27   Accounts in the form of a daybook containing information on an enterprise that was apparently designed to employ poor and dependent persons in Philadelphia. Entries record purchases of yarn, flax, cotton, and other supplies, as well as payments made for spinning, weaving, carding, hackling, etc., suggesting the mode of operation in the putting-out system of manufacture. Christopher Marshall and Adam Wentzell were involved in the work of the society.

WILLIAM MARTINE
1 vol., 1783–85.

28   Martine: New England merchant.

Journal of a general store dealing principally in dry goods, hardware, sugar, molasses, rum, butter, and salt. The business grew from four to five transactions monthly in 1783 to over 300 monthly in Oct.—Dec. 1785.

MARYLAND SALT WORKS
1 vol., 1770–1811.   Force manuscripts.
29   Includes fragments of accounts kept by several persons over a long period but comprises chiefly the transactions at a combined saltworks and general store, apparently owned by Charles Wallace and operated by the Gilliss Polk family of the Maryland Eastern Shore, 1778–79.

JONATHAN MASON
1 vol., 1784–97.   Force manuscripts.
30   Mason (1756–1831): Boston, Mass., businessman, lawyer, Federalist politician; member, General Court, 1786–96, 1805–8, U.S. Senate, 1800–1803, and U.S. House of Representatives, 1817–20; director of the Boston branch of the Bank of the U.S.
      Mason's accounts with the Bank of Massachusetts, 1784–97, reveal considerable short-term borrowing that fluctuated significantly from year to year.

JOHN MILTON
1 folio, 1784–96.   Force manuscripts.
31   Milton: Georgia official.
      A 28-page booklet containing Milton's "account against the State of Georgia," Jan. 1784—Dec. 1796, for administering oaths, swearing in officials, and issuing commissions and proclamations.

SHAPLEY MORGAN
1 vol., 1748–1834.
32   Morgan (1740–1800): Sgt., Capt. Christopher Morgan's company, Connecticut Militia, 1785–86.
      Chiefly Morgan's personal accounts, 1785–99, but includes diverse and fragmentary entries relating to many business matters. Accounts continuing after 1801 are apparently those of Eneas Morgan.

ELIJAH MORRILL
3 vols., 1760–84.
33   Morrill (d. 1767): Salisbury, Essex County, Mass., blacksmith.
      Includes Morrill's daybook, 1760–61, which portrays the daily transactions of a Massachusetts blacksmith; a receipt book, 1768–84, maintained in conjunction with the settlement of Morrill's estate; and the account book of Ezra Morrill, 1771–83. The receipt book records the decisions of a committee appointed by probate to divide Morrill's property and the payments made to the estate by his debtors. Ezra Morrill's accounts were begun as an "iron book," listing purchases of scrap iron for blacksmith work, but he apparently diversified his business, and by the late 1770's the accounts are those of a small trader.

ROBERT MUNDELL
34   See Henry Riddell, entry no. 44.

JAMES MURDOCH & COMPANY
2 vols., 1773–75.
35   Murdoch: Glasgow merchant.
      Journals of the Virginia operations of the Glasgow firm James Murdoch & Co. Includes an original journal of a store in Pittsylvania County, Sept. 1773—Aug. 1775, and a contemporary true copy of a journal of a store in Halifax County, Sept. 1774—Aug 1775.

JOHN DE NEUFVILLE AND SON
1 vol., 1779–80.   Force manuscripts.
36   Neufville: Amsterdam merchant.

Mostly invoices of cargoes shipped to America by Neufville and Son, Oct. 1779—Dec. 1780. Provides considerable information on the quantity and variety of American imports during the war, and on American merchants trading with the Dutch. About one-tenth of the entries are in French, including 10 pages pertaining to supplies obtained for ships under John Paul Jones' command at Texel, Jan. 1780.

See also Barthélemy Terrasson Papers, entry no. 1070.

ROBERT CARTER NICHOLAS
1 folio, 1769–70.

37   Nicholas (1728–80): Virginia planter, politician; treasurer of Virginia, 1766–78.

Consists of papers pertaining to the funeral expenses and the estate of Lord Botetourt collected by Nicholas as chairman of the legislative committee appointed to settle financial affairs of the deceased Governor. Includes lists of personal property sent to the Governor's heirs and the accounts of payments to the estate maintained by his agent, W. Marshman.

JOHN NORTON & SONS
2 vols., 1764–84.

38   Norton: Tobacco merchant of London and Virginia.

Includes a book of accounts with the banking firm Cliff, Walpole & Clark (later Walpole, Clark, Bourne & Pott) recording the balances maintained by Norton & Sons, 1766–84, and a warehouse book recording the company's tobacco shipments from Virginia, 1771–76. The banking accounts reveal the expansion and decline of the company's operations in Virginia. Warehouse records preserve a detailed account of tobacco shipped, the quantity and value of purchases from individual planters, the ships and captains transporting tobacco, and consignees.

ORANGE COUNTY, VIRGINIA, STOREKEEPER'S LEDGER
1 vol., 1784–1801.

39   Fragmentary accounts of an unidentified Virginia storekeeper [Thomas Herman?], apparently of Orange County, Va. Most of the accounts record the purchases of a few dozen customers during the period June—Sept. 1784, although a small number of entries were added years later.

PARKINSON & BURR
1 vol., 1787.

40   Parkinson and Burr: New York merchants.

Journal of accounts, May—Aug. 1787, pertaining to the operations of a diversified company heavily engaged in importing tea (which was traded to firms in Baltimore, New London and Hartford, Conn., Newport, R.I., Boston, and Canada), wine, and brandy, and in exporting provisions to the West Indies and tobacco to France. Also provides insight into the practices of marine insurance underwriters.

PHYSICK FAMILY
39 vols., 1759–1872.

41   Edmund Physick (d. 1804): Pennsylvania merchant; agent for the Penn family estates after the Revolution.

Includes six account books pertaining to the financial affairs of Edmund Physick during the Revolutionary era; three volumes concerning Physick's administration of the estate of the Philadelphia silversmith, Philip Syng (1703–89), and four volumes relating to the administration of the estates of James and Robert Bremner. Also a John Penn receipt book, 1774–76, the earliest entries of which are expenses incurred in building the Governor's mansion, Lansdowne House.

JOHN PRINGLE

1 vol., 1775–85.   Force manuscripts.

42

Pringle: Philadelphia merchant.

Irregularly kept accounts, three-fourths of which consist of a journal covering the period Apr. 1780—Mar. 1781. Includes lists of debts owed Pringle, 1784–85, invoices of cargoes exported, and sales records showing distribution of shipments imported. Pringle, apparently heavily involved in the Chesapeake trade, dealt with Richard Harrison & Co. of Alexandria, Gale, Jackson & Steward of Somerset County, Md., and William Patterson of Baltimore and exported tobacco to France, Holland, and the West Indies.

PEYTON RANDOLPH

1 vol., 1774–76.

43

Randolph (1721–75): Member, Virginia House of Burgesses, 1764–74; pres., Virginia Convention, 1774, 1775, Continental Congress, 1774, 1775.

Entries include the last will and testament of Peyton Randolph, Aug. 1774; inventories and appraisals of Randolph's estates in James City, York, Charlotte, and Albemarle Counties; and at Martin's Hundred, lists of slaves and sundry accounts. Most are in the hand of Peyton Randolph.

HENRY RIDDELL

1 vol., 1777–80.   Force manuscripts.

44

Riddell: Factor for John Glassford & Co. interests in Charles County, Md.

Consists of accounts kept by Robert Mundell acting in behalf of Henry Riddell after the latter fled Maryland in 1776. Mundell was chiefly concerned with settling Riddell's outstanding accounts and collecting rents from tenants on Glassford property in Benedict, Nottingham, St. Marys, Leonard Town, Nanjemay, and Georgetown, Md.

CHARLES RIDGELY

1 vol., 1774–80.

45

Ridgely (1733–90): Maryland planter, businessman, Hampton, Baltimore County; two-thirds owner, Charles Ridgley & Co. ironworks, 1774–76; member, State legislature, 1777–87; land speculator; purchased major share of the confiscated Nottingham Co. ironworks, 1780; anti-Federalist.

Records of Ridgely's company provide a comprehensive view of the operation of a Maryland ironworks. The accounts, covering primarily the period Mar. 1774—Oct. 1775, consist of five sections: (1) a "time" book recording the number of days worked by each man in two coal crews, with notations indicating days lost through illness, injury, drunkenness, etc., (2) accounts of the coal production of each crew; (3) accounts of ore hauled by 11 teamsters; (4) accounts of pig iron "weighed off" four to five times monthly at the Northampton furnace; and (5) accounts of iron hauled to Baltimore or sold at the furnace. Includes notations on the formation and liquidation of Ridgely's partnership (1774–76) with Darby Lux, Daniel Chamier, and Pleasance Goodwin and fragmentary accounts of iron sales, 1779–80.

JOHN RUTLEDGE

1 vol., 1761–83.   Microfilm available.

46

Rutledge (1739–1800): South Carolina lawyer; member, Continental Congress, 1774-75, 1782–83; gov., 1776–77, 1779–82.

Business accounts showing debits and credits of Rutledge, chiefly between 1761 and 1775. The accounts are in poor condition, numerous entries being completely obscured or mutilated.

Owned by Mrs. St. Julien R. Childs, Charleston, S.C., 1948.

SMITH, HUIE, ALEXANDER & COMPANY
2 vols., 1784–96.

47   Smith, Huie, Alexander & Co.: Glasgow firm.

Consists of a ledger (with a typed index) of the firm's store in Dumfries, Va., May 1784—Sept. 1785, and an indexed journal, Sept. 1786—Aug. 1787. James Reid apparently managed the company's Dumfries store, as well as the warehouses located at Dumfries and Quantico.

JOHN STUMP
1 vol., 1743–86.

48   Stump (1728–97): Cecil County, Md., planter.

Transactions of a middling planter, owner of several hundred acres and a few slaves, who diversified farm production to avoid dependence upon tobacco. Offers limited view, though over a long period, of prices and wages in Maryland's Eastern Shore.

TRIGG FAMILY
1 vol., 1760–97.

49   Trigg: Spotsylvania County, Va.

An account book and scrapbook containing records of estate sales and the division of estate assets. The records indicate the personal property holdings and debts of several small planters and prevailing prices at estate sales during the Revolution. Includes accounts for the estates of Henry and Mary Brock, 1763; Abraham Simpson, 1771; Rev. James and Sarah Marye, 1782; Capt. John Carter, John Z. Lewis, and Robert Lewis, 1784; and Martha Goodloe, 1786.

ZEPHANIAH TURNER
1 vol., 1764–79.

50   Turner: Charles County, Md., planter-storekeeper; commissioner for settlement of Virginia accounts, 1783–84.

Accounts Turner kept during the period 1764–68 for settlement of the estate of his father, Sam Turner, which apparently included a plantation and general store. He subsequently kept his personal accounts in the book, but after 1771 only sporadic entries appear.

ROBERT UNDERHILL & COMPANY
3 vols., 1786–89.

51   Underhill: Westchester County, N.Y., merchant; Quaker.

Journal and two-volume ledger of a general store. Includes an index to over 400 customers trading with Underhill and provides a record of the variety of consumer goods available and prevailing price levels at the end of the Confederation period.

WADSWORTH FAMILY
1 box, 1776–1903.

52   Elisha Wadsworth: West Hartford, Conn., merchant.

Contains miscellaneous bills of exchange, receipts, and fragmentary accounts, offering limited insight into everyday life of Connecticut farmers, artisans, and storekeepers during the Revolutionary era. Most are from the general store kept by Elisha Wadsworth.

WILLIAM A. WASHINGTON
1 vol., 1776–92.

53   Washington (1757–1801): Virginia planter—Wakefield, Blenheim, and Haywood, Westmoreland County; son of George Washington's half brother Augustine.

Ledger of Washington's accounts, irregularly maintained during the years 1776–92. The diversity of the economic life of Virginia planters is seen in the wide variety of products traded in the area and the range of goods purchased.

WILLIAMS, CARY & COMPANY
1 vol., 1784–96.

54   Williams, Cary & Company: Alexandria, Va., firm.

Accounts of the trustees managing the division of property of Williams, Cary & Co. after it was apparently liquidated in 1785. Includes lists of 45 creditors of the firm who participated in five property divisions and of payments made to the estate. Contains miscellaneous inventories as well as affidavits connected with the final settlements in Alexandria, 1794–96.

Military and Public Accounts

WILLIAM ALEXANDER
1 vol., 1777–79.   Force manuscripts.

55   Alexander: Capt., 7th Pennsylvania Regiment, Jan. 1777—Apr. 1780.

Indexed account book kept by Alexander during the period he commanded a company of the 7th Pennsylvania. Entries for each man in the company record pay and expenditures, as well as dates of enlistment, deaths, and desertions. Includes a comprehensive clothing account and a record of disbursements from paymaster John Knight to Alexander.

ANONYMOUS ACCOUNT BOOK AND SCRAPBOOK
1 vol., 1710–1863.   Force manuscripts.

56   A ledger, 1710–13, into which were pasted several miscellaneous pay orders, payrolls, and newspaper clippings dated from the 1770's and 1780's. The payrolls are for six companies of the 3d Virginia Regiment, 1777–78.

WILLIAM BAUSMAN
3 vols., 1779–82.

57   Bausman (1724–84): Member, Lancaster, Pa., committee of correspondence and committee of public safety; barrackmaster, 1777, and assistant deputy quartermaster, 1779–82.

Accounts and receipts kept by Bausman as assistant deputy quartermaster primarily concerning the purchase of horses, forage, and supplies for dragoons.

NATHANIEL APPLETON
1 vol., 1780–93.

58   Appleton: Commissioner of the Continental Loan Office in the State of Massachusetts, 1777–93.

Receipts relating to the transportation and issuance of paper currency at Boston, chiefly for the period July 1780—Aug. 1782. Also includes a few Congressional resolutions and letters of instruction from the Treasury Office bearing on Appleton's duties as Continental loan officer and documents containing information on U.S. funding operations at the Boston Loan Office, 1790–93.

THOMAS BLAKE
1 vol., 1782–83.

59   Blake: Paymaster, 1st New Hampshire Regiment; 1st lt., Mar., 1780.

Receipt book for the period Mar. 1782—Dec. 1783.

JAMES BLANCHARD
1 vol., 1780–81.

60   Blanchard: Paymaster, 2d New Hampshire Regiment, 1778–81.

Account book for the 2d New Hampshire, 1780–81, containing entries for approximately 400 men in the regiment.

BRANDENBURG TROOPS
1 box, 1777–86.

61   Account book, in German, showing subsidies received by the London agent, J. W. Hesse, for the Brandenburg troops sent to America in the pay and service of Great Britain.

SILAS BURBANK
1 vol., 1777.

62   Burbank: Massachusetts Regiment, Jan. 1777; capt., July 1777.
Payroll of Burbank's company, June 1777, plus two lists of supplies belonging to the company.

COMMISSARY GENERAL OF PRISONERS
1 vol., 1777–78.

63   Commissary General of Prisoners Elias Boudinot's book of accounts, listing expenditures for 93 American officers held by the British in New York, Sept. 1777—May 1778.

CONNECTICUT, CONTINENTAL LOAN OFFICE RECEIPT BOOKS
17 vols., 1781–1809.   Force manuscripts.

64   Receipt books of William Imlay, Continental loan officer in Connecticut, for interest payments made on outstanding loan office certificates and for new certificates issued upon cancellation of those of earlier issue. Eight volumes contain receipts signed before 1790.

CONTINENTAL ARMY, PAYMASTER GENERAL RECORDS
6 vols., 1780–85.

65   Consists of four manuscript registers of "certificates of indebtedness," a volume of receipts for certificates issued to Maryland troops by John White, and a volume recording warrants issued to John Pierce when he was deputy paymaster general, 1780–81. "Certificates of indebtedness" were issued by deputies working under Pierce to Continental soldiers and officers in settlement of their accounts with the United States from Jan. 1783 to Sept. 1785. Registers include the following data: number and letter of each certificate, date of certificate, to whom due, when due, and amount. They cover the following series of certificates: Nos. 5,245–10,203 (Conn., N.J., and Mass. troops), 15,439–18,693 (Mass. and N.H.), 20,466–25,550 (N.H. and N.J.), and 86,628–93,679 (Md. and N.C.). The fourth volume, a fragment, has many missing pages. Information contained in the collection was published in a comprehensive compilation under the title *Register of the certificates, issued by John Pierce, Esquire, Paymaster General, and Commissioner of the Army accounts, for the United States*, 4 vols. (New York, 1786). Comparison of the manuscript and the printed registers reveals a number of variations in the spelling of names. The receipts issued by John White, 1784–85, cover certificates numbered 80,851–89,168. The "Record of Warrants issued to John Pierce" consists of a daybook maintained in the paymaster's office listing warrants issued to Pierce, Feb. 1780—June 1781, for settlement of accounts of various soldiers, officers, and agents having claims against the Army. Entries identify recipients of warrants and specify amount and purposes for which they were issued.

CONTINENTAL ARMY, PAYROLL RECORDS: ABSENTEES, VARIOUS REGIMENTS
1 vol., 1 folio index, 1779–80.

66   Contains name, rank, and company assignment of men absent from various units and therefore omitted from the payrolls, July 1779—July 1780, with reasons assigned for the omissions. Modern index is provided.

JULIUS DEMING
1 vol., 1778–80.

67   Deming (1755–1830): Commissary of issues employed with Henry Champion, deputy commissary general for the Eastern Department.

Primarily Deming's accounts with Connecticut, Rhode Island, and New York drovers and butchers for the delivery of stock to various camps during the period June 1778—Apr. 1780.

DANVILLE, KENTUCKY, GENERAL STORE
1 vol., 1785–86.

68   Daybook containing information about price levels, availablility of dry goods and hardware, prevailing prices, and the volume of business transacted in a frontier community.

ZEPHANIAH HALSEY
1 vol., 1780–82.

69   Halsey: Blooming Grove, Orange County, N.Y., followed the main American Army to Yorktown, Va., in 1781 and returned to Newburgh in November.

Accounts pertaining to the delivery of horses to various quartermaster officials, Sept. 1780—Apr. 1782.

JOSEPH HOWELL, JR.
1 vol., 1776–92.

70   Howell: Paymaster, 2d Pennsylvania Regiment, Aug.—Oct. 1778; commissioner of Army accounts and acting paymaster general, U.S. Army, Aug. 1778—May 1792.

Includes information on several hundred officers of all ranks from ensign to major general whose cases for back pay and miscellaneous unsettled claims came before Howell's office.

WILLIAM HUNT
3 vols., 1775–78.

71   Hunt: Assistant commissary of issues, Watertown, Mass.

Two daybooks and a journal contain Hunt's accounts of military stores received and issued between May 1775 and Aug. 1778.

ENOS KELSEY
1 folio, 1777.

72   Kelsey: Maj., New Jersey Militia, 1776–79.

Contains a few dozen receipts pertaining to Kelsey's delivery of supplies to the Continental Army at Princeton, N.J., May—June 1777.

JOHN LIGHT
1 vol., 1780–85.

73   Light: Lancaster, Pa.

Accounts of forage issued for the 4th Regiment of Dragoons, Dec. 1780—May 1783, plus Light's personal accounts, chiefly pertaining to the sale of liquor which he apparently distilled, 1784–85, after his return to Lancaster, Pa.

ROBERT MACKENZIE
1 scroll, 1776–92.

74   Mackenzie: Paymaster, British provincial forces in North America, 1778.

This copy of the accounts, which passed the Treasury commissioners in 1790, was made from the Roll of Foreign Accounts in 1792.

MARYLAND, JOURNAL OF ACCOUNTS AND SCRAPBOOK
1 vol., 1776–1862.　　　Force manuscripts.

75　　Journal of military supply accounts of the State of Maryland with various officers and agents, Jan.—Sept. 1781. Various receipts, bills, and indentures dating 1781–84, plus sundry engravings and documents dating to 1862 have been pasted into the volume.

MARYLAND, WESTERN SHORE
1 vol., 1781–83.　　　Force manuscripts.

76　　Ledger of accounts of Maryland treasurer of the Western Shore, Thomas Harwood, July 1781—May 1783. Entries pertain to Harwood's transactions with dozens of persons engaged in a variety of activities, civil and military, for the most part relating to expenses incurred in defense of the State during the campaign of 1781. Payments cover wages and salaries, supplies, provisions, medicine, forage, transportation, recruitment, and care of the sick, wounded, and prisoners.

MARYLAND, JOURNAL B, No. 1 AND No. 2
2 vols., 1778–91.　　　Force manuscripts.

77　　Journal of the treasurer of the State of Maryland covering daily transactions of his office, Mar. 1778—Nov. 1785. Entries pertain to various military expenses incurred by the State for supplies, transportation, recruitment, medical care, and tending prisoners, plus the pay of sundry civil and military officers, accounts with the United States, redemption of loan office certificates, and salt bounty payments. The journal was audited in 1791. Once used as scrapbooks, the volumes also contain muster rolls and payrolls of various companies of the 1st New Hampshire, 3d New York, and 11th Virginia Continental Regiments, 1777–80.

4TH MASSACHUSETTS REGIMENT
4 vols., 1779–83.

78　　Two volumes of quartermaster receipt books, 1779–82, maintained successively by Benjamin Ray, Jubez Bill, Joel Pratt, and Africa Hamlin. A third volume contains weekly returns, supply accounts, and company rolls of Capt. Seth Banister's 3d company, Nov. 1781—Mar. 1783, and of Capt. William North's 2d company, Aug. 1782—Mar. 1783. Volume 4 contains the same information for Capt. Caleb Clap's 8th company, Jan. 1782—Mar. 1783.

JOSHUA MERSEREAU
1 vol., 1777–79.

79　　Mersereau: Deputy commissary of prisoners for New England.

　　Composed of three sections containing miscellaneous accounts of officials concerned with provisioning British prisoners held in New England; Ebenezer Prout's accounts of provisions supplied the convention troops; disbursements from d'Estaing and Gérard to Mersereau, apparently for American-held prisoners who had been captured by the French; and the journal of a deputy commissary for prisoners kept in Rutland, Vt., Dec. 1777—Sept. 1778.

DANIEL MILLS
1 vol., 1775–77.

80　　Mills: Capt., 4th New York Regiment, June 1775; capt., 2d New York Regiment, Nov. 1776.

　　Accounts of wages paid to men of Mills' company. Accounts of several of the men were settled by Lt. Charles Parsons after Mills' death, Apr. 1777.

SAMUEL MONTGOMERY
1 vol., 1777–78.

81   Montgomery: Capt., 7th Pennsylvania Regiment, Mar. 1777—Jan. 1781.
Accounts of wages paid to men of Montgomery's company and to officers of Col. William Irvine's 7th Pennsylvania Regiment.

JOHN MORTON
1 vol., 1776–82.

82   Morton: Capt., 4th Virginia Regiment, Feb. 1776—Mar. 1777; lt. col., Virginia Militia; deputy commissary of Prince Edward County.
Accounts of men of Morton's company, 1776, plus accounts for provisions received when he was deputy commissary of Prince Edward County, 1780–82.

EBENEZER MOTT
1 vol., 1781.

83   Mott: Quartermaster, Col. Wiesenfels' 4th New York Regiment.
Small receipt book with entries dated at Fishkill and Saratoga, N.Y., Sept.—Nov. 1781.

MICHAEL NOURSE
2 vols., 1781–1855.   Force manuscripts.

84   Nourse: Chief Clerk, Registers Office, U.S. Treasury.
Includes a ledger labeled "Statements of the Financial Affairs of the last Confederated Government of the United States from February 1781, to September 1789." The volume was compiled in 1857 from public records by Michael Nourse.
See also U.S. Treasury, General State of Receipts and Expenditures, entry no. 96.

PHILADELPHIA TROOP OF LIGHT DRAGOONS
1 reel, microfilm, 1780–87.

85   Ledger of the Philadelphia Troop of Light Dragoons, 1780–87, used by Alexander Nesbitt and John Lardner to settle accounts of the troop pursuant to a resolution of **Mar.** 1786.

SAMUEL POTTER
1 vol., 1776–1809.

86   Potter: Capt., 3d New Jersey Regiment, Feb. 1776—Mar. 1777; lt. col., 1st Regiment, Essex County Militia, 1777–78.
Contains accounts for men of the 3d New Jersey Regiment stationed near Albany, N.Y., Feb. 1776—May 1777, fragmentary personal accounts, 1777–86, and a portion of a daybook, 1787.

RICHMOND, MASSACHUSETTS, TAX ROLL
1 folio, Dec. 1, 1779.

87   Records number of polls, tax on real estate, and tax on personal estates of 76 men listed.
See Anita Newcomb McGee Papers, 1688–1932, Library of Congress.

EDWARD ROGERS
1 vol., 1776–84.

88   Rogers: Capt., Col. Gay's Connecticut regiment, June—Dec. 1776; capt., Col. Enos' Connecticut State Regiment, 1777–79; justice of the peace, Cornwall, Conn.
Accounts for the men of Rogers' Connecticut companies, 1776–79, listing arms, clothing, and wages drawn by each man. The last 10 pages record his judgments on some 100 cases brought before his justice court, 1782–84.

PHILIP SCHUYLER
2 vols., 1775–77.

89   Schuyler (1733–1804): Maj. gen., Continental Army; commander in chief, Northern Department, 1775–77.

One volume contains Schuyler's accounts with numerous officers under his command and with the Government of the United States, July 1775—Aug. 1777. The second volume contains lists of warrants drawn by Schuyler for the various units under his command, Mar.—Aug. 1777. The recipient of each warrant and the purposes to which it was directed are specified.

EBENEZER SMITH
1 vol., 1780–96.

90   Smith: Capt., 13th Massachusetts Regiment, Mar. 1779; justice of the peace.

Contains a roll of the men in Smith's company of the 13th Massachusetts Regiment, 1781, and clothing accounts for the company, 1780–83. The volume was later used as a justice of the peace docket book, 1787–93, after Smith returned home to New Marlborough, Mass., and contains a list of marriages performed, 1787–96.

JOHN SODER
1 vol., 1776–77.

91   Accounts of wages paid men of Capt. Soder's company of the 3d battalion, Pennsylvania Militia, Aug. 1776—Sept. 1777.

WILLIAM TAYLOR
1 vol., 1778–83.

92   Taylor: 1st lt., 2d Massachusetts Regiment, Jan. 1777.

Two receipt books, bound together, pertaining to quartermaster issues in Col. John Bailey's 2d Massachusetts Regiment, July—Oct. 1778 and July 1782—June 1783.

LAWRENCE TREMPER
2 vols., 1782–83.

93   Tremper: Lt. in Col. Marinus Willett's regiment of New York Militia.

Two small booklets of miscellaneous receipts and accounts pertaining to Tremper while he was at Albany and Fort Herkimer.

See also Lawrence Tremper, journal, entry no. 448.

U.S. COMMISSION AT THE COURT OF FRANCE
1 vol., 1776–85.   Force manuscripts.

94   Consists of a 51-page "journal of cash" and a 47-page ledger of accounts pertaining to the American commission in France, Dec. 1776—May 1779, bound into a single volume. Transactions recorded in the journal were posted in the ledger. Includes the Government's accounts with several American commissioners and agents (John Adams, Silas Deane, Franklin, Arthur Lee, and William Lee), and with merchants, agents, and ship captains with whom the commissioners transacted business. Also includes two loose sheets of accounts pertaining to Franklin, Dec. 1776—June 1785.

Filmed by the National Historical Publications Commission as part of the "Pre-Federal Accounting Records in the Library of Congress," NP–M7, Roll 1.

U.S. REGISTER OF THE TREASURY, STATEMENT OF ACCOUNTS
1 vol., 1785–1803.   Force manuscripts.

95   A two-page statement with 13 accounts, showing each State's quota under various acts of Congress. Includes amounts paid pursuant to each requisition and balance remaining in 1785 and a consolidated "Statement of Taxes required by Congress; . . . Payments made by the several States, on Account of their respective Quotas on the Requi-

sitions for Paper Money; with the Balances due thereon." Bound with an 1803 copy of a "Report" of the commissioners appointed to settle accounts between the United States and individual States pursuant to act of Aug. 5, 1790.

U.S. TREASURY, GENERAL STATE OF RECEIPTS AND EXPENDITURES
1 vol., 1781–90.   Force manuscripts.

96   Series of 21 general accounts of receipts and expenditures under authority of Congress, Nov. 1784—Sept. 1789, plus a 14–page "General Account" of Robert Morris as superintendent of finance, Feb. 1781—Nov. 1784, and a two-page letter of transmittal from Joseph Nourse, Mar. 4, 1790. The 21 general accounts, which are essentially quarterly fiscal reports, contain information on Congress, the Armed Forces, Indian affairs, foreign interest, and various departments of Government. Also includes records of pensions, annuities, grants, and the civil list of the President's household. The accounts were prepared in 1790 by the Treasury for a committee of the House of Representatives.
     Filmed by the National Historical Publications Commission as part of the "Pre-Federal Accounting Records in the Library of Congress," NP–M7, Roll 2. See also Michael Nourse, account book, entry no. 84.

U.S. TREASURY, REVOLUTIONARY WAR CLAIMS
1 vol., 1786–96.

97   Alphabetical list of men who had claims for military service outstanding against the U.S. Treasury at the end of the war, with notations signifying final disposition of their claims during the years 1786–96.

U.S. TREASURY, THIRD AUDITOR'S OFFICE RECORDS
12 vols., 1775–1832.

98   Two volumes of the journal of the Auditor's Office in New York consisting of the daily record of the disposition of sundry accounts of Revolutionary War officers examined during Apr. 1786–Nov. 1791. Pagination of the two volumes, 3984-6247. The journal is interrupted by the insertion of extensive lists of names at the beginning of the second volume (p. 5010–6084). Five oversize ledgers contain a comprehensive compilation of the accounts of Army officers with the U.S. Government for the years 1775-84, for which an index was prepared after the office's original alphabetical lists of officers had been burned during the destruction of public buildings in 1814. An additional volume contains "accounts current for pay, commutation, and gratuity" of officers and soldiers from Delaware, Maryland, New Jersey, New York, Pennsylvania, and Virginia, which show the back pay owing to each man, the amount of five years' salary received in commutation of half pay for life, payments made, and the type and denomination of treasury certificates issued to each person upon settlement of his account. A separately bound modern index has been prepared for the volume.

VERMONT
1 folio, 1777–86.   Force transcripts.

99   Accounts of the State of Vermont with the following men: Ethan Allen, Ira Allen, Thomas Butterfield, Thomas Chittenden, Jonas Fay, Edward Harris, Roswell Hopkins, John Knickerbacor, Matthew Lyon, John Payne, Moses Robinson, Judah Spooner, and Paul Spooner. Contains considerable information on their military and political activities relative to the organization of the Government and in behalf of the land claims of the State. Detailed accounts of Ethan and Ira Allen provide a virtual journal of activities for certain periods of service.

NEHEMIAH WADSWORTH
1 vol., 1777–88.

100   Wadsworth: Connecticut merchant.
     Accounts dealing with Wadsworth's procurement of horses and payments to com-

panies of teamsters from Hartford, Litchfield, Norfolk, Glastonbury, Suffield, Colchester, and Simsbury, Conn., Feb.—Dec. 1777. Includes four pages of a daybook Wadsworth maintained at Hartford in Dec. 1788.

DAVID WATERBURY
1 vol., 1776–77.
101   Waterbury: Col., 5th Connecticut Regiment, May—Dec. 1775; brig. gen., Connecticut State Line, June 1776—81.
Indexed account book, listing arms, clothing, and pay received by men of Waterbury's Stamford company of the 5th Connecticut Regiment, Apr. 1776—Apr. 1777.

JOHN WEITZEL
1 vol., 1779–81.
102   Weitzel: Assistant commissary of issues.
Contains receipts for rations and supplies issued by Weitzel to various Pennsylvania units, some of which were at Fort Rice and Fort Hambright.

JOHN WHITMAN
1 vol., 1776–1811.
103   Whitman: Capt., Pennsylvania Militia, Berks County.
Miscellaneous accounts of supplies and payments for transportation of troops to Lancaster, Pa., 1776–77.

WILLIAM WILSON
1 vol., 1780.
104   Wilson: Quartermaster, 1st battalion of Philadelphia County Militia.
A small receipt book pertaining to supplies Wilson issued in Aug. 1780.

ADAMS FAMILY COLLECTION
2 boxes, 1776–1914.   *NUCMC* 69-2025
105   Adams: Massachusetts family.
Consists primarily of John Quincy Adams letters, 1796–1850, but includes three letters of John Adams from the period of the Revolution: a 1776 letter urging the fortification of Boston; a letter of Mar. 24, 1779, discussing the decline of American virtue; and a letter of Apr. 10, 1780, concerning Russia's Declaration of the League of Armed Neutrality and the value of privateering.

THE ADAMS PAPERS
608 reels, microfilm, 1639–1889.   *NUCMC* 62–1621
106   John Adams (1735–1826): Massachusetts lawyer-politician; American statesman and President of the U.S. Abigail Smith Adams (1744–1818): Wife of John Adams. John Quincy Adams (1767–1848): Son of John and Abigail, President of the U.S.
Letters, diaries, accounts, journals, and miscellaneous documents. Most of the material for the Revolutionary era pertains to the political, social, and economic affairs of John and Abigail Adams and family, particularly their eldest son John Quincy. Miscellaneous non-Adams materials include the journal of Samuel C. Johonnot, Nov.—Dec. 1779; the diary of Stephen Peabody, 1769–71; and the journal of Samuel Tucker, Feb.—Sept. 1778. The following reels contain documents from the period of the Revolution: 1–17, 89–115, 125–26, 180–92, 197, 199, 217–23, 241, 256, 330, 341–73, 601–4, and 607.
Selected items are being published in letterpress editions under the general editorship of Lyman H. Butterfield. Published guides are available. Originals on deposit in Massachusetts Historical Society.

SAMUEL ADAMS PAPERS
19 vols., 1635–1826.   Photostats.   *NUCMC* 70–1689

107   Adams (1722–1803): Member, Massachusetts General Court, 1765–74, 1781, Continental Congress, 1774–82; gov., 1794–97.

Since Adams was a leader in the protest movement in Massachusetts from 1764–1774, his papers contain numerous letters and documents relating to prewar events. His correspondence while he was a delegate to Congress discusses the outbreak of hostilities, the issue of independence, the business of the War Office, Arthur Lee's public and private reports, the French Alliance, Continental debts, the Articles of Confederation, and the organization of the Army. Correspondence from the Confederation period deals primarily with the problem of the loyalists, war debts, Indian affairs, boundaries, Society of the Cincinnati, the weakness of Congress, Shays' Rebellion, and the Constitution. A few letters touch upon the role of the Negro in Revolutionary America. Miscellaneous documents in the collection include instructions and resolutions of the General Court and the Boston town meeting; letters of Peter Oliver and Thomas Hutchinson; reports from Massachusetts colonial agents in England; and the journal of the General Court, 1773–74.

Principal correspondents: Elizabeth Adams, John Adams, James Bowdoin, Samuel Cooper, Dennys De Berdt, Horatio Gates, Elbridge Gerry, Samuel Holten, Thomas Hutchinson, Lafayette, Arthur Lee, Richard Henry Lee, William Lee, James Lovell, John Lowell, Peter Oliver, Samuel Purviance, Jr., and James Warren.

Originals in New York Public Library.

ALDEN FAMILY PAPERS
4 vols., 1710–1844.   *NUCMC* 67–580

108   Seth Alden (1709–84): South Bridgewater, Mass., farmer, mill owner, and blacksmith; son of Deacon Joseph Alden. Joseph Alden (1748–1803): Son of Seth; farmer, mill owner, and militia captain; drafted in 1776 for service for coastal defense. Seth Alden, Jr. (1741–75): Farmer.

Family letters, receipts, and mill and blacksmith accounts, 1737–77. Includes miscellaneous accounts of Joseph Alden, 1760–88, and Seth Alden, 1771–81; deeds of the Alden family and Trask family of Sutton, 1766–82; the will of Seth Alden and related legal papers; accounts of the south precinct of Bridgewater, 1771–73, kept by Seth Alden, treasurer, and the south precinct school tax for 1782; and miscellaneous muster rolls for the local militia.

Principal correspondents: Daniel Alden, Joseph Alden, Seth Alden, Jonah Edson, Timothy Edson, Thomas Leach, and Thomas Odiorne.

WILLIAM ALEXANDER PAPERS
2 vols., 1774–82.   Force transcripts.

109   Alexander (Lord Stirling) (1726–83): Col., 1st New Jersey Regiment, 1775; brig. and maj. gen., 1776–83; commander in chief, Northern Department, Oct. 1781—Jan. 1783.

Chiefly letters to Alexander from members of Congress, various Revolutionary officers, and political figures in New York and New Jersey. Most of them concern the procurement of supplies, munitions, and recruits, intelligence on enemy maneuvers, and the disposition of troops under Alexander's command. Also includes returns for several units in Alexander's division, a list of commissioned officers in the Massachusetts and Connecticut Continental Lines, 1781–82, and photographs of portraits of Lord and Lady Stirling.

Principal correspondents: Elias Boudinot, William Burnet, Abraham Clark, George Clinton, Henry Clinton, John Conway, Elias Dayton, Henry Dearborn, John Jacob Faish, Franklin, Peter Gansevoort, Nathanael Greene, William Livingston, James Lovell, Alexander McDougall, Richard Kidder Meade, Robert Morris, William Patterson, Timothy Pickering, Arthur St. Clair, Philip Schuyler, John Stark, Sarah Stirling, William Thompson, Tench Tilghman, Jonathan Trumbull, Samuel Tucker, Washington, and Anthony Wayne.

Originals in New York Historical Society.

ALEXANDRIA, VIRGINIA, PROCEEDINGS OF THE TRUSTEES OF THE TOWN
1 box, 1749–67.

110   Minutes of the meetings of the trustees. Items of business include the sale of public lots, purchases, surveys, and the maintenance of streets and public buildings, such as the school and the warehouse. Includes lists of persons present at each meeting.

ETHAN ALLEN PAPERS
1 folio, 1773–84.   Force transcripts.

111   Allen (1738–89): Connecticut native; land speculator and farmer in New Hampshire Grants; col., Green Mountain Boys, 1770–84; led independence movement for Vermont against New York, New Hampshire, and Great Britain.

Correspondence of Vermont's leaders concerning the major issues relating to that region during the Revolution. Includes Allen's accounts of the capture of Ticonderoga and the invasion of Canada, about 25 letters concerning Vermont's attempt to gain recognition by the Continental Congress, and reports to Washington on British activities in Canada. Negotiations with the British are discussed in depth in correspondence of the Allens and British officials.

Principal correspondents: Ira Allen, Thomas Chittenden, George Clinton, Roger Enos, Jonas Fay, Horatio Gates, and Justice Sherwood.

Originals in the possession of Henry Stevens in 1843.

IRA ALLEN PAPERS
1 folio, 1769–73.   Force transcripts.

112   Allen (1751–1814): Connecticut native and brother of Ethan Allen; land speculator; political leader of Vermont.

Consists of the section of Allen's unpublished autobiography that was written at Pelagie Prison in 1799 and covers the years 1769–73. It discusses the Allen brothers' commercial and land dealings in Vermont and the struggle against New York's exercise of authority in the New Hampshire Grants.

ALMANAC COLLECTION

113   A small collection of miscellaneous almanacs, some annotated:
Nathaniel Ames, *An Astronomical Diary; Or, An Almanack* (Boston, 1775).
Joseph Crukshank, *Poor Will's Pocket Almanack* (Philadelphia, 1783).
Daniel George, *George's Cambridge Almanack; or, the Essex Calendar* (Salem, 1787).
Nathaniel Low, *An Astronomical Diary; Or, Almanack* (Boston, 1774, 1778, 1780, 1788-90).
Thomas Moore, *Gaine's New-York Pocket Almanack* (New York, 1787).
David Sewall, *An Astronomical Diary, or Almanack* (Portsmouth, N.H., 1786).

Additional annotated almanacs are scattered through the Library's collections, chiefly in the journals and diaries section of the Manuscript Division holdings and in the Rare Book Room.

ELIZABETH JACQUELIN AMBLER PAPERS
1 vol., 1781–1823.   Photostats.

114   Ambler (b. 1765): Daughter of Jacquelin Ambler (1742–98), Yorktown, Va., merchant, and Rebecca Burwell; wife of (1) William Brent of Stafford and (2) Col. Edward Carrington of Cumberland.

Includes seven letters from Elizabeth Jacquelin Ambler to Mrs. Mildred Dudley and an unnamed friend in Bristol. The letters concern personal and family matters and domestic problems related to the war, particularly the distress of the people of Virginia during the invasions of 1781.

AMBLER FAMILY PAPERS
2 vols., 1 folio, 1638–1809.

NUCMC 66–1381

115   Ambler: Yorktown, Va., mercantile family.

Consists of land grants, deeds, surveys, bonds, and indentures chiefly relating to the region about Jamestown and the Fairfax proprietary estates of the Northern Neck. Includes the will of Richard Ambler, 1765; articles of agreement concerning the purchase of land by Edward Ambler from Robert Carter Nicholas, 1765; several deeds for land purchased by Edward, Jacquelin, and John Ambler, 1765–88; a letter from Samuel Jordon to Robert Carter Nicholas concerning a land survey, 1773; and a land claim based on warrants held by John Ambler and George Nicholas, 1783.

AMERICAN DANISH COLONIES PAPERS
1 box, 1776–84.

116   Contemporary copies in both Danish and English of records concerning the seizure of two Danish merchant ships off the Danish West Indies in 1778. Includes reports of the Admiralty Courts, depositions of Danish and British officers and sailors, and related papers.

Principal correspondents: Gov. William M. Burt, C. Clausen, Lord George Germain, and Adm. James Young.

AMERICAN INDIANS, MISCELLANY
16 boxes, 1638–1958.

117   Material includes copies of five treaties Georgia Governors made with the Creek Indians, 1726–71. Also an address to the Six Nations by commissioners from New York, 1776.

AMERICAN REVOLUTION MANUSCRIPTS
1 vol., 1777–79.   Transcripts.

118   The first and smaller part of this material consists of correspondence of Sir Henry Clinton with Secretaries of State George Germain and Charles Jenkinson and with Lord Jeffery Amherst, commander in chief of British forces. Also, an exchange of letters between Generals Clinton, Washington, and William Phillips on the provisioning and exchange of prisoners. The second part contains correspondence from Gen. Frederick Haldimand, reports from various sources on American strength and activities on the western frontier, and miscellaneous accounts and returns. Several letters are in cypher. Miscellaneous items include transcriptions of four intercepted letters from Patrick Henry, George Rogers Clark, David Rogers, and Bernardo de Gálvez concerning Virginia's attempt to obtain supplies from Spanish Louisiana, 1778–79.

AMERICAN STAMP ACT PAPERS
1 vol., 1764–68.   Bancroft transcripts.

119   Official correspondence and miscellaneous papers relating to the Stamp Act. Includes Orders in Council, letters between Gen. Thomas Gage and the Secretary of State, circular letters to Governors in America and the West Indies, memorials from commissioners of customs in America, extracts from Privy Council Registers, and a general return of the distribution of troops in North America, 1765.

AMORY FAMILY PAPERS
5 boxes, 1697–1823.

120   Thomas Amory (1722–84): Boston, Mass., merchant and distiller; loyalist. John Amory (1728–1802): Boston dry goods merchant; loyalist in England, 1774–84. Jonathan Amory (1726–89): Boston dry goods merchant; loyalist; handled the family business in America during the war.

Letters and accounts falling chiefly within the periods 1697–1740 and 1802–4, with scattered letters, bills of exchange, and minor accounts from the Revolutionary era. The latter documents concern the mercantile affairs of John and Jonathan Amory, but they include a report from Samuel Elliot in London on the debates over the repeal of the Townshend duties.

Principal correspondents: Messrs. Blanchard & Lewis and Samuel Elliot.

ANDRÉ–ARNOLD COLLECTION
1 vol., 1 box, 1 folio, 1780.   Photostats.

121   Benedict Arnold (1741–1801): Gen., Continental Army; traitor. John André (1751–80): Maj., British Army; aide-de-camp to Sir Henry Clinton.

Copies of documents found in Major André's boot at the time he was apprehended, Sept. 23, 1780. Also proceedings of André's trial; the sketch he made of himself on the eve of his execution; and related correspondence between Generals Washington, Clinton, Arnold, and James Robertson.

Originals in New York Historical Society.

ARMSTRONG FAMILY PAPERS
1 vol., 1762–1814.   Force transcripts.

122   John Armstrong, Sr. (1717–95): Pennsylvania surveyor; brig. gen., Continental Army, 1776–77; maj. gen., Pennsylvania Militia, 1778; member, Continental Congress, 1778–80. John Armstrong, Jr. (1758–1843): Maj. and aide-de-camp to Gen. Horatio Gates, 1777–83; author of the Newburgh Addresses, 1783; member, Continental Congress, 1787–88, U.S. Senate, 1800–1804; minister to France, 1804–10; secretary of war, 1813–14.

Chiefly papers from the headquarters of the Northern Department, 1777–79. Includes returns and muster rolls, court-martial proceedings, and routine correspondence with various officers in the commissary department. Also material relating to the younger Armstrong's membership in a fraternal organization, "the worshipful Society of the Starkites," and personal and family correspondence.

GUY ATKINSON PAPERS
1 box, 1781–1835.

123   Includes a series of letters from Atkinson to his family in Ireland describing the commercial and social scene in Virginia. The activities and finances of family members in Ireland are reported in letters to Atkinson.

Principal correspondents: Rev. Guy Atkinson, James Atkinson, and Mary Atkinson.

WILLIAM A. ATLEE PAPERS
1 box, 1759–1816.   Force manuscripts.   *NUCMC* 67–585

124   Atlee (1735–93): Lancaster, Pa., jurist; member and chairman, Lancaster County committee of inspection, Dec. 1774, July 1776—July 1777; deputy commissary of prisoners, 1777–82; judge, Pennsylvania Supreme Court, 1777–93.

Chiefly correspondence pertaining to Atlee's activities as deputy commissary of prisoners. Six letters Atlee received from his brother Samuel, 1776–78, a British-held prisoner on Long Island, contain information on the treatment of American prisoners of war. Also includes personal and business letters Atlee wrote to his wife, Esther, while he was sitting on the supreme court in Philadelphia and on judicial circuit around the state. Eight letters to Atlee from Chief Justice Thomas McKean and six letters from Judge George Bryan, 1780–91, comment on judicial and political issues of the day.

Principal correspondents: John Beatty, Elias Boudinot, Thomas Bradford, James Gordon, Henry Haller, Thomas Hartley, Moses Hazen, Robert Hooper, Samuel Purviance, Jacob Rush, Abraham Skinner, William Smallwood, and War Office secretaries Joseph Carleton, Joseph Nourse, Richard Peters, Timothy Pickering, and Benjamin Stoddert.

See also Lancaster County, Pennsylvania, Committee of Safety, Minutes, entry no. 474.

JACOB BAILEY PAPERS
1 box, 1756–81.

125 Bailey (1731–1808): Harvard graduate, 1755; missionary for the Society for the Propagation of the Gospel at Pownalboro, Maine, 1760–79; loyalist émigré; Episcopal priest, Nova Scotia, 1779–1808.

Correspondence describing the problems of an Episcopal priest in the district of Maine before and during the Revolution. Civilian violence and harrassment of Bailey and his family in rural Pownalboro are the major topics of discussion during the war years. Other letters, mainly to Bailey, concern missionary work on the frontier, wartime inflation, and the difficulties that religious minorities faced in New England. Five letters written from Nova Scotia in 1781 reflect a loyalist's concern over prospects for returning home and restitution of or reimbursement for lost property.

Principal correspondents: Jonathan Bowman, A. A. Campbell, Sylvester Gardiner, William Gardiner, George Lynde, and W. Wheeler.

SIMEON BALDWIN PAPERS
1 folio, 1784–88.   Photographs.

126 Baldwin (1761–1851): Connecticut lawyer-jurist; Yale tutor, 1782–85; clerk, U.S. District Court, 1789–1806; judge, Connecticut Court of Errors, 1806–18.

Seven letters from Jabez Colton of Somers, Conn., to his brother-in-law, Simeon Baldwin, concerning family matters. Colton also discusses religion, local politics, and the possibility of his emigrating to the frontier.

JOSEPH BALL LETTERBOOK
1 vol., 1743–80.   Microfilm available.

127 Ball (d. 1760): Lawyer and landowner in England and Virginia; half brother of Mary Washington and uncle of George Washington.

After Ball's death his son-in-law, Rawleigh Downman (ca. 1720–81) of Westham, Essex County, England, used the remaining pages of Ball's letterbook to record his personal and business correspondence. Letters written before the summer of 1765, the time Downman removed to Virginia to assume active control of Morattico, the Ball estate in Lancaster County, concern crops, livestock, slaves, tobacco shipments, family matters, and Rawleigh Downman's preparations to take up residence in Virginia. Correspondence from Morattico, 1765–80, concerns tobacco sales, purchases, and the management of Downman's business interests in England.

Principal correspondents: Messrs. Edward & Samuel Athawes & Son, John Backhouse, William Chamberlayne, William Cheslyn, Messrs. Clay & Midgley, James Gildart, George Kemp, and Stephen Renaud.

BALTIMORE, COMMITTEE OF SAFETY
1 vol., 1774–76.   Force manuscripts.

128 Journal of the proceedings of the committee of safety of Baltimore, Nov. 1774—Oct. 1776, containing information on business brought before the committee and decisions in cases bearing on significant aspects of the Revolutionary movement in Maryland. Also includes lists of members of the committee, of the county's committees of observation and inspection, and of delegates to the provincial assembly; copies of letters to and from the committee; and intercepted correspondence from England to Gov. Robert Eden. The committee's concerns extended to Pennsylvania and Virginia, and included foreign trade as well as local defense. Miscellaneous entries include payrolls of several companies in Col. Daniel Morgan's and Col. Abraham Buford's Virginia regiments, Oct.—Nov. 1778.

JAMES D. AND DAVID R. BARBEE PAPERS
18 boxes, 1784–1951.   *NUCMC* 60–571

129 Barbee: Washington, D.C., Methodist ministers.

Includes one letter from Thomas Towles, member of the Virginia House of Delegates, to an unnamed recipient in Richmond, June 1784, concerning matters then before the Assembly: the support of religion, church property, foreign trade, taxes, British debts, the recovery of slaves taken during the war, and future importation of Negroes.

BARNARD FAMILY PAPERS

6 boxes, 1714–1901. *NUCMC* 62–4621

130 Ebenezer Barnard (1727–99): Hartford, Conn., merchant and militia captain. Ebenezer Barnard, Jr. (1748–1827): Hartford merchant. Cyprian Barnard (1753–1832): Merchant skipper, prisoner of war. Timothy Barnard (1756–1847): Maj., commissary department, merchant, and land speculator.

Revolutionary material consists largely of letters between the Barnard brothers, Ebenezer, Cyprian, and Timothy. Twelve letters from Timothy chiefly to Ebenezer Barnard written from various encampments and cities between Williamsburg and Boston, 1782–88, concern military supplies (some of which he purchased through his brother), maneuvers, and the capture of his older brother Cyprian by the British. Timothy's postwar correspondence concerns business ventures in Virginia and New York and family matters. Thirteen letters from Cyprian to Ebenezer, 1782–89, discuss business and family matters. Miscellaneous items include receipts, deeds, indentures, accounts, and memorandum books.

MRS. CHRISTIAN BARNES PAPERS

50 items, 1768–84.

131 Barnes: Wife of Henry Barnes (1723–1808), a Marlborough, Mass., loyalist merchant who removed to England, Feb. 1776.

Letters from Mrs. Barnes to friends in Cambridge, Brush Hill, and Boston, Mass., and London, most of which concern personal and social matters. Three letters written in 1770 describe the sufferings of the Barnes family at the hands of the Massachusetts Sons of Liberty and contain occasional references to the Boston Massacre, the nonimportation agreement, and various committees of safety.

Principal correspondents: Dorothy Forbes, Catherine Goldthwaite, Elizabeth Inman, and Elizabeth Smith.

JOHN BARRY PAPERS

2 boxes, 1770–1801. *NUCMC* 69-2028

132 Barry (1745–1803): Philadelphia shipmaster and shipowner; capt., Continental Navy.

Documents pertaining to the Revolutionary career of Barry include the logbook kept on the voyages of the schooner *Industry* to St. Croix, New York, Virginia, and Nevis, 1770–72; lists of officers and men on board the *Alliance*, Mar. 1781 and Dec. 1782; a letterbook kept on the *Alliance*, Oct. 1782—Apr. 1783; and accounts on the sale of prize ships taken by the *Alliance*. Correspondence between Robert Morris and Barry reflects the problems of supply and the use of the Navy for personal gain. Letters between Barry and Lafayette concern prospects for peace in 1782.

Principal correspondents: Thomas Barclay, Franklin, James Geagan, and Henry Johnston, and the firms of Howland & Cort, McCall & Lewis, and Morris & Swanwick.

BARTLETT FAMILY PAPERS

29 boxes, 1710–1951.   Finding aid and microfilm available.   *NUCMC* 70–937

133 Josiah Bartlett (1729–95): Kingston, N.H., physician; member, assembly, 1765–75, and Continental Congress, 1775–79; State judge, 1779–90; pres. New Hampshire, 1790–92.

Material from the period of the Revolution includes correspondence and medical notes of Josiah Bartlett. Bartlett's letters discuss the high cost of shipbuilding, the battle of Bennington, and events in Congress. Letters of Ezra, Josiah's son, describe student life at Phillips Exeter Academy, 1786, and those of his wife, Mary, concern family and local matters, 1776–78. Also includes a few indentures, deeds, and contracts.

BARTON–JENIFER FAMILY PAPERS
1 box, 1781–1876.   *NUCMC* 70–938

134   Seth Barton: Baltimore, Md., merchant. Daniel of St. Thomas Jenifer (1723–90): Maryland planter; proprietary agent.
        Contains 12 commercial letters to Seth Barton from business associates in England and America, 1787. Also a letter from Charles Carroll to St. Thomas Jenifer commenting on the war in the Southern Department and foreign affairs, 1781, and miscellaneous accounts and receipts.

BASSETT FAMILY PAPERS
1 vol., 1693–1837.   *NUCMC* 67–586

135   Burwell Bassett (1734–93): Member, Virginia House of Burgesses, 1762–75, and Virginia Convention, 1774, 1776. Burwell Bassett, Jr. (1764–1841): Member, State legislature, 1787–89, 1793–1805, 1819–21, and U.S. House of Representatives, 1805–13, 1815–19, 1821–29.
        Includes invoices for the sale of tobacco, 1763–73, giving information on rates, freight charges, profits, and commissions. Also miscellaneous letters and receipts.

JOHN D. BATCHELDER AUTOGRAPH COLLECTION
12 vols., 15th—20th centuries.   Finding aid available.   *NUCMC* 61–2074.

136   Mainly a collection of signed photographs of stage personalities, annotated theater programs, and personal correspondence. Items bearing on the Revolution appear in volumes 1, 4, 5, 6, 7, 9, and 11. They include a 1783 note by John Adams, a purported page from Benedict Arnold's account book, a certificate signed by Capt. John Barry, requisitions for supplies signed by Gen. Thomas Gage and Francis Marion, and letters by David Humphreys, Maj. Pierre L'Enfant, and Joseph Reed, 1781, 1788. Also includes clipped signatures of many Revolutionary figures and post-Revolutionary letters by Henry Lee, Henry Knox, Lafayette, and George Mason.

HENRY BECK PAPERS
1 vol., 1786.

137   Copies of melodies and songs. Contains no hymns or religious pieces. Music Division.

GEORGE BEDINGER PAPERS
1 vol., 1780–1880.   Draper Mss., series A, WHi.   Microfilm, 1 reel.

138   Bedinger (1756–1843): Virginia and Kentucky frontiersman, soldier, and politician.
        Pertinent material, largely in the form of notes taken by Draper in conversation with Bedinger, consists of Bedinger's recollections of his services during the Revolution. Also includes genealogical notes, land warrants, and letters and affidavits from descendants regarding various episodes in the life of Bedinger.
        See Reuben Gold Thwaites, ed., *Descriptive List of Manuscript Collections of the State Historical Society of Wisconsin* (Madison, 1906), p. 2.

THOMAS BEE PAPERS
1 box, 1783–1812.

139   Bee (1740–1812): South Carolina lawyer and judge; lt. gov., 1779–80; member, Continental Congress, 1780–82.
        Includes 15 letters sent to Bee between 1781 and 1783. Six letters from the Marquis de Barbé-Marbois concern personal and business affairs; four from Col. John Laurens concern the progress of the southern campaign; and three from the Chevalier de Cambray concern plans to settle in South Carolina and the reward he expects for his service in America.

JEREMY BELKNAP PAPERS
4 vols., 1683–1775.   Force transcripts.
140   Belknap (1744–98): Massachusetts and New Hampshire antiquarian, Congregational minister, and author.

Consists of correspondence, orders from the Governor and council of New Hampshire, extracts from council minutes, deeds, and reports. Subjects of the correspondence include the appointment of John Thomlinson as agent for New Hampshire, paper currency, repeal of the Stamp Act, trade, and various legal matters.

Principal correspondents: Theodore Atkinson, Gov. William Shirley, and Gov. Benning Wentworth.

Originals in New Hampshire Historical Society.

ANDREW BELL PAPERS
2 vols., 1777–1838.
141   Bell (1757–1847): New Jersey loyalist; secretary to Sir Henry Clinton and Sir Guy Carleton, 1778–82.

Correspondence of Andrew Bell with his sister, Cornelia Bell Paterson, and various friends and acquaintances in Canada, England, and British-occupied New York. The letters relate personal and family news and vividly depict the plight of the loyalists during the American Revolution. Twenty-five love letters Bell wrote to Mrs. Susanna Moore, a widow he secretly married in Sept. 1782, contain personal news and frequent allusions to some ill-defined scheme he harbored for advancing his career. The remaining correspondence concerns loyalist claims, political developments in England, and the whereabouts and circumstances of several of Bell's loyalist friends.

Principal correspondents: O. Barberie, Grove Bend, Jonathan Burnett, Charles Cooke, Andrew Goeranson, Heathcote Johnston, Robert Mackenzie, and Patrick Stuart.

The Andrew Bell–Cornelia Bell Paterson correspondence is published in the *Proceedings of the New Jersey Historical Society* (4th series), vol. 15 (1930), p. 508–17; vol. 16 (1931), p. 56–67, 186–201.

WINSLOW M. BELL, BERMUDIANA COLLECTION
9 boxes, 1674–1916.
142   Bell: Phoenix, Ariz., bibliophile.

Notes and transcripts made by Winslow M. Bell during the preparation of his histories of Bermuda. Two boxes of "Notes on Papers in the Bermuda Public Library" contain extracts from the records of King's Bench, 1780–87, entry books of King's Bench, 1704–82, Colonial Office records, 1782–1811, and Custom House records, 1694–1799. Four boxes contain typescripts of the records of the Courts of Assize, Oyer and Terminer, 1704–64. Material also includes laws, 1690–1788, a small collection of manuscript deeds, estate inventories, and ship accounts, and drafts of three histories of Bermuda written by Bell that appeared in the Bermuda *Gazette*: "The Tribes of Old Bermuda," "Bermuda through the Centuries," and "Tales and Traditions of Old Bermuda."

BENJAMIN BELLOWS PAPERS
1 folio, 1778–83.   Force transcripts.
143   Bellows (1712–1802): Founder of Walpole, N.H.; member, State legislature; col., New Hampshire Militia.

Letters concerning the Connecticut River towns during the Vermont controversy, the major question being whether the towns should unite and join either New Hampshire or Vermont. Also discussed are Vermont's negotiations with the British. Includes records of the Cheshire County Convention.

Principal correspondents: Ira Allen, Josiah Bartlett, Josiah Goldsmith, Samuel Livermore, William Page, John Sullivan, Meshech Weare, and Beza Woodward.

SIR FRANCIS BERNARD PAPERS

1 vol., 1768–69.   Force transcripts.

144   Bernard (1712–79): Lincoln, England, barrister, 1737–58; gov., New Jersey, 1758–60, and Massachusetts, 1760–69.

Letters and official reports of Bernard as Governor of Massachusetts reveal his problems in attempting to maintain calm while enforcing the Townshend Acts in the face of what he called "the Faction." Includes nine of Bernard's reports to Lord Shelburne, Jan.–Mar. 1768, and 50 reports to Lord Hillsborough, May 1768–July 1769, describing attacks on customs commissioners, control of law enforcement by "the Faction," reactions to the landing of troops, use of Crown appointments for political purposes, troubles with the Massachusetts Council and General Court, and problems with the courts of law.

Transcribed in 1834 from a letterbook owned by Obadiah Rich of London.

JOSEPH V. BEVAN COLLECTION

1 box, 1733–1825.   Force transcripts.

145   Bevan (1798–1830): Georgia editor and archivist.

Mostly military correspondence, accounts, Government records, military rolls, etc., collected by Bevan for a history of Georgia. Several James Habersham letters, 1738–75, discuss issues such as the Stamp Act, Georgia's opposition to British trade and Indian policies, selection of a colonial agent, and Crown interference in the Georgia Legislature. Lachlan McIntosh papers, 1777–84, provide information on military activities on the southern and western borders. Letters from Jonathan Martin and Felix Warley describe wartime events within the State, and list land forfeitures for Richmond County. Also includes extracts from Maj. John Habersham's journal of the siege of Charleston, 1780; a collection of papers on Georgia Indians containing several Elijah Clark, Anthony Wayne, John Wilkinson, and Nathanael Greene letters on the 1782 expedition against the Cherokees; records leading to Hawkins' Treaty with the Choctaw Indians, 1785; Richard Winn's memoir on the southern campaign, 1780; and scattered rolls and accounts of the Georgia Continental Line, 1778–79.

ROBERT BEVERLEY LETTERBOOK

190 items, 1761–93.

146   Beverley (ca. 1738–1800): Virginia planter; loyalist; remained quietly at Blandfield, Essex County, throughout the war.

Chiefly commercial correspondence between Beverley and his agents in London and Liverpool. The letters express criticism of British economic policy and approval of moderate American protest until 1775. A 10–page apologia to William Fitzhugh, July 1775, reveals the apprehensions of an Anglophile who feared Parliamentary encroachments less than the tactics of American republicans. Five letters from Beverley to his son William in England, 1781–83, document the maintenance of personal contacts in the mother country during the war and the revival of trade at the war's end.

Principal correspondents: Samuel Athawes, John Bland, and Samuel Gist.

WILLIAM BINGHAM PAPERS

25 items, 1776–79.

147   Bingham (1752–1804): Philadelphia, Pa., banker; agent to the French West Indies for Congress and for the firm of Willing and Morris, 1776–80; member, Continental Congress, 1787–88, State legislature, 1790–95, U.S. Senate, 1795–1801.

Consists mainly of letters to Bingham in Martinique from Willing, Morris and Company and from Robert Morris, 1776–79. The letters provide a picture of wartime commercial conditions—fluctuating prices, availability of goods, insurance rates, and privateering. They indicate the manifold transactions, public and private, carried on by Thomas Willing, Robert Morris, and Bingham; Morris' changing attitude toward privateering and the activities of his brother Thomas in Europe; and the spectacular growth of Bingham's personal fortune.

See also Miscellaneous Manuscripts Collection, entry no. 560.

EPHRAIM BLAINE PAPERS
19 vols., 1765–1805.   Force manuscripts.   *NUCMC* 66–1385

148   Blaine (1741–1804): Pennsylvania merchant and farmer; commissary to the 8th Pennsylvania Regiment, 1776; deputy commissary general of purchases, Middle Department, 1777–79; commissary general, 1780–82; merchant at Pittsburgh after the war.

Consists of five volumes of original correspondence, 1766–1805, two letterbooks, 1777–78 and 1780–83, two cashbooks, an account book, a memo book, and eight volumes of miscellaneous accounts. Correspondence for the period 1765–74 primarily concerns mercantile matters but includes two letters from John Dickinson, who represented Blaine in a legal case in Philadelphia in 1769. The letters Blaine wrote as deputy commissary general of purchases, which are addressed to a network of assistants in Pennsylvania, Maryland, New Jersey and Delaware, concern general economic conditions, price levels, availability of transportation, and the status of troops posted in the region. His correspondence as commissary general, which is more national in scope, reflects the overall organization of the department and its relationship with Congress and the states.

Supplementing this correspondence are the two cashbooks, 1778–80, containing a record of payments received by Blaine while serving as deputy commissary; a memorandum book, 1782–84, containing notes on business trips made to settle accounts at the close of the war; and an account book containing abstracts of accounts with the U.S., 1777–79, 1780–81, and 1794–95. The remaining eight volumes, chiefly commissary accounts, also include portions of three daybooks, 1765–66, 1769–70, and 1779–81; accounts for goods sold through the store operated by E. Blaine & Co. at Pittsburgh, 1783–84; and three comprehensive returns on the organization and personnel of the commissary department.

Principal correspondents: Washington, various presidents of Congress, Governors and legislative leaders in Pennsylvania, Maryland, New Jersey, and Delaware, and officials of several Congressional boards and committees. Also Peter Aston, Clement Biddle, Alexander Blaine, Anthony Broderick, Robert Buchanan, William Buchanan, Isaac Carty, John Chaloner, Henry Champion, Peter Colts, Robert Dodd, Azariah Dunham, Nehemiah Dunham, George Eichelberger, Patrick Ewing, Royal Flint, Robert Forsyth, Jacob Giles, Sebastian Graff, Udney Hay, Henry Hollingsworth, Robert Hooper, John Howell, Joseph Hugg, Thomas Huggins, Andrew Levy, Nicholas Lutz, William Maclay, John McAlister, Robert McGermont, Charles Miller, Henry Miller, George Morgan, Jacob Morgan, George Murdock, John Patton, David Redick, Thomas Richardson, George Ross, Matthias Slough, Jeremiah Wadsworth, Conrad Theodore Wederstrandt, James White, and Donaldson Yates.

JAMES G. BLAINE FAMILY PAPERS
49 boxes, 1777–1943.

149   Blaine (1830–1920): Member, Maine Legislature, 1859–62, U.S. House of Representatives, 1863–76, U.S. Senate, 1876–81; secretary of state, 1881, 1889–92.

Box 34 contains a folder marked "Special Autograph Collection," which includes a letter from George Washington, Aug. 21, 1781, concerning the march of the American Army from New York to Yorktown, Va.

THEODORICK BLAND PAPERS
1 box, 1742–83.

150   Bland (1742–90): Virginia doctor and planter; col., 1st Continental Dragoons, 1777–79; member, Continental Congress, 1780–83.

Includes various orders issued by Bland and letters to Bland from Lt. Col. John Banister, Col. Christian Febiger, and Thomas Smith. Banister's letter of May 1781 describes the British attack on Richmond under Maj. Gen. William Phillips.

SAMUEL BLODGET PAPERS
1 box, 1758–1813.   *NUCMC* 62–4563
151   Samuel Blodget, Jr. (1724–1807): Haverhill, Mass., dry goods merchant.
Miscellaneous receipts and bills of exchange of Samuel and his father, Samuel, Sr., make up most of the material for the Revolutionary era. Includes scattered legal documents, mercantile orders, and a surveyor's report on the Blodget farm in Foffstown, N.H.

WILLIAM BLOUNT COLLECTION
1 box, ca. 1783–1823.
152   Blount (1749–1800): North Carolina soldier and statesman; Territorial Governor, Tennessee; paymaster, various North Carolina units during the American Revolution.
Includes a few items from the 1780's: a copy of the articles of agreement between Col. James Robertson and William Blount for the survey of land awarded to officers and soldiers from North Carolina; a list of men who served under Jesse Bean for the protection of the Carolina frontier, 1788; a return of men enlisted by William Roberts for duty on the frontier, 1789; and payrolls for soldiers serving under Capt. Alexander Brown, 1788, Maj. Robert King, 1788–89, Capt. John Crawford, 1788, and Capt. David Haley.

BOARD OF COMMISSIONERS FOR SUPERINTENDING EMBARKATION OF THE BRITISH ARMY FROM NEW YORK, MINUTES
153   1 vol., 1783.   Force manuscripts.
Testimony presented to the board relating to ownership of slaves being taken on board ships preparing to embark from New York, May 30—Aug. 7, 1783. The board was appointed by Sir Guy Carleton pursuant to the seventh article of the Treaty of Paris, which attempted to prevent the "destruction, or carrying away any Negroes, or other property, of the American inhabitants," during the British evacuation.
See also Carleton Papers, P.R.O. 30/55, entry no. 1576.

WILLIAM BOND PAPERS
1 reel microfilm, 1768–1833.   *NUCMC* 66–1553
154   Bond (d. 1776): Lt. col., Thomas Gardner's Massachusetts regiment; col., 25th Continental Infantry.
Printed forms (filled in), commissions, broadsides, military returns and lists of officers, receipts, orders, and correspondence. Bond's letters, written in 1776, chiefly to his wife Lucy, concern personal and family matters. Also includes routine letters to Gen. Nathanael Greene and Joseph Trumbull and letters from Gen. Philip Schuyler and Stephen Moylan. A letter from Chaplain Ebenezer David to Mrs. Bond, Aug. 1776, relates the news of her husband's death.
Originals owned by Elizabeth S. Sellen, 1946.

DANIEL BOONE PAPERS
33 vols., chiefly 19th century.   Draper Mss., series C, WHi.   Microfilm, 8 reels.
155   Boone (1734–1820): Frontier scout, surveyor, and soldier.
Primarily anecdotes and reminiscences collected by Lyman C. Draper in conversation or correspondence with numerous descendants and acquaintances of Boone. Most original documents in the collection—signatures, commissions, accounts, land patents, survey books, letters, and miscellaneous legal papers—appear in volumes 25–27.
See also Thwaites, *Descriptive List of Manuscript Collections*, p. 2–5.

ELIAS BOUDINOT PAPERS
2 boxes, 1773–1812.
156   Boudinot (1730–1821): New Jersey lawyer and politician; member, Continental Congress, 1777–84, pres., 1782–84; commissary general of prisoners, 1777–78; acting

secretary of foreign affairs, 1783–84.

Letters and documents concerning the handling of prisoners during the Revolution. Topics discussed in the correspondence include paroles, complaints of cruel treatment, supplies and provisions, the confinement of loyalists, and prisoner exchanges. Several letters written while Boudinot served as President of Congress and Acting Secretary of Foreign Affairs concern peace negotiations.

Principal correspondents: John Adams, John Campbell, Franklin, John Hancock, Sir William Howe, John Jay, Henry Knox, Henry Laurens, Robert R. Livingston, William Livingston, Richard Peters, Timothy Pickering, Washington, and Ezekiel Williams.

ELIAS BOUDINOT PAPERS

1 vol., 1776–83.   Force transcripts.

157   Boudinot (1730–1821): See entry no. 156.

Letters between Boudinot and Sir William Howe, Joshua Loring, Washington, and others concerning the treatment and exchange of prisoners. Includes a list of prisoners held by the British in New York, 1777, with Boudinot's assessment of conditions, and lists of American prisoners of war, 1776–78.

PETER BOUNETHEAU PAPERS

1 folio, 1685–1897.

158   Bounetheau: Charleston, S.C., militia officer.

Contains miscellaneous petitions and commissions of Bounetheau, including a petition to Lord Cornwallis for the return of a Negro slave "borrowed" by Maj. Charles Cochran, Aug. 1780, and Bounetheau's commissions as a militia officer, notary public, and deputy quartermaster general.

SYLVANUS BOURNE PAPERS

41 vols., 1774–1854.   *NUCMC* 62–4998

159   Bourne: Barnstable, Mass., merchant; U.S. consul at Hispaniola, 1791–92; vice consul at Amsterdam, 1794.

Part of one volume includes letters of the Bourne family written during the Revolution, which reveal how little the war affected some parts of Massachusetts. Also minor accounts of Bourne, records dealing with the estate of his father, Melatiah, and a short journal, Apr. 1789, describing Bourne's trip to New York with Vice-President-elect John Adams.

Principal correspondents: Melatiah Bourne, Joseph Hinckly, John Hodgson, Joseph Pitcairn, and various members of the Bourne family.

BOZMAN-KERR COLLECTION

3 boxes, 1669–1883.   Finding aid available.

160   John Leeds Bozman (1757–1823): Maryland lawyer and minor public official. John Leeds Kerr (1780–1844): Nephew of Bozman; member, U.S. House of Representatives, 1825–29, 1831–33, U.S. Senate, 1841–43. John Bozman Kerr (1809–78): Son of John Leeds Kerr; member, U.S. House of Representatives, 1849–51.

Correspondence of three men from Talbot County on the Eastern Shore of Maryland. Includes 12 letters chiefly from John Leeds Bozman to David Kerr and John Leeds, 1784–86, and from William Vans Murray to Bozman, 1787–89. Bozman's letters, written from London, and Murray's from Bristol, England, and Cambridge. Md., concern personal and family matters. Also includes a list of shipping fees received at the port of Oxford, Md., 1765–66, showing names of vessels and dates of arrival.

JOHN BRADFORD LETTERBOOKS

2 vols., 1776–82.

161   Bradford: Continental agent at the port of Boston, Mass.

Correspondence concerning building contracts for Continental vessels; the acquisition, transport, and distribution of naval supplies; ship schedules, cargoes, and destinations; captured vessels; and stores received from France. Also contains information on prizes, naval engagements, and ships lost at sea, and accounts of goods forwarded to the Continental Army.

Principal correspondents: Capt. John Adams, Samuel Adams, John Brown, Caleb Cushing, John Dorsius, William Ellery, Franklin, Horatio Gates, John Green, William Greene, John Hancock, Benjamin Harrison, Joseph Hewes, Capt. John Inglis, Leonard Jarvis, John Jay, Richard Henry Lee, Francis Lewis, William Lux, Capt. John Moody, Robert Morris, Thomas Morris, John Philip Nerkle, Joseph Nourse, Richard Peters, Timothy Pickering, John P. Rathbourn, John Ross, John Daniel Schweighauser, Daniel Tillinghast, Washington, Abraham Whipple, and William Whipple. Also the firms of Messrs. Clarkson and Livingston and Messrs. Morris, Pliarne, Penet & Co., commercial committee, marine committee, secret committee of Congress, and the Board of Trade.

SAMUEL BRADY AND LEWIS WETZEL PAPERS
16 vols., 1757–1871.   Draper Mss., series C, WHi.   Microfilm, 4 reels.

162   Brady (1756–95): Revolutionary officer, frontiersman, Indian fighter. Wetzel (1763–1808): Frontiersman and Indian fighter.

Primarily Lyman C. Draper's correspondence of the 1840's, 1850's, and 1860's with amateur historians and descendants of Brady and Wetzel. In addition to this correspondence, Draper collected newspaper clippings and various manuscript "narratives," but he failed to locate any substantial body of original manuscripts describing the adventures of Brady and Wetzel on the Pennsylvania–Ohio frontier. The material on Wetzel is particularly sparse.

Volume 1 contains approximately 100 original documents, 1757–1822, chiefly correspondence, military records, and accounts of Indian activities. Volumes 12–13 contain miscellaneous notes and documents, including Draper's own manuscript on Samuel Brady.

JOSEPH BRANT PAPERS
22 vols., chiefly 19th century.   Draper Mss., series F, WHi.   Microfilm, 8 reels.

163   Brant (ca. 1740–1807): Mohawk chief; educated at Wheelock's Indian school; led his tribesmen against the American Colonies during the Revolution.

Chiefly transcripts, notes, and miscellaneous printed material concerning the Revolutionary struggle on the western frontiers of New York and Pennsylvania. Material includes copies of select papers of Sir William Johnson, Brant's brother-in-law, and notes on persons associated with Brant. One volume of original documents includes letters from border leaders on both sides, Indian treaties, speeches, and petitions, 1771–99.

See also Thwaites, *Descriptive List of Manuscript Collections*, p. 7–9.

BRECKINRIDGE FAMILY PAPERS
1112 units, 1750–1950.

164   Breckinridge: Virginia and Kentucky frontier family.

Six volumes of this large collection contain the papers of John Breckinridge (1760–1806), lawyer and statesman of Botetourt County, Va., and Kentucky. Includes correspondence between Breckinridge and his mother, Lettice Preston Breckinridge; papers and documents concerning speculation in land by George May, John May, William Preston, Thomas Marshall, John Brown, William Christian, and Thomas Walker; and letters from various members of the Breckinridge family concerning Indian affairs, 1782–84. Several letters from Archibald Stuart give an overview of the controversy concerning ratification of the Constitution, 1788.

Principal correspondents: John Brown, Joseph Cabell, Arthur Campbell, Paul Carrington, William Fleming, Patrick Henry, and John Marshall.

ISAAC BRIGGS PAPERS
1 box, 1691–1886.   *NUCMC* 69–2030

165   Briggs: Wilkes County, Ga., and Cecil County, Md., planter.
Contains a few surveys, land grants, and business papers relating to Briggs' speculation in land in Georgia during the postwar period. Also letters and abstracts of records
from the Quaker yearly and quarterly meetings for London, Philadelphia, and Cecil
County, Md.

BRITISH INTELLIGENCE, NEW YORK
1 vol., 1778.

166   Anonymous diary-like record of information taken from deserters and spies on the
location, condition, and maneuvers of American troops in New York, July—Nov. 1778.
Probably recorded by a British officer stationed near Kings Bridge, Manhattan Island.

BROADSIDES AND MISCELLANEOUS MATERIALS
2 folios, 1754–1873.

167   Includes printed oaths of allegiance signed by James Young, Aug. 1778, William
Bartram, June 1777, and James Bryson, 1778, all of Pennsylvania, as well as a deed in
the name of Asa Mixer, 1783, a photostat of the parole of Jared Ingersoll, Sr., 1778, and
interest vouchers, pension vouchers, Treasury Office receipts, and related items, issued by
the Pennsylvania Council of State, 1783–88.

DANIEL BRODHEAD PAPERS
3 vols., 1775–81.   Draper Mss., series H, WHi.   Microfilm, 1 reel.

168   Brodhead (1736–1809): Lt. col., 2d and 4th Pennsylvania Regiments, 1776; col., 8th
Pennsylvania Regiment, 1777; commandant, Fort Pitt, Mar. 1779—Sept. 1781; brig. gen.,
Sept. 1783.
Material concerning military affairs at Fort Pitt and operations against the Indians
on the western frontier. Documents for 1775–78 deal with western intelligence and Congressional Indian policy before Brodhead took command at Fort Pitt. The remaining documents, which make up the bulk of the collection, include addresses to the Indians, "Indian talks and treaties," and military correspondence. Several Washington letters, 1779–80,
concern attacks planned in coordination with Sullivan's expedition against the Iroquois,
and possible followup expeditions against Detroit. A letterbook kept by Brodhead at
Fort Pitt, Oct. 1780—Dec. 1781, contains copies of his correspondence with the quartermaster department, militia leaders in the western parts of Pennsylvania and Virginia,
and officers on detached command.
Principal correspondents: Ephraim Blaine, John Clark, John Gibson, Rev. John
Heckewelder, Samuel Huntington, William Irvine, Jefferson, Thomas McKean, Richard
Peters, Joseph Reed, Baron von Steuben, William Taylor, Washington, Anthony Wayne,
and Rev. David Zeisberger.
See also Thwaites, *Descriptive List of Manuscript Collections*, p. 9-10.

JAMES BROWN PAPERS
5 vols., 1765–1867.   *NUCMC* 62–4647

169   Brown (1766–1835): Kentucky lawyer; secretary of state, Kentucky, 1792; secretary,
New Orleans Territory, 1804; member U.S. Senate, Louisiana, 1813–17, 1819–21; minister
to France.
Contains two letters relating to Brown's business affairs in New Orleans, surveyor's
maps showing land in West Florida belonging to the heirs of John Stuart, and a return
for the southern Army, 1781. Most material in the collection concerns Brown's later political career.

ALEXANDER BRUCE PAPERS
1 vol., 1776–81.

170   Manuscript copy of an essay by Bruce first published anonymously at Edinburgh in 1759 under the title "An Enquiry into the cause of the pestilence, and the diseases in fleets and armies." This edition, prepared with copies of several letters pertaining to the problems of disease and sanitation during the War for Independence, was never published. Letters by Bruce are to the Earl of Mansfield, 1776, Sir Grey Cooper, 1778, John MacPherson, 1779, and the Earl of Dalhousie, 1781. The one letter to Bruce is from Maj. George Hay, 1781.

SAMUEL BURCH PAPERS
4 boxes, 1775–1865.   *NUCMC* 62–4568

171   Burch: Lawyer; clerk, U.S. House of Representatives.
Includes a copy of a ledger containing Benjamin Franklin's European account, 1777; two letters by Gen. Baron de Kalb written on the eve of his departure for America with Lafayette, 1777; and copies of letters by La Luzerne, Robert Morris, John Pierce, and Marquis de Barbé–Marbois, 1784.

AARON BURR PAPERS
4 boxes and 1 folio, 1788–1810.

172   Burr (1756–1836): Lt. col., Continental Army; Member, U.S. Senate, 1791–97; Vice President of the U.S.
Includes a letter from Burr to Christopher P. Yates, Oct. 1788, inquiring about the existence of a mortgage or judgment against James Wilson of Philadelphia.

J. KELSEY BURR, JR., COLLECTION
3 boxes, 1774–1865.   *NUCMC* 70–940

173   Burr: New Jersey collector.
Includes papers of the Philadelphia area barrackmaster for the American Army, 1777–80. Col. Isaac Melcher's papers include accounts, receipts, and orders for wood, cut and hauled, 1777–80; accounts of wood and candles issued, 1778; and accounts of wagons in the public service at Pennsbury Manor, Pa., 1779.

LAURENCE BUTLER PAPERS
1 box, 1784–93.

174   Butler: Westmoreland County, Va., planter and surveyor; served in various regiments of the Virginia Continental Line, 1776–83.
Series of 11 letters from Butler to Mrs. Anna Francesca Cradock of Leicestershire, England, whom he met on a trip to Paris. Butler describes his return from Europe, his trips to Kentucky, and the formation of the Federal Government.

PIERCE BUTLER PAPERS
1 box, 1787.   Photostats.

175   Butler (1744–1822): South Carolina planter; member, State legislature, 1778–82 and 1784–89, Continental Congress, 1787, Constitutional Convention, 1787, and U.S. House of Representatives, 1789–96, 1802–6.
Notes on the Constitution during the 1787 convention, including Butler's 12 objections to the Constitution as of Aug. 30, drafts of the fugitive slave clause, and notes on several drafts of the Constitution. Also notes on Franklin's proposal on representation and on the debates over taxation.
Originals owned by Owen Wister in 1940.

JOHN BUYERS DOCKET BOOK
1 vol., 1781–1802.

176   Buyers (1749–1821): Northumberland County, Pa., justice of the peace.

Contains information on social and economic conditions in Northumberland County during the 18th century. About three-fourths of all cases recorded concern the collection of debts. The remaining cases involve judgments against persons accused of Sabbath-breaking, breaches of the peace, and assault, and the assignment of terms of service for children bound out by the county. Also records weddings conducted by Buyers and oaths of allegiance administered to former loyalists who settled in the county between 1785 and 1787.

SIMON CAMERON PAPERS
29 boxes, 1 folio, 1738–1906.

177   Cameron (1738–1809): Indian scout and manager of the Pennsylvania estate of Donald Cameron.

Contains about 50 letters of George Frey of Middletown, N.J., concerning the shipment of hemp and salt, as well as scattered material relating to the Revolutionary military career of William Baxter and a later pension claim, documents pertaining to the arrest of Maj. Nathaniel Mitchell, the parole of Henry Hamilton, 1780, and miscellaneous deeds and receipts.

CAMPBELL–PRESTON–FLOYD FAMILY PAPERS
12 vols., 6 boxes, 1741–1931.

178   Campbell, Preston, Floyd: Related families on the Virginia frontier.

Documents from the period of the Revolution, chiefly wills, accounts, surveys, deeds, and business and personal correspondence, apppear in the first two volumes. Letters concern the burning of Norfolk, Va., the battle of Point Pleasant, operations against the Indians during Dunmore's War, and the battle of King's Mountain. Other pertinent items include survey books, 1768–87, a commonplace book containing extracts from a speech by Governor Botetourt to the Virginia House of Burgesses, 1769, and Thomas Hanson's journal of a surveying expedition into Kentucky, 1774.

Principal correspondents: Daniel Brodhead, Jr., Arthur Campbell, David Campbell, Elizabeth Campbell, Margaret Campbell, William Campbell, William Christian, Nathanael Greene, Isaac Hall, Sarah Henry, Andrew Lewis, George Lewis, Abner Nash, Robert Preston, William Preston, Evan Shelby, Isaac Shelby, and David Ward.

GUY CARLETON PAPERS
1 vol., 1774–77.   Force manuscripts.

179   Guy Carleton (1724–1808): Lt. gov., Quebec, 1766–68, gov., 1768–78, 1786–96; British northern commander, 1775–78; commander in chief in America, 1782–83.

Contemporary copies of letters from secretaries Dartmouth and Germain concerning the period of Carleton's defense of Canada, 1776, and the administration's reaction to his conduct. Initially focused on measures for the relief of Quebec, the correspondence shifts to plans for reinforcing Carleton, cooperating with General Howe on the frontiers of New York, and utilizing the Indians. Includes Germain's critical reaction to Carleton's failure to capture Ticonderoga and his decision to withdraw from Lake Champlain.

CHARLES CARROLL OF CARROLLTON PAPERS
3 vols., 1661–1829.

180   Carroll (1737–1832): Maryland planter; member, Continental Congress, 1776–78, Board of War, 1776–77, State legislature, 1777–1800, and U.S. Senate, 1789–92.

Chiefly 18th–century accounts and records from the Carroll family estates. Also includes Charles Carroll's personal accounts of expenditures and taxes, 1778–88, 1800, sheriff's accounts for Baltimore and Anne Arundel Counties and Poplar Island, and letters relating to mercantile activities and land speculation.

Principal correspondents: Daniel Dulany and Joseph Ensor.

DANIEL CARROLL OF DUDDINGTON PAPERS
10 boxes, 1662–1910.   *NUCMC* 64–768

181   Carroll (1764–1849): Maryland lawyer and landowner.

Scattered through three of the above boxes are legal and financial papers, 1763–89, chiefly receipts, accounts, indentures, certificates, and survey records. Much of this material relates to the estate of Charles Carroll, Jr., who died in 1771. Other clients include John Beall, Robert Carter, Ignatius Fenwick, and Notley Young.

JOHN CARROLL PAPERS
1 box, 1785.

182   Carroll (1735–1815): Jesuit priest; apostolic prefect to the United States from 1784; Bishop of Baltimore, Md., and founder of Georgetown University, 1789.

A collection of four, long letters in English, French, and Latin written by Father John Carroll explains and describes many of the problems that faced Catholics and the Catholic Church in post-Revolutionary America. Among the views expressed was the fear that governance of Catholics from Rome could lead to retraction of civil rights because of the American fear of foreign interference.

ROBERT CARTER PAPERS
3 boxes, 1795–1805.   *NUCMC* 66–1391

183   "Councillor" Carter (1728–1804): Virginia and Maryland planter and iron manufacturer; resided primarily at Nomini Hall.

Business letters from Robert Carter to Landon Carter, William Hammond, and an anonymous recipient. Letters received include one each from Rev. James Manning and Rev. Asa Hunt concerning the effects of their preaching in the Northern States, 1786–88, and one from Rev. John Leland expressing approval of a theological treatise by Carter. Also two daybooks, Feb.—Dec. 1775, and Apr. 1789—June 1790, recording commercial activity on Carter's estates; a ledger, 1759–99, containing miscellaneous accounts, bills, and agricultural notes and formulas; a journal, Aug. 1784—Mar. 1789, containing accounts and lists of estates, tenants, slaves, and livestock; and three memorandum books, 1774–89, with miscellaneous accounts, inventories, rent rolls, and agricultural formulas. Six volumes of religious writings (five undated) consist largely of prayers and extracts from the Bible.

JAMES L. CATHCART PAPERS
3 boxes, 1785–1817.   *NUCMC* 63–333

184   Cathcart (1767–1843): Midshipman, Continental Navy, 1779, 1782; merchant seaman; prisoner at Algiers, 1785; secretary to the dey of Algiers until 1796; consul to Tripoli, 1797; diplomatic agent to Tunis, 1798–1801; consul at Algiers, Tunis, and Madeira, 1807–15.

Includes Cathcart's journal, a "Precise Account of Negotiation Between the United States and the Regencies of Algiers, Tunis, and Tripoli Since They Commenced Depredations of U.S. Commerce in 1785," describing his activities in Algiers. Also contains such items as a list of ships and sailors captured by Algeria. Published by Jane B. Newkirk, ed., *The Captives* . . . (La Porte, Ind., 1899).

CATHOLIC CHURCH, DIOCESE OF LOUISIANA AND THE FLORIDAS
12 reels microfilm, 1576–1803.

185   Documents from the period of the American Revolution consist largely of Spanish records concerning the finances of Charity Hospital at New Orleans, requests of fugitives

for sanctuary, registers of persons in Louisiana, and at Mobile, and Pensacola, West Florida, religious requirements for settlement of Americans in Spanish Louisiana, and the destructive fire that swept New Orleans in April 1788.

Sponsored by National Historical Publications Commission. Originals in University of Notre Dame Archives.

GEORGE CHALMERS COLLECTION
69 vols., 1641–1824.   Force manuscripts.

186   Chalmers (1742–1825): Scottish historian; practiced law in Maryland, 1763–75; went to London, 1775; author of *Political Annals of the Present United Colonies* (1780) and *Introduction to the History of the Revolt of the British Colonies* (1782); and chief clerk to the privy council committee on trade and foreign plantations, 1786.

Primarily material concerning British trade during the 17th and 18th centuries. Includes official correspondence and documents, tabular data on the volume of trade, and an annotated copy of Sir Charles Whitworth's *State of the Trade of Great Britain in its Imports and Exports, Progressively from the Year 1697* (London, 1776). Also West Indian reports and papers containing information on population, slaves, and economic conditions; material on West Florida; an account of prices of furs and skins sold by Hudson Bay Co., 1787–89; two volumes pertaining to Newfoundland; and papers concerning shipping, duties, and prices at Quebec.

A few items pertain to Chalmers' legal practice in Maryland and personal matters. One volume relating to the British evacuation of Charleston includes copies of letters of British officers in South Carolina and of Lord Shelburne, Gen. Nathanael Greene, and Gov. John Mathews, as well as an original of the "Articles of Agreement" of Oct. 6, 1782. Also census reports from New Hampshire towns; a list of laws concerning the established church in Virginia, 1758–77; the orderly book of Thomas Ainslie, Sept. 1775—May 1776; the orderly book maintained at New York headquarters, Apr. 1752—July 1771, by Thomas Moncrieff and others; Capt. Walter Home's memorandum book; and five British Navy logbooks pertaining to the *Vestal* and the *Aeolus*.

See also P.R.O./Adm. 51, 52, entry nos. 1409–10.

SOCIETY OF THE CINCINNATI PAPERS
1 box, 1784–1810.   Force manuscripts and transcripts.

187   Ledger of the Society of the Cincinnati in Virginia containing accounts of expenditures and income from membership fees. Also a roll of autographs of Virginia officers subscribing to the constitution of the society, 1783. The transcripts include a journal of the organization of the society, May 10–13, 1783; a journal of proceedings of the first meeting, May 3–14, 1784; a list of delegates from several States; and a roll of the members of the South Carolina Society, 1793.

SOCIETY OF THE CINCINNATI PAPERS
22 boxes, 6 folios, 1776–1936.

188   Contains correspondence, journals, and minutes of society meetings, 1783–1811, concerning the society's organization, recruiting efforts, and the controversy over hereditary membership. Also lists of members in France, 1789; records of State societies, with membership lists for the 1780's for New Hampshire, Rhode Island, New York, New Jersey, South Carolina, and Virginia; and miscellaneous accounts and receipts. Small collections within the collection include the A. R. Parker Papers, 1770–82, which contain several items of Nathanael Greene as quartermaster general and Baron von Steuben's plan for organizing six brigades; Henry Laurens' notes on the readiness of South Carolina and Georgia, 1778; and the Nathaniel Pendleton Papers, 1781–1815. Pendleton, a captain in the Virginia Line and aide-de-camp to General Greene, wrote several letters concerning military supply and a possible mutiny in the southern Army, 1781–82.

Principal correspondents: John S. Dart, Comte d'Estaing, Horatio Gates, Henry Knox,

Marquis de la Rouerie Tuffin (Armand-Charles), La Luzerne, Benjamin Lincoln, Lachlan McIntosh, William Moultrie, Rochambeau, William Smallwood, and Washington.

RICHARD CLAIBORNE PAPERS
1 box, 1780–82.

189   Claiborne: Lt., 1st Continental Artillery, Jan. 1777; brigade maj., Gen. George Weedon's brigade, Nov. 1777; deputy quartermaster general for Virginia, 1780–82.

Letters from Claiborne chiefly to Richard Young, assistant deputy quartermaster at Fredericksburg, Va., concerning the business of the quartermaster department. Other correspondents include Gov. Benjamin Harrison, Thomas Marks, and Colonel Peabody.

GEORGE ROGERS CLARK PAPERS
64 vols., 18th—19th centuries.   Draper Mss., series J, WHi.   Microfilm, 17 reels.

190   Clark (1752–1818): Capt., Virginia Militia; brig. gen., Virginia State Line.

The largest and most important series of the Draper collection. Pertains chiefly to the early history of Kentucky and western operations in the Revolution. Original documents appear in volumes 7–12 and 39–63, with scattered letters and documents in volumes 17–18, 27, and 30–32. Volumes 13–35 contain mostly secondary material.

Principal correspondents: James Adler, Matthew Arbuckle, Isaac Bowman, John Bowman, Joseph Bowman, Daniel Brodhead, John Brown, Arthur Campbell, John Campbell, Abraham Chapline, Jonathan Clark, William Clark, John Crittenden, George Croghan, John Croghan, William Croghan, Valentine Dalton, Walker Daniel, William Davies, John Dodge, Lord Dunmore, William Finney, John Floyd, John Gibson, John Girault, Henry Hamilton, John Hardin, Josiah Harmar, Benjamin Harrison, Patrick Henry, William Irvine, Jefferson, Guy Johnson, Arthur Lee, J. M. P. Legros, John Marshall, Thomas Marshall, John May, James Monroe, John Montgomery, George Morgan, John Nevill, Oliver Pollock, Worden Pope, Edmund Randolph, Philippe François de Rocheblave, George Rogers, Isaac Shelby, George Slaughter, John Taylor, Charles M. Thruston, John Todd, Levi Todd, Stephen Trigg, and John Willis.

See also Thwaites, *Descriptive List of Manuscript Collections*, p. 10–14.

JONATHAN CLARK PAPERS
2 vols., 1728–94.   Draper Mss., series L, WHi.   Microfilm, 1 reel.

191   Clark (1750–1811): Capt., 8th Virginia Continental Regiment, 1776–77; maj. and lt. col., 10th Virginia Regiment, 1778–80; elder brother of George Rogers Clark.

Among the military papers of the collection are pay rolls and muster rolls, returns of prisoners, receipts, intelligence reports, orders from superior officers, and letters. Topics discussed in Clark's correspondence include Governor Dunmore's gunpowder plot, western lands, military maneuvers, the invasion of Virginia, and family matters.

Principal correspondents: Abraham Bowman, Richard Campbell, George Rogers Clark, John Clark, William Croghan, William Darke, Robert Harrison, Peter Helphenstine, John Herndon, Henry Lee, Thomas Marshall, Daniel Morgan, Peter Muhlenberg, John Page, William Russell, Charles Scott, James Wood, and William Woodford.

See also Thwaites, *Descriptive List of Manuscript Collections*, p. 15.

WILLIAM CLARK PAPERS
6 vols., 1780–1822.   Draper Mss., series M, WHi.   Microfilm, 1 reel.

192   Clark (d. 1791): Lt., Illinois Regiment; cousin of George Rogers Clark.

Documents from the Revolutionary era include letters and copies of letters from officers in the Illinois Regiment, papers relating to the Illinois grant, accounts, returns of stores and provisions, pay records, muster rolls, surveys, deeds, and copies of addresses delivered to the Indians.

Principal correspondents: John Armstrong, Abraham Chapline, Benjamin Clark, John Dodge, Harry Innes, Richard Tarrell, and John Thruston.

See also Thwaites, *Descriptive List of Manuscript Collections*, p. 15–16.

WILLIAM BELL CLARK COLLECTION
1 box, 1770–1950.   Photostats and typescripts.

193   Clark (1889–1968): Naval historian.
Includes a copy of Capt. John Barry's account of the defense of the *Raleigh*, 1778; copies of letters and papers relating to the Continental sloop of war *Independence*, 1776–78, copies of papers from the brig *Lexington*, 1777; extracts from the logs of British ships *Liverpool*, *Roebuck*, *Fowey*, and *Kingfisher*, and the Continental schooner *Wasp*, 1776; and transcripts of British Foreign Office and Admiralty Office papers.
In Naval Historical Foundation Collection, Library of Congress.

LEVINIUS CLARKSON PAPERS
1 box, 1 folio, 1772–93.

194   Clarkson: Charleston, S.C., merchant.
Business correspondence of Clarkson with his father-in-law, David Van Horne of New York, and William Neate of London. Concerns Clarkson's attempts to establish himself in the slave trade in South Carolina. Includes an assessment of economic conditions in the State. Miscellaneous items include two letters from Jacob Read to Mrs. Ann Van Horne, 1772 and 1790, and undated bills, receipts, and invoices.

THOMAS J. CLAY PAPERS
33 vols., 6 boxes, 1737–1927.

195   Clay: Kentucky planter family; descended from John Clay, a Baptist minister in Henrico and Hanover Counties, Va., during the Revolutionary period.
Documents concerning the business affairs of John Clay, Thomas Hart, and Jesse Benton in the 1770's and 1780's, including receipts, deeds, land claims, and surveys in Augusta and Fayette Counties, Va., and the Kentucky and Ohio regions. Most of the correspondence pertains to Hart's business activities, particularly land preemption claims in the 1780's, with Benton as his agent. Also includes John Clay's will and related chancery documents, as well as a report on Tory strength in Hillsborough County, N.C., 1781.
Principal correspondents: William Blount, Daniel Boone, and Samuel Hughes.

HEINRICH URBAN CLEVE PAPERS
1 vol., 1777–78.   Force manuscripts.

196   Cleve (d. 1808): Capt., Col. von Rhetz's regiment; aide-de-camp to Maj. Gen. Friedrich Riedesel; captured at Saratoga, N.Y.
Contemporary transcripts of eight letters from Cleve to friends and relatives in Lower Saxony. The letters, written from St. Anne, Canada, Mar. 1777, contain descriptions of living conditions of Hessian soldiers during the hard Canadian winter, geography and climate of the area, flora, hunting and fishing, Indian culture, and difficulties of winter travel. Also includes a description of a British military festival held at Quebec in honor of the victory of Gen. Guy Carleton over Gen. Robert Montgomery, Jan. 1, 1776, remarks on military training, and plans for a campaign in the Lake Champlain area. The volume ends with a serial letter, Nov. 1777—July 1778, Cleve wrote from Cambridge, Mass., where the Convention Army was sent after Burgoyne's surrender, concerning the battle of Saratoga, the march to Cambridge, observations on the life, manners, and customs of New Englanders, and prison life in Cambridge.

GEORGE AND JAMES CLINTON PAPERS
1 vol., 1 box, 1776–89.   Part photostats and typescripts.

197   George Clinton (1739–1812): Member, Continental Congress, 1775–76; brig. gen., New York Militia and Continental Army, 1777–83; gov., New York, 1777–95; Vice President of the U.S. James Clinton (1733–1812): Brother of George Clinton; col., 3d New York Regiment, 1775; col., 2d New York Regiment, 1776; brig. gen., Continental Army, 1776–83.

Letters to and from James and George Clinton. Seventeen letters from James Clinton to Governor Clinton, Washington, and various Continental and militia officers in New York concern reconnaissance, troops disposition, supply, Sullivan's expedition against the Iroquois, and defenses on the western frontier, 1779–82. Eight letters from Governor Clinton to Generals James Clinton, Horatio Gates, Lafayette, Alexander McDougall, Philip Schuyler, and Washington pertain to military affairs in New York, 1777–78. Typescripts and photostats are of correspondence between Governor Clinton and the New York delegates in Congress, 1777–83. Delegate letters written by James Duane, Ezra L'Hommedieu, Robert R. Livingston, Alexander Hamilton, and John Morin Scott concern Burgoyne's invasion, Lafayette's proposed Canadian invasion, the battle of Camden, foreign affairs, finance, the Vermont problem, and the passage and ratification of the Articles of Confederation.

Sir Henry Clinton Papers
10 vols., 54 pamphlets, 1780–92.

198   Clinton (ca. 1738–95): Commander in chief of the British Army in America, 1778–82.
Originally part of Clinton's personal library. Volumes containing Clinton's manuscript annotations were used by B. F. Stevens to prepare *The Campaign in Virginia 1781. An Exact Reprint of Six Rare Pamphlets on the Clinton-Cornwallis Controversy, . . .* 2 vols. (1888). Included are five copies of Clinton's *Narrative of Lieutenant-General Sir Henry Clinton* (1783), Cornwallis' *Answer . . .* (1783), and Clinton's *Observations on Some Parts of the Answer of Earl Cornwallis, . . .* (1783). Also John Burgoyne, *A State of the Expedition from Canada* (1780), David Ramsay, *The History of the American Revolution* (1791), and the *Memoirs of the Life of the Late Charles Lee . . .* (1792).
Most pamphlets in the collection are reproductions of all or parts of the above volumes. They include "A Narrative of Sir Henry Clinton's Co-operation with Sir Peter Parker, on the Attack on Sullivan's Island . . ."; "Letters between Clinton and the Commissioners for Auditing the Public Accounts"; "A View of Evidence Relative to the Conduct of the American War . . ."; and "Parting Word; or, A Summary Review of the Controversy between Clinton and Cornwallis."

Julia A. Clore Collection
1 reel microfilm, 1 box photostats, 1775–1935.

199   Clore: Collector of Kentucky historical documents.
Includes several receipts from the Transylvania region, 1777.

Cadwallader Colden Papers
24 items, 1686–1830.   Part photostats.

200   Colden (1688–1776): Lt. gov., New York, 1761–76; scientist; author.
Letters to Colden from Lt. Col. James Abercrombie and Gen. Thomas Gage, May 1775; letter from Cadwallader Colden, Jr., to Sir Henry Clinton concerning personal relief, Nov. 1778; and letter from Aaron Burr to Cadwallader Colden, Jr., concerning Burr's business affairs, 1784. Includes commissions of Cadwallader Colden, Jr., New York, militia colonel. 1774, and commissary to British prisoners of war, 1780, and of John Colden, major, New Jersey Volunteers, 1776; and an essay entitled "Man's Truest Interest is in the Prosperity of his Country," 1778.

Colebrooke, Nesbitt, Colebrooke, & Franks Papers
1 vol., 1 box, 1756–89.   *NUCMC 71–1345*

201   Colebrooke, Nesbitt, Colebrooke, & Franks: British merchants.
Letters, contracts, memoranda, reports, and accounts relating to the provisioning of British forces in North America, 1759–79, by contractors James Colebrooke, Arnold Nesbitt, George Colebrooke, and Moses Franks. Includes letters from agents in America and letters to various military and Government officials. Also a small memorandum book and a folio containing "accounts current" with the Treasury Office, 1760–75.

STEPHEN COLLINS & SON COLLECTION
183 vols. and boxes, 1702–1857.   Finding aid available.

202   Collins (1733–94): Philadelphia, Pa., merchant. Zaccheus Collins (1764–1831): Son of Stephen Collins; entered business with his father, 1784.

Volumes 1–56 contain personal and commercial correspondence, primarily incoming letters from merchants in London, Manchester, Nottingham, and Leeds, England and in America, Burlington, N.J., Boston, Baltimore, and New York, with drafts of some outletters, 1758–1803. Volumes 57–69, the Collins letterbooks, 1760–1801, record business transactions, family news, Stephen Collins' death, and the continuation of the firm under Zaccheus Collins. Also contains receipt books, journals, daybooks, ledgers, sales books, and invoices.

The collection includes the papers of William Barrell (d. 1776) whose estate was administered by Stephen Collins, and correspondence between Collins and Colburn Barrell, a loyalist exile who later declared bankruptcy. Also the Solomon Fussell (d. 1762) business papers, 1738–62; two account books of John Glover of New York, 1773–83; three account books of James Millar of Bucks County, Pa., 1768–80; a daybook of John Pemberton kept at Alexandria, Va., 1785; and correspondence between Zaccheus Collins and his brother-in-law Richard Bland Lee.

Principal correspondents: Samuel Allinson, Jonathan Amory, John Barrell, Joseph Barrell, Nathaniel Barrell, Theodore Barrell, Walter Barrell, William Berry, David Bowen, Wright Brickell, Henry Chapman, Minton Collins, William Cox, Tench Coxe, James Cumming, Samuel Elam, Samuel Eliot, Charles Emory, John Fitzgerald, Joseph Foster, William Freeman, James Gibbon, John Glover, William Gray, Samuel Greg, James Henderson, Andrew Hollingsworth, Michael Hutchinson, Duncan Ingraham, Robert Innes, Holton Johnson, Rinaldo Johnson, George Joy, John Kennedy, David Knox, William Langdon, Alexander Leckie, Thomas Lee, Joseph Leland, Thomas Lightfoot, Robert Lilly, Benjamin Longstreth, Alexander Macaulay, Daniel Mifflin, Joseph Musgrove, William Neate, John Okely, Edward Parrish, Thomas Pearsall, Thomas Pleasants, William Redwood, Jacob Reed, Jr., John Relph, Thomas Rennard, Nathaniel Ridgely, Walter Roe, Epes Sargent, James Seagrove, John Shephard, Paschal Smith, Robert Smith, John Story, James Swan, John Taylor, John Thurman, William Tilghman, William Vans, Josiah Watson, John Watts, and Jasper Yeates; and the firms of Amory, Taylor & Rogers; Benjamin & John Bower; John & John Brown; Nathaniel & Robert Denison; Harford & Powell; Harrison, Ansley & Co.; Hayley & Hopkins; Robert & Nathan Hyde; Jokes, Coulson & Co.; Robert & Alexander McKim; Mildred & Roberts; Neate & Pigou; Scott & Gill; Sears & Smith; Smithson & Greaves; and Sterling & Norcross.

STEPHEN COLLINS LETTERBOOK
1 reel microfilm, 1783–93.

203   Collins (1733–1794): See entry no. 202.

Mercantile correspondence with Collins' business associates and a few friends whom he served as agent. Several letters contain lists of goods and prices.

Principal correspondents: Colburn Barrell, John Fitzgerald, William Gray, Richard Lee, Thomas Lee, Alexander Macaulay and Josiah Watson; and the firms of John & John Brown; Harrison, Ansley & Co.; Knox & Cowan; Robert & Alexander McKim; Pearsall & Glover; and Taylor & Rogers.

Originals in Historical Society of Pennsylvania.

COMMISSIONS MISCELLANY COLLECTION
1 box, 1715–1918.

204   Consists of British, Belgian, Spanish, Mexican, and U.S. Federal, State, and colonial commissions. Benedict Arnold, George Clinton, Arthur St. Clair, Adam Stephens, and David Waterbury, Jr., are among those represented.

CONNECTICUT, MISCELLANY
4 boxes, 1646–1837.   Part photostats.

205   Contains military correspondence relating to Daniel Morgan's and William Thompson's rifle companies, 1775; correspondence concerning Washington's conference with Rochambeau, 1780; a list of minutemen in Mansfield, Conn.; and various legal documents—wills, deeds, indentures, etc. Also a copy of John Murry's sermon on the Thanksgiving for Peace, 1783, information on Connecticut's boundary claims based on records from 1597, and the province's case for its Susquehanna grants.
    Principal correspondents: John Chester, Lord Hillsborough, Jedediah Huntington, and Jonathan Trumbull.

CONNECTICUT, MISCELLANY
1 vol., 1637–1783.   Force transcripts.

206   Correspondence from the period of the Revolution concerning military affairs, political and economic conditions in Connecticut, land claims of the Susquehanna Company, Indian affairs, loyalists, Hutchinson's manuscript history of the Massachusetts Colony, and smallpox epidemics. Also includes scattered returns, poems, proclamations, petitions, committee reports, and official records.
    Principal correspondents: Benjamin Coit, Joshua Coit, Silas Deane, Eliphalet Dyer, Samuel Gray, Roger Griswold, Jedediah Huntington, Samuel Huntington, Thomas Hutchinson, Samuel Langdon, Richard Law, Thomas Moffatt, Samuel H. Parsons, Richard Peters, Timothy Pickering, Samuel Purviance, Peter Robertson, Roger Sherman, Ezra Stiles, Benjamin Thompson, Jonathan Trumbull, Joseph Trumbull, Joseph Ward, Washington, and Thomas Young.

CONSTABLE, RUCKER & COMPANY PAPERS
23 letters, 1786–95.

207   Constable, Rucker & Co.: New York mercantile firm.
    Contains commercial correspondence of Robert Morris, consisting of 20 letters to the firm of Constable, Rucker & Co., 1786–87, and three letters to James and William Constable, 1790–95. The letters are primarily of a business nature but also contain information on Morris' political views.
    See also Robert Morris Papers, entry no. 819.

CONTINENTAL ARMY RETURNS
54 vols., 1775–83.   Force transcripts.

208   Transcripts of documents in the Washington Papers, Library of Congress. Includes a one-volume index. The transcripts are arranged under such subjects as pay and hospital returns, military stores, resignations of officers, quartermaster general, arrangement of officers, regimental returns, brigade returns, deserters, inspection, general returns, etc.
    See also the Library's unpublished guide to the Peter Force Papers, series VII D.

CONTINENTAL CONGRESS, BOARD OF TREASURY REPORTS
3 vols., 1785–87.   Photostats.

209   Reports of the Board of Treasury on memorials, letters, claims, and resolutions presented to the commissioners of the Treasury. Reports for Apr. 1785—Sept. 1787, contain the responses of commissioners Arthur Lee, Walter Livingston, and Samuel Osgood to routine petitions and claims. Others are in the form of letters to Congress containing the findings and recommendations of the commissioners.
    Originals in New York Public Library.

CONTINENTAL CONGRESS COLLECTION OF EDMUND C. BURNETT
28 boxes, 1774–89.   Part photostats.

210   Burnett (1864–1949): Historian, editor; employed by the Carnegie Institution of Washington, 1907–36.

Documents and working files related to the publication of Burnett's *Letters of Members of the Continental Congress*, 8 vols. (Washington, D. C., 1921–36). Includes several boxes of printer's copy for the volumes and a quantity of "duplicates, discards, &c." culled from Burnett's files. The most valuable material in the collection consists of the photostats (boxes 15–18), most of which are of letters either omitted or abridged in the published volumes. Also includes several letters intended for inclusion in a planned supplement and a collection of ciphers (box 26) that Burnett used to decode many of the printed letters.

For correspondence related to Burnett's work on the *Letters* project, see J. Franklin Jameson Papers, Library of Congress.

CONTINENTAL CONGRESS, COMMISSION
1 folio, 1778.   Force transcripts.

211   "Journal of the Commissioners appointed By the States of New Hampshire, Massachusetts, Connecticut, Rhode Island, New York, and New Jersey & Pennsylvania for the Purpose of regulating the Prices of Labor, &c. agreeable to the Fifth Article of the Resolves of the Continental Congress, of the 22 Novr. A.D. 1777." The Journal covers the proceedings of the commissioners, who convened Jan. 15, 1778, and includes their report to Congress, Jan. 30, 1778.

See Worthington C. Ford, ed., *Journals of the Continental Congress* (Washington, D.C., 1904–37), vol. 9, p. 956–57. Original in New Hampshire Historical Society.

CONTINENTAL CONGRESS, JOURNAL
1 reel microfilm, 1774.

212   Contemporary copy of the journal of the First Continental Congress, Sept. 5—Oct. 21, 1774, in the hand of a clerk, who apparently transcribed the material to that point for use of the secretary of Congress, Charles Thomson. Entries for Oct. 22—26, 1774, which are in Thomson's hand, appear to have been made during the last four days of the 1774 session, but they are in a more abbreviated form and somewhat different order from those in the published journal.

Original in the possession of James O. Keene in 1953.

CONTINENTAL CONGRESS, MISCELLANY
3 boxes, 2 folios, 1775–95.   Part photostats.

213   Chiefly miscellaneous correspondence of members of Congress and of its various officers, committees, and boards. Includes petitions of and to Congress, accounts, agreements, and committee orders, plus drafts of reports, resolves, amendments, and lists of delegates prepared by the secretary, Charles Thomson. Includes 15 letters of William Bingham, agent for Congress in Martinique, to the Secret Committee and to Robert Morris; lists of delegates in attendance, 1781 and 1785–88; an account of expenditures, Jan. 1779—Jan. 1780; and "drafts" against Congress issued to Beaumarchais, June 1779. Also several letters to Congress from Army and Navy officers, and various State officials, and photostats of documents in the Papers of the Continental Congress containing specimens of the handwriting of 156 members of Congress.

CONTINENTAL CONGRESS PAPERS
90 boxes, 1775–89.   Force transcripts.

214   Copies of approximately 80 percent of the Papers of the Continental Congress, which are now in the National Archives. The copies were made by Peter Force about 1840, when the collection was at the Department of State. They consist of the following "items": 1, 11, 12A, 13–16, 18–45, 47–53, 55–73, 77–85, 88–90, 93–103, 105, 109–11, 114, 116–19, 132–33, 135–41, 145, 147–68, 173–74, 177, 184–94; and a "Marine Committee Letter Book, 1776–1780."

Correspondence in the letterbook is published in Charles O. Paullin, ed., *Out-Letters of the Continental Marine Committee and Board of Admiralty, August, 1776—Sep-*

tember, 1780, 2 vols. (New York, 1914). See also National Archives "Pamphlet Accompanying Microcopy No. 247," *Papers of the Continental Congress, 1774–89* (Washington, D.C., 1961).

JOHN SINGLETON COPLEY PAPERS
1 vol., 1 folio, 1767–1809.   *NUCMC* 64–1217
215   Copley (1738–1815): American painter and native of Boston, Mass.; migrated to England in 1774; member, Royal Academy, 1783.
Includes a small number of letters from John Copley to his wife, 1775–77, in which the artist gives his impressions of English and European paintings. The letters reveal little interest in political or military affairs in the Colonies, though on July 22, 1775, Copley did write of his aversion to war and urged his wife to emigrate to England. Several letters contain negative remarks on American social and cultural life.
Principal correspondents: Richard Clark, Joseph Greene, and Mary Pelham.
See also Copley–Pelham Papers, P.R.O./C.O.5, entry no. 1416.

JOHN SINGLETON COPLEY PAPERS
1 reel microfilm, 1767–1815.
216   Copley (1738–1815): See entry no. 215.
Personal and business correspondence of Copley. Includes three letters to his wife concerning family matters, 1774–75; a personal letter from Mrs. Mary Pelham, Copley's mother-in-law, 1778; and business letters to Isaac Winslow, 1776, and John Greenwood, 1775. Also an undated statement of "The Case between the City of London and Mr. Copley."
Originals in Boston Public Library.

FRANCIS COWHERD PAPERS
1 folio, 1781–1833.
217   Cowherd (d. 1833): Capt., 2d Virginia Continental Regiment, 1780.
Contains a certificate of exchange for Lt. Hamilton, a British prisoner of war, Charleston, Feb. 27, 1781.

CRANCH FAMILY PAPERS
1 box, 1758–1882.
218   Cranch: Massachusetts family; connected with the Adams family by marriage.
Contains a few personal and family letters from the Revolutionary era.
Principal correspondents: Richard Cranch, Eunice Paine, and Josiah Quincy.

WILLIAM CRANCH PAPERS
1 vol., 1758–1882.
219   Cranch: Washington, D.C., lawyer and judge.
Letters of Eunice Paine to her mother, Mary Cranch, concerning family matters and local news. Also includes William Cranch's comments on the aristocratic behavior of John Hancock, 1778, Richard and Mary Cranch's letters of advice to their son William, and post–1790 letters of John and John Quincy Adams.
Principal correspondents: Mary Cranch, Richard Cranch, William Cranch, Eunice Paine, and Polly Palmer.

REBEKAH CRAWFORD AND LINDA CLARKE-SMITH COLLECTION
22 boxes, 6 folios, 1715–1934.
220   Includes miscellaneous deeds and receipts from New Jersey, five undated poems, and a report on fortifications at Gibraltar, 1768.

CRESAP FAMILY PAPERS
1 box, 1784–1856.

221   Thomas Cresap (1702–88): Old Town, Md., surveyor; miller; justice of the peace; and founder of the Ohio Company. Daniel Cresap (1727–98): Member, Maryland committee of safety. Michael Cresap (1742–75): Old Town, Md., trader; soldier.

Documents include surveyors records and court testimony relating to Cresap family landholdings in the Ohio region and in Augusta County, Va., 1763–75, the will of Rebecca Arnold of Baltimore, 1788; and the will of Thomas Cresap.

MICHEL-GUILLAUME JEAN DE CRÈVECOEUR PAPERS
1 vol., 1783–88.   Transcripts.   *NUCMC* 70–944

222   Crèvecoeur (1735–1813): Native of Caen, France; Orange County, N.Y., farmer; author; French consul in New York, 1783–90.

Crèvecoeur's correspondence while serving as French consul in New York. Subjects discussed include politics, French packet service, agriculture, literature, medicine, wagon-making, American culture, and the Continental Congress. Most of the letters are from Crèvecoeur to the Duc de la Rochefoucauld D'Anville (in both French and English). Also includes Mrs. Julia M. Kunkle's study of Crèvecoeur's *Letters from an American Farmer* (London, 1782).

Principal correspondents: George Clinton, Pierpont Edwards, Robert R. Livingston, William Livingston, John Warren, and Washington.

See also Manuscrits Français, Nouvelles Acquisitions, Letters to Saint Jean de Crèvecoeur, entry no. 1177.

WILLIAM CROGHAN PAPERS
3 vols., 1779–1814.   Draper Mss., series N, WHi.   Microfilm, 1 reel.

223   Croghan (1752–1822): Capt., 8th Virginia Continental Regiment, 1776–78, maj., 1778–80; settled in Kentucky, 1783.

Miscellaneous in character, the Croghan papers include payrolls and muster rolls for the Virginia regiments in which Croghan served; a typescript of survey notes kept on an expedition into the western parts of Virginia and North Carolina, 1784; personal and business letters from Daniel Clark, Lardner Clark, John Connor, John Dodge, Hugh Heward, and Presley Nevill, 1787–88; and letters from Croghan to James Wilkinson, Dr. Chapline, 1788, and Charles Scott, 1786. Also includes the journal of Sgt. Thomas McCarty covering the march of the 3d Virginia Regiment from Virginia to New York and the campaign in New Jersey, 1776–77, and two journals presumably kept by Croghan, which cover the march of Virginia troops from New York to South Carolina in the winter of 1779–80, and the return of a Virginia Line detachment from the Charleston captivity, Feb. 7–28, 1781.

The McCarty journal is published in *Proceedings of the New Jersey Historical Society*, vol. 82 (Jan. 1964), p. 29–46.

See also Thwaites, *Descriptive List of Manuscript Collections*, p. 16–17.

WILLIAM CROGHAN FAMILY PAPERS
1 box, 1784–1851.

224   William Croghan: See entry no. 223.

Documents from the Revolutionary era include miscellaneous survey records, plats, and maps of land in the Ohio region and western Virginia.

PAUL CUFFE PAPERS
2 reels microfilm, 1765–1963.

225   Cuffe (1759–1817): Westport, Mass., Negro-Indian; merchant seaman and shipowner at New Bedford, Mass.; known for transporting free Negroes to Sierra Leone at his own expense.

Family papers from the Revolutionary era include miscellaneous deeds, contracts, legal papers, notes, and bills of Cuffe Slocum and Paul Cuffe. Also petitions to the General Court and local selectmen on behalf of free blacks and the rights of citizenship, and Cuffe's plan for farming, 1780. Indexed at the beginning of each reel.

JABEZ L. M. CURRY PAPERS
24 vols., 7 boxes, 1637–1939.   *NUCMC* 60–1701

226   Curry (1825–1903): Alabama lawyer and educator; member, U.S. House of Representatives, 1857–61, and Confederate Congress.

Includes two small items in an autograph collection from the Revolutionary era: a 1785 Benjamin Franklin letter referring M. P. Chevallie to Thomas Jefferson for settlement of his claims against Virginia and the Confederation Congress, and a receipt for John Adams' subscription to a French periodical.

NATHANIEL CUSHING PAPERS
1 box, 1666–1851.

227   Cushing (1762–1827): Pembroke, Mass., merchant.

Includes receipts and account sheets concerning Cushing's business activities, 1783–89, and several manuscript fragments containing data relating to members of the Joseph Nash family, 1760–78.

NATHANIEL CUSHING PAPERS
1 box, 1760–1930.

228   Cushing (1762–1827): See entry no. 227.

Bills, accounts, and receipts concerning Cushing's business activities.

CUTTS FAMILY PAPERS
1 box, 1755–1905.   *NUCMC* 69–2032

229   Samuel Cutts: New England shipbuilder and merchant. Anna Cutts: Wife of Samuel; daughter of Rev. Edward Holyoke, pres., Harvard College.

Contains three letters to Mrs. Anna Holyoke Cutts from Edward Holyoke, Sarah Bradstreet, and a sister, 1763–75, and one letter from Samuel Cutts to his daughter Nancy, 1784, concerning personal and family matters.

CHARLES DABNEY PAPERS
1 box, 1769–1809.   Photostats.

230   Dabney (1744–1829): Lt. col., 2d Virginia State Regiment, 1777–78; col., Virginia Militia, 1778–81.

Contains three letters to Dabney from Mary Ambler, 1769, concerning Dabney's business affairs, and William Croghan, 1785 and 1789, regarding land Dabney received for his military service. Also includes survey receipts, a sketch of Dabney's land holdings in Kentucky, a document describing a change in the location of his land claims, and a receipt issued by the land office upon registration of his claim.

DAG REGISTER
1 vol., 1780–83.   Force manuscripts.

231   Journal, in Dutch, concerning Anglo-Dutch diplomatic and commercial relations and the Anglo-Dutch war, which arose over Holland's clandestine trade with the American Colonies. Includes copies of diplomatic correspondence and treaties, lists of Dutch warships, and numerous patriotic poems.

NATHAN DANE PAPERS
1 box, 1785–1814.

232   Dane (1752–1835): Massachusetts lawyer-legislator; member, Massachusetts General Court, 1782–85, Continental Congress, 1785–88.

    Miscellaneous letters touching on major developments during the Confederation period: the need to revise the Articles of Confederation; inaction in Congress; financial difficulties; the admission of new States to the Confederation and the organization of territories; Shays' Rebellion; and negotiations with Spain over transit on the Mississippi River.

    Principal correspondents: Caleb Davis, Thomas Dwight, Nathaniel Gorham, Samuel Henshaw, Stephen Higginson, Rufus King, and Theodore Sedgwick.

NATHAN DANE AND JONAS CLARK PAPERS
1 box, 1780–1830.

233   Dane (1752–1835): See entry no. 232. Clark, Jr. (1760–1828): Maine merchant.

    Four letters of Jonas Clark to his father, the Rev. Jonas Clark, concern his capture by the British, 1782, a convention held at Falmouth, Maine, 1785, to consider separation from Massachusetts, and business prospects in Maine, 1785. Also includes a love letter from Nathan Dane to Polly Dane, 1783, and a letter from John Avery to Nathan Dane on Massachusetts claims and bounties under Congressional authority, 1788.

JOHN DAVIS PAPERS
11 vols., 1755–83.   *NUCMC* 66–1393

234   Davis (d. 1827): Capt., Pennsylvania Militia; assistant quartermaster for Carlisle, Pa., 1775; assistant quartermaster for western Pennsylvania, northern Maryland, and northern Virginia, 1777–78; deputy quartermaster for western Pennsylvania, 1778–83.

    Documents from the period of the war include letters, receipts, accounts, and commissions relating to the colllection and disbursement of military supplies. Material also includes letters concerning the use of Hessian prisoners as laborers, selling of supplies to the British, and reorganization of the Quartermaster Department, 1778.

    Principal correspondents: Mark Bird, George Campbell, David Duncan, Nathanael Greene, William Irvine, Samuel Miles, Richard Peters, Charles Pettit, Timothy Pickering, and James Wilson.

WILLIAM DAWSON PAPERS
2 vols., 1728–75.   *NUCMC* 66–1394

235   Dawson (d. 1752): Anglican clergyman; commissary of Virginia; pres., College of William and Mary.

    Contains personal and business correspondence between Mrs. William Dawson and Robert Carter Nicholas.

SILAS DEANE LETTERBOOKS
4 vols., 1777–84.   Force transcripts.   *NUCMC* 62–1479

236   Deane (1737–89): Connecticut merchant; statesman; member, Continental Congress, 1774–76; agent to France, 1776–78.

    Most of the letters in these volumes are published in the New York Historical Society *Collections* (1887–89), vols. 20–22. The unpublished correspondence deals with Deane's return to America in 1778, his efforts to clear himself of charges of misuse of public funds, his extensive commercial activities, especially with his brothers Barnabas and Simeon Deane, and his assessment of American military fortunes and political developments in Congress.

    Principal correspondents: Edward Bancroft, Beaumarchais, Samuel Chase, Barnabas Deane, Simeon Deane, Franklin, Conrad Alexandre Gérard, Sir George Grand, Nathanael Greene, John Hancock, Benjamin Harrison, Jean Holker, Lafayette, Le Ray de

Chaumont, Jonathan Trumbull, Vergennes, Washington, Joseph Webb, and Jonathan Williams.

Originals in Connecticut Historical Society. See also Silas Deane, account books, entry no. 13.

DENNYS DE BERDT PAPERS
1 vol., 1765–70.   *NUCMC* 69–2035

237   De Berdt (1694–1770): London merchant; colonial agent for Massachusetts and Delaware, 1765–70.

A letterbook kept by De Berdt while colonial agent for Massachusetts includes reports of his activities in the repeal of the Stamp and Townshend Acts, the landing of troops in Boston, and the removal of Sir Francis Bernard as Governor of Massachusetts. The letters reveal how the increasingly radical actions of the Massachusetts Sons of Liberty surprised and frustrated the basically sympathetic De Berdt.

Principal correspondents: Samuel Adams, Thomas Cushing, Thomas McKean, Caesar Rodney, William Smith, and Samuel White.

Published in Massachusetts Colonial Society, *Publications*, XIII (1912).

DECLARATION OF INDEPENDENCE COLLECTION
1 box, 1776.   Photostats.

238   Copies of miscellaneous letters and documents pertaining to the Declaration of Independence and the Virginia Declaration of Rights.

DELAWARE MISCELLANY
4 vols., 3 boxes, 1 folio, 1684–1835.

239   Consists largely of official State papers: correspondence and addresses between the Governor and the assembly; council minutes; records of the proceedings of the assembly; resolutions, proclamations, and commissions; and a "diary" of transactions of government under Gov. John Dickinson, Nov. 1781—Dec. 1782. Also pay certificates, military accounts and returns, oaths of allegiance, deeds, indentures, and a list of taxables, 1776.

DELMONTE COLLECTION
2 vols., 14 boxes, 1592–1871.

240   Domingo Delmonte y Aponte (d. 1853): Cuban scholar and author.

Includes about 40 letters and documents pertaining to Cuban and American affairs during the period of the Revolution. Of primary interest are two letters from Bernardo de Gálvez to Diego Navarro concerning military operations against Baton Rouge and Manchac, La., and Pensacola, West Florida, Aug. and Sept. 1779; a report on the failure of a combined squadron of French and Spanish ships to intercept Adm. George Rodney's fleet in the Straits of Bahama, July 1782; a letter with instructions from Juan Manuel de Cagigal, Captain-General of Cuba, to D. Nicholas de Arredondo, Governor of Santiago de Cuba, concerning a possible British invasion, Oct. 1782; and a royal order regarding attempts by foreign agents to revolutionize Spanish America, Dec. 1783.

ASBURY DICKINS PAPERS
1 box, 1749–1941.

241   Dickins: Chief clerk, U.S. Treasury Department, 1815–24.

Chiefly letters of the Dickins family in the 19th century. A few items from the Revolutionary era, notably a letter of Raymond DeMere, May 1777, describe conditions in Maryland and Pennsylvania and the attitude of the inhabitants toward the Revolution.

DAVID DICKSON PAPERS
1 box, 1773.

242   Dickson: Tennessee settler; retired from the British Army.
Surveys, patents letters, and plats for 2,000 acres of land near Fort Natchez granted to Dickson, a reduced brigade major in the British Army.

DIGGES–L'ENFANT–MORGAN COLLECTION
5 vols., 2 boxes, 1674–1912.

243   Documents concerning Pierre L'Enfant's work in designing the U.S. Capital. Includes material pertaining to L'Enfant's recruiting for the Society of the Cincinnati in France. Also two letters of Jean Holker acknowledging the receipt of large sums of money from Jean de Neufville for the purchase of U.S. loan certificates, 1778–79.
Principal correspondents: Comte d'Estaing, Comte de Grasse, William Moultrie, Marquis de Vaudreuil, and Washington.

ANDREW JACKSON DONELSON PAPERS
19 vols., 6 boxes, 1779–1943.

244   Doneslon (1799–1871): Lawyer; Army officer; diplomat.
Contains a Dunlap & Claypool printing of the Constitution with annotations by Edmund Pendleton, Pendleton's address, June 7, 1788, to the Virginia Convention, and an annotated copy of the *Journal of the Convention of Virginia*, June 1788.

JAMES DUANE PAPERS
1 vol., 1 folio, 1624–1780.   Force transcripts.   *NUCMC* 60–2701

245   Duane (1733–97): New York lawyer, jurist, land speculator; member, Continental Congress, 1774–83; mayor, New York City, 1784–89.
Transcribed from the original manuscripts in the New York Historical Society, Duane's "State of the Evidence and Argument in Support of the Historical Rights and Jurisdiction of New York Against the Government of New Hampshire and the Claimants Under It and Against the Commonwealth of Massachusetts," 1781, forms the greater part of the collection. In the dispute over New York's claim of Vermont, Duane supported New York, using proclamations, council minutes, extracts from New York and Connecticut newspapers, and letters reporting violence between Vermonters and New York agents.
Principal correspondents: William Cockburn, Benjamin Hough, John Muro, Benjamin Spencer, and Peter Yates.

CHARLES W. F. DUMAS PAPERS
2 vols., 1775–93.

246   Dumas (1725–96): German native; resided in Holland as a man of letters before the war; secret agent for the Continental Congress at The Hague, 1776; translator and secretary to John Adams; U.S. chargé d'affaires at The Hague.
Diplomatic correspondence from the Revolutionary and post-Revolutionary periods. Includes contemporary copies of letters to and from Dumas concerning prisoners of war, the League of Armed Neutrality, the French alliance, negotiations with Holland, peace negotiations, and a treaty of commerce with England.
Principal correspondents: John Adams, Committee for Foreign Affairs of the Continental Congress, Franklin, John Paul Jones, Lafayette, and Arthur Lee.

WILLIAM DUNBAR PAPERS
1 box, 1775–1802.

247   Dunbar (b. 1748): Scottish immigrant to Philadelphia, Pa., 1770; Indian trader in Mississippi Valley, 1770–72; planter near Baton Rouge, La., 1774–92.
Extracts of letters describing the effects of the American Revolution on people living in Florida and Louisiana. Also letters from Dunbar to John Ross of Philadelphia con-

cerning economic opportunities in the Mississippi Valley, disruptions caused by the war, and James Willing's raid.

Originals in Mississippi Department of Archives.

DUNLOP FAMILY PAPERS

16 boxes, 1750–1930. *NUCMC 63–342*

248   James Dunlop, Sr. (1724–90): Petersburg, Va., tobacco and grain merchant. James Dunlop, Jr. (1755–1825): New York merchant, loyalist. George Dunlop: Lt., 74th Highland Regiment, British Army.

Business and family correspondence between James Dunlop, Sr., James Dunlop, Jr., George Dunlop, Henrietta Dunlop of Glasgow, and the Glasgow firm of James Ritchie & Co. Includes letters written by George Dunlop during his confinement as a prisoner of war at Lancaster, Pa., 1781–82, and material concerning economic conditions during and after the Revolution.

Principal correspondents: James Anderson, Dugald Bannatine, David Buchanan, Robert Dobson, John Dunlop, Thomas Dunlop, Laurence Hill, John Laird, Thomas Montgomery, William Robertson, David Ross, John Simpson, John Wallace, William Woddrop, and Hugh Wyllie.

PIERRE EUGÈNE DU SIMITIÈRE PAPERS

5 vols., 1742–84.   Force manuscripts.

249   Du Simitière (1736–84): Artist, antiquary, naturalist; Swiss immigrant to America, 1765, residing chiefly in New York City and Philadelphia, Pa.; curator, American Philosophical Society, 1776–81.

Three memorandum books of notes, tracing Du Simitière's interest in America. The notes primarily concern pamphlets, newspaper articles, collected or desired artifacts and curiosities, and his own paintings. One volume contains notes on articles related to the American Revolution in Pennsylvania. Also includes a commonplace book containing notes on anagrams, Greek script, heraldry, and drafts of poems, and Du Simitière's letterbook.

Principal correspondents: George Clinton, Robert Morris, Joseph Reed, and John Sullivan.

DUTILH AND WACHSMUTH PAPERS

1 folio, 2 letterbooks, 1784–1800. *NUCMC 66-1401*

250   Dutilh and Wachsmuth: Philadelphia, Pa., merchants.

Business correspondence of the firm Dutilh & Wachsmuth. Letters to the firm include about 25 dated before 1790, chiefly from Dubey & Co. of New York, and Samuel and John Smith of Baltimore. The two indexed letterbooks, Jan. 1784—Aug. 1785 and Sept. 1788—July 1789, contain letters mainly to European houses, although the number of American correspondents increases in the second volume. Most of the letters are in French, a few in Dutch and English.

Principal correspondents: Augier frères, Cognac; Pieter Baelde, Rotterdam; Corn. Balguerie, Rotterdam; A. B. Beerenbrock, Antwerp; Jan Berckemeyer, Hamburg; Lancel Carez, Lisle; P. G. Chion, Charleston; Christian Dutilh, Rotterdam; Jacob Dutilh, Port au Prince; James Dutilh, Cap Francois; Fontaine & Morin, Wilmington; Thomas Fonteyn, Delft; François & Co., Port au Prince; Haas & Co., Amsterdam; Christian Iongeneel, Rotterdam; Lonchon frères, L'Orient; G. Pastor, Borcette; Rolland & Co., Amsterdam; Rykevorsel & Ellinckhuysen, Rotterdam; John Richard, Richmond; St. Martin & fils, Amsterdam; Savary de Valcoulon, Richmond; Louis Tessier, London; Philip Thieriot, Bordeaux; Valck, Burger & Schouten, Baltimore; A. J. Verstolk, Rotterdam.

See also Samuel Smith Papers, entry no. 1040.

GABRIEL DUVALL PAPERS

2 boxes, 1765–1920.

251   Duvall (1752–1835): Annapolis, Md., lawyer-merchant; clerk, Maryland Convention and House of Delegates, 1775–78; member, executive council, 1782–85, State legislature, 1787–94 and 1796–1800, and U.S. House of Representatives, 1794–96; comptroller, U.S. Treasury, 1802–11; justice, U.S. Supreme Court, 1811–35.

Correspondence of Duvall during the 1780's concerns the Maryland borders, confiscation of property, land and monetary speculation, and postwar business. Includes indentures, deeds, inventories, a 1775 list of non-associators for Annapolis, Md., and a list of attorneys practicing at the Maryland General Court, 1775–1800. Duvall's record book contains family genealogical information, as well as extracts from contemporary publications.

Principal correspondents: Benjamin Duvall, Col. W. Forest, and William Stevenson.

EARLY STATE RECORDS MICROFILM COLLECTION

1,770 reels microfilm, 1613–1930.

252   The State Records Microfilm Project, jointly undertaken by the University of North Carolina and the Library of Congress (1941–51), attempted to microfilm all official printed and manuscript records of the States that could be located in the continental United States. The collection, arranged by class, by State, then chronologically, brings together more than 2,700,000 pages of material.

Ten of the collection's 11 basic classes contain material related to the Revolution: Legislative records, Statutory law, Constitutional records, Administrative records, Executive records, Court records, Local records, Indian records, Newspapers, and Miscellany.

In addition to official records, such as legislative journals, law codes and session statutes, constitutions and constitutional conventions, court minute books, dockets, and records of administrative officers and institutions, the project includes newspapers and broadsides for the 17th and 18th centuries, which are often the only surviving record of provincial acts and related activities. The collection of material related to the American Indian Nations enables scholars to view Indian-white interrelationships from the perspective of documents in tribal archives. Few "personal" collections were filmed, though the records of Maryland and Pennsylvania include Calvert and Penn family papers.

Two extensive guides to the collection, published by the Library of Congress and the University of North Carolina, are available from the Photoduplication Service of the Library of Congress: *A Guide to the Microfilm Collection of Early State Records* (Washington, 1950) and *A Guide to the Microfilm Collection of Early State Records, Supplement* (Washington, 1951), both compiled by William S. Jenkins.

EAST FLORIDA PAPERS

16,000 items, 1595–1858.   Finding aid and microfilm available.

253   Archives of the Spanish Government in East Florida, in Spanish, primarily from the period 1783–1821. The bulk of the material concerns the broad issues of Spanish policy in America: government finance, commerce, agriculture, boundaries, legal matters, defense, and Indian affairs. Includes correspondence of the Captain-General in Havana; the Exchequer; the Departments of Grace and Justice, the Indies, and State; British authorities, 1784–88, and the U.S. Government. Commercial papers consist of the records of the British trading firm of Panton, Leslie, & Co., and registers of arriving and departing vessels. Also includes court records, census returns, registrations for marriages, and information on loyalist investments in Florida.

Principal correspondents: Sir Guy Carleton, Bernardo de Gálvez, José Gálvez, Georgia commissioners, Nathanael Greene, John Houstoun, Alexander McGillivray, Estevan Miró, Lord North, William Panton, Patrick Tonyn, Vergennes, and Manuel Vicente de Zéspedes.

Select documents from the Indian papers are published in translation in John W. Caughey, *McGillivray of the Creeks* (Norman, Okla., 1938), p. 61–255. See also Joseph B. Lockey, comp., *East Florida, 1783–1785* (Berkeley, 1949).

EDGEHILL–RANDOLPH PAPERS
1 reel microfilm, 1775–1827.

254   Edgehill–Randolph: Virginia planter families.
The correspondence of Francis Eppes and Thomas Jefferson provides insight into the life of Jefferson and the operation of Monticello plantation in the 1780's. Includes four letters of Eppes to Jefferson, 1775–76, describing the activities of Lord Dunmore and the growth of opposition to him.
Originals at Massachusetts Institute of Technology.

ELIZABETH CITY PARISH, VIRGINIA, VESTRY BOOK
1 vol., 1751–1833.   Photostats.

255   Includes professions of faith; accounts of parish expenses and levies expressed in pounds of tobacco and cash; and lists of church members and officers by precinct. Also contains information of expenditures for the care of orphans.

ANDREW ELLICOTT PAPERS
7 vols., 1777–1820.

256   Ellicott (1754–1820): Maryland mathematician and surveyor; surveyed Pennsylvania-Virginia boundary, 1784–85, Pennsylvania-New York boundary, 1786, New York border, 1790, District of Columbia, 1791, U.S. border with Florida, 1796–1800.
Includes personal letters from Ellicott to his wife written during the Revolutionary era, some of which contain descriptions of the land and people Ellicott encountered on his surveying expeditions. Also letters between Bishop James Madison and Ellicott concerning scientific experiments and surveys.
Principal correspondent: David Rittenhouse.

ALFRED L. ELWYN PAPERS
2 vols., 1774–89.   Force transcripts.

257   Elwyn (1804–44): Minister and collector.
Largely correspondence of the maritime committee of Congress with John Langdon, Continental agent at Portsmouth, N.H., 1775–79. Subjects discussed include possibilities for peace, with particular reference to the Peace Commission of the Howes, the construction and supply of naval vessels, the progress of the war, currency depreciation, and the struggle over ratification of the Articles of Confederation.
Principal correspondents: Josiah Bartlett, William Ellery, Richard Henry Lee, James Lovell, Robert Morris, John Sullivan, and William Whipple.

WILLIAM ENNALS PAPERS
1 vol., 1771–74.

258   Ennals: Maryland planter.
Memorandum book containing daily entries for income and expenses for a farm on the Eastern Shore of Maryland on the eve of the Revolution. Also contains records of the county court, 1771–73.

WILLIAM EUSTIS PAPERS
6 vols., 1761–1885.   *NUCMC* 64–1563

259   Eustis (1753–1825): Boston, Mass., physician; surgeon, Continental Army, 1776–83; secretary of war, 1809–13; gov., 1823–25.
Revolutionary documents comprise wills, deeds, and probate records relating to the estates of the grandfather and father of William Eustis.

JEREMIAH EVARTS PAPERS
1 box, 1784–1831.   Photostats.

260   Evarts (1781–1831): Lawyer, philanthropist, and editor; son-in-law of Roger Sherman.

Contains a letter from Gouverneur Morris to Roger Sherman, Jan. 1784, concerning American commerce and relations with Britain and France.

THOMAS EWING AND FAMILY PAPERS
289 boxes, 23 vols., 1754–1941.   Finding aid available.   *NUCMC* 65–905

261   Thomas Ewing (1789–1871): Ohio lawyer; son of George, Revolutionary War officer and farmer; member, U.S. Senate, 1831–37; and secretary of the treasury, 1841–43.

Scattered items relating to the Revolution include two letters of M. Ewing, one concerning speculation in Continental dollars. Also includes a 1786 will of John Filson of Chester County, Pa.

FAIRFAX FAMILY PAPERS
1 box, 1739–1832.

262   Fairfax: Proprietary family in Northern Neck of Virginia.

Consists primarily of legal documents of Lord Thomas Fairfax—wills, indentures, deeds —most of which are dated before 1763. Also includes the Col. William Fairfax Papers, containing amateur historian E. H. Schutz's notes, photographs, and maps of Belvoir, the Fairfax plantation house on the Potomac, based on excavations at the site and theoretical reconstruction.

See Fairfax Estate Executors, account books, entry no. 16.

SOL FEINSTONE COLLECTION ON THE AMERICAN REVOLUTION
3 reels microfilm, 1741–1862.   Finding aid available.   *NUCMC* 66–1065

263   Feinstone (1890—): Collector, Washington Crossing, Pa.

Autograph documents, as well as transcripts and drafts of letters. Correspondence concentrates largely on political and military aspects of the war. About 30 letters from Dr. Samuel Adams to Sally Preston Adams, 1776–81, concern personal and family matters and military affairs, and 25 pieces relate to the Stamp Act. Miscellaneous documents include military accounts, receipts, commissions, orders, returns, and pay certificates. Also committee reports, proclamations, broadsides, petitions, deeds, handbills, estate inventories, court records, indentures, sermons, and poems. Additional longer items include Capt. Jacob Bowers' book of accounts for Col. Henry Bicker's 2d Pennsylvania Regiment, 1777; the diary of a New England clergyman, 1775, kept in Thomas' *New England Almanac*; and two orderly books kept at Peekskill, N.Y., Oct. 6–29 and Dec. 8–26, 1776, containing division, brigade, and regimental orders. The collection is arranged alphabetically and includes a table of contents and a list of correspondents.

Originals in the David Library of the American Revolution, Washington Crossing State Park, Pa.

NICHOLAS FISH PAPERS
3 boxes, 1776–1845.   Part photostats and typescripts.

264   Fish (1758–1833): New York lawyer and businessman; lt. to maj., Continental Army, 1776–84; maj., U.S. Army, 1785–86; adjt. gen., New York Militia, 1786; U.S. supervisor of revenue for New York, 1793.

Includes one box of letters containing information on the organization of the Army, 1785–86, and describing the problems of service on the Ohio frontier. Also copies of Fish's commissions.

Principal correspondents: John Armstrong, Michael Connolly, Jonathan Doughty, Dr. John Elliot, H. Hamtramck, Josiah Harmar, Henry Knox, John Smith, and John C. Van Herrman.

JOHN FISHER PAPERS
10 vols., 1777–1802.

265   Fisher: New York merchant before and after the Revolution; assistant deputy quarter-

master at Fishkill, N.Y., during the war.

Accounts, letters, receipts, orders, personnel and supply lists concerning the supply of troops stationed in New York and New Jersey, 1777–83. Also in the collection are returns of military stores at Basking Ridge, N.J., 1777, and at Fishkill Landing, 1778–79, 1782; invoices of sloops loaded at Tarrytown and Fishkill, 1778, 1780–81; an account of expenses for procuring masts for the French Navy in Pennsylvania and Connecticut, 1779; monthly reports of vessels in public service on the Hudson River, 1781–82; payrolls for water department at Fishkill, 1781–82; final accounts at Fishkill Landing, 1783; a daybook for supplies at Fishkill, 1778–79; and forage accounts, 1780–81. Approximately 50 items relate to Fisher's business affairs before and after the Revolution.

Principal correspondents: William Betts, Joseph Browne, John Campbell, Daniel Carty, D. Hale, Udney Hay, Robert Henry, John Keese, Richard King, James McMaster, Uriah Mitchell, Lionell Smith, Andrew Taylor, George Trimble, and Timothy Whiting.

SAMUEL FISHER PAPERS
1 box, 1758–81.   Part photostats.

266   Fisher (1733-1816): Wrentham, Mass., farmer; 2d lt., Massachusetts Militia, Timothy Ruggles' regiment, 1759; capt., 4th Suffolk County Regiment, 1776–81.

Roster lists, receipts, letters, and related documents concerning Fisher's militia company in the 4th Suffolk Regiment. Also includes draft lists and bounty accounts for Wrentham during the Revolution.

Principal correspondents: Seth Bullard, Benjamin Hawes, James Spencer, and Ephraim Wheelock.

JOHN FITCH PAPERS
9 vols., 1783–1826.   Force manuscripts.

267   Fitch (1743–98): Connecticut native, metal craftsman and surveyor; Pennsylvania resident when he built his first steamboat, 1787; operated steamboat on Delaware River, 1788–91.

Three volumes of diaries, surveyors notebooks, and personal accounts for the period 1783–91, describing Fitch's surveying work in the Ohio River Valley and the early years of boat building, as well as pamphlets related to the controversy between Fitch and James Rumsey. Many of Fitch's letters seek monetary or lobbying support.

Principal correspondents: Samuel Briggs, George Clymer, Thomas Johnson, Charles Pettit, Samuel Smith, and Washington.

JOHN FITZGERALD PAPERS
1 box, 1756–98.

268   Fitzgerald: Alexandria, Va., merchant.

Commercial correspondence between Fitzgerald and merchants and customers in New York, Philadelphia, Baltimore, and various Virginia towns. Most of the letters were written between 1770 and 1793.

Principal correspondents: Henry Bedinger, Thomas Bond, Thomas Burling, Daniel Carroll, John Clayton, George Diggs, Thomas Fitzsimmons, Jonathan Hudson, Elias Jones, William Kilty, Joseph LaCoste, Thomas Lee, William Lyles, John McHenry, David McMechen, Thomas H. Marshall, George Meade, John F. Mercer, Messrs. Patton & Dalrymple, John Ridout, Messrs. Samuel & John Smith, Benjamin Stoddert, John Vaughan, Jeremiah Wadsworth, and James Wood.

EBENEZER FOOTE FAMILY PAPERS
1 box, 1751–1871.

269   Charles A. Foote (1785–1828): New York attorney; officer in the War of 1812; member, U.S. House of Representatives, 1823–25.

Contains a medical prescription and recipe of Dr. J. Wainwright, Oct. 1781.

FORBES FAMILY PAPERS

47 reels microfilm, 1732–1931.   *NUCMC* 60–799

270   John Forbes (1740–83): British official in East Florida. John Murray Forbes (1771–1831): U.S. consul at Copenhagen and Hamburg; agent for U.S. at Buenos Aires. James Grant Forbes (1769–1825): Merchant.

Includes correspondence of loyalist James Murray concerning British attitudes toward America in the early 1770's and the life of a loyalist in Boston and Nova Scotia. Also postwar business correspondence of James Grant Forbes relating to trade with the West Indies, and personal letters between James Murray Forbes, a law student at Brookfield and Lancaster, Mass., and his mother Dorothy Forbes, 1788–91. A small notebook kept by Dorothy Forbes in the 1770's contains birth dates and poems.

Principal correspondents: Ralph B. Forbes and Elizabeth Murray.

The collection was filmed under the auspices of the National Historical Publications Commission. A published guide is available. Originals in Massachusetts Historical Society, Baker Library, Harvard Business School, and several private collections.

PETER FORCE COLLECTION

3 boxes, 1762–1814.   Force transcripts.

271   Force (1790–1868): Collector and editor.

Originals of nearly all these letters and documents are in other groups of the Peter Force Papers. The material, focusing on military activities during the years, 1777–80, was copied by Force's son, William Q. Force, probably for unpublished volumes of the *American Archives.* Included are letters of Washington, Henry Knox, Robert H. Harrison, William Woodford, Jonathan Hale, John Armstrong, and Benedict Arnold; minutes of the Committee on the Arrangement of the Army, 1778; and large numbers of muster rolls and supply records.

More detailed descriptions of most of these papers are found in other entries in this guide dealing with the original manuscripts from which they were transcribed.

PETER FORCE HISTORICAL MANUSCRIPTS

40 boxes, 1501–1866.   Force Papers, Series IX.

272   Force (1790–1868): See entry no. 271.

Miscellaneous letters and documents collected by Force, chiefly originals. Material is chronologically arranged except for undated items in boxes 39–40, which are arranged alphabetically by subject and author. Documents from the period of the Revolution are in boxes 9–34, but there are a few items of obvious Revolutionary origin among the undated material. Documents generally include personal, political, and military correspondence; military certificates, returns, intelligence reports, paroles, and accounts of battles and skirmishes; business and legal papers; minutes, proceedings, and resolutions of various State legislatures; petitions, proclamations, indentures, and various public and private records.

Principal correspondents: John Adams, Ethan Allen, Jonathan Ashley, Theodore Atkinson, William Atlee, Jeremy Belknap, Samuel Buell, Archibald Bulloch, George Clinton, Cadwallader Colden, Nicholas Cooke, Lord Dunmore, James Easton, Samuel Finley, James Freeman, Thomas Gage, Charles Garth, Germain, Elbridge Gerry, Nicholas Gilman, John Glover, James Gordon, Richard Gridley, David Griffith, James Habersham, Josiah Harmar, Burr Harrison, Moses Hazen, Adm. Richard Howe, Robert Howe, John Hurd, John Jay, Thomas Johnson, Jr., Henry Knox, Lafayette, Samuel Leslie, Robert R. Livingston, William Logan, Thomas McKean, Lord North, Andrew Oliver, James Otis, Samuel H. Parsons, Edmund Pendleton, Richard Peters, Timothy Pickering, Peyton Randolph, George Ross, Arthur St. Clair, John Schuyler, Jr., Abraham Skinner, William Smith, Ezra Stiles, John Sullivan, Charles M. Thruston, John Tomlinson, Jonathan Trumbull, William Tryon, Samuel Tucker, Anthony Wayne, Eleazar Wheelock, William Whipple, James Wilkinson, Israel Williams, William Williams, James Wilson, and William Woodford.

ISAAC FOSTER FAMILY PAPERS
2 folios, 1769–1899.   *NUCMC* 67–600

273   Isaac Foster (1740–81): Charlestown, Mass., physician, 1766–75; acting director, Cambridge Hospital, 1775–76; accompanied the Army in the New York and New Jersey campaigns, 1776; deputy director of hospitals, Eastern Department, 1777–80. Mary Russell Foster: Wife of Isaac Foster.

Correspondence between Isaac Foster, his wife, Mary, and his father, Isaac Foster, Sr., concerning military and domestic affairs. Several letters Foster wrote from New York City during the summer of 1776 describe popular reaction to the Declaration of Independence and the British buildup of forces on Staten Island. Letters written from Philadelphia during three trips he made to that city concern his efforts to acquire funds for the medical department and higher rank for himself. Mrs. Foster's correspondence, written chiefly from Boston, concerns family matters and personal sufferings caused by the war. Both Foster and his wife provide a detailed account of the British raid on Danbury, Conn., 1777. Also includes Foster's will and miscellaneous accounts for military pay.

FRANCE, MISCELLANY
6 boxes, 4 vols., 1483–1932.

274   Includes the minutes of the Clerical Provincial Assembly at Auch, France, Sept. 1782, which discuss the calling of the Clerical General Assembly by the King to gain support for the war's settlement. Also wills, bills of sale, notarized testimony, and other scattered legal documents.

BENJAMIN FRANKLIN PAPERS
38 vols., 15 boxes, 4 folios, 1728–1907. Part transcripts and photostats. Microfilm available. Finding aid available.

275   Franklin (1706–90): Printer, author, scientist, statesman, and diplomat.

The first series (17 vols.) of the original Henry C. Stevens Collection consists primarily of papers concerning Franklin's diplomatic career, including the Records of the United States Legation, Paris; the petition of the Continental Congress to George III, Oct. 1774; Franklin's "Craven Street Letter Book," Aug. 1772—Sept. 1773; and Richard Oswald's correspondence with Lord Shelburne and the American commissioners, 1782–83. Also Franklin's "Journal," May—July 1782, containing notes pertaining to the opening of negotiations with Britain; his account of negotiations in London, 1774–76, published in Francis Wharton, *Revolutionary Diplomatic Correspondence of the United States*, 6 vols. (Washington, D.C., 1889); and correspondence with David Hartley, 1775–81. The second series contains miscellaneous letters and papers, 1726–90, filed chronologically, and the papers of William Temple Franklin, who for a time was his grandfather's secretary in Paris.

The Franklin Papers Miscellany contains correspondence with Polly [Mary] Stevenson, 1760–79, published in James M. Stifler, *My Dear Girl* (New York, 1927); letters to Sir Joseph Bank, Dr. Jan Ingenhousz, Jean Baptiste Le Roy, and Edward Nairne concerning scientific subjects; and unpublished letters to Franklin from Beaumarchais, Robert W. Jones, Barbé-Marbois, John de Neufville, Samuel Noble, Joseph Priestley, and Anthony Wayne, and from Franklin to Richard Bache, C. W. F. Dumas, Felix Frecon, David Hartley, Philip Mazzei, Benjamin Rush, Granville Sharp, and Dufourney de Villiers.

Photostats include letters of Benjamin and William Franklin to William Strahan, 1748–81; notes for Franklin's autobiography to 1778; letters from Franklin to William Temple Franklin, Sarah F. Bache, and Benjamin F. Bache; and letters from William Temple Franklin to Louis Le Veillard, 1786–92. Originals in Pierpont Morgan Library. Also a photostat of the original autograph of Franklin's autobiography; the original is in the Huntington Library.

Other items in the miscellany include the manuscript of Louis Le Veillard's French translation of the autobiography; three drafts of Condorcet's "Éloge de Franklin;" Franklin's letter to Count Mercy, the Austrian minister in Paris, concerning a treaty of commerce; and facsimile copies of Franklin's Postmaster General ledger, 1776–78, and of Rembrandt Peale's drawing of Franklin.

See Worthington C. Ford, *List of the Benjamin Franklin Papers in the Library of Congress* (Washington, D.C., 1965), and *Proceedings of the American Philosophical Society*, vol. 99 (1955), p. 359–80. A new definitive edition of the Franklin papers is now being prepared by the Yale University Press (New Haven, Conn., 1959–   ).

WILLIAM FRANKLIN PAPERS
1 vol., 1775–76.   Force manuscripts.

276   Franklin (1731–1813): Son of Benjamin Franklin; gov., New Jersey, 1763–75; pres., Associated Loyalists.

Franklin's view of the causes of the Revolution up to 1776 are revealed in a long letter to Lord Dartmouth. Also includes Franklin's messages to the New Jersey Assembly, a contemporary copy of the records of the Assembly, Nov.—Dec. 1775, and John DeHart's letter of resignation from the Continental Congress.

FRONTIER WARS PAPERS
24 vols., 1742–1826.   Draper Mss., series U, WHi.   Microfilm, 6 reels.

277   Original documents and papers prepared by Lyman C. Draper concerning Indian wars in the Northwest, 1788–95, and western operations during the War of 1812. Revolutionary materials, volumes 1–3 and 14, include papers describing the Cherokee expedition, 1776; the defense of the Virginia and Pennsylvania frontiers, 1777; Evan Shelby's Chickamauga campaign, 1779; and journals, commissions, muster rolls, and land warrants from the papers of Gen. Richard Butler, Continental soldier, superintendent of Indian affairs, 1784–91, and commissioner for Indian treaties, 1785–88. The collection also contains original papers concerning the Hopewell treaties, 1785–86; a narrative of Col. William Sudduth, a Kentucky pioneer, 1783–94; and copies of journals kept on Sullivan's expedition, 1779, by Ebenezer Elmer, Samuel M. Shute, James Norris, and Thomas Blake.

Principal correspondents: Matthew Arbuckle, John Bowyer, James Callaway, Arthur Campbell, William Christian, John Gibson, Edward Hand, Benjamin Harrison, Josiah Harmar, Patrick Henry, Abraham Hite, Jefferson, Andrew Lewis, William McClanachan, Samuel McDowell, Samuel Moorhead, Lacklan Morgan, John Page, William Preston, William Russell, David Shepherd, and Thomas Walker.

See also Thwaites, *Descriptive List of Manuscript Collections*, p. 27–30.

BENJAMIN FRY AND FAMILY PAPERS
1 folio, 1784–1857.

278   Fry: Newport, R.I., merchant; 1st lt., Rhode Island State Regiment, 1775–76; capt., Rhode Island Militia, 1776–77.

Contains 13 letters between Fry and James Bentham of Charleston, S.C., concerning problems of interstate business. Includes details on financing, building, and the operation of a packet between Newport, R.I., and Charleston, S.C.

HUGH GAINE NOTEBOOK
1 box, 1779–81.

279   Gaine (1726–1807): New York printer; bookseller.

Entries describe the arrival and departure of British ships at New York harbor; Maj. Henry Lee's raid on Paulus Hook, 1779; Sir George Collier's Penobscot expedition, 1779; Benedict Arnold's arrival at New York and subsequent expeditions against Virginia and New London, Conn., 1780–81; and the arrival of Cornwallis at New York following his release on parole.

ALBERT GALLATIN PAPERS
46 reels microfilm, 1761–1880.

280   Gallatin (1761–1849): Swiss immigrant; member, U.S. House of Representatives, 1795–1801; secretary of the treasury, 1801–14; diplomat.

Reels 1–2 contain correspondence and accounts relating to Gallatin's career as a French tutor at Cambridge, Mass.; his removal to Pennsylvania, 1783; letters and papers concerning western lands and Pennsylvania politics. Also a notebook and diary, 1787–88; an account book, Mar. 1789—Sept. 1790; and miscellaneous deeds, patents, and petitions. Most of Gallatin's personal correspondence during this period is in French.

Principal correspondents: Alexander Addison, Jean Badollet, George Bryan, Alexander J. Dallas, Francis Deakins, Pierre Eugène du Simitière, E. Dutilh & Co., Franklin, Suzanne Gallatin, Patrick Henry, Thomas Madison, John Marshall, Thomas Mifflin, John Moyland, Catherine Pictet, David Redick, Edward Shippen, Philippe Strubing, and Abraham Trembley.

The material was filmed under the auspices of the National Historical Publications Commission. See also *NUCMC* 60–2702.

JOSEPH GALLOWAY PAPERS
1 box, 1742–1823.

281   Galloway (1731–1803): Speaker, Pennsylvania Assembly, 1766–74; member, Continental Congress, 1774; joined the British in New York, 1776; with General Howe during occupation of Philadelphia, 1777–78; pamphleteer in England after 1779.

Chiefly material pertaining to Joseph's wife, Grace Growden Galloway (d. 1782). Pertinent items include about 60 letters exchanged between Grace and her husband and daughter Elizabeth after Galloway fled to New York. Also includes letters of John Pemberton, John De Normandie, and Deborah Morris and a small booklet containing a record of the travels of William Roberts of Portsmouth, Va., 1770–1809.

JOSEPH GALLOWAY PAPERS
2 vols., 1779–ca. 1785.   Force manuscripts.

282   Galloway (1731–1803): See entry no. 281.

Contains drafts of four letters and essays written by Galloway and intended for publication in England—two variant drafts of a letter to General Burgoyne in response to published remarks from Burgoyne's speeches before the House of Commons, a letter to Lord Howe, and a draft of Galloway's Plan of Union as he reformulated it, about 1785. The second volume in the collection is Israel Maudit's annotated copy of Galloway's pamphlet *The Examination of Joseph Galloway . . . Before the House of Commons* (London, 1779).

The Plan of Union is published in Julian P. Boyd's *Anglo-American Union: Joseph Galloway's Plans to Preserve the British Empire, 1774–1788* (Philadelphia, 1941), p. 157–72.

GALLOWAY–MAXCY–MARKOE FAMILY PAPERS
64 vols., 28 boxes, 1654–1888.   *NUCMC* 70–950

283   Samuel Galloway (d. 1785): Tulip Hill, Md., merchant.

Revolutionary materials focusing on Maryland economic life include 22 volumes of correspondence (vols. 6–23, 56–61), 24 business ledgers and journals, and several small rent, cash, invoice, and miscellaneous account books. Samuel Galloway's commercial activities also involved his sons John and Benjamin, his son-in-law, Thomas Ringgold, Jr., and his brother Joseph (d. 1805). The family's personal correspondence includes letters from Samuel's in-laws, John, Samuel, and Benjamin Chew of Philadelphia, and James Cheston of Annapolis, husband of Samuel's daughter Ann.

Principal correspondents: Benjamin Chambers, Cornelius Conaway, Richard Davis, Michael Earle, James Gibson, Sylvanus Grove, William Hemsley, James Hollyday, Reese

Meredith, Thomas Philpot, James Russell, Stephen Steward, Edward Tilghman, James Tilghman, Richard Tilghman, William Tilghman, William Tippell, Jeremiah Watkins, and William Young, and the firms Paul & James Benson, Clark & Manwaring, Josiah & Samuel Coates, Thomas Eden & Co., Mayne & Co., Thomas Ringgold & Son, and Sims White & Son.

GARRETT FAMILY PAPERS
147 boxes, 1778–1925.

284   Garrett: Baltimore, Md., merchant family.
Includes a letter from Charles Carroll of Carrollton to John Francis Gardiner, Annapolis, Nov. 1782, concerning payment on a bond, and a signed receipt for partial payment, Oct. 1778.

CHARLES GARTH PAPERS
1 box, 1 folio, 1765–75.   Force transcripts.

285   Garth (ca. 1734–84): Colonial agent for South Carolina, 1762–75, Maryland, 1765–66, and Georgia, 1763–66; Member of Parliament from Devizes borough, Wiltshire, 1765–80.
Correspondence between Garth and the South Carolina committee of correspondence concerning South Carolina's relations with England, 1765–75, and the development of Revolutionary sentiment in South Carolina. Also includes Garth's petitions and memorials to the English government and his itemized expense account, as well as a notebook, 1765–66, pertaining to the Stamp Act crisis.
Principal correspondents: Christopher Gadsden, Thomas Lynch, John Rutledge, and Joseph Wilson.

HORATIO GATES PAPERS
2 vols., 1776–77.   Force transcripts.

286   Gates (1728–1806): Brig. and maj. gen., Continental Army; adjutant general, 1775; pres., Board of War, 1777; commander in chief, Northern Department, 1777–78, Eastern Department, 1779, and Southern Department, 1780.
Gates' official correspondence as adjutant general and as commander in chief, Northern Department. Includes letters to Congress concerning the progress of the war, rank disputes, and assignment of commands, letters from persons seeking commissions and special favors, and family correspondence. Also letters between various Continental officers, Gates' instructions to Continental and militia units, information obtained from German soldiers captured at Bennington, intelligence reports, accounts of battles and skirmishes, military returns, and documents relating to Burgoyne's surrender at Saratoga. Miscellaneous documents include an address to the chiefs of the Six Nations, May 1777; petitions from American prisoners of war, loyalists seeking permission to enter Canada, and persons in New Hampshire suffering from British depredations; and an orderly book containing general orders issued at Fort Albany, N.Y., April 19—June 3, 1777.
Principal correspondents: Charles Armand, John Armstrong, Jr., Burgoyne, William Clajon, George Clinton, Thomas Cushing, John Ettwein, John Fellows, Peter Gansevoort, Alexander Hamilton, John Hancock, Moses Hazen, William Heath, Hugh Hughes, James Irvine, John Jay, Thaddeus Kosciuszko, Lafayette, Henry Laurens, Charles Lee, Francis Lewis, Benjamin Lincoln, William Livingston, James Lovell, Alexander McDougall, Thomas Mifflin, John Nixon, Samuel Patterson, William Patterson, Richard Peters, Enoch Poor, Israel Putnam, Joseph Reed, Arthur St. Clair, Philip Schuyler, Roger Sherman, John Stark, Joseph Trumbull, Richard Varrick, Artemas Ward, Washington, and James Wilkinson.
Originals in New York Historical Society.

"GENERAL SULLIVAN"
1 vol., 1777–80.

287   Logbook for the privateer *General Sullivan*. Includes minutes of the meetings of the ship's proprietors, 1777–79, a list of goods seized on the prize brigatine *Charlotte*, and miscellaneous accounts.

EDMUND C. GENÊT PAPERS
19 vols., 32 boxes, 1734–1895.   Microfilm and finding aid available. *NUCMC* 59–224

288   Genêt (1763–1834): French diplomat; acting secretary of the French Legation in England, 1783–87; charge d'affaires at St. Petersburg, 1787–92; minister plenipotentiary to the U.S., 1792–93; New York farmer.

Contains correspondence to Genêt and his father, Edme, head of the Bureau of Interpretation in the Foreign Office, from American agents in France. Principal concerns include aid for the United States, information on French and British supply operations, the Silas Deane affair, trade, and campaigns in America. Also includes French translations of letters from John Paul Jones to the Ministry of Marine; diplomatic correspondence and instructions concerning Franco-American relations; essays by Genêt on American government, the Army, loyalists, and science; a draft history of the Genêt family; and extracts and clippings from French, British, and American newspapers.

Principal correspondents: John Adams, Edward Bridger, Francis Dana, Franklin, Alexander Gillon, Ralph Izard, Edmund Jenings, Arthur Lee, William Lee, J. Lindblom, Matthew Ridley, Vergennes, and Thomas Wilcox.

GEORGIA, COLONIAL RECORDS
16 reels microfilm, 1732–83.

289   Transcripts of papers of the royal governors and their correspondence with ministers in England; also official letterbooks and entry books. Materials on these reels are not published in Allen D. Candler, ed., *The Colonial Records of the State of Georgia*, 26 vols. (Atlanta, 1904–1916). Reels 2, 3, 9, and 12–15 contain material from the Revolutionary era. Topics include trade, legislation, land grants and quit rents, the silk industry, Indian affairs and treaties, administrative expenses, and the dispute with South Carolina over lands south of the Altamaha River. References to the Stamp Act, the burning of rice, loyalist claims—particularly the large claim of Governor Wright—and the reoccupation of Georgia by the British in 1779.

Principal correspondents: Henry Seymour Conway, Cornwallis, Dartmouth, Egremont, Germain, John Graham, James Habersham, Earl of Halifax, Hillsborough, William Knox, Duke of Richmond, Shelburne, and James Wright.

For additional information see the index on reel 16. See also P.R.O./C.O.5, entry nos. 1506–17.

GEORGIA, COMMITTEE OF CORRESPONDENCE
1 folio, 1762–71.   Force transcripts.

290   Correspondence and accounts with colonial agents William Knox and Benjamin Franklin. Transcribed from originals in the office of the secretary of state, Milledgeville, Ga., 1833.

GEORGIA, EXECUTIVE COUNCIL
1 folio, 1785–89.   Force transcripts.

291   Official correspondence of the Executive Council of Georgia.

GEORGIA, GENERAL ASSEMBLY
1 vol., 1755–89.   Force transcripts.

292   Legislative acts and extracts of acts passed by the Georgia Commons House of Assembly. Transcribed from originals in the Georgia Department of State, 1833.

GEORGIA, GOVERNORS
1 vol., 1754–78.   Force transcripts.

293   Includes proclamations of James Wright, John Houstoun, John A. Treutlen, and Archibald Bulloch, copied from originals in the Georgia Department of State, 1833. Subjects include exports, Indian affairs, the Articles of Confederation, public morality, and a variety of other matters.

GEORGIA, MISCELLANY
1 box, 1733–1855.

294   Includes a land warrant for Jacob Weed, May 1787, and a petition from loyalists at Queensborough to Gov. James Wright asking better protection against Indians and renegade whites, Mar. 1780.

GERMAN TROOPS IN AMERICA
1 vol., 1776–83.

295   Transcripts of documents in the British War Office Records, London. Includes list of troops from Hesse-Cassel, showing date raised, commanding officers, and station. Also records of correspondence with the War Office pertaining to German troops in America.

GERMANS IN THE REVOLUTIONARY WAR
1 vol., undated.

296   Memoir, in German, of the service of Hessian soldiers in the Revolution.

ELBRIDGE GERRY PAPERS
8 boxes, 2 vols., 1744–1836.   Part photostats.

297   Gerry (1744–1814): Member, Massachusetts General Court, 1772–73, Continental Congress, 1776–85, and Constitutional Convention, 1787; special envoy to France, 1797; gov., Massachusetts, 1810–11; Vice President of the U.S.
        Chiefly copies of documents in Massachusetts depositories dealing with political affairs in the Continental Congress and in Gerry's home state. Many of the items are published in Burnett, *Letters of Members of Congress.*
        Principal correspondents: John Adams, Samuel Adams, James Bowdoin, Nathaniel Cutting, Richard Devens, William Eustis, James Lovell, James Madison, Harrison Gray Otis, Nathaniel Peabody, William Shippen, Artemas Ward, James Warren, and Mercy Warren.

ELISHA GILBERT PAPERS
1 folio, 1775–81   Force transcripts.

298   Gilbert: New Lebanon, N.Y., militia captain, Col. William R. Whiting's regiment.
        Muster and marching orders from Whiting to Gilbert offer insight into the activities of the militia in the King's district of New York. Also includes payrolls, muster rolls, and related letters.
        Principal correspondents: Jonathan Warner and Asa Waterman.

DAVID GILLESPIE AND ANDREW ELLICOTT PAPERS
1 vol., 1777–1801.

299   Ellicott (1754–1820): Surveyor and mathematician.
        Items from the period of the Revolution include an obituary note and eulogistic poem by Lt. Col. Alexander Martin on the death of Gen. Francis Nash, Oct. 1777.

NICHOLAS GILMAN PAPERS
1 box, 1776–1824.   *NUCMC* 64–1567

300   Gilman (1755–1814): New Hampshire officer and politician; member, Continental Congress, 1786–88, Constitutional Convention, 1787, U.S. House of Representatives, 1789–97, U.S. Senate, 1804–14.

The bulk of the papers dated before 1789 pertain to the activities of Gilman's father, Nicholas, Sr. (1731–83), and his brother Nathaniel (1759–1847), who were successively commissioners of the Continental Loan Office in New Hampshire. Includes accounts and receipts of Nicholas, Sr., containing information on the transfer of loan office certificates and interest paid to holders, 1780–82. Nathaniel's papers include instructions and letters from William Duer, secretary of the Board of Treasury, and from U.S. Treasurer Michael Hillegas, in addition to miscellaneous documents relating to his work as receiver of Continental taxes in New Hampshire.

MORDECAI GIST PAPERS

1 vol., 1777–79.   Force transcripts.   *NUCMC* 69–878

301   Gist (1742–92): Nephew of Christopher Gist; maj., Col. William Smallwood's regiment, 1776; col., 3d Maryland Continental Regiment, 1776–78; brig. gen., Continental Army, 1779–81.

Letters from Gist to the Maryland delegates in Congress, Gov. Thomas Johnson, friends and business associates in Baltimore, and various Continental and militia officers. Subjects include family affairs, recruiting, apprehension of deserters, prisoners of war, rank disputes, supplies, troops dispositions, Tory disturbances on the Eastern Shore of Maryland, and the organization of the Army. Also included are accounts of battles and skirmishes, reconnaissance reports, orders, and returns.

Principal correspondents: William Carmichael, Samuel Chase, William Crawford, Nathanael Greene, Benjamin Griffith, R. H. Harrison, Thomas Johnson, Baron de Kalb, David Moore, Lewis Nicola, William Paca, Richard Peters, Thomas Price, Charles Ramsey, Nathaniel Ramsey, Caesar Rodney, William Smallwood, William Smith, James Sterett, Mary Sterett, William Sterett, John Steward, Lord Stirling, John Stone, and Washington.

Originals in New York Public Library.

GIST FAMILY PAPERS

1 box, 1776–1865.   Part photostats.

302   Mordecai Gist (1742–92): See entry no. 301.

Three letters between Gist and his wife concern personal matters and the progress of the war in 1778. Letters from John McLure discuss social, political, economic, and military developments in Baltimore and vicinity, 1777, and those from John and William Sterett pertain to business affairs, 1777–78 and 1785. Letters to Gist following his removal to Charleston in the postwar period describe social and economic conditions in Maryland and comment on the market for American products, chiefly tobacco, in France. Also includes a list of the officers in Gist's regiment and a draft of military installations around the Delaware and Schuylkill Rivers.

Principal correspondents: Paul Bentalou, Pierre Changeur, J. D. Chase, John Pierce, C. Richmond, J. Swan, and Francis Spencer Warrington.

Photostats are of originals in Maryland Historical Society.

JOHN GLASSFORD & COMPANY PAPERS

228 vols., 1753–1844.   Finding aid available.   *NUCMC* 62–4657

303   John Glassford: Glasgow merchant.

Records of several Glasgow companies trading in Maryland and Virginia. Chiefly journals, ledgers, inventories, invoice lists, and letterbooks pertaining to stores in Benedict, Bladensburg, Georgetown, Leonard Town, Lower Marlborough, Newport, Nottingham, Piscataway, Port Tobacco, Rock Creek, and Upper Marlborough, Md.; and Alexandria, Boyd's Hole, Cabin Point, Colchester, Dumfries, and Norfolk, Va. Firms represented include John Glassford & Co.; Glassford, Henderson & Co.; Glassford, Gordon, Monteath & Co.; Simon, Baird & Co.; James Brown & Co.; Bogle, Scott & Co.; Jamieson, Johnstone & Co.; Shortridge, Gordon & Co.; and James Gordon & Co.

Also contains material concerning the activities of some of the Scottish factors in the region, including James Brown, Archibald Campbell, Colin Campbell, Peter Campbell, John Chambers, Mungo Fairlie, Robert Ferguson, Thomas Gantt, Alexander Hamilton, Alexander Henderson, Archibald Henderson, Richard Henderson, Thomas Jones, Robert Peters, Henry Riddell, John Riddell, David Walker, and John Wardrop.

Miscellaneous items include the Alexander Hamilton (James Brown & Co. factor at Piscataway) letterbook, 1773–76, 1784–90; the Robert Ferguson (Glassford factor) letterbook, 1787–88; "Tobacco Inventories" and "Invoices of Tobacco Shipped," 1760–75; "Debt Transactions," 1785–92; and "Lists of Debts" contracted prior to 1776 at Glassford stores.

The Hamilton letters have been published in the *Maryland Historical Magazine,* vols. 61, 62, 65, and 66.

See also Alexander Hamilton, entry no. 316.

HENRY GLEN PAPERS

1 vol., 1776–80.   Force transcripts.   *NUCMC* 70–324

304   Glen (1739–1814): Continental deputy quartermaster general at Schenectady, N.Y., 1776–80; member, New York Provincial Congress, 1774–76, State legislature, 1786–87, and U.S. House of Representatives, 1793–1801.

Letters written by Glen while serving as deputy quartermaster at Schenectady, N.Y., concerning the acquisition and distribution of supplies and provisions. The letters are addressed to militia and Continental officers stationed along the Hudson River and in forts along New York's western frontier.

Principal correspondents: Elisha Avery, Peter Bellinger, James Clinton, Jacob Cuyler, Isaac Degraff, Jellis Fonda, Peter Gansevoort, Horatio Gates, James Gray, John Hansen, Udney Hay, Morgan Lewis, James Livingston, William Popham, Philip Van Rensselaer, Joseph Savage, Goose Van Schaick, and Ebenezer Winship.

Originals in New York Public Library.

SIMON GRATZ AUTOGRAPHS

2 vols., 1719–1873.

305   Gratz: Pennsylvania clergyman.

Letters from Revolutionary era clergymen concerning price control, inflation, hiring of soldiers, Baptists, and Indians. Among the clergymen represented are Charles Backus, Jacob Cushing, Samuel Hopkins, Joseph Huntington, Joseph Lee, Joseph Lothrop, Joseph Lyman, Nathan Perkins, Silvanus Ripley, Ebenezer Thayer, Jonathan Todd, William Williams, and Anson Woolworth.

SAMUEL GRAY PAPERS

1 vol., 1754–81.   Force transcripts.   *NUCMC* 64–1275

306   Gray: Deputy commissary general of issues, Eastern Department, Continental Army.

Official correspondence with Charles Stewart (1729–1800), commissary general of issues, and with local deputies in New England and southern New York concerning the acquisition and distribution of military stores and provisions. Includes some war news and reports of maneuvers and encampments.

Principal correspondents: James Burnside, Moses Church, Peter Colt, John Elderkin, Ebenezer Gray, Alexander Greene, Nathanael Greene, Samuel H. Parsons, James Richardson, Alexander Scammell, John Squire, Jr., Frederick Tracy, and Jonathan Trumbull.

Originals in Connecticut Historical Society.

GREAT BRITAIN, ARMY IN AMERICA

2 vols., 1728–92.

307   Contains annual records of the paymaster general for British forces, 1763, 1766, and 1769–74, showing general and staff officers' per diem and annual expenses at each post in America.

GREAT BRITAIN, ARMY IN IRELAND AND NORTH AMERICA
1 vol., 1751–71.   Force manuscripts.

308   Copybook of Richard Maitland, deputy adjutant general of forces in North America, and Thomas Moncrieff, major of brigade. Contains instructions and orders for troops in Ireland, 1751–52, and at New York and Boston in North America, 1767–71.

GREAT BRITAIN, BOARD OF TRADE REPORT
1 vol., July 1766.

309   A report to George III on the South Carolina Stamp Act controversy, bound with 15 enclosures concerning efforts to remove the clerk of the court of common pleas, Dougall Campbell, for compliance with the act. Enclosures include letters of Lt. Gov. William Bull; resolutions, orders, and letters of the assembly; an opinion and letters of judges of the court of common pleas; and petitions of Dougall Campbell, Apr.—May 1766.

GREAT BRITAIN, COMMITTEE ON TRADE AND FOREIGN PLANTATIONS
3 vols., 1784–86.

310   Contemporary copy of minutes of the committee of council that was successor to the Board of Trade, Mar. 5, 1784—Aug. 23, 1786.
    See also P.R.O./B.T.5, entry no. 1413.

NATHANAEL GREENE LETTERBOOKS
2 vols., 1781–82.   Force manuscripts.

311   Greene (1742–86): Brig. gen., Rhode Island Militia, 1775; brig. and maj. gen., Continental Army, 1775–83; quartermaster general, Feb. 1778–Aug. 1780; commander in chief, Southern Department, Oct. 1780—Aug. 1783.
    Greene's official correspondence as commander in chief, Southern Department, Jan.—Feb. 1781 and Jan.—Apr. 1782. Addressed chiefly to American officers serving in the department and to Governors of States from Maryland to Georgia on such subjects as British and American maneuvers, the critical need for supplies and reinforcements, and lesser administrative problems.
    Principal correspondents: John Adams, John Barnwell, Abraham Buford, Thomas Burke, Richard Caswell, Benjamin Harrison, William Henderson, Patrick Henry, Isaac Huger, Thomas Jefferson, Thaddeus Kosciuszko, La Luzerne, Thomas Sim Lee, Alexander Leslie, John A. Lillington, Benjamin Lincoln, Josiah Martin, Daniel Morgan, Robert Morris, Abner Nash, Andrew Pickens, Lord Rawdon, Rochambeau, Griffith Rutherford, John Rutledge, Charles Scott, Baron von Steuben, Jethro Sumner, Thomas Sumter, Washington, Anthony Wayne, and various Presidents of Congress.

NATHANAEL GREENE PAPERS
5 vols., 1 box, 1775–85.   Part photostats.

312   Greene (1732–86): See entry no. 311.
    Four volumes (Peyton H. Skipwith Collection) contain letters received by Greene during the southern campaign—chiefly reconnaissance reports, accounts of battles and skirmishes, reports and instructions from Congress, correspondence with British officers in Charleston on the treatment of prisoners, 1780–83, and returns on casualties, supplies, and reinforcements. A few letters in the first volume describe the general progress of the war, 1778. Letters for 1779 include responses of several high-ranking Continental officers to an inquiry by Greene on the propriety of his having assumed a field command at the battle of Monmouth while serving as quartermaster general. Documents after 1780 comprise letters from citizens in South Carolina who complain of being plundered by American soldiers; a bound copy of the Cherokee Treaty of 1781; captured enemy dispatches; and addresses delivered in honor of General Greene during his return trip north in 1783. The remaining volume consists of a letterbook, Aug.—Dec. 1780, containing

official correspondence from the southern campaign. Boxed items include photostats of scattered letters and documents relating to military affairs, chiefly in the Southern Department.

Principal correspondents: Benedict Arnold, Edward Carrington, Cornwallis, Horatio Gates, Mordecai Gist, John Hancock, Henry Knox, Lafayette, John Laurens, Robert Lawson, Charles Lee, Robert R. Livingston, George Lux, Thomas McKean, John Marshall, Gouverneur Morris, Peter Muhlenberg, Charles Pettit, Timothy Pickering, William Pierce, Joseph Reed, Caesar Rodney, Arthur St. Clair, William Smallwood, Edward Stevens, John Twiggs, and Otho H. Williams.

ARISTACHUS AND SETH GRIFFIN PAPERS
1 box, 1787–1819.   Transcripts.

313   Griffin: Granby, Connecticut family.

Miscellaneous and personal accounts. See U.S. Work Projects Administration finding aid, group 7.

HABERSHAM FAMILY PAPERS
1 box, 1787–1892.   *NUCMC* 66–1412

314   James Habersham: Georgia planter; gov., 1771–72.

Contains three 18th–century letters from James Habersham to a brother concerning attendance in the Georgia Legislature, Indian problems, paper money, and family matters.

HALE FAMILY PAPERS
12 vols., 9 boxes, 1698–1914.   *NUCMC* 59–139

315   Hale: Massachusetts family.

Letters of Lucy Hill Everett to Rebecca Huse concerning family matters, 1781–88. Also an inventory of the personal estate of John Hill, a letter describing Hill's death in 1777, and a William Vinal letter, 1764, publicly admonishing Rhoda Willcox for spreading calumny and scandal in Newport, R.I.

Principal correspondents: Oliver Everett, Capt. Benjamin Franklin, Alexander Hill, and Alexander S. Hill.

ALEXANDER HAMILTON
35 items, 1784–96.

316   Hamilton: Piscataway, Md., lawyer.

Fragmentary letterbook of business correspondence, 1784–85, pertaining to debts owed James Brown & Company, a firm Hamilton served before the outbreak of war.

Principal correspondents: Francis Brown, Thomas Contee, and George Mason.

See also James Brown & Co., letterbook, and John Glassford & Co. letterbooks, in John Glassford & Company Papers, entry no. 303.

ALEXANDER HAMILTON PAPERS
111 vols., 3 boxes, 1 folio, 1714–1849.   Microfilm and finding aid available.

317   Hamilton (1757–1804): Capt., New York Independent Artillery Company, 1776–77; lt. col. and aide-de-camp to Washington, 1777–81; member, Continental Congress, 1782–83; secretary of the treasury, 1789–95.

The Hamilton papers are arranged in two series. Documents from the period of the Revolution, chiefly letters received, are in volumes 1–8 of series one and volumes 1–2 of series two. All letters to and from Hamilton are printed in Harold C. Syrett, ed., *The Papers of Alexander Hamilton*, vols. 1–5 (1961–62). Also in the collection are numerous letters between persons with whom Hamilton was associated during and after the war concerning military and political affairs, and various financial and legal matters. These letters are calendared in the published papers. Additional related items include an account book for Hamilton's artillery company, 1776–77, and two printed drafts of the U.S. Constitution, Aug. and Sept., 1787, with annotations by Hugh Williamson.

Principal correspondents: William Allison, Fisher Ames, Charles Armand, John Banks, Elisha Boudinot, Ephraim Bowen, George Cabot, Edward Carrington, John B. Church, George Clinton, Francis Dana, Jonathan Dayton, James Duane, James Hamilton, Robert G. Harper, Jean Holker, John Jay, Jefferson, Rufus King, Lafayette, Henry Laurens, John Laurens, Charles Lee, Henry Lee, Robert R. Livingston, James McHenry, James Madison, Richard Kidder Meade, Gouverneur Morris, William Vans Murray, Timothy Pickering, Charles Cotesworth Pinckney, Edmund Randolph, Benjamin Rush, Philip Schuyler, Theodore Sedgwick, Baron von Steuben, Lord Stirling, Benjamin Stoddert, Francis Upton, Jeremiah Wadsworth, Washington, Anthony Wayne, Otho H. Williams, Thomas Willing, John Witherspoon, Oliver Wolcott, John Wynkoop, and the firm of Beekman and Cruger.

THOMAS HAMILTON PAPERS
2 vols., 1 box, 1781.   Force manuscripts.

318   Hamilton (d. 1786): Capt., 1st Virginia State Regiment, 1777–81; assistant deputy quartermaster, Staunton District of Virginia, Feb.—Dec. 1781.

Military receipts, accounts, and returns of supplies and provisions furnished by the quartermaster department in Virginia. Also includes returns of persons employed at supply depots in Richmond and Staunton. Most disbursements were to troops involved in the campaign against Cornwallis.

HAMILTON–McLANE FAMILY PAPERS
5 boxes, 1725–1903.

319   Hamilton (1757–1804): See entry no. 317.

Mrs. Madeline E. (Hamilton) Bartholf collection. Contains letters and copies of letters from the correspondence of Alexander Hamilton chiefly concerning legal and political affairs, and the routine business of the treasury office. Also includes miscellaneous correspondence pertaining to the war; a personal letter Hamilton wrote to his wife, Elizabeth, 1786; letters and papers of Angelica Schuyler Church, Philip Schuyler's eldest daughter, 1784–86; and scattered accounts, receipts, and legal papers.

Principal correspondents: John Carter, Stephen DeLancey, Nathanael Greene, John Hancock, William Samuel Johnson, Henry Laurens, John Laurens, Robert R. Livingston, William Livingston, Thomas McKean, Archibald McLean, Rochambeau, Philip Schuyler, Robert Troup, William Tryon, Francis Upton, Washington, and George Webb.

HAMOND NAVAL PAPERS
3 reels microfilm, 1766–1825.   *NUCMC* 69–1275

320   Sir Andrew Snape Hamond (1738–1828): Commander of warships *Arethusa*, 1771–73, and *Roebuck*, 1775–80; lt. gov., Nova Scotia; commander of British base at Halifax, 1781–82.

Chiefly official documents relating to British naval operations in American waters during the Revolution. Includes Hamond's autobiography and a personal account of his activities in the war.

Principal correspondents: Marriot Arbuthnot, Robert Digby, Adam Duncan, Dunmore, George Keith Elphinstone, Germain, Thomas Graves, William Hotham, Lord Howe, John Montagu, John Orde, Peter Parker, Molyneux Shuldham, Philip Stephens, and William Tryon.

The collection was filmed under the auspices of the National Historical Publications Commission. For further details see Paul P. Hoffman, ed., *Guide to the Naval Papers of Sir Andrew Snape Hamond, bart., 1766–1783 and Sir Graham Eden Hamond, 1799–1825* (Charlottesville, 1966).

JOHN HANCOCK PAPERS
7 vols., 1774–76.   *NUCMC* 64–1219

321   Hancock (1737–93): Massachusetts merchant; member, General Court, 1766–72; pres., Massachusetts Provincial Congress, 1774; member and pres., Continental Congress, 1775–80, 1785–86; gov., 1780–85, 1787–93.

Contains Hancock's presidential letterbooks and rough journals of the Continental Congress covering the period of the First Congress. Material in the letterbooks consists largely of reports from military headquarters on the organization and supply of the Army, the siege of Boston, the defense of Rhode Island and New York, the Canadian expedition, and problems with the Indians. Also lists of the employees in the commissary and quartermaster departments, Jan. 1776; inventories of supplies left in Boston after the British evacuation; minutes of a conference between Congressional delegates, representatives of the New England states, and Washington to settle problems of supply, army discipline, and recruits, 1775; and a journal kept by Benedict Arnold during his march through the Maine wilderness, 1775.

Principal correspondents: Albany Committee, Guy Johnson, James Livingston, Richard Montgomery, New York Assembly, and Philip Schuyler.

EDWARD HAND PAPERS
4 vols., 1 box, 1775–84.   Force transcripts.   *NUCMC* 60–3011

322   Hand (1744–1802): Lt. col., William Thompson's Pennsylvania Rifle Battalion, 1775; lt. col., 1st Continental Infantry Regiment, 1776; col., 1st Pennsylvania Regiment, 1777; brig. gen., 1777–80; adjutant general, 1781–83; member, Continental Congress, 1784–85.

Hand's correspondence while he was commandant at Fort Pitt, chiefly with subordinate Continental officers, frontier militia officers, and political figures in Virginia and Pennsylvania concerning military affairs on the western frontier: skirmishes with the Indians, troop dispositions, supplies, the activities of British agents among the Indians, and efforts to establish contact with Spanish officials in Louisiana. Also his correspondence while he served as commandant at Albany, N.Y., and Minisink, Pa., 1779–84, chiefly concerning preparations for Sullivan's expedition against the Iroquois, and letters from Dr. Jasper Yeates to Hand concerning personal, family, and business affairs. Of particular interest are Dr. Yeates' comments on the trial of Dr. William Shippen. Miscellaneous items include addresses to the Indians, returns of troops and supplies, petitions, memoranda, proclamations, and records of courts of inquiry, councils of war, and courts-martial.

Principal correspondents: Matthew Arbuckle, Daniel Brodhead, James Chem, Richard Claiborne, George Rogers Clark, George Clinton, James Clinton, William Crawford, John Davis, Alexander Fowler, John Gibson, Abraham Heite, Patrick Henry, Richard Law, Richard Henry Lee, Francis Lewis, Benjamin Lincoln, Archibald Lochry, David McKee, Samuel Moorhead, George Morgan, Lacquill Morgan, Robert Morris, John Page, Richard Peters, Timothy Pickering, John Piper, Casimir Pulaski, Moses Rawlings, Daniel Roberdeau, Benjamin Rush, William Russell, Philip Schuyler, David Shepherd, Abraham Smith, Devereaux Smith, Richard Spaight, John Stark, Baron von Steuben, John Sullivan, Charles Thomson, and David Zeisberger.

Originals in Historical Society of Pennsylvania.

JOSIAH HARMAR PAPERS
2 vols., 1778–99.   Draper Mss., series W, WHi.   Microfilm, 1 reel.

323   Harmar (1753–1813): Capt. through col., Pennsylvania Continental Line, 1776–83; commanded troops on the northwestern frontier, 1784–92; adjutant general for Pennsylvania, 1793–99.

Extracts from the papers of Harmar. Revolutionary material chiefly concerns the Rhode Island expedition, 1778, the campaign of 1779 in New York, Sullivan's expedition against the Indians, 1779, and campaigns in New York and New Jersey, 1780. Includes information on Indian affairs and western lands, 1784–88. Chronological and name indexes appear at the beginning of each volume.

Originals in possession of Harmar's son, William, in 1849.

WILLIAM HENRY HARRISON PAPERS

9 vols., 2 boxes, 1734–1939.   Microfilm available.   *NUCMC* 59–182

324   Harrison (1773–1841): Virginia statesman, soldier, and President of the U.S.

Includes a letter from Benjamin Harrison, Jr., to Richard Willing of Philadelphia concerning accommodations for Virginia delegates to Congress, Aug. 1774.

HARROD FAMILY PAPERS

1 folio, 1757–1868.   Photostats.

325   Harrod: Frontier family.

Genealogical notes on the Harrod family compiled in 1845. Begins with John Harrod of Little Cove, Pa., whose brothers and sons were among the first settlers of Kentucky.

CHARLES C. HART AUTOGRAPH COLLECTION

1 box, 1476–1942.   Photostats.

326   Hart: Washington, D.C., collector.

Includes a Robert Morris letter to Jonathan Hudson, Nov. 1779, instructing him to convert goods and bills of exchange to Continental currency; an indenture for dividing the land granted to the Illinois Regiment, 1788; and a Washington letter, May 1778, concerning the British evacuation of Philadelphia and the Conway Cabal.

HARWOOD FAMILY PAPERS

1 reel microfilm, 1767–1940.

327   Andrew A. Harwood (1802–84): Vice admiral, U.S. Navy; commander, USF *Constitution*.

Contains a few items of Benjamin Franklin, Richard Bache, Alexander Hamilton, Aaron Burr, and Benedict Arnold. Franklin mentions the British offer to recognize American independence in 1782. Includes Hamilton and Burr letters concerning the collection of debts, an account of indebtedness of Samuel Huntington to Benedict Arnold, and a 1776 letter in which Mrs. William Franklin comments on the treatment of her husband.

Originals in Stanford University Library.

HASBROUCK FAMILY PAPERS

1 vol., 1 folio, 1675–1879.

328   Abraham Hasbrouck (1707–91); Jonathan Hasbrouck (1763–1846); and A. Bruyn Hasbrouck (1791–1879): Kingston, N.Y., farmers.

Includes indentures, chiefly lease agreements; a list of births and deaths, 1738–1846; and a brief diary with entries mainly concerning crops, weather, family illnesses, and deaths. The volume also contains an entry for Oct. 16, 1777, describing depredations committed by the British. Desultory entries, 1776–91.

EBENEZER HAZARD PAPERS

18 boxes, 1632–1814.   Force transcripts and manuscripts.

329   Hazard (1744–1817): Antiquarian; postmaster general, 1782–89.

Material collected by Hazard for his *Historical Collections; Consisting of State Papers and other Authentic Documents,* 2 vols. (Philadelphia, 1792–94). Includes notes and newspaper clippings, 1768–76, contained in several scrapbooks labeled "Politicks" and transcripts of the proceedings of the New Hampshire Assembly, 1770–78, and of extracts from the journal of the Fourth Provincial Congress dated 1775–76. Also a pen-and-ink reproduction of the Stamp Act caricature "The Repeal" and personal letters to Jedediah

Morse, chiefly concerning a planned atlas of the United States.
See also Ebenezer Hazard, journal, entry no. 405.

JOHN H. HAZELTON COLLECTION
22 items, 1725–1884.

330   Hazelton: Lawyer and author.
Includes a contemporary copy of Gen. Robert Howe's letter to Maj. Joseph Lane, Jan. 3, 1779, complaining of Lane's disregard of orders to evacuate Sunbury, Ga., before its capture on Jan. 9. Also routine administrative letters from Gen. James Wilkinson to Gov. Richard Caswell, Aug. 1779; and from James M. Simmons to Gov. Edward Telfair, Dec. 1786.

MOSES HAZEN PAPERS
3 vols., 1776–83.

331   Hazen (1733–1803): Col., 2d Canadian Regiment, 1776–81; brig. gen., 1781–83.
Muster rolls of the 2d Canadian Regiment, also known as "Congress' Own," and "Hazen's Own." Contains a few miscellaneous entries in the first volume concerning supplies and accounts.

WILLIAM HEATH PAPERS
2 vols., 1774–83.   Force transcripts.   *NUCMC* 60–2707

332   Heath (1737–1814): Col. and maj. gen., Massachusetts Militia, 1775; brig. and maj. gen., Continental Army, 1775–83.
Letters and documents chiefly concerning military affairs in the Eastern Department. Correspondence is primarily between Heath and various Continental and militia officers in New York and New England; political figures in Massachusetts, Connecticut, and New York; members of Congress; and Generals Washington and Burgoyne. Major topics include the siege of Boston, the defense of the City of New York, the supply and disposition of troops under Heath's command in the New York highlands, and the Convention Army. Miscellaneous documents include records of councils of war, court-martial proceedings, resolutions of Congress, petitions, returns of troops and supplies, and accounts of battles and skirmishes.
Principal correspondents: John Adams, Samuel Adams, Benedict Arnold, George Clinton, Elbridge Gerry, John Glover, John Hancock, Henry Knox, Henry Laurens, Benjamin Lincoln, William Livingston, Joshua Loring, Alexander McDougall, John Nixon, Samuel Parsons, William Patterson, William Phillips, Timothy Pickering, Enoch Poor, Philip Schuyler, John Morin Scott, Jonathan Trumbull, and Anthony Wayne.

PATRICK HENRY PAPERS
1 box, 1 folio, 1762–1881.

333   Henry (1736–99): Virginia lawyer and statesman; member, Continental Congress, 1774–75; gov., 1776–79, 1784–86.
Includes an account book, 1771–78, with undated notations in Henry's hand; George Mason's commentary on Ohio valley land settlement; and Col. Samuel Meredith's memoir of Henry's life (Meredith's second wife was Jane Henry, sister of Patrick Henry). Also includes miscellaneous family papers, 1777–1813.
Principal correspondents: William DuVal, William Grayson, Richard Henry Lee, William Lee, Philip Mazzei, William Moultrie, William Nelson, David Ross, and Caleb Wallace.

HENRY FAMILY PAPERS
1 item, 1769–1911.   Photostat.

334   Henry: Virginia family.
Genealogical notes recorded in the Henry family Bible.

HESSIAN OFFICERS, LETTERS
1 box, 1 folio, 1776–81.

335   Seventeen personal letters, in French and "Foreigner's English," from Capt. Johann Ewald and Capt. von Stamford chiefly to Miss Jeanette d'Horne (or Van Horne) and Miss Ann d'Horne, 1777–81, and a certificate of protection for Joseph Talman of Burlington County, N.J., issued on the authority of Lt. Gen. Leopold von Heister, 1776.

HESSIAN TROOPS, PAPERS
1 package, 1775–82.   Photostats.

336   Miscellaneous documents in the Wolfenbüttel, Bamberg, and Munich archives. Includes two letters from Johann Andreas Voigt and Wilhelm Wicke to Major General Riedesel appealing for reinforcements, 1780; two letters from Duke Charles of Brunswick to Riedesel concerning negotiations with Britain over the use of Hessian troops, 1775; and two Washington letters to Riedesel and Henry Clinton on the exchange of prisoners, 1778, 1781. Also contains paroles, orders, countersigns, illustrations of Brunswick uniforms, and a draft of an oath for German soldiers enlisting for service in America, as well as drafts of treaties between George III and the Duke of Brunswick, the Prince of Hesse-Cassel, and the Landgrave of Hesse regarding troops for America, 1775–76, and a printed proclamation from the Duke of Brunswick and Lüneburg on recruitment of "foreign" volunteers.

HISPANIC MANUSCRIPTS COLLECTION

337   Most Hispanic manuscripts in the Library of Congress are described with the collections in which they appear. For additional items see the three-volume unpublished guide to Hispanic materials available in the Manuscript Division.

HANNAH HOBART PAPERS
1 box, 1783–89.

338   Hannah Pratt Hobart (1732–1804): Wife of Enoch Hobart (1712–76), a Philadelphia, Pa., mariner; mother of John H. Hobart, Bishop of the Diocese of New York, 1816–30.
    Chiefly social correspondence between Hannah Hobart and the Enoch Story family of Philadelphia and London. Story, a Pennsylvania loyalist attainted for treason during the occupation of Philadelphia, took his family to England when Howe evacuated the American Capital in June 1778. Five letters from Hannah Hobart to Enoch and Mary Story concern family matters; eight letters to Hannah concern family matters and the plight of loyalists in England; and two letters from Enoch Story, Jr., to Master Enoch Hobart describe the former's love for his native land and his great respect for Washington.

JEAN HOLKER PAPERS
41 vols., 1777–1822.   *NUCMC* 69–2039

339   Holker (1745–1822): French merchant; French consul at Philadelphia, Pa., 1778–81; speculator in money and military supplies.
    Correspondence concerning Holker's attempts to capture the markets in flour and ship masts through contracts with the French Navy, and his large scale speculation in both land and currency using the money of French investors. Also Holker's accounts, including a journal of accounts, 1779–81, which provides a daily record of his public and private transactions; monthly balance accounts and correspondence with Robert Morris, 1778–79, accounts with merchants such as Daniel Bell, Simeon Deane, John Mitchell, Daniel Parker, Mark Pringle, William Smith, and William Turnbull; and Holker's official accounts with the French Marine Department and the French Marine Agency at Boston, 1778–80.
    Principal correspondents: Edward Bancroft, François Barbé-Marbois, Daniel Bell, Lawrence Betbeder, Boullangé, B. Burchell, Simeon Deane, François Del'horme, Demerr,

Desmarais, William Duer, John Edgar, Thomas Fitzsimmons, Royal Flint, Franklin, Conrad Alexandre Gérard, George Grand, Matthew Hough, Robert Johnston, Seth Johnston, Jolidon, Jean Lacour, de la Freté, John Langdon, D. Le Griffon, Jacques Donatien Le Ray de Chaumont, William Livingston, Robert Morris, N. V. Muhlberger, Thomas Mumford, Daniel Parker, J. Plombard, Mark Pringle, Matthew Ridley, John Ross, Thomas Russell, John Rutledge, Sabatier, Melancton Smith, Robert Smith, Barthélemy Terrasson, William Turnbull, de Valnais, Jonathan Williams, and the firms Jolly & Talazae and Roulhac and Company.

See also Barthélemy Terrasson Papers, entry no. 1070, and Archives Nationales, Affaires Etrangères, entry no. 1150.

SAMUEL HOLTEN PAPERS
5 boxes, 1744–1843.   *NUCMC* 59–32

340   Holten (1738–1816): Danvers, Mass., physician; member, General Court, 1768, Essex County Convention and Massachusetts Provincial Congress, 1774, Continental Congress, 1779–80, 1783, 1784–85, and U.S. House of Representatives, 1793–95.

Includes a comprehensive "valuation" of the town of Danvers, 1768, and instructions from the town while Holten was attending sessions of the General Court. Also correspondence for the periods Holten was in Congress, including file copies of 112 Holten letters not published in Burnett, *Letters of Members of Congress.* The letters contain information on Congressional business, Massachusetts political affairs, and public and private activities of Holten and several of his friends.

Principal correspondents: Samuel Adams, Nathaniel Appleton, John Avery, James Bowdoin, Thomas Cushing, Manasseh Cutler, Nathan Dane, William Gordon, Nathaniel Gorham, John Hancock, Israel Hutchinson, Rufus King, Richard Henry Lee, Benjamin Lincoln, James Lovell, Isaac Osgood, Joseph Palmer, George Partridge, Nathaniel Peabody, Joseph Reed, David Sewall, Jeremiah Shelden, William Story, James Sullivan, Thomas Wallcut, and John Witherspoon.

See also Samuel Holten, account books, entry no. 23.

FRANCIS HOPKINSON COLLECTION
1 vol., 1 folio, 1759–65.

341   Hopkinson (1737–91): Philadelphia, Pa., lawyer, writer, and artist; member, Continental Congress, 1776.

Includes a personal letter of Benjamin Franklin to Hopkinson, London, Aug. 15, 1765. Music Division.

PETER HORRY PAPERS
1 box, 1779–1807.   Force transcripts.

342   Horry (1747–1815): Capt., 2d South Carolina Regiment, 1775; maj., lt. col., South Carolina Continental Line, 1776–80; served under Brig. Gen. Francis Marion in the South Carolina Militia, 1780–81.

Contains letters, orders, and memoranda chiefly relating to military campaigns in the Southern Department, 1779–82, particularly the activities of Brig. Gen. Francis Marion. Subjects covered include the exchange and treatment of prisoners, enemy maneuvers, battles, and the problems of supply.

Principal correspondents: Nesbit Balfour, George Campbell, Guy Carleton, Christopher Gadsden, Nathanael Greene, Isaac Huger, John Laurens, Benjamin Lincoln, Francis Marion, John Mathews, William Moultrie, Augustine Prevost, John Rutledge, John Saunders, Thomas Sumter, Washington, and John Watson.

Originals in the possession of Robert W. Gibbes, 1853.

HUGH HUGHES PAPERS

6 vols., 1768–1875.

NUCMC 63–359

343   Hughes (d. 1804): Col., Continental Army; deputy quartermaster, New York, 1776–81.

Four letterbooks, Mar. 1781—Dec. 1782, primarily containing Hughes' official correspondence as deputy quartermaster for New York, concern the acquisition and distribution of military provisions and supplies. The volumes are unnumbered and overlap chronologically. Volume I (1786–93) of the two remaining volumes contains 32 letters Hughes wrote to Timothy Pickering, various militia and Continental officers in New York, and members of his immediate family. The letters to Pickering concern the wartime business of the quartermaster department and the settlement of accounts during the postwar period. Also includes an unsigned letter in the hand of Charles Tillinghast describing the struggle over ratification of the Constitution; a letter by James Duane and Ezra L'Hommedieu to Gov. George Clinton concerning the location of the Capital and western land claims, Oct. 1783; a schedule of rates and prices during the war; a lengthy commentary on the Constitution of 1787 in Hughes' hand; and general and garrison orders for the post at Fishkill, N.Y.

Principal correspondents: John Campbell, William Clajon, Thomas Collins, William Denning, Alexander Hamilton, John Harrison, Charity Hughes, Charles Pettit, Ralph Pomeroy, Peter Townsend, John Tyson, Washington, Jacob Weiss, Daniel Wistar, and David Wolfe.

HUIE, REID, & COMPANY PAPERS

3 boxes, 1784–96.

344   Huie, Reid, & Company: Dumfries, Va., store of a Scottish trading firm.

Account books, daybooks, a letterbook, inventories, and loose correspondence. Letters addressed to merchants at Glasgow, London, and Rotterdam, in Europe, and in the Chesapeake Bay area in America contain detailed information on the tobacco market. Correspondence with Virginia and Maryland planters includes scattered references to the hiring out of slaves.

Principal correspondents: Richard Brent, Robert Brent, Mary Burwell, Archibald Campbell, John Campbell, Landon Carter, George Gibson, Robert Hunter, William Hunter, Jr., Thomas Lee, and the firms Hartshorne & Donaldson, and Smith, Huie, Alexander, & Company.

DAVID HUMPHREYS PAPERS

2 folios, 1781–1802.

345   Humphreys (1752–1818): Capt., Connecticut Line, 1777; aide-de-camp to Generals Israel Putnam, Nathanael Greene, and Washington, 1778–83.

Two photographs showing both sides of the handle of a sword presented to Humphreys by Congress in appreciation of his services as Washington's aide-de-camp, with a description of the weapon. Also includes Humphreys' poem "An Ode, to his Excellency, Gen'rl Washington," written in 1776.

WILLIAM HUNT PAPERS

3 vols., 1775–78.

346   Hunt: Watertown, Mass., assistant commissary of issues.

The Hunt papers consist of two daybooks and a journal containing accounts of stores received and issued between May 1775 and Aug. 1778.

ILLINOIS–WABASH LAND COMPANY PAPERS

1 reel microfilm, 1769–1822.

347   Minutes of meetings of the Illinois and Wabash Land Companies; a list of names of original purchasers and proprietors of lands in the Illinois country; and indentures, deed

rolls, terms of settlement, and miscellaneous data pertaining to lands purchased from the Indians.

Originals in Historical Society of Pennsylvania.

INDEPENDENCE HALL COLLECTION

1 box, 1652–1845.   Photographs.

348   Miscellaneous letters, commissions, and receipts concerning supply and the military operations of Nathanael Greene, Henry Knox and Washington. Includes a letter of the Dutchess County committee of safety pertaining to imprisonment of loyalists, 1776, and an Arthur Lee letter consulting Col. William Johnson regarding an exchange of prisoners with the Indians, 1784. The collection also includes private business letters and material related to the Philadelphia Bank, 1780.

Principal correspondents: James Bradford, Benjamin Franklin, Edward Hand, William Johnson, and Arthur Lee.

Originals in National Museum in Independence Hall, Philadelphia, Pa.

JARED INGERSOLL PAPERS

2 boxes, 1740–79.   Force transcripts.

349   Ingersoll (1722–81): New Haven, Conn., lawyer and public official; Connecticut agent in London, 1758–61, 1764–65; stamp distributor, 1765; judge, vice-admiralty court at Philadelphia, 1768–75.

Includes papers concerning Ingersoll's mast contract with the Admiralty, the Stamp Act, the Susquehanna Affair, the vice-admiralty court, and approximately 20 letters of Ingersoll to his nephew, Jonathan Ingersoll, revealing his political and moral positions on the Revolution, 1775–79.

Principal correspondents: Andrew Adams, Joseph Chew, Eliphalet Dyer, Thomas Fitch, Benjamin Gale, William S. Johnson, Andrew Oliver, Roger Sherman, Jedediah Strong, Matthew Talcott, Nathaniel Whiting, and Samuel Willis.

HARRY INNES PAPERS

28 vols., 6 boxes, 1772–1850.

350   Innes (1752–1816): Virginia lawyer; member, State legislature and Bedford County escheator, 1779–82; Kentucky resident after 1785; attorney general and Federal judge for Kentucky district.

The early papers relate to Innes' service as escheator in Bedford County and as supply commissioner during the Revolution. Correspondence, 1786–94, concerns his extensive legal practice, political alliances, and views on Indian affairs. Also includes letters from Innes to Senator John Brown and various Virginia officials, 1785–88.

Principal correspondents: John Aylett, William Campbell, John May, Edmund Pendleton, Edmund Randolph, Isaac Shelby, Peyton Short, and James Wilkinson.

IRELAND, HOUSE OF COMMONS DEBATES

91 vols., 1776–89.   *NUCMC* 62–4531

351   A contemporary copy of the debates of the Irish House of Commons and an original set of shorthand notes of the debates reflect attitudes toward the American Revolution in both Ireland and England. Printed volumes of debates of the Irish House begin in 1781.

WILLIAM IRVINE PAPERS

2 vols., 1776–1834.   Draper Mss., series AA, WHi.   Microfilm, 1 reel.

352   Irvine (1741–1804): Carlisle, Pa., doctor; col., Jan. 1776, brig. gen., May 1779, Continental Army; prisoner of war, 1776–78; commandant at Fort Pitt, Nov. 1781—Oct. 1783; Pennsylvania agent to direct location of military bounty lands, 1785; member, Continental Congress, 1786–88.

Contains military correspondence to Irvine from officers in Pennsylvania, 1777–78, New

Jersey, 1780–81, and Virginia, 1781. Nearly half the material in the collection deals with Irvine's command at Fort Pitt, at which time he was occupied with the pacification of the Indians in the aftermath of the Gnadenhutten massacre, preparations for an assault against militant Shawnees at upper Sandusky, and regaining the initiative after the defeat of Col. William Crawford's expedition. Also included are materials on the condition of the western garrisons, problems of supply and troop morale, and disturbances caused by frontiersmen settling west of the Ohio River. Irvine's postwar correspondence reflects the concerns of former officers from the Carlisle area who speculated in western lands, were prominent in the Society of the Cincinnati, and supported Federalist positions on constitutional and economic issues.

Principal correspondents: John Armstrong, Jr., John Armstrong, Sr., Daniel Brodhead, Richard Butler, William Crawford, John Dickinson, Richard Hampton, Samuel Hay, Henry Knox, Lafayette, Benjamin Lincoln, James Marshall, David Redick, Joseph Reed, John Rose, Washington, Anthony Wayne, and the Board of War.

See also Thwaites, *Descriptive List of Manuscript Collections*, p. 33–34.

ANDREW JACKSON PAPERS
186 vols., 1775–1860.   Microfilm available.   *NUCMC* 63–363
353   Jackson (1767–1845): Lawyer; soldier; President of the United States.

Volume 1 contains about 100 items from the period of the American Revolution, chiefly receipts, surveys, survey books and records, and memorandums. Also includes accounts, a power of attorney, bills of sale, deeds, indentures, promissory notes, and miscellaneous correspondence. Volume 158 contains a letter from John Haring to Lieutenant Hays, Orangetown, Aug. 1779, concerning military affairs.

HENRY JACKSON PAPERS
4 vols., 1778–82.
354   Jackson (1747–1809): Col., one of the 16 additional Continental regiments, 1777–80; 9th Massachusetts Regiment, 1781–83.

Muster rolls and returns of troops under Jackson's command, some of which show dates enlisted, rank, length of service, age, size, hair color, complexion, trade, State, and place of birth.

NEIL JAMIESON PAPERS
23 vols., 1757–89.
355   Jamieson: Norfolk, Va., resident, 1757–76; partner in the firm Glassford, Gordon, Monteath & Co., Glasgow merchants; fled with Governor Dunmore to New York, 1776; remained in New York until 1785.

Mercantile correspondence focusing chiefly on Jamieson's activities in the lower Chesapeake. Includes extensive material on several Glasgow trading firms. Correspondence for the period, 1760–76, concerns routine business matters. There are numerous letters to James Glassford, who managed the firm in Norfolk during Jamieson's absences. Much of the material for the years 1776–83 consists of accounts concerning Jamieson's supply of the British Army in America. Also contains information pertaining to West Indian trade, particularly tobacco; a summary of the firm's holdings in 1776, prepared for the Loyalist Claims Commissioners in Halifax in 1786; and a few letters of George Wythe and Robert Carter Nicholas, who handled legal affairs for Jamieson in Williamsburg.

Principal correspondents: William Aisquith, William Aylett, William Balmain, Alexander Blair, Carter Braxton, Neill Buchanan, John Campbell, Robert Christie, Alexander Cuninghame, Robert Donald, James Dunlop, Mathias Ellegood, Adam Fleming, James Gibson, Robert Gilchrist, Alexander Henderson, Joseph Hewes, Thomas Irving, Andrew Leitch, Thomas Lilly, James Lyle, Alexander McCaul, John Mitchell, Thomas Montgomerie, Arthur Morson, Robert Purviance, Samuel Purviance, Richard Redwar, Henry Riddell, Hector Ross, Daniel Sanford, John Taylor, Jr., James Warden, John Wood, and the firms Bogle & Scott, Ferguson, Murdock & Co., Mayne & Co., Robert Herries & Co., Robertson, Jamieson & Co., William Robertson & Co., Henry Tucker & Son, and Jesson Welsh & Co.

JOHN JAY PAPERS

1 vol., 1 folio, 1776–89.   Photostats.   *NUCMC* 60–2717 and 61–3334

356   Jay (1745–1829): New York lawyer; member, Continental Congress, 1774–76, pres., 1778–79; minister to Spain, 1779–82; peace commissioner, 1782–84; secretary for foreign affairs, 1784–90; chief justice, U.S. Supreme Court, 1789–95; gov., 1795–1800.

Letterbook, 1779–82, containing Jay's correspondence while he was Minister Plenipotentiary to Spain and notes on conferences with Floridablanca and other Spanish officials. Most of the letters concern diplomatic relations between the United States, Great Britain, Spain, and France. Folio item is George Mason's "Objections to the Constitution of Government formed by the Convention," 1783, endorsed by James Madison and Jay, 1789.

See also U.K., Windsor Castle, Jay Papers, entry no. 1292.

THOMAS JEFFERSON PAPERS

50,000 items, 1651–1856.   Microfilm available.

357   Jefferson (1743–1826): Virginia lawyer and statesman; member, Continental Congress, 1775–79, 1783–84; gov., 1779–81; U.S. minister to France, 1784–89; secretary of state, 1790–93; Vice President and President of the U.S.

The Jefferson Papers, containing such diverse items as account books, farm books, and interest calculations, in addition to voluminous personal and official correspondence, constitute a basic collection for the study of political, economic, military, and diplomatic aspects of the American Revolution. Documents in the collection from the period of the Revolution are published in full in Julian P. Boyd, ed., *The Papers of Thomas Jefferson* (Princeton, 1950—   ), vols. 1–16. An index, published separately, is available for volumes 1–12.

The Library also has a microfilm copy of the control files from *The Papers of Thomas Jefferson*, with a clarifying statement on its use that gives the location of materials in other depositories. Eventually, all known Jefferson documents will be included in the collection either in manuscript or reproduced form.

THOMAS SIDNEY JESUP PAPERS

16 vols., 8 boxes, 1780–1907.

358   Jesup (1788–1860): Virginia soldier; quartermaster general, U.S. Army, 1818–60.

Contains one letter (perhaps a tracing) from George Rogers Clark to his father, John Clark, notifying him of his successful expedition against the Shawnees, Aug. 1780.

JOSHUA JOHNSON LETTERBOOK

1 vol., 1785–88.   Force manuscripts.

359   Johnson (1742–1802): London merchant; brother of Thomas Johnson, gov. of Maryland; father-in-law of John Quincy Adams; American agent in France during the American Revolution; first American consul at London, 1790–97.

Contains about 350 commercial letters written by Johnson while serving as agent for Messrs. Charles Wallace and John Muir of Annapolis, Md. Also includes letters of Charles Carroll of Carrollton, Daniel Carroll of Dudington, Francis Charlton, Overton Cosby, James Gittings, John Jay, Thomas Johnson, Henry Nichols, Jr., John Seawell, David Sterett, John Sterett, and Joseph Wilkinson. French merchants corresponding with Johnson include Nicholas Darcel and Messrs. Helie and LeRoy.

OBADIAH JOHNSON PAPERS
1 vol., 1777–81.   Force transcripts.

360   Johnson: Col., 21st Regiment, Connecticut Militia.

Chiefly orders from Brig. Gen. John Douglas, commander of the Connecticut Militia, regarding recruits and the disposition of the troops under Johnson's command. Also includes a query, with answers, on the pay and bounties received by Connecticut Continental soldiers; a list of the officers in the 5th brigade of the Connecticut Militia; copies of orders issued by Generals William Maxwell, Adam Stephen, John Sullivan, and Washington; and special instructions from Gov. Jonathan Trumbull.

SIR WILLIAM JOHNSON PAPERS
1 vol., 1755–74.   Force manuscripts.

361   Johnson (1715–74): New York land baron; superintendent of Indian affairs on the northern frontier, 1763–74; maj. gen., New York Militia, 1772–74.

Consists chiefly of drafts of letters by Johnson concerning the conversion and education of Indians, particularly as related to the work of the Society for the Propagation of the Gospel; Indian grievances over land; the training of ministers for the Church of England and the controversy over an American bishop; the erection of churches; and cures for venereal and other diseases. Also includes a plan by William Smith for training ministers of the Dutch Reformed Church in New Jersey.

Principal correspondents: Samuel Auchmuty, Thomas Barton, Thomas Bateman, Thomas Brown, Daniel Burton, Samuel B. Chandler, Thomas B. Chandler, Cadwallader Colden, Myles Cooper, Eli Forbes, Joseph Gorham, Matthew Graves, Charles Inglis, Samuel Johnson, Harry Munro, John Ogilvie, Richard Peters, William Smith, and Eleazar Wheelock.

Johnson's correspondence is published in *The Papers of Sir William Johnson,* 13 vols. (Albany, 1921–63).

WILLIAM SAMUEL JOHNSON PAPERS
1 vol., 1745–90.   *NUCMC* 63–364

362   Johnson (1727–1819): Stratford, Conn., lawyer; colonial agent in London, 1767–71; member, Stamp Act Congress, 1765, Continental Congress, 1784–87, and U.S. Senate, 1789–91; pres., Columbia College, 1787–1800.

Chiefly letters and documents relating to the Stamp Act controversy. Includes Johnson's drafts of the petition to the King drawn up by the Stamp Act Congress, notes on debates, and drafts of Connecticut's address to the King, July 1766, following the repeal of the Stamp Act. Also includes Johnson's notes on the effectiveness of nonimportation, 1768–69; a copy of a plan for the union of Great Britain and the colonies through proportional representation; Johnson's notes in Congress on the debate over negotiations with Spain for navigation of the Mississippi River, 1786; and reports by Samuel H. Parson on conditions in the Ohio Valley in the 1780's.

Principal correspondents: Roger Alden, Montfort Browne, Donald Campbell, and John Rutledge.

WILLIAM JOHNSTON FAMILY PAPERS
29 items, 1775–1866.

363   Johnston: Fairfax County, Va., family.

Includes four letters from George Johnston, a captain in the Virginia Continental Line, to Leven Powell concerning military operations in Virginia and New Jersey, 1776–77, a few personal letters of the Johnston family, 1777–78, and letters to William Johnston from Benjamin Harrison, 1783, and Edward Carrington, 1784.

JOHN PAUL JONES PAPERS
10 vols., 1775–88.   Force manuscripts.   Microfilm available.

364   Jones (1747–92): Lt. and capt., Continental Navy, 1775–83.

Contains letters received and autograph drafts of letters sent. Also includes a contemporary copy, in French, of an autobiography Jones wrote in the form of a "Memoire" to Louis XVI.

Principal correspondents: John Adams, Edward Bancroft, Continental Congress, Franklin, John G. Frazer, Esek Hopkins, Lafayette, Arthur Lee, John Manley, Marine Committee, James Moylan, John de Neufville & Son, John Ross, Daniel Tillinghast, Jonathan Williams, and various French officials.

Jones' correspondence is catalogued in *A Calendar of John Paul Jones Manuscripts in the Library of Congress* (Washington, D.C., 1903). The "Memoire" is a duplicate copy of the volume described under entry no. 1166, except in the selection and number of letters appended. An English translation of the "Memoire" will be published by the Library of Congress as part of its American Revolution Bicentennial Program.

JOHN PAUL JONES PAPERS
1 reel microfilm, 1777–1817.

365   Jones (1747–92): See entry no. 364.

Includes an account kept by the marine committee of expenses in equipping the *Ranger*, June—July 1777, and letters and drafts of letters, 1778–89, from Jones to Thomas Jefferson, John Ross, Jonathan Nesbitt, Gouverneur Morris, and William Carmichael concerning money for prize ships brought into French ports, and personal and business affairs. Also an original letter and a transcript of a letter from Henry Vernon to Jones, 1788, pertaining to Jones' service in the Russian Navy.

Originals in collections of Grand Lodge of the Masons Library, Massachusetts.

JOHN PAUL JONES PAPERS
3 boxes, 1 vol., 1776–92.   Transcripts and photostats.

366   Jones (1747–92): See entry no. 364.

Copies of documents in Russian archives, 1785–89, chiefly concerning Jones' service in the Russo-Turkish War, his activities in the Continental Navy, and his appointment as U.S. consul for Algeria.

Principal correspondents: William Carmichael, Joseph Hewes, Jefferson, Robert R. Livingston, and Washington.

ROGER JONES FAMILY PAPERS
35 vols., 3 boxes, 1662–1890.

367   Jones: Virginia family; descendants of Capt. Roger Jones, who came from England with Lord Culpeper in 1680. Thomas Jones (d. 1786): Clerk of Northumberland County; merchant; planter.

Documents from the period of the Revolution, primarily the papers of Thomas Jones, consist chiefly of receipts, invoices, accounts, indentures, bills, ledgers, daybooks, personal and business correspondence, and legal papers. Several memorandum books concern plantation operations, and letters to Jones from his brother Walter, a medical student at Edinburgh, describe student life abroad, 1766–69. Also contains extensive lists of "clerk fees," 1762–75; letters of John Warden, a tutor on the Jones estate, 1771–72; a "journal," 1774–91, kept by schoolmaster Robert Lucas, also an employee of Jones; a partial inventory of Jones' estate; and accounts of shoemakers, goldsmiths, and pewterers with whom he did business.

Principal correspondents: Elisha Betts, Robert Gilchrist, Charles Goore, Catesby Jones, John Morton Jordan, William Molleson, William Peachey, James Russell, and the firms of Bogle & Scott, and Farrell & Jones.

Journals and Diaries

THOMAS ANDERSON
1 vol., May 1780—Apr. 1782.   Force transcript.
368   Anderson: Cpl., ens., lt., 1st Delaware Regiment, 1776–83; quartermaster, 1778–83.
Contains descriptions of troop movements and battles in the southern campaigns.
Extracts printed in *Historical Magazine*, n.s., vol. 1 (1867), p. 207–11.

ANONYMOUS
1 vol., Jan.—Dec. 1773.
369   Surveyors work notes and job descriptions entered in a copy of *Poor Will's Pocket Almanack* (Philadelphia, 1770).
Rare Book Room.

ANONYMOUS
1 vol., Jan.—Dec. 1773.
370   Scattered notes on garden and farm production entered in Isaac Bickerstaff's *Boston Almanack* (Boston, 1773).
Rare Book Room.

ANONYMOUS
1 vol., June 10, 1774—Apr. 16, 1777.
371   Record of loans and other business accounts with people such as Hugh Galt, Aaron Bridges, Elizabeth Wiles, and Timothy Burgess. Entered in a copy of *The Virginia Almanack* (Williamsburg, 1774).
Rare Book Room.

ANONYMOUS
1 vol., 1777.
372   Miscellaneous notes and accounts, including a few notes on the war, entered in *Father Abraham's Pocket Almanack* (Philadelphia, 1777).
Rare Book Room.

ANONYMOUS
1 vol., 1778.
373   Miscellaneous notes and accounts entered in the *Lancaster Pocket Almanack* (Lancaster, 1778).
Rare Book Room.

ANONYMOUS
3 vols., Mar. 22, 1779—Dec. 24, 1781.
374   A Salem, Mass., lawyer kept this occasional diary, which lists political and military events throughout the Colonies and records his attendance at court. Interleaved in Fleet's *A Pocket Almanack* (Boston, 1779, 1780, 1781).
Rare Book Room.

ANONYMOUS
1 vol., June—Dec. 1783.
375   Journal of an unidentified doctor from New Haven, Conn., describing a trip from Boston to England and Holland. Records his impressions of London and Portsmouth

and gives an account of a conversation with Richard Price on the causes and outcome of the American Revolution.

ANONYMOUS
1 vol., Jan. 1—Dec. 30, 1785.

376   Farmer's journal of animal husbandry and crop production interleaved in Isaac Bickerstaff's *Almanack* (Springfield, Mass., 1785).
Rare Book Room.

ANONYMOUS
1 vol., Feb. 5—Nov. 15, 1788.

377   Entries for departures of ships from Philadelphia with destinations and captains. Entered in a copy of *Poor Will's Pocket Almanack* (Philadelphia, 1788).
Rare Book Room.

ANONYMOUS, AMERICAN PRISONERS
2 vols., 1777–79.

378   One volume consists of a journal kept by American sailors held captive at Forton Prison near Portsmouth, England. Entries record escape attempts, punishments, and visits by officials and citizens from Portsmouth and vicinity. Also includes news of the war obtained from British newspapers and prison officials. The companion volume, containing 58 bawdy songs and ballads, suggests how the prisoners entertained themselves during their confinement.
   Journal published in the *New England Historical and Genealogical Register*, vols. 30–33 (1876–79).

ANONYMOUS, JOURNAL OF FRENCH NAVAL OPERATIONS
1 vol., 1778–82.

379   French journal kept by an officer aboard *le Robuste*, a warship of 80 guns. Copied in part from other sources, the journal provides accounts of French naval activity in American waters. These include attacks on Dominique and St. Lucia, 1778, and on St. Vincent and Grenada, 1779; the battle off Martinique and the English attack on St. Vincent, 1780; the loss and recapture of St. Eustatius, 1781; the attack on St. Christopher, the battle of the Saints, and the expedition to Hudson Bay, 1782.

NATHAN BEERS
1 vol., Aug. 1777—Jan. 1782.   Force transcript.

380   Beers (1753–1849): Enlisted under Benedict Arnold, Apr. 1775; paymaster and 1st lt., Samuel B. Webb's Connecticut Regiment, May 1778—June 1783; Swift's Connecticut Regiment, June—Nov. 1784; merchant; steward of Yale College.
   Account of the Connecticut Regiment's movements from West Point through the Rhode Island expedition and into winter quarters at Morristown, N.J., its participation in the Springfield raid, June 1780, and its operations along the Hudson River and in Connecticut during the next two years. Includes accounts of the regiment's expenses for supplies and rations.

CLAUDE BLANCHARD
1 vol., July 1780 and Oct. 1781.

381   Blanchard (1742–1802): Commissary with Rochambeau's French Auxiliary Army, 1780–83.
   Extracts by William Duane from Blanchard's journal containing Blanchard's personal reactions to the French approach to Rhode Island and the opening of the battle of Yorktown.
   Published in Thomas Balch, ed., *The Journal of Claude Blanchard* (Albany, 1876).

CHRISTIAN BOERSTLER
3 vols., 1784–1830.

382   Boerstler (b. 1750): German immigrant; school teacher, minister, doctor, near Hagerstown, Md.

Includes a journal, 1784–1816, an account book, 1787–1802, and an autobiography, 1801, all three in German. The autobiography contains additions made in 1812 and 1830. Journal entries describe Boerstler's life near Zweibrucken in the Palatinate as a schoolmaster's son, the hardships he experienced in immigrating to America, 1784, and his first years near Hagerstown during the postwar depression. Boerstler's account book provides information on the financial affairs of a practicing country doctor. Also includes a manuscript translation of the autobiography by a descendant, J. W. Lowe, 1901.

JAMES BOOTH
1 vol., 1778.

383   Miscellaneous notes and accounts entered in the *British and American Register*, . . . (New York, 1778).

Rare Book Room.

JOHN BROWN
1 vol., 1776–78.

384   Brown: Ens., 1st North Carolina Militia, Nov. 1775; 2d lt., Jan. 1776; capt., Apr. 1777; returned home to Halifax, N.C., Apr. 1778.

John Brown, who entered the militia on Oct. 5, 1775, kept a diary intermittently from 1776 to 1778, with regular entries for the period Apr. 28—July 14, 1777. Most of the journal consists of minor records of company rations, expenses, enlistments, casualties, and desertions, along with records of personal debts, loans, and purchases.

GEORGE BRYAN
1 vol., 1764.

385   Bryan (1731–91): Philadelphia, Pa., merchant, politician, and jurist; member, Pennsylvania Assembly, 1764–65, 1779; judge, court of common pleas, 1764–76, the supreme executive council, 1777–79; justice, Pennsylvania Supreme Court, 1780–91.

Entered in the blank portion of *The Gentleman and Citizen's Almanack* (Dublin, 1760), Bryan's journal describes the political struggle between the proprietary and antiproprietary factions in Pennsylvania. Bryan argues that Quaker support of the antiproprietary faction was an attempt to shift the onus of frontier massacres away from themselves and onto the proprietor. Includes a multipage discussion of Benjamin Franklin's role in the struggle, including the suggestion that Franklin expected to be the royal governor of Pennsylvania.

ELIHU CLARK, JR.
1 vol., Apr.—Dec. 1775.   Force transcript.

386   Clark: Colchester, Conn., blacksmith; clerk, Levi Wells' company, 2d Connecticut Regiment, May 1775.

A vivid account of the social life of a bachelor before and after he entered the Army. Includes descriptions of the camp life of the common soldier around Boston and observations on the battle of Bunker Hill and the panic of Clark's company during the British cannonade.

CHARLES CUSHING
1 vol., June—Sept. 1776.   Force transcript.

387   Cushing (1744–1809): Hingham, Mass.; capt., Col. William Heath's regiment, May—Dec. 1775; capt., 24th Continental Regiment, 1776.

Describes the retreat of Gen. John Sullivan's fever-ridden army from St. John's to

Ticonderoga. According to Cushing's record, confusion, mutiny, and pilfering were endemic. The final section is an account of Cushing's journey home from Ticonderoga.

JACOB CUSHING
43 vols., 1749–1809.   Force manuscripts.
388   Cushing (1730–1809): Waltham, Mass., Congregational minister.
Diary of a smalltown minister, noting sermons, fees, marriages, funerals, etc. Interleaved in almanacs.

JACOB CUSHING
2 vols., Jan. 1, 1777—Dec. 31, 1778.
389   Cushing (1730–1809): See entry no. 388.
Diary records weather, church services, deaths, births, and sickness in the community. Interleaved in a copy of Daniel George's *An Almanack* (Boston, 1777) and Isaac Bickerstaff's *New England Almanack* (Norwich, Conn., 1778).
Rare Book Room.

EMILY T. DONELSON
1 vol., Dec. 1779—Apr. 1780.
390   Donelson: Kentucky settler.
An account of daily life on a flotilla of ships voyaging from Fort Patrick on the Holstein River to Big Salt Lick on the Cumberland River. Includes descriptions of the hazards of river travel, such as Indian attacks, rapids, waterfalls, and storms. Also lists the names of settlers on the vessels.
In Andrew J. Donelson Papers, Library of Congress.

[WILLIAM DOUGLAS?]
1 vol., Jan.—Dec. 1775.
391   Douglas: Minister, Goochland County, Va.
Record of expenses and accounts for his salary, and entries for farm production. Interleaved in *The Virginia Almanack* (Williamsburg, 1775).
Rare Book Room. See also William Douglas, orderly book, entry no. 876.

AUGUST W. DUROI
2 vols., Feb. 1776—Mar. 1779.
392   DuRoi: Lt. and adjutant in the service of the Duke of Brunswick under Gen. John Burgoyne.
An extensive account, in German, of Burgoyne's preparations and subsequent New York campaign to its disastrous ending at Saratoga. Also an account of the march of the Convention Troops from Boston to Virginia, with DuRoi's comments on the countryside and people along the route. Volume two contains an orderly book for July—Aug. 1777, a table of the value of all coins used in America, and a list of the population of each State.
Journal translated and published by Charlotte Epping, ed., *Journal of DuRoi the Elder* (Philadelphia, 1911).

MICHAEL ERRICKSON
1 vol., May—Aug. 1779.
393   Errickson: Monmouth, N.J.; sgt., 4th New Jersey Regiment.
Thin journal of the march of the 4th New Jersey from Elizabethtown to the Wyoming Valley, where it joined Gen. John Sullivan's forces for the expedition into Iroquois country.

ROBERT FARMER
1 vol., Mar.—July 1781.   Force transcript.

394

Farmer (d. 1804): Birdsboro, Pa., loyalist; ens., Royal American Regiment.

Daily account of British and Spanish actions during the siege of Pensacola, Fla., given by an officer in a regiment of loyalists in the British Army. Covers the return of English prisoners to New York, July 1781.

Published in *Historical Magazine*, vol. 4 (1860), p. 166–71.

JOHN FELL
1 vol., Nov. 1778—Nov. 1779.

395

Fell (1721–98): Member, New Jersey Provincial Congress, 1775, provincial council, 1776, Continental Congress, 1778–80.

Diary of events and proceedings in the Continental Congress: committee meetings, incoming correspondence, finance, supply, foreign affairs, etc. Contains little material on the internal political divisions or debates.

Published in part in Burnett, *Letters of Members of Congress*.

JABEZ FITCH
2 vols., Aug.—Dec. 1775; Jan.—Apr. 1776.   Volume 2 in Force manuscripts.

396

Fitch (1737–1812): Norwich, Conn., farmer, teacher, and soldier; lt., 8th Connecticut Regiment, 1775; 17th Continental Regiment, 1776; prisoner of war, Aug. 1776—Dec. 1777.

The first volume, published in the Massachusetts Historical Society, *Proceedings*, 2d ser., vol. 9 (1894–95), p. 40–91, records routine activities in the American camp during the siege of Boston. The second volume contains an account of the occupation of Dorchester Heights, a maneuver in which Fitch participated, and the resulting evacuation of Boston. Also includes descriptions of the ruins of Charlestown and Castle Island after the British withdrawal.

For Fitch's experiences as a prisoner of war see W. H. W. Sabine, ed., *The New York Diary of Lieutenant Jabez Fitch from August 22, 1776 to December 15, 1777* (New York, 1954).

CHRISTOPHER FRENCH
3 vols., 1756–64, 1776–78.

397

French: British officer; served in the 22d Regiment of Foot in ranks from ensign to major, 1744–77; lt. col., 52d Regiment of Foot, Oct. 1777–78; prisoner of war, 1775–76.

Consists of 11 booklets, bound in three separate volumes. Only four booklets (1 volume) relate to the Revolution. French describes the progress of the war, his treatment as a prisoner at Hartford, Conn., and the details of his escape, Dec. 1776. A chronic complainer, he wrote demanding letters to anyone who would listen, including the commander in chief. Copies of many of these letters appear in the journal along with a few responses. Also songs and verse, chiefly doggerel, villifying the Americans.

A 12th booklet, also pertinent to the period, is in the collections of the Connecticut Historical Society and is published in the Society's *Collections*, vol. 1 (1860), p. 189–225.

A FRENCH TRAVELER IN THE COLONIES
2 vols., Dec. 1764—Sept. 1765.   Photostats.

398

The writer of this anonymous journal was apparently a French agent, though not the well-known agent of Choiseul, M. DePontleroy. Describes the traveler's trip from France to Jamaica, Havana, and South Carolina by ship and then by horseback through North Carolina, Virginia, Maryland, Delaware, Pennsylvania, and New Jersey to New York City. Concentrating on the economic activity and military preparedness of the Colonies, he also discusses the contemporary political upheaval over the Stamp Act, the best known part of the journal being a report of the debates on Patrick Henry's anti-Stamp Act resolutions in the House of Burgesses.

The two volumes can be divided into four sections: (1) journal, in English, Dec. 1764—Sept. 1765; (2) journal, in French, Jan.—Mar. 1765, almost identical to the English version of that time span; (3) section, in French, describing the major seaports and the ease with which they could be captured; (4) critique of an anonymous plan to attack Jamaica.

Original journals in the Bibliothèque du Service Central Hydrographique de la Marine, Paris, vol. 76, no. 2. The English portion of the journal and the French remarks on seaports have been published in the *American Historical Review*, vol. 26 (1920–21), p. 726–47; vol. 27, (1921–22), p. 70–90.

GASPARD GABRIEL, BARON DE GALLATIN
4 vols., 1780–81.

399   Gallatin (b. 1758): Native of Geneva, Switzerland; 2d lt., Regiment de Royal Deux Ponts, 1780–83.

Journal, in French, kept during the American expedition of Comte de Rochambeau. Includes descriptions of the voyage to America, the debarkation at Newport, R.I., the march to Virginia, and the siege of Yorktown.

A translation of the portion of the journal dealing with the siege of Yorktown appeared in the *Magazine of American History*, vol. 7 (Oct. 1881), p. 283–95.

NEHEMIAH GALLUP
1 vol., Sept.—Nov. 1776.

400   Gallup: Ledyard, Conn.; in Capt. John Morgan's company, 8th Connecticut Militia.

Records the march of a unit from Connecticut to New York City and its subsequent retreat, during which most of the men and officers, according to Gallup, deserted.

GEORGETOWN, MARYLAND
1 vol., 1751–1801.

401   Consists of records of the commissioners and aldermen of Georgetown, Md., showing town lots, lists of owners, improvements, etc. Information on the actual meetings is confined to members present and the time and place of meetings. Contains no records for 1775–81.

See also Hugh T. Taggart Collection, entry no. 1065.

CALEB GIBBS
1 vol., Apr.—Nov. 1780.

402   Gibbs (1755–1818): Charlestown, Mass.; adjutant, 14th Continental Infantry, Jan. 1776; commander, Washington's Life Guards, Mar. 1776—July 1778; maj., 2d Massachusetts Regiment, Jan. 1781—Sept. 1783; lt. col. to 1784.

Journal kept on a march from Morristown, N.J., to North Windsor, N.Y. Although Gills knew and recorded the major movements of the American, French, and British forces during this period, his descriptions contain little detail. Interleaved in a *Continental Pocket Almanac* (1780).

HAMBURGH
1 vol., 1763.   Force transcript.

403   Hamburgh: Apparently a trader who accompanied British troops sent to occupy the former French outposts following the French and Indian War.

Written after Hamburgh's trip, the journal emphasizes navigational qualities of the rivers and lakes and locates landing sites closest to Indian villages. Gives a general description of the country and the routes of travel in the Lake Huron and Lake Michigan region.

THOMAS HASKINS

1 vol., Nov. 1782—Oct. 1783; Oct. 1784—May 1785.

404   Haskins (b. 1760): Maryland preacher, native of Eastern Shore; rode cricuit for Methodist Church in Frederick County, Md., Chester County, Pa., and Delaware.

A graphic view of the activities, emotions, and motivations of an itinerant minister, who saw his journal as a source of inspiration to his friends. Haskins recorded the subject and impact of each sermon and religious lecture-class on himself and his congregations.

EBENEZER HAZARD

2 vols., 1775–76.

405   Hazard (1744–1817): Postmaster in New York City, 1776; postmaster general, 1782–89.

Scattered notes on military and political events during the New York campaign. Entered in Gaines' *Universal Register* (New York, 1775, 1776).

Rare Book Room. See also Ebenezer Hazard Papers, entry no. 329.

WILLIAM HETH

1 vol., Feb.—July 1776.

406   Heth (1750–1807): Lt., Capt. Daniel Morgan's rifle company, 1775; captured at Quebec, Jan. 1776; maj., 11th Virginia Regiment, Nov. 1776; lt. col., 3d Virginia Regiment, Apr. 1777; captured at Charleston, S.C., May 1780.

While a prisoner in Quebec, Heth recorded the entry and exit of ships and troops, conditions of prison life, attempted escapes, and rumors on the progress of the war. There is also a brief account of his expenses while in prison.

Published in Winchester Historical Society, *Annual Papers*, vol. 1 (1931), p. 27–118.

RICHARD B. HINCKLEY

1 vol., Mar. 27—Dec. 17, 1780.

407   Hinckley (d. 1816): Boston merchant.

Records of ship departures and arrivals at Boston. Entered in Fleet's *A Pocket Almanack* (Boston, 1780).

Rare Book Room.

ROBERT HONEYMAN

1 vol., Jan. 1776—Mar. 1782.

408   Honeyman (1747–1824): Hanover County, Va., physician and planter.

A neutral during most of the war, Honeyman provides a detailed account of political, military, and economic developments throughout the Colonies, apparently gathered from newspapers, rumors, and personal contacts with friends in other Colonies. Also includes periodic accounts of the rising prices during the war and Honeyman's eyewitness account of the siege of Yorktown.

Honeyman's journal of a trip to Newport, R.I., in 1775, is published in Phillip Padelford, ed., *Colonial Panorama: Dr. Robert Honeyman's Journal for March and April, 1775* (San Marino, Calif., 1939). For the section covering the siege of Yorktown, see Richard K. MacMaster, "News of the Yorktown Campaign: the Journal of Dr. Robert Honyman, April 17—November 25, 1781," *Virginia Magazine of History and Biography*, vol. 79 (Oct. 1971), p. 387–426.

ADAM HUBLEY

1 vol., May—Oct. 1779.

409   Hubley (1740–93): Philadelphia, Pa., auctioneer; maj., lt. col., 10th Pennsylvania Regiment, 1776–78; col., 11th Pennsylvania Regiment, 1779.

Journal kept by Hubley during General Sullivan's expedition against the Iroquois, 1779. Includes descriptions of the country along the route of march and skirmishes with the Indians, particularly at Newtown.

Published in Frederick Cook, ed., *Journals of the Military Expedition of Maj. General John Sullivan against the Six Nations of Iroquois in 1779* . . . (Auburn, N.Y., 1887), p. 145–67. See also Daniel Livermore, journal, entry no. 417.

WILLIAM JENNISON
1 vol., Apr. 1776—Aug. 1780.

410   Jennison (1757–1843): Native of Mendon, Mass.; adjutant, Massachusetts "Five Months Infantry," May—Dec. 1776; lt. of marines, frigate *Boston*, 1777–83.

The first section, a memoir of Jennison's service during the New York campaign, describes Washington's retreat from Long Island, Aug. 1776. The actual diary covers Jennison's service aboard the *Boston*, 1777–79, and, following his capture by the British in 1779, prison life at Halifax. Jennison was released in 1780 and participated in the futile efforts of the U.S. Navy for the relief of Charleston, S.C.

Extracts published in *Pennsylvania Magazine of History and Biography*, vol. 15 (1891), p. 101–8.

ROBERT KIRKWOOD
1 vol., Mar.—Dec. 1777; Apr. 1780—Apr. 1782.   Force transcripts.

411   Kirkwood (1730–91): Delaware farmer; 1st lt., Delaware Regiment, Jan. 1776; capt., Dec. 1776; maj., Sept. 1783; capt., U.S. Infantry, Mar. 1791.

Journal kept by Kirkwood during his service in the southern campaign, 1780–81. Includes brief accounts of marches, skirmishes, and battles, with a casualty return for the battle of Eutaw Springs. Also in the volume is Kirkwood's orderly book for the Philadelphia campaign. Entries include general orders, court-martial proceedings, and returns of men and supplies.

Published in the *Papers of the Historical Society of Delaware*, vol. 56 (1910). Reprinted by Kennikat Press, 1970.

JEAN FRANCOIS DE GALAUP, COMTE DE LAPÉROUSE
2 vols., May 31, 1782—Oct. 12, 1782.

412   Lapérouse (1741–88): French naval officer; commanded expedition to Hudson Bay, 1782; led an exploratory voyage around the world, 1785–88.

Journal of Lapérouse's expedition against the English trading forts on Hudson Bay. The account was probably maintained by Paul de Monneron, a captain of the French corps of engineers who was assigned to the mission. The journal and an anonymous English translation provide a detailed picture of the expedition's hardships and triumphs. Lapérouse's force of three ships and 300 soldiers destroyed Forts Prince of Wales and York at a loss estimated at between 10 and 12 million livres and forced the Hudson Bay Company to suspend trade in that region until 1785.

MILTON S. LATHAM
1 vol., Apr. 1780—Mar. 1783.

413   Latham: French officer with Rochambeau.

Military journal, in French, covering the embarkation of Rochambeau's forces at Brest in the spring of 1780, the march from Newport, R.I., where they disembarked, to Yorktown, and the siege of York.

JOHN LAWRENCE
1 vol., Mar. 1765—Jan. 1771.   Force manuscripts.

414   Lawrence (d. 1796): Burlington, N.J., lawyer, justice, and politician; member, provincial assembly, 1771–75; loyalist.

Casebook listing defendants, issues, and decisions in cases in which Lawrence participated. Provides insight into the rationale of court decisions.

SUSAN LEAR
1 vol., May—Aug. 1788.   Transcript.

415   Susan Lear (b. 1770): Wife of James Duncan (1756–1844), of Pennsylvania.
Detailed and lively account of a trip by stage and packet from Philadelphia to Boston.
Accompanied by Mrs. Barnabas Binney and Mrs. Nicholas Brown, Miss Lear attended
stage plays in New York, visited Brown and Harvard colleges, and traveled in the vicinity
of Providence and Boston. Entries provide a panorama of the daily lives and social and
religious activities of the people in whose homes she visited.

BENJAMIN LINCOLN
3 vols., Oct.—Dec. 1778; Sept.—Oct. 1779.

416   Lincoln (1733–1810): Maj. gen., Continental Army, 1776–83; commander in chief,
Southern Department, 1778–80.
Lincoln's 1778 diary covers the trip from Oblong, N.Y., to Georgetown, S.C., following
his appointment to the command of the Southern Department. Entries concern distances
traveled, stopovers, and scenery. The later diary, kept during the siege of Savannah, records
plans for the siege and the disposition of troops in the early stages of the battle.
See also Benjamin Lincoln Papers, entry no. 488.

DANIEL LIVERMORE
1 vol., May 1779—June 1780; May 1782.   Force transcript.

417   Livermore (1749–98): New Hampshire carpenter; served in ranks from ens. to maj.,
3d New Hampshire Regiment, 1775–83.
Journal of General Sullivan's expedition against the Iroquois nation, 1779. Includes
observations on the country along the route of march and ethnic origins of people living
in northern Pennsylvania and western New York. Also describes the battle at Newtown
and the destruction of Indian villages and provisions. The section of the journal for May
1782 describes Livermore's march from Concord, N.H., to rejoin the 3d New Hampshire
Regiment at Saratoga, N.Y.
Extracts printed in Frederick Cook, ed., *Journals of the Military Expedition of Maj.
General John Sullivan against the Six Nations of Iroquois in 1779* . . . (Auburn, N.Y.,
1887), p. 178–91. Reprint by Benchmark Publishing Company, 1970. See also Adam
Hubley, journal, entry no. 409.

ROBERT McCREADY
1 vol., Nov. 1776.

418   McCready (1752–1846): Pennsylvania and Maryland school teacher, 1773–76; pvt.,
York County Battalion, on duty in New York, 1776; resided at Fort Pitt, 1776–78.
Brief account of a military surveying expedition from Fort McIntosh to Fort Laurens
under Col. Lachlan McIntosh. Contains surveyor's traverse readings for the line of march
in the Ohio region between Beaver Creek and the Tuscarawas River.

GEORGE McCULLY
1 vol., July—Aug. 1783.

419   McCully (d. 1793): Ens., 2d Pennsylvania Battalion, Mar. 1776; 2d lt., Sept. 1776; 1st
lt., 3d Pennsylvania Regiment, Jan. 1777; capt., Oct. 1777; retired, Jan. 1781.
Diary kept by McCully on a trip from Pennsylvania to the Ohio Valley in company
with Ephraim Douglas. The purpose of the expedition was to notify Indian tribes in the
area of the peace treaty with Great Britain. Records meetings with chiefs of the Delaware,
Wyandot, and Shawnee tribes and discussions with whites held captive by the Indians and
Indian traders.
Published in C. M. Burton, "Ephraim Douglas and His Times," *Magazine of American
History*, extra no. 10 (1910), p. 39–49.

FRIEDERICH WILHELM VON DER MALSBURG
1 vol., Feb.—Dec. 1776.   Transcript.
420   Malsburg: Capt., Dittfurth Regiment.
Journal, in German, concerning the activities of Capt. Malsburg's Hessian regiment during the New York campaign.
See also Foreign Reproductions, Marburg, entry no. 1239.

EDWARD MARTIN
1 vol., Dec. 1786.
421   Brief journal describing a trip by packet from New York to Providence, R.I., and by stagecoach from Providence to Boston.

MEMORANDUM BOOK, BRITISH ARTILLERY OFFICER
1 folio, 1764 and 1774.
422   Artillery manual containing tables and formulas for the correct loading and firing of ordnance used by the British. Includes notes taken during target practice.

SAMUEL MILES
1 vol., 1776.
423   Miles: Col., Pennsylvania Rifle Regiment, Mar. 1776; captured in the battle of Long Island, Aug. 1776; exchanged, Apr. 1778.
"Diary" written on Nov. 17, 1776, in which Miles presents a defense of his actions before and during the battle of Long Island.

GARRETT MINOR
7 vols., 1774, 1780–81, 1784–85, 1788–89.
424   Plantation and family records and accounts. The 1781 almanac contains brief notes on military activities in Virginia. Entered in *The Virginia Almanack* (Williamsburg, 1774, 1780; Richmond, 1781, 1784–85, 1788–89).
Rare Book Room. See also Garrett Minor Papers, entry no. 542.

THOMAS MOFFAT
1 vol., July 1775—Oct. 1777.   Force manuscripts.
425   Moffat (1700–87): Scottish physician; immigrated to America in 1746; resided in Newport, R.I., 1750–69; comptroller of customs in New London, Conn., 1769–75.
Contains scattered entries relating to Moffat's mission to London in 1775 to meet with Lord North; activities of the British fleet during the capture of New York, 1776; and the problems of pensioned loyalists who went to England.

NEW YORK CITY, COMMITTEE OF SAFETY
1 vol., Sept. 1775—Aug. 1776.   Force manuscripts.
426   Written by a member of the committee of safey in New York City, the journal contains reports of military and political developments in other Colonies and countries. Sources of news include newspapers, incoming ships' crews, messages from civil and military authorities, and personal acquaintances. Regular entries end Nov. 9, 1775.

REVEREND LEWIS OGDEN
1 vol., 1778.
427   Miscellaneous notes and accounts attached to a copy of *The Burlington Almanack* (Burlington, Vt., 1778).
Rare Book Room.

JAMES PEMBERTON
1 vol., Jan. 2—Sept. 10, 1773.

428   Pemberton (1723–1809): Philadelphia, Pa., merchant and Quaker leader.
Notes on arrivals and departures of his ships, giving captains and destinations. Entered in a copy of *Poor Will's Pocket Almanack* (Philadelphia, 1773).
Rare Book Room.

JOHN PEMBERTON
1 vol., Mar. 17—Dec. 31, 1775.

429   Pemberton (1727–1795): Philadelphia, Pa., merchant and Quaker missionary; brother of James Pemberton.
Notes on births and deaths and on major battles in 1775. Entered in a copy of *Poor Will's Pocket Almanack* (Philadelphia, 1775).
Rare Book Room.

[JOHN PEMBERTON?]
2 vols., Jan.—Aug. 1778; Jan. 13—Oct. 11, 1784.

430   Pemberton (1727–1795): See entry no. 429.
Itinerary and expense accounts of a trip through Delaware and eastern Pennsylvania, 1778, and a journey between Philadelphia and Harper's Ferry by way of Baltimore, 1784. Interleaved in *Poor Will's Pocket Almanack* (Philadelphia, 1778, 1784).
Rare Book Room.

EDWARD PENINGTON
3 vols., Jan. 28, 1779—Dec. 10, 1781.

431   Penington (1726–1796): Philadelphia, Pa., merchant; political leader; loyalist.
Diary of expenses and garden production, with notes on weather. A few entries are in code. Entered in *Poor Will's Pocket Almanack* (Philadelphia, 1779, 1780, 1781).
Rare Book Room.

[EDWARD PENINGTON?]
1 vol., Feb. 25—Nov. 18, 1786.

432   Penington (1726–1796): See entry no. 431.
Miscellaneous records of expenses and loans entered in a copy of *Poor Will's Pocket Almanack* (Philadelphia, 1786).
Rare Book Room.

PENNOCK FAMILY
1 vol., Jan. 20—Nov. 28, 1771.

433   Pennock: Pennsylvania family.
Notes on business transactions, loans, a trip to Philadelphia and on the history of the Pennsylvania Charter. Interleaved in a copy of *Poor Will's Pocket Almanack* (Philadelphia, 1771).
Rare Book Room.

PHILADELPHIA CALENDAR
1 vol., 1775.

434   Anonymous diary interleaved in a German religious almanac. Appears to have been maintained by a German farmer who kept cursory notes on crops, visitors, and local events, occasionally adding relevant scriptural notations.

ABRAHAM PHILLIPS
1 vol., Sept.—Dec. 1781; June 1782—Feb. 1783.

435   Phillips: Hillsborough, N.C., school teacher and soldier; served in Continental Army, 1778–81.

Journal for the last three months of 1781 describing skirmishes with loyalists in the back country of North Carolina and Virginia. The latter section deals with Phillips' personal accounts and school records.

ISRAEL PUTNAM
1 vol., Dec. 1772—Mar. 1773.   Force transcripts.

436   Putnam (1718–90): Pomfret, Conn., farmer and soldier; officer, Connecticut Militia, 1755–64; accompanied Phineas Lyman to Natchez, 1772–74, to examine land granted to Connecticut veterans of the Havana expedition of 1762; maj. gen., Continental Army, 1775–79.

Description of the voyage from New York through the West Indies to Pensacola, West Florida. Records in detail the difficulties encountered in securing approval of a land grant from the British governor and subsequent negotiations. The journal ends when Putnam and Lyman reach the Mississippi River.

Published in *The Two Putnams, Israel and Rufus* (Hartford, 1931), p. 113–33.

THOMAS RODNEY
1 vol., 1778.

437   Rodney (1744–1811): Delaware statesman; member, Continental Congress, 1781–82, 1786.

Scattered notes, accounts, and price lists. Entered in a copy of *Father Abraham's Pocket Almanack* (Philadelphia, 1778).

Rare Book Room.

ABNER SANGER
1 vol., Oct. 1774—Dec. 1782.

438   Sanger (1739–1822): Keene, N.H., farmer and laborer; private, New Hampshire Militia, 1760, 1775; loyalist confined to Keene during the Revolution.

Diary providing a graphic picture of the daily activities of a farmer in a small frontier community (population 756 in 1776). Reveals Sanger's fear of Whig retaliation for his loyalist sympathies, but best portrays the life of persons not directly involved in the war. Also describes the disruption of the courts during the controversy between Vermont and New Hampshire over control of the Connecticut River towns.

Diary for 1774–77 published in *Repertory*, vols. 1–2 (Keene, N.H., 1924–27).

JUNIPERO SERRA
1 vol., Mar.—July 1769.   Photostat.

439   Serra (1713–84): Franciscan friar; led military-missionary expedition to California, 1769; resident missionary at San Diego.

Diary describing an expedition from Baja California to San Diego to establish Spanish missions. Includes vivid descriptions of lower California and Indians living in the vicinity of the Spanish missions.

Published in Ben F. Dixon, ed., *Journal of Padre Serra* (San Diego, 1964). Original in Mexican National Archives.

HENRY SEWALL, JR.
1 vol., June 1783.

440   Sewall (1753–1845): York, Maine, farmer and soldier; aide-de-camp to Gen. William Heath, 1779–83.

Brief journal kept at Newburgh, N.Y., during the disbanding of the Army and the peace celebration.

Published in *Maine Farmer* (1872).

WILLIAM SEYMOUR
1 vol., Apr. 1780—Jan. 1783. Force transcripts.

441   Seymour: In ranks from pvt. to sgt. maj., Delaware Continental Regiment, 1777–82; attached to Robert Kirkwood's Light Infantry, 1781–82.

Journal kept during the southern campaigns of Gens. Horatio Gates and Nathanael Greene. Provides insight into the problems of morale and desertion in the Army under Gates. Also includes descriptions of the battles of Camden, Cowpens, Guilford Courthouse, and Eutaw Springs and the almost daily skirmishes with British regular and loyalist troops in the Carolinas, 1782–83.

Published in *Pennsylvania Magazine of History and Biography,* vol. 7 (1883), p. 286–98, 377–94.

SALLY SHAW
1 vol., Jan. 18—Dec. 25, 1777.

442   A housewife from Lancaster, Pa., notes her expenses and experiences on trips to Philadelphia, Reading, and Easton, Pa. Entered in a copy of *Poor Will's Pocket Almanack* (Philadelphia, 1777).

Rare Book Room.

RICHARD SMITH
1 vol., Sept.—Oct. 1775; Dec. 1775—Mar. 1776.

443   Smith (1753–1803): Burlington, N.J., lawyer and politician; member, Continental Congress, 1774–76; treasurer of New Jersey, 1776–77.

Journal of proceedings in the Continental Congress. Contains more detail than the journal of Samuel Ward and covers periods when John Adams was not in attendance. Also reveals the multitude of minor issues that occupied the attention of the delegates.

Published in *American Historical Review,* vol. 1 (1895–96), p. 288–310, 493–516.

EPHRAIM SQUIER
1 vol., Sept.—Nov. 1775; Sept.—Nov. 1777.

444   Squier (1748–1841): Ashford, Conn.; pvt., Connecticut Militia, 1775; served under Benedict Arnold during the Quebec expedition, 1775; sgt., 3d Connecticut Regiment, 1776–77.

The only surviving journal kept by a member of Lt. Col. Roger Enos' division during the march to Quebec. Squier's unit returned to Boston before reaching its destination. Entries reflect the low morale of the troops before and during the expedition and the difficulties encountered on the march. In the second part of the journal, Squier recounts his march to Stillwater, N. Y., and experiences at the battle of Saratoga.

The journal of the march to Canada is published in Kenneth Roberts, ed., *March to Quebec* (New York, 1938), p. 619–28. The journal of the Saratoga campaign is published in the *Magazine of American History*, vol. 2, pt. 2 (1878), p. 685–94.

BENJAMIN STEVENS
1 vol., Feb.—May 1776. Force transcripts.

445   Stevens (1754–1838): Canaan, Conn.; pvt., Charles Burrall's regiment; assistant to Nathaniel Stevens, deputy commissary of issues at Hartford, Conn., 1777–83.

Journal describing a march to Montreal and the subsequent surrender of Stevens' unit at The Cedars. Reveals the frustrations and fears of short-term enlistees, and the hardships Stevens experienced during his brief imprisonment near St. Ann. Ends abruptly with the approach of a rescue force in May 1776.

Published in *Daughters of the American Revolution Magazine,* vol. 45 (1914), p. 137–40.

EZRA STILES

2 boxes, 1770–90.   Force transcripts.

446   Stiles (1727–95): Scholar, lawyer, and clergyman; pastor of churches in Rhode Island, Massachusetts, and New Hampshire, 1755–78; pres., Yale College, 1778–95.

Extracts from the literary diary and journal of Stiles concentrating on political and military activities during the Revolutionary era. Entries include notes from newspapers, personal observations, and information gained through conversation and correspondence. Also copies of letters and documents relating to the attempted enforcement and repeal of the Stamp Act and Townshend Acts. Most of Stiles' voluminous religious, educational, and personal commentaries are omitted. Used in conjunction with Franklin B. Dexter, ed., *The Literary Diary of Ezra Stiles,* 3 vols. (New York, 1901), the transcripts provide a reasonably complete text of Stiles' diary and journal.

SAMUEL TALMADGE

1 vol., Aug. 1778—Sept. 1779.   Toner transcripts.

447   Talmadge (1755–1825): Brookhaven, Long Island; sgt., ens., 4th New York Regiment, 1776–77; adjutant, 1778–81; transferred to 2d New York Regiment, 1781.

Talmadge's journal traces the movements of Gen. James Clinton's brigade from White Plains, N.Y., through winter quarters at Johnstown, N.Y., to the junction with General Sullivan's army at Tioga, N.Y., in the summer of 1779. Includes a brief account of Sullivan's expedition against the Iroquois.

Copied into John Barr's journal, Toner Collection.

LAWRENCE TREMPER

1 vol., Mar. 1783—Nov. 1784.

448   Tremper: Lt. and quartermaster, Col. Marinus Willett's regiment, New York Militia, 1783–84.

Records the daily routine at several minor forts in northern New York. Includes brief descriptions of the negotiations with the Indians and some minor accounts, but the bulk of the journal revolves around Tremper's numerous love affairs.

See also Lawrence Tremper, account book, entry no. 93.

CHRISTOPHER VAIL

1 vol., July 1775—Aug. 1782.   Force transcripts.

449   Vail (1758–1846): Son of a sea captain from Sag Harbor, Long Island; served in Connecticut Militia, 1775–77, and on American privateers and ships of war, 1778–82; prisoner, 1779 and 1781.

Diary of Vail's experiences in the Connecticut Militia, his service on American frigates and privateers, and his imprisonment by the British. Includes descriptions of prison life at Antigua and aboard British warships, and a seaman's view of the battle off Martinique, 1780.

MARQUIS DE VAUDREUIL

1 vol., Apr. 1782.   Force transcripts.

450   Louis Philippe Rigaud, Marquis de Vaudreuil (b. 1723): French naval officer; commanded 15-vessel squadron in the West Indies expedition, 1782–83.

Translated extract from Vaudreuil's journal of the battle of the Saints, Apr. 1782, and the aftermath of the engagement. Provides an inside view of one of the decisive battles of the war.

SAMUEL VAUGHAN
1 vol., June—Sept. 1787.

451   Vaughan (b. 1720): Jamaica and London merchant; toured the United States in 1784–85 and 1787 to view sites of Revolutionary War battles and to inspect land for possible speculation; invested in land in Maine.

Description of the countryside and towns through which Vaughan passed during a 1,437–mile trip into Pennsylvania and Virginia. Also includes a list of expenses.

BARON VON CLOSEN
5 vols., Apr. 1780—June 1783.   Transcript.

452   Hans C. F. I. L. von Closen-Haydenburg (1754–1813): Sub-lt., French Army, 1769; in ranks lt. to 2d capt., 1774–80; served in America in the Royal Deux-Ponts Regiment and as aide-de-camp to Comte de Rochambeau, 1780–83.

French journal of Rochambeau's American expedition. Covers the embarkation at Brest in the spring of 1780, campaigns in North America and the West Indies, and the return to France in June 1783. Parts of the journal were written some time after the events, and large segments are devoted to the reminiscences of central figures in the war. The original journal and memoirs were destroyed in 1921, but a folio volume of photographs of illustrations from the original has been maintained with this transcript by Worthington C. Ford.

Published in Evelyn M. Acomb, ed., *The Revolutionary Journal of Baron Ludwig von Closen, 1780–1783* (Chapel Hill, 1958).

JOSEPH WARE
1 vol., Sept. 1775—June 1776.   Force transcripts.

453   Ware (1753–1805): Needham, Mass., farmer and soldier; sgt., Samuel Ward's company, 1775–76.

Journal of Benedict Arnold's expedition against Quebec. Recounts the hardships of the march through northern Maine and provides a complete list of American casualties and prisoners. Also names Americans who joined the British in Quebec following the repulse of Arnold's attack, Jan. 1, 1776.

Extracts published in *New England Historical and Genealogical Register,* vol. 6 (1825), p. 129–50.

MRS. LUND WASHINGTON
1 vol., 1779–96.

454   Mrs. Washington: Born Elizabeth Foote; lived at Mount Vernon and nearby Hayfield.
Religious diary. Includes remarks on her role as a wife and mother.

RICHARD WHEELER
1 vol., 1767–93.

455   Wheeler (1739–99): Stonington, Conn., farmer and storekeeper.

Includes a journal kept by Wheeler, Mar. 1772—Jan. 1777, that records farm activities and services he provided other farmers in the area. Accompanying accounts provide a detailed record of his barter-trade activities. Wills and deeds relating to the Wheeler family property in Stonington are interleaved.

JOHN WHITE
8 vols., 1774–76, 1778, 1787–90.

456   White: Salem, Mass., merchant and privateer ship captain.

Interleaved in eight almanacs, White's journal contains observations on events in Salem, Mass., and Machias, Maine. Entries concern ship arrivals and departures, inflation, and the scarcity of salt and other products. Also includes remarks on political and military events between 1774 and 1778.

WILLIAM WILLIAMS
1 vol., Jan.—Apr. 1774.

457   Williams (1731–1811): Lebanon, Conn., merchant and judge; town clerk, 1753–96; member, provincial assembly, 1757–61, 1763–76, 1780–84; member, Continental Congress, 1776–77; district judge, 1776–1804.

Brief records of court sessions, public meetings, and elections; few details or observations. Includes minor accounts, 1777–78.

See also William Williams Papers, entry no. 1127.

WILLIAM WINTHROP
1 vol., Jan. 28—Aug. 28, 1780.

458   Records of ship sailings and dockings at the port of Boston. Recorded in a copy of Fleet's *A Pocket Almanack* (Boston, 1778).

Rare Book Room.

THEODORE WOODBRIDGE
1 vol., Aug.—Oct. 1780, 1781–83.

459   Woodbridge (1748–1810): Glastonbury, Conn., farmer and soldier; 1st lt., 4th Connecticut Regiment, 1777; maj., 7th Connecticut Regiment, 1778; brigade maj., 1779–81; moved to Salem, Pa., after the war.

Written while Woodbridge was at Washington's headquarters, the diary contains notes on military life, particularly desertions and dueling in the American Army. Includes comments on the history of Rome, the rise of Christianity, world travel books, beekeeping, and agricultural publications. Also contains information on early meetings and the rules governing the Society of the Cincinnati.

LEVI WOODBURY
1 vol., Jan—June 1781.

460   Woodbury: Massachusetts sea captain.

Records daily occurrences, sail changes, positions, wind, and speed during various cruises of the ships *Nonesuch, Rhea, Amherst, Nancy,* and *Montgomery.* Woodbury identifies himself as captain or prize master on these ships, but his record contains contradictory information on dates for the voyages of the *Nonesuch, Rhea,* and *Nancy.* These ships sailed from Cape Ann and Boston.

RICHARD AUGUSTUS WYVILL
1 vol., 1778–1814.   Force manuscripts.

461   Wyvill: Ens., 1780, and lt., 38th Regiment of Foot, British Army.

Memoir of Wyvill's military career, beginning with his training at a military school in Strasburg, Alsace, and continuing until his retirement on the Isle of Jersey. Wyvill served in America during the last two years of the Revolution. His memoir contains descriptions of regular and leisure activities at British headquarters in New York, impressions of the inhabitants, and an account of the evacuation of New York, Nov. 1783.

JULIAN AUTOGRAPH COLLECTION
1 box, 1481–1932.

462   Includes two George Washington items—a 1791 debt transfer and a 1786 Potomac Company receipt—and a Patrick Henry supply order, 1763.

George G. Kelly Family Papers
1 box, 1761–1865.

463   Kelly: New Hampshire farming family.
Includes six deeds of David Gove of Hampton Falls, N.H., the probate records of Daniel Gove of Templeton Falls, N.H., and the birth and death records of the Ingraham family, 1773–96.

James Kent Papers
26 vols., 1779–1847.   *NUCMC* 59–222

464   Kent (1763–1847): New York lawyer and minor politician; first law professor, Columbia College, 1794–98 and 1824–26; judge, New York Supreme Court, 1798–1814; chancellor, New York Court of Chancery, 1814–23; author, *Commentaries on American Law.*
Letters between Kent and his friends discussing legal studies, politics, and personal matters.
Principal correspondents: Simeon Baldwin, James M. Hughes, Moses Kent, Sr., and John Smith.

James Kent Letter
1 item, 1787.

465   Kent (1763–1847): See entry no. 464.
Four-page letter from James Kent to N[athaniel] L[awrence] Dec. 21, 1787, providing insight into the views of New York Federalists and anti-Federalists during the controversy over the ratification of the Federal constitution.
Law Library.

Simon Kenton Papers
13 vols., 1755–1839.   Draper Mss., series BB, WHi.   Microfilm, 3 reels.

466   Kenton (1755–1836): Frontier scout and Indian fighter associated with George Rogers Clark.
Volume 13 contains a few original documents from the period of the Revolution, chiefly land warrants, receipts, affidavits, and letters from Kentucky, Ohio, and Illinois pioneers. Includes a letter from John Brown to John Preston concerning land claims, June 1787.
See also Thwaites, *Descriptive List of Manuscript Collections*, p. 34–35.

Kentucky Manuscripts
30 vols., 1775–1853.   Draper Mss., series CC, WHi.   Microfilm, 8 reels.

467   Papers collected by Lyman C. Draper concerning the early history of Kentucky. Contains the Richard Henderson papers pertaining to transactions of the Louisa and Transylvania land companies and including Henderson's journal of a visit to Kentucky, Mar.—July 1775; the William Whitley papers, 1775–1813; and the James McAfee papers including McAfee's journal of a trip from Botetourt County, Va., through the Kentucky wilderness, June—Aug. 1773. John Filson's journals, 1785–86, describe a trip from Vincennes to the falls of the Ohio River, Aug. 1785, a voyage from Pittsburgh to Vincennes, and his defeat on the Wabash, June 1786.
See also Thwaites, *Descriptive List of Manuscript Collections*, p. 35–39.

Rufus King Papers
25 letters, 1784–1815.

468   King (1755–1827): New England lawyer-politician; member, Continental Congress, 1784–87, U.S. Senate, 1789–95 and 1813–25; U.S. minister to Great Britain, 1796–1803 and 1825–26.
Primarily concerns foreign affairs while King was Minister to Great Britain. Three

letters mention King's views of a prospective U.S. mint, Shays' Rebellion, and scientific research during the Confederation period.

Principal correspondents: Daniel Kilham and John Lowell.

KING'S MOUNTAIN MANUSCRIPTS
18 vols., 1753–1859.   Draper Mss., series DD, WHi.   Microfilm, 8 reels.

469   Transcripts and original documents collected by Lyman C. Draper in preparation for writing *King's Mountain and Its Heroes* (Cincinnati, 1881). Includes papers of Arthur Campbell (1743–1811), William Campbell (1745–81), Evan Shelby (1720–94), and Isaac Shelby (1750–1826) concerning frontier warfare and Indian affairs during the Revolution, the establishment of the State of Franklin, and early Kentucky politics. Also includes papers of John Sevier (1745–1815) pertaining to North Carolina politics and western expansion; papers of Andrew Hampton bearing on the conduct of the war in North Carolina; and the diary of Lt. Anthony Allaire, 1780.

See also Thwaites, *Descriptive List of Manuscript Collections*, p. 39–45.

JACOB KINGSBURY PAPERS
3 vols., 1727–1856.   *NUCMC* 62–4544

470   Kingsbury (1756–1837): Pvt., Continental Army, 1775; lt. through col., U.S. Army; inspector general, 1813–14.

Contains 13 deeds of David and Zebadiah Hartshorn for land in Scotland, Norwich, and Franklin, Conn.

HENRY KNOX PAPERS
56 reels microfilm, 1719–1825.   *NUCMC* 60–2588

471   Knox (1750–1806): Boston bookseller; col., Continental Regiment of Artillery, 1775–76; brig. gen. and chief of artillery, 1776–81; maj. gen., 1781–83; commander in chief, 1783–84; secretary of war, 1785–94.

Documents from the prewar period include Knox's business correspondence as proprietor of the London Book-Store. His wartime papers contain numerous letters from Continental officers, members of Congress, State officials, and friends, along with sundry bills, receipts, ledgers, maps, military returns, and muster rolls. Postwar letters and documents, including the official correspondence of the U.S. secretary of war, concern western lands, land speculation, military pensions and accounts, Shays' Rebellion, Indian affairs, and frontier garrisons. The collection also contains correspondence of the Knox family, papers of Knox's wife and her family, and Waldo family papers dealing chiefly with Maine lands.

Principal correspondents: John Adams, John Avery, Clement Biddle, William Bingham, Christopher Brown, Edward Carrington, Chastellux, Joseph Clark, David Cobb, Samuel Cooper, Richard Cranch, John Crane, John B. Cutting, Horatio Gates, Elbridge Gerry, Nathanael Greene, Elihu Hall, Alexander Hamilton, John Hancock, Josiah Harmar, William Heath, David Hopkins, Joseph Howland, William Irvine, Henry Jackson, Rufus King, Lafayette, John Lamb, Tobias Lear, Benjamin Lincoln, Thomas Longman, Joshua Loring, David MacClure, Alexander McDougall, William Miller, John Moriarty, Andrew Oliver, Robert Treat Paine, Samuel H. Parsons, Richard Peters, Timothy Pickering, Joseph Pierce, James Rivington, Isaac Sears, Samuel Shaw, Samuel Stringer, John Sullivan, James Swan, Robert Towle, John Troutbeck, Jeremiah Wadsworth, Jonathan Waldo, Thomas Walker, Artemas Ward, Washington, James Webber, and Benjamin West.

Filmed by Massachusetts Historical Society. Originals in New England Historic Genealogical Society.

JACOB G. KOCH PAPERS
13 boxes, 1783–1842.

472   Koch: Philadelphia insurance underwriter.

Contains two account books, one for Jan.—Aug. 1783, in Dutch, and one dated Dec. 1787—Dec. 1798.

LAFAYETTE PAPERS

7 vols., 6 boxes, 2 folios, 1095–1834.　　　Part photostats and facsimiles.

473　　Lafayette (1757–1834): French volunteer; maj. gen., Continental Army, 1777–81.

Revolutionary material consists of an orderly book kept by members of the staffs of Generals Lafayette, Enoch Poor, and Edward Hand, Aug. 5—Sept. 16, 1780; copies of Lafayette letters in the Stuart W. Jackson Collection, Yale University Library, concerning the status of French officers in the Continental Army, 1777, and the U.S. Constitution, 1787; letters from Lafayette to Henry Laurens, Robert Morris, and William Woodford, 1778, concerning military and business affairs; and a copy of a letter from Gen. Nathanael Greene to Lafayette concerning the southern campaign, 1781.

LANCASTER COUNTY, PENNSYLVANIA, COMMITTEE OF SAFETY, MINUTES

1 vol., 1774–77.　　　Force manuscripts.

474　　Material concerning the organization and composition of the Revolutionary movement in Pennsylvania. Includes membership records, information on issues coming before the committee, and its interaction with other county committees.

LANDSDALE–MOYLAN–VAN HORNE PAPERS

1 folio, 1771–1816.　　　Photostats.

475　　Thomas Landsdale: Maj., 3d Maryland Continental Regiment. Stephen Moylan (1737–1811): Mustermaster general, 1775–76; quartermaster general, 1776; col., 4th Continental Dragoons, 1777–83.

Correspondence to Thomas Landsdale and Stephen Moylan concerning military supply and the disposition of troops in Pennsylvania and Connecticut, 1777–83.

Principal correspondents: Clement Biddle, William Franklin, Alexander Hamilton, Timothy Pickering, Tench Tilghman, and Washington.

COMTE ANDRAULT DE LANGERON PAPERS

5 vols., 1761–85.

476　　Comte de Langeron (1765–1851): Lt., Regiment Bourbonnais, 1782–83.

Records of the French military during the Revolution. Includes lists of the numerical strength of the French fleet at Brest, 1776–78; signals and rules for division of prizes in the French Navy; regimental rosters of troops at Brest, 1777–79; charts and reports on D'Orvilliers' defeat of Admiral Keppel, 1778; intelligence reports on the British Navy, 1779; troop assignments on the French fleet, 1779; rosters of troops at St. Malo; and a report on the siege of Savannah, 1779. Also includes shipping lists, rosters, equipment lists, and embarkation orders for Rochambeau's army and the supporting French fleet, 1780–81.

LANSINGBURGH, NEW YORK, TOWN RECORDS

1 vol., 1771–1810.

477　　Items from the Revolutionary era include records of town elections and meetings; rules for the governance of the town, Jan. 1771; and a vote supporting the central committee of New York, 1775.

HENRY LAURENS PAPERS

1 vol., 1 folio, 1732–1811.　　　Part photostats.　　　*NUCMC* 62–4890

478　　Laurens (1724–92): South Carolina planter and merchant; pres., provincial congress, 1775; member and pres., Continental Congress, Nov. 1777—Dec. 1778; prisoner of war, Sept. 1780—Dec. 1781; peace commissioner.

Letters to Laurens concerning personal and family matters, 1772–87, events in South

Carolina before and during the Revolution, defenses, military maneuvers, and diplomatic affairs. Miscellaneous items include receipts for money provided soldiers returning to South Carolina; accounts; extracts from secret journals of Congress, 1779–81; a list of military stores sent to South Carolina, 1779; sundry medical and agricultural recipes; and "A Narrative of my proceedings in the case of Mr. Laurens," concerning Laurens' imprisonment. The folio contains photostats of Lord Hillsborough's order committing Laurens to the Tower of London, and select entries from the Tower register. The collection also includes letters to Col. John Laurens, son of Henry Laurens, concerning his mission to Europe to raise money and supplies, 1781, and political and military affairs.

Principal correspondents: William Aylett, Thomas Bee, Joseph Browne, William Drayton, John Lewis Gervais, Alexander Hamilton, Baron von Holtzendorff, Ralph Izard, J. John Joyner, Joseph Kershaw, Mary Laurens, John Lloyd, William Manning, Richard Peters, John Rutledge, John Christian Senff, John Stevens, John Stoddart, William Thomson, Washington, Holtzendorff, and Moses Young.

HENRY LAURENS FAMILY PAPERS
19 reels microfilm, 1732–1882. *NUCMC* 63–293

479   Henry Laurens (1724–92): See entry no. 478; John Laurens (1754–82): Lt. Col., Continental Army, 1778–82; aide-de-camp to Washington; special envoy to France, 1781.

Includes Laurens' commercial, private, and presidential letterbooks, 1762–64, 1767–79, 1782–83; letters from Roderique, Hortales, & Company to committees of Congress, 1776–79; original letters and copies of letters to Laurens concerning politics, the administration of the Army, war plans, foreign affairs, the business of Congress, and personal matters; and miscellaneous returns and documents relating to the conduct of the war. Also a journal, June–July 1775, and papers, 1775–76, of the South Carolina council of safety; correspondence of the Laurens family, 1774–83; business correspondence of the Countess of Huntington, 1770–84, and copies of letters from the Rev. W. Piercy to the Countess, 1773–83; papers concerning Indian affairs, 1776, and the treaty of peace, 1781–83; papers relating to Gérard and Lafayette, 1778–79; and papers concerning the court-martial of Brig. Gen. William Thompson, 1778. Additional items include the Austin, Laurens, and Appleby letterbooks, 1785–87, and copybook of invoices, 1759–63; a John Laurens account book, 1767–75; papers of John Laurens, 1777–81; Laurens' manuscript reply to Christopher Gadsden, "Philolethes," 1763; and miscellaneous military returns and records for South Carolina, 1775–81.

Principal correspondents: John Adams, William Bell, Thomas Day, John Ettwein, Franklin, Horatio Gates, John Lewis Gervais, Alexander Gillon, Girard, William Heath, John Houstoun, Robert Howe, Jedediah Huntington, Ralph Izard, Baron de Kalb, Lafayette, Henry Laurens, Jr., James Laurens, John Laurens, Martha Laurens, Mary Laurens, William Livingston, Samuel Otis, Timothy Pickering, Jacob Read, Baron von Steuben, Lord Stirling, George Walton, and Washington.

Originals in South Carolina Historical Society. A brief guide to the microfilm edition prepared by the Society outlines contents of each reel.

JONATHAN AND RICHARD LAW PAPERS
1 folio, 1742–84.   Force transcripts.

480   Jonathan Law (1674–1750): Connecticut lawyer; gov., 1741–50. Richard Law (1733–1806): Connecticut lawyer; State judge from 1773, U.S. judge from 1789; member, Continental Congress, 1774, 1776–77, 1780–83.

Letters of Richard Law concerning events in Congress and reports on British and American military maneuvers, 1777. Also correspondence of Samuel Huntington and Jonathan Trumbull concerning British and American activities around New York and Roger Sherman's description of a proposed law compilation for Connecticut, 1783.

ARTHUR LEE PAPERS

1 vol., 1776–77.   Force transcript.

481   Lee (1740–92): Diplomat; member, Continental Congress, 1782–84; brother of Richard Henry Lee.

Account of Lee's experiences as commissioner to the French Court from the Continental Congress, 1776–77. The limitations of the commissioners can be seen in the reports on his missions to Spain, Prussia, and the Austrian Empire. Also reflects his resentment of Benjamin Franklin and his distrust of Silas Deane. Scattered extracts from diplomatic and commercial correspondence are included.

RICHARD BLAND LEE PAPERS

122 letters, 1700–1825.

482   Lee (1761–1827): Virginia statesman.

Contains correspondence pertaining to the political leanings of prominent Virginians. Principal correspondents: Theodorick Bland, Charles Lee, Henry Lee, Richard Henry Lee, William Lee, James Madison, Bishop James Madison, David Stuart and George Turberville.

LEE FAMILY PAPERS

8 reels microfilm, 1742–95

483   Lee: Virginia family. Arthur Lee (1745–92; Francis Lightfoot Lee (1734–97); Richard Henry Lee (1732–94); William Lee (1739–95); and others.

A project sponsored jointly by the University of Virginia Library and the National Historical Publications Commission combining on film the papers of the Lee family of Virginia. Includes holdings of Lee papers at the American Philosophical Society, Harvard University Library, Historical Society of Pennsylvania, Library of Congress, Minnesota Historical Society, University of Virginia Library, and Yale University Library. Consists of correspondence with members of the Continental Congress, military officers, diplomats and agents abroad, French authorities, State leaders, and family friends. The letters cover a broad range of topics but focus chiefly on mercantile, political, diplomatic, and military affairs. Also contains papers of Robert Morris, John Ross, and William Brigham; miscellaneous pamphlets; and proceedings of the secret committee of Congress, Sept. 1775—Sept. 1777.

Principal correspondents: John Adams, Samuel Adams, John Berkenhout, John Bondfield, Thomas Cushing, Silas Deane, Alexander Dick, John Dickinson, Charles Frederic Dumas, John Emery, Franklin, James Gardoqui, Ralph Izard, Jefferson, Edmund Jenings, John Paul Jones, Lafayette, Charles Lee, Thomas Lee, John Lloyd, James Lovell, John Page, Mann Page, Jr., Edmund Pendleton, Comte de Sarsfield, Comte de Sartine, William Shippen, Jr., Adam Stephen, Vergennes, Washington, George Weedon, and Jonathan Williams.

A published *Guide to the Microfilm Edition of the Lee Family Papers, 1742–95* is available from the University of Virginia Library. See also *NUCMC*.

LEE FAMILY PAPERS

4 boxes, 1753–1927.

484   Lee: Virginia family.

Includes a transcript of a letter from Richard Henry Lee to an unknown recipient, Nov. 1786, concerning recognition of Col. Henry Lee for services in the war. Also contains material assembled by Edmund C. Burnett pertaining to ciphers used by Arthur Lee and Richard Henry Lee, 1776–79.

THOMAS SIM LEE PAPERS

1 box, 1771–1820.   Photostats.

485   Lee (1745–1819): Maryland statesman; gov., 1779–83; member, Continental Congress, 1783.

Contains 20 letters to Lee, 1771–89, commenting on Chesapeake society and customs, economics, and politics.

Principal correspondents: Daniel Carroll, William Fitzhugh, James Forbes, William Goddard, John Hanson, Daniel of St. Thomas Jenifer, Arthur Lee, Richard Lee, Jr., and John Rutledge.

LEE–PALFREY PAPERS
4 boxes, 1780–1900.

486   Lee–Palfrey: Massachusetts commercial and literary families.

Includes a William Palfrey letter, June 1780, reporting commercial losses from Phila-delphia, Pa., and a letter from Jonathan Palfrey of Machias, Maine, concerning family health and welfare.

JOHN LEWIS PAPERS
2 boxes, 1752–1828.

487   Lewis (1754–1823): North Yarmouth, Maine, surveyor; member, committee of safety for Cumberland County, 1775, provincial congress, 1774–75, and Massachusetts General Court, 1776, 1783–84; town selectman, 1775–96; superintendent of manpower and supplies for Cumberland County, 1779–81; justice of the peace.

Much of the material, 1776–82, pertains to Lewis' work as county superintendent and includes muster rolls, supply lists, census information, enlistment lists, and correspondence with the State government. Several letters written in the 1760's concern surveys of towns such as New Marblehead, New Gloucester, Edgecomb, and New Boston.

Principal correspondents: Committee of Proprietors of New Boston, committee of safety, Enoch Ilsley, Asa Lewis, Nathaniel Sparhawk, and William Story.

BENJAMIN LINCOLN PAPERS
13 reels microfilm, 1635–1964.   Finding aid available.

488   Lincoln (1733–1810): Brig. and maj. gen., Massachusetts Militia, 1776–77; maj. gen., Continental Army, 1777–83; commander in chief, Southern Department, 1778—May 1780; secretary of war, 1781–83.

The Benjamin Lincoln Papers were filmed under the auspices of the National Histor-ical Publications Commission. A guide, prepared by Frederick S. Allis, Jr., and Wayne A. Frederick and available from the Massachusetts Historical Society under the title *Guide to the Microfilm Edition of the Benjamin Lincoln Papers* (1967), includes a 15-page biographical sketch of Lincoln, the provenance of the collection, and a list of corres-pondents identified by period, locale, or subject matter of letters to Lincoln. Individual reel descriptions provide information on the outside dates of documents represented, the kind of material, and its basic emphasis.

Revolutionary material appears in the first nine reels. Documents for the years 1763–74 include deeds, wills, receipts, bills of sale, acquittances, and copies of court records. Those for 1775 include six letters from Lincoln to officials in Hingham, Mass., and copies of resolutions passed by the Provincial Congress and the General Court of Massachusetts. From 1776 to 1783 the focus is on military affairs, viz., general and divisional orders, court-martial proceedings, intelligence reports, returns on troops and supplies, and correspond-ence from Congress, Washington, and various Continental and provincial officers under Lincoln's command. This material relates primarily to Lincoln's service as commander of the Massachusetts Militia during the siege of Boston, as a Continental general in the Jersey and Saratoga campaigns, as commander in chief in the Southern Department, and as secretary of war in the Confederation government. Postwar documents pertain largely to Lincoln's service as commander of the Massachusetts Militia during Shays' Rebellion, customs collector for the port of Boston, and member of special commissions on land claims and Indian affairs.

Originals in Massachusetts Historical Society. See also Benjamin Lincoln, diary, entry no. 416.

RICHARD LIPPINCOTT PAPERS
1 vol., 1782.

489   Lippincott (1745–1826): New Jersey loyalist; capt., Associated Loyalist Militia.

Proceedings of the court-martial of Capt. Richard Lippincott, April 1782, for hanging Capt. Joshua Huddy of the New Jersey Militia, a prisoner of war. Also includes related correspondence from William Franklin, Henry Clinton, Germain, and Washington.

For a full account of the episode see Katherine Mayo, *General Washington's Dilemma* (New York, 1938).

ROBERT R. LIVINGSTON PAPERS
1 box, 1765–76.

490   Livingston (1746–1813): Member, Continental Congress, 1775–76, 1779–80; secretary of foreign affairs and chancellor of New York.

Includes correspondence concerning patronage in the Continental Congress, the resignation of Philip Schuyler, dangers of peace negotiations in 1776, and the prospect of a loyalist triumph in New York in 1776. Also contains resolves against the Stamp Act proposed by the elder Robert Livingston.

Principal correspondents: George Clinton, William Duer, John Jay, Gouverneur Morris, Edward Rutledge, Philip Schuyler, and Tench Tilghman.

LIVINGSTON PAPERS
10 reels microfilm, 1695–1839.   Finding aid available.

491   Livingston: New York and New Jersey patrician family. William Livingston (1723–90): Gov., New Jersey, 1776–90; member, Continental Congress, 1774–76. Robert R. Livingston (1746–1813): Member, Continental Congress, 1775–76, 1779–80; secretary of foreign affairs and chancellor of New York. Philip Livingston (1716–78): New York delegate to Stamp Act Congress; member, Continental Congress, 1775–78. James Livingston (1747–1832), Henry B. Livingston (1750–1831), and H. Brockholst (1757–1823): Soldiers, Continental Army.

Material from the Revolutionary era consists largely of correspondence of William Livingston. The letters touch on all major and many minor aspects of the war but focus chiefly on the mobilization and defense of New York and New Jersey. Also includes William's casebooks from 1759, fee bills, deeds, indentures, wills, and accounts; documents and letters relating to the dispute over the malpractice of Samuel Ogden as justice of the peace; and personal and estate accounts.

Principal correspondents: John Beatty, Abraham Clark, David Clarkson, Henry Clinton, Philemon Dickinson, Nathanael Greene, William Hooper, Francis Hopkinson, John Jay, Henry Laurens, Margaret Livingston, Hugh Mercer, Thomas Mifflin, Robert Morris, Abraham Ogden, Charles Pettit, Edmund Randolph, John C. Symmes, Washington, and John Witherspoon.

See also *NUCMC*.

LIVINGSTON FAMILY PAPERS
2 boxes, 1 packet, 1732–1823.

492   Livingston: See entry no. 491.

Miscellaneous deeds, accounts, and letters. Includes two minor accounts of Robert Livingston with New York merchants, 1768, 1783; an indenture for the purchase of land; and a letter from Nicholas Quackenbush, deputy quartermaster, to Robert Livingston discussing the need for iron, 1780.

Principal correspondents: Henry Cruger and William Patterson.

LOUISIANA, MISCELLANY
14 vols., 9 boxes, 1 folio, 1493–1919.

493   Includes a manuscript volume in Spanish containing copies of documents pertaining to the history of Florida and Louisiana, 1493–1780. Materials from the period of the Revolution concern Britain's declaration of war against Spain, preparations in Louisiana for an attack on the British posts in West Florida, an expedition to Castillo de San Marcos, and the capitulation of Fort Charlotte. Also contains typescripts of four letters from Charles Lee, Patrick Henry, George Morgan, and the Virginia committee of safety, 1776–78; records of land grants in Louisiana, 1785–99; miscellaneous letters and petitions, 1763–89; and papers concerning fortifications, surveys, commerce, and various internal matters.

NICHOLAS LOW FAMILY PAPERS
167 boxes, 8 vols., 1773–1920.

494   Nicholas Low (1739–1826): New York merchant in the firm of Low & Wallace, land speculator and legislator; brother of Isaac Low (1735–91), New York merchant, political leader, loyalist.

Revolutionary era material, approximately one-fifth of the whole, primarily concerns the career of Nicholas Low—his commercial activities centered in New York City, land development in upstate New York, and the recovery and development of American commerce after the war. Contains a large number of letters to Low from merchants in Europe, the West Indies, and American ports; from Low's exiled loyalist brother Isaac in England; his nephew Isaac Low; and various members of his sister's family who were exiled in England and Ireland. Also includes miscellaneous accounts, bills and receipts, and a large ledger concerning Low's business activities in the late 1780's.

Principal correspondents: John Blackburn, James Caldwell, Lewis Chollet, Sam Chollet, Richard Curson, Philip Cuyler, Henry Drinker, Edward Forbes, Benjamin Fuller, Robert Gilmor, Joseph LaCoste, William Lawrence, Abraham Lott, George Meade, John Mitchell, Moses Myers, Thomas Russell, Alexander Wallace, Gertrude Low Wallace, Hugh Wallace, William Wallace, John Wilcocks, and Sam Wilcox; and the firms Bourdieu, Chollet & Bourdieu; Daniel Bowden & Son; Hananel and Jacob Mendes Da Costa; Robert Hazelhurst & Co.; Mordecai Lewis & Co.; Samuel and Moses Myers; Nelson, Heron & Co.; Rocquette & Elsevier; Nicholas & Jacob van Staphorst; and Wilhem and Jan Willink.

WILLIAM LOWNDES PAPERS
2 reels microfilm, 1754–1941.   *NUCMC 64–556*

495   Lowndes (1782–1822): South Carolina planter; member, U.S. House of Representatives, 1810–22.

The Lowndes papers were filmed under the auspices of the National Historical Publications Commission. Documents from the period of the Revolution include the will of Lowndes' uncle, William Jones, 1768; scattered receipts; a business letter from Henry Laurens to William Lowndes, May 1777; and papers of William's father, Rawlins Lowndes (1721–1800), chiefly business correspondence with foreign merchants, 1778, 1786.

Originals in the Southern Historical Collection, University of North Carolina Library.

JOHN LOWNES LETTERBOOK
1 box, 1760–69.

496   Lownes: Philadelphia, Pa., merchant; Quaker.

Chiefly commercial correspondence with merchants in England, America, and the West Indies. A letter to William Freeman, Nov. 1765, reveals Lownes' opposition to the Stamp Act.

LOYALIST PAPERS, PROCEEDINGS OF THE LOYALIST COMMISSIONERS
36 vols., 2 boxes, 1783–90.

497   Consists of evidence and testimony of loyalists who migrated to Canada, collected by American Loyalist Claims Commissioners Thomas Dundas and Jeremy Pemberton at Halifax, St. John, Quebec, and Montreal. Includes estate valuations, descriptions of landholdings, statements of military service, estimates of total losses, and amounts claimed and allowed. After the information in these records was transcribed into entry books submitted to the Government, Dundas apparently retained the collection. It was acquired by the Smithsonian Institution in the 1860's and later transferred to the Library of Congress.

Published in *Second Report of the Bureau of Archives for the Province of Ontario, 1904,* 2 vols. (Toronto, 1905).

See also P.R.O./A.O.12–13, entry nos. 1559–60, F.O.4, entry no. 1562, and T.79, entry no. 1590.

"LOYALIST RHAPSODIES"
1 vol., 1775–86.   Force manuscripts.

498   Songs and verse composed by loyalists Jonathan Odell and Joseph Stansbury. The poems cover a variety of subjects but emphasize the glories of Britain and aspects of the Revolutionary War.

DUNCAN MCARTHUR PAPERS
50 vols., 4 boxes, 1783–1848.   *NUCMC* 60–1452

499   McArthur (1772–1839): Ohio settler; member, State legislature, 1805-14, 1817–18, 1821–23, 1826, 1829–30; gov., 1830–32.

Includes land patents and associated documents for land in Kentucky, 1783–86, with warrants for David Anderson, John Harris, John P. Harrison, Augustin Slaughter, and Stephen Southal. Also includes the will of William G. Mumford, 1786.

JAMES MCFARLAND PAPERS
12 items, 1775–82.   Force manuscripts.

500   McFarland: Pennsylvania militia officer, 1775–82.

Includes McFarland's commissions as second lieutenant and captain in the Cumberland County militia, 1775 and 1780; his appointment at quartermaster for Col. Thomas Gibson's 2d Battalion, Cumberland militia, 1779; a requisition for troops from Bedford County, 1781; and Henry Epple's petition to the Pennsylvania committee of safety for a commission, 1775.

JAMES C. MCGUIRE COLLECTION
2 folios, 1775–89.   Force transcripts.

501   McGuire: Washington, D.C., bibliophile.

Most of the collection consists of letters of Edmund Pendleton to James Madison, 1780–83, discussing economic, military, and political developments on the State and local level. Also includes an Orange County, Va., resolve praising Patrick Henry's actions against Lord Dunmore, 1775, and ciphers used by Jefferson, Robert Livingston, Madison, Monroe, Pendleton, and Edmund Randolph.

Pendleton's letters are published in David John Mays, ed., *The Letters and Papers of Edmund Pendleton, 1734–1803,* 2 vols. (Charlottesville, Va., 1967). Originals owned by James C. McGuire in 1857.

JAMES MCHENRY PAPERS
10 vols., 7 boxes, 1775–1862.   Part photostats and typescripts.

502   McHenry (1752–1816): Medical staff member, Cambridge Hospital, 1776; prisoner of war, Nov. 1776—Mar. 1778; aide-de-camp to Generals Washington, 1778–80, and

Lafayette, 1780–81; member, Continental Congress, 1783–86; secretary of war, 1796–1800.

McHenry's papers, arranged in three series, contain letters concerning the arrest and trial of Dr. William Shippen, director general of Continental Army hospitals; the progress of the war; Continental finance; negotiations for peace; and the siege of Yorktown, 1781. Miscellaneous documents include a general return of noncommissioned officers and privates in service at the commencement of several campaigns, a draft of Washington's resignation as commander in chief of the Continental Army, and a draft of the Declaration of Independence. Also two boxes containing typescripts of letters McHenry received during the war, drafts and copies of letters sent, and personal and official papers.

Principal correspondents: John Adams, John Beatty, Barnabus Binney, John Cochran, Nathanael Greene, Alexander Hamilton, Robert Howe, James Hutchinson, Lafayette, John Morgan, Benjamin Rush, William Sterett, Lord Stirling, Charles Thomson, Tench Tilghman, Robert Troup, and Washington.

Many of McHenry's letters are printed in B. C. Steiner, *Life and Correspondence of James McHenry* (Cleveland, 1907). His correspondence on the siege of Yorktown, chiefly to Gov. Thomas Sim Lee of Maryland, is published in *A Sidelight on History* (New York, 1931).

ALEXANDER McKEE PAPERS

1 vol., May—June, 1774.   Force manuscripts.

503   McKee (d. 1799): Deputy agent for Indian affairs, district of Fort Pitt, 1772.

Minutes of negotiations between British and Virginia agents and the Delaware and Six Nations Indians at the home of Col. George Croghan in Pittsburgh, Pa. Includes messages and speeches of whites and Indians during the sessions following Cresap's Massacre and before the outbreak of war with the Shawnee later that year.

JOHN McKESSON COLLECTION

1 folio, 1775–83.   Force transcripts.

504   McKesson: Secretary, New York Provincial Assembly, 1775; commissary of prisoners for New York; clerk, New York Supreme Court.

Copies of correspondence of the New York Provincial Assembly concerning the New York war effort, particularly troop movements and supply distribution. Letters of Charles Inglis to Cadwallader Colden report British and American activities at New York City and Long Island, 1776.

EDWARD McPHERSON PAPERS

45 vols., 56 boxes, 1738–1900.   *NUCMC* 65–915

505   Robert McPherson (ca. 1730–89): York County, Pa., sheriff, 1762–65, treasurer, 1767–69, and chairman of the county committee of inspection, 1776; Pennsylvania assemblyman, 1765–67, 1781–84; member, Pennsylvania Constitutional Convention, 1776; col., York County militia, 1775. William (d. 1813): Son of Robert; lt., Miles' Pennsylvania rifle regiment, 1776; maj. and aide-de-camp to Gen. Benjamin Lincoln, 1781–83; prisoner of war, Aug. 1776—Apr. 1778. Edward (1830–95).

Contains four boxes of miscellaneous family financial papers, account books, memo books, surveys, deeds, and indentures. Includes records of the Hance Hamilton estate, 1757–95, which was administered by Robert McPherson, some of McPherson's tax collection records, returns of the York County militia, 1774–83, and a daybook, June 1785—Dec. 1786, of a general store apparently operated by McPherson and Samuel Gettys. One box consists of financial papers related to the Marsh Creek Presbyterian Church, founded in 1740, with which Robert McPherson was prominently identified for four decades. Also includes a few letters to Robert concerning his activities as a Revolutionary leader in York County, 1764–83, a dozen letters from his son-in-law David Grier concerning the war in New York and Pennsylvania, 1776–81, and several letters from Robert to his son William and other members of the family.

Principal correspondents: John Dickinson, George Duffield, Robert Galbraith, Charles McClure, Henry Miller, John Nixon, and Richard Peters.

JAMES MADISON PAPERS

108 vols., 8 boxes, 1723–1859.   Microfilm available.   *NUCMC* 63–375

506   Madison (1751–1836): Member, Virginia Convention, 1776, Continental Congress, 1780–83, 1787–88; President of the U.S.

The Madison papers are arranged in six series, three of which contain material from the period of the Revolution, chiefly concerning politicial and military affairs and family matters. In 1965 the Library of Congress published an index to the Madison Papers, which includes a complete description of the collection and a manual for the 28-reel microfilm edition. A modern comprehensive edition of the papers is in progress.

See William T. Hutchinson and William M. E. Rachal, eds., *The Papers of James Madison* (Chicago, 1962–   ). See also the James Madison Ephemera (recent acquisitions) for a personal and political letter from Madison to his father, 1781, and a political letter from Washington to Madison, 1789.

MAINE, MISCELLANY

3 boxes, 1701–1934.   Part photostats.

507   Church records dominate the material from the Revolutionary era. Includes records of the First Church of Christ, Wells, 1701–1811, which trace the development of the institution, documents relating to the organization of the Congregational Church in Winthrop, 1776, miscellaneous survey plats and records of the Warren town meeting, 1783–86, and the typescript of Elizabeth Ring's *A Reference List of Manuscripts Relating to the History of Maine* (Orono, Maine, 1938).

WILLIE P. MANGUM PAPERS

30 vols., 3 boxes, 1771–1906.   *NUCMC* 63–373

508   Mangum (1792–1861): North Carolina politician; member, U.S. House of Representatives, 1823–26, and U.S. Senate, 1831–36, 1840–53.

Volume 1 contains a few deeds for land in North Carolina, 1771–89.

MARINE MISCELLANY

1 box, 1768–86.

509   Includes an agreement between the officers and crew of the schooner *Polly*, Mar. 1768; an account of Arnold Hazard's expenditures on voyages in the brig *Hope*, 1773; Richard Graves' account with Messrs. Kennady, Keel & Co. for building the *Sturdy Beggar*, 1776; an order from the marine committee to Çapt. Ebenezer Peck, commander of the privateer sloop *Wooster*, with a list of the officers and crew of the *Wooster*, 1778; accounts for the ship *Washington*, 1785; and miscellaneous papers, 1782, 1786.

JOHN MARSHALL PAPERS

6 vols., 2 boxes, 1776–1835.   Photostats.

510   Marshall (1755–1835): Lt., capt. lt., and deputy judge advocate for various units of the Virginia Continental Line, 1776–81; chief justice, U.S. Supreme Court, 1801–35.

Material from the period of the Revolution consists of letters from Marshall to John Alexander, Alexander Hamilton, Cadwallader Jones, James Monroe, and George Muter concerning political and legal matters and personal affairs, 1781–88, and personal and family correspondence of Mrs. Edward Carrington, formerly Elizabeth Jacquelin Ambler. Marshall's account book records sums paid and received for sundry articles and services, 1783–92.

See also *NUCMC* 67–185.

MARTIN FAMILY PAPERS
1 box, 1740–1887.   *NUCMC* 65–916
511   Martin: Virginia planter family.
        Family and business matters concerning Goochland County, Va., are the major topics
of seven letters, 1772–85, exchanged between members of the family in England and
Virginia. In June 1774, the impending Revolution led John Martin to express the fear that
he would never see England again.
        Principal correspondents: Elizabeth Martin, Henry Martin, and Elizabeth Phelps.

MARYLAND, INTENDANT OF REVENUE, LETTERBOOK
1 vol., 1785–87.   Force manuscripts.
512   Correspondence of Intendant Daniel of St. Thomas Jenifer, Mar. 1785—Oct. 1786, concerning fiscal operations of the State of Maryland and economic development in the
Chesapeake Bay region. Specific topics discussed include taxation, money and land policies,
confiscated British and loyalist property, imports, the tobacco contract, and the State's
creditors and debtors.

MARYLAND, MISCELLANY
7 boxes, 4 folios, 1632–1936.
513   Contains correspondence, accounts, indentures, petitions, deeds, and survey sketches,
including letters of William Hindman, Maryland delegate to Congress; Daniel of St.
Thomas Jenifer, Intendant of Revenue; and Govs. Thomas Johnson, Thomas Sim Lee,
and William Paca. A book of receipts of Paymaster General John Pierce concerns disbursements to several Maryland agents for settling accounts with troops in various State
units, 1784–85. Also includes the resolves of the city of Annapolis requesting Congress
to locate the Federal capital in Annapolis, May 1783; a photostat of the "Minutes of the
Harford County Committee," Dec. 1774—May 1777, obtained from the Harford County
Historical Society, containing lists of "Non-Associators" with a record of fines levied
against them; and a 1776 Harford County census of the white and black population of
each "hundred."

MARYLAND, MONTGOMERY COUNTY, RECORDS OF PRINCE GEORGE'S PARISH
1 vol., 1711–1832.   Photostats.
514   Contains vestry minutes, 1719–1832. Records are missing for the years 1773–89. Also
a register of births, 1726–98, sporadically maintained after 1766; a ledger of parish
accounts, 1727–71; and material concerning parish lands, taxes, and the rectors and
vestrymen of the parish.

MARYLAND, VICE-ADMIRALTY COURT
1 vol., 1754–75.   Force manuscripts.
515   Proceedings of the Vice-Admiralty Court, held at Annapolis before Judge George
Steuart, 1754–73, containing charges brought against defendants, petitions, and decrees
of the court. Also includes copies of commissions issued to officials in various positions
related to the court, and the commissions of Judge Robert Smith and Register George
Ranken, 1775.

MARYLAND COUNCIL OF SAFETY, PROCEEDINGS AND CORRESPONDENCE
3 vols., 1773–77.   Force transcripts.
516   Consists of material from the Maryland Hall of Records, much of which has been
published in volumes 11–13 of the *Archives of Maryland*. Documents include a "Constitution of the Council of Safety," June 1775; "Association of the Freemen of Maryland,"
July 1775; journals of the proceedings of the July convention, 1775; proceedings and
correspondence of the council of safety, 1773–77; and journals of the committee of observation for Elizabeth Town District, 1775–77.

MARYLAND HALL OF RECORDS
256 reels microfilm, 17th—19th centuries.

517   Official letters and papers divided into the following categories, each containing documents from the period of the Revolution: wills, balance books, inventories, accounts, testamentary proceedings, provincial court judgments, Baltimore County deeds, Anne Arundel County deeds, Anne Arundel County wills, the Rainbow Series, court of appeals, Western Shore General Court, and Eastern Shore General Court. The most important category for the study of the Revolution is the Rainbow Series, which is subdivided into the "Black Books," "Blue Books," "Brown Books," and "Red Books." Of these the "Red Books" is the largest and most comprehensive, containing correspondence of Maryland delegates in Congress; minutes of the Maryland Convention, 1775, and the committee of safety, 1776–77; correspondence of Congress and the War Office to the Governor of Maryland; etc. Published calendars are available for the Rainbow Series. Reels 253–56 contain indexes to numerous court records, inventories, wills, and accounts in the collection.

See also James M. Magruder, *Index of Maryland Colonial Wills, 1634–1777, in the Hall of Records, Annapolis, Md.* (Baltimore, 1967).

MASCARENE FAMILY PAPERS
1 reel microfilm, 1687–1839.

518   Mascarene: Massachusetts loyalist family.

Includes about 70 personal and family letters to Mrs. Margaret Holyoke Mascarene of Cambridge and Boston, Mass., from her sister-in-law, Margaret Mascarene Hutchinson; her nephew, Thomas Perkins; and Thomas Lane, a merchant seaman and family friend, 1764–89. Lane's letters, written from various ports between Maine and South Carolina, contain occasional references to climate and points of interest. Letters of Thomas Perkins, a merchant of Bristol, England, contain scattered references to his business activities, particularly in the cod fisheries off Newfoundland. Mrs. Hutchinson, a Massachusetts refugee living at Halifax and the most heavily represented correspondent, writes chiefly of marriages, births, illness, deaths, etc., but her letters also reflect the plight of American loyalists as they attempted to adjust to life in Nova Scotia.

MASON COUNTY, KENTUCKY, HISTORICAL SOCIETY PAPERS
2 reels microfilm, 1777–1879.

519   Miscellaneous collection concerning early Kentucky history. Includes three small, unidentified account books; copies of a few George Rogers Clark letters, 1781–82; depositions, undated but apparently ca. 1820, describing Clark's activities in the West, 1777–82; and various receipts and notes.

GEORGE MASON PAPERS
2 boxes, 3 folios, 1750–1890.   Part photostats.   Microfilm available.

520   Mason (1725–92): Virginia planter and statesman; delegate, Virginia Conventions, 1775, 1776; member, House of Delegates, 1777–81; author of Virginia Declaration of Rights and Virginia Constitution, 1776.

Contains miscellaneous documents pertaining to the tobacco trade, Mason's landholdings, and family matters. Also includes a letter from Mason to Washington, Oct. 1769, and the first draft of the Virginia Declaration of Rights, which is separated from the collection for permanent exhibition in the Library.

Published in Robert A. Rutland, ed., *The Papers of George Mason*, 3 vols. (Chapel Hill, N.C., 1970).

JOHN MASON FAMILY PAPERS
1 reel microfilm, 1781–1834.

521   Mason (1766–1849): Son of George Mason of Gunston Hall.

Contains correspondence between Mason and his father, primarily concerning family and business matters, including one letter written by George Mason from the Richmond ratifying convention, 1788. Other John Mason letters pertain to the beginning of the French Revolution.

Originals owned by Philip Dawson.

KENDER MASON PAPERS
1 box, 1778–80.

522   Contains a vellum scroll with terms of Mason's victualer's contract with the British Army for feeding 3,000 men stationed in East Florida, Feb. 1778—June 1780, including chronological lists of payments.

WILLIAM S. MASON LIBRARY COLLECTION, MINUTES OF THE FRENCH LEGATION IN THE UNITED STATES
3 boxes, 1777–96.   Photostats.

523   Extracts from records, journals, dispatches, and correspondence of the French legation at Philadelphia. Includes statistical studies on population, commerce, agriculture, and ship registrations. Also La Luzerne's letterbook of dispatches, 1779–82, containing information on the war and affairs in Congress; summaries of the correspondence of Barbé-Marbois and Vergennes, 1784–85; and extracts from the journal of De Moustier, Minister Plenipotentiary to the U.S. in 1788.

Originals in William S. Mason Library, Evanston, Ill.

MASSACHUSETTS, BOARD OF WAR
9 vols., 1776–81.   Force transcripts.

524   Minutes of the Board of War concerning the purchase, distribution, and sale of goods both in Massachusetts and in the overseas trade. Records of the board, 1776–78, contain data on the recruitment and movement of men for the Army and Navy. Correspondence, 1776–81, relates to the purchase of war material in Europe and foodstuffs, mostly flour, from the Southern Colonies.

Principal correspondents: Samuel Arnold, Stephen Bruce, John Clark, John Clauston, Nicholas Cooke, James Devereux, Jonathan Fisk, William Frost, Joseph Gardoqui & Sons, Elbridge Gerry, Alexander Gillon, Jonathan Glover, Jacques Gruel & Co., William Haynes, Leonard Jarvis, Holton Johnson, Nathan Leech, Joseph Loring, Morris, Penet & Co., Henry Newman, Hugh Orr, Timothy Parsons, Robert Purviance, Samuel Purviance, Samuel P. Savage, Daniel Tillinghast, James Warren, George Williams, and Alexander Wilson.

Originals in Massachusetts State Archives.

MASSACHUSETTS, BOUNDARY
1 folio, 1767.   Force transcripts.

525   Detailed minutes of a meeting concerning the Massachusetts–New York boundary, held at New Haven, Conn., kept by New York delegates William Nicole, William Smith, Jr., and Robert R. Livingston, Sr.

MASSACHUSETTS, COMMITTEES
1 folio, 1775–83.   Force transcripts.

526   Concerns the work of New England committees during the Revolution, including reports on paper currency, Springfield, 1777; wages and price control, New Haven, 1778; the Massachusetts embargo, Boston, 1779; and the control of prices, Philadelphia, 1779. Also contains reports of Indian commissioners and agents, 1777–80, material concerning trade with the Indians, and reports on the Stockbridge, Oneida, Penobscot, St. Francis, St. John's, Mickmac, and Passamaquody Indians.

Originals in Massachusetts State Archives.

MASSACHUSETTS, COUNCIL MESSAGES
2 folios, 1775–77.   Force transcripts.

527   Orders and instructions of the council concerning recruitment and supply of the Army. Some items deal with loyalists and civilian and military prisoners. The collection is indexed.
     Originals in Massachusetts State Archives.

MASSACHUSETTS, DUKES COUNTY
1 folio, 1712–1812.   Force manuscripts.

528   Legal papers containing records of the court of general sessions, court of common pleas, and the sheriff. Includes summonses, judgments, pleas, attachments, appeals, writs of seizure, debt indentures, and probate records. Also contains a bill of expenses for John Hancock's ship *Lydia*, 1766.

MASSACHUSETTS, GENERAL COURT, PETITIONS TO
4 vols., 1776–79.   Force transcripts.

529   Petitions and other letters of appeal to the General Court concerning economic hardship, military service, release from jail, parish incorporation, religious freedom, care of prisoners, land grants, relief from taxes, loyalist emigration, and licensing of privateers. Several letters reflect the problems of imprisoned loyalists and British soldiers.
     Originals in Massachusetts State Archives.

MASSACHUSETTS, GENERAL COURT, RESOLVES
11 vols., 1776–77.   Force transcripts.

530   Calendared resolves for Nov. 1776—Aug. 1777, indicating the extent of the General Court's power during the Revolution. Includes minor accounts, some of delegates to the Continental Congress.
     Published in *Resolves and Orders of the Congress, Council, and General Court of the State of Massachusetts Bay* (Boston, 1777).

MASSACHUSETTS, PROVINCIAL CONGRESS
1 vol., July—Nov. 1775.   Force transcripts.

531   Records of the Massachusetts General Court sitting as the Provincial Congress pertaining to governmental actions taken during the first summer of the war.
     The journals of the Massachusetts Provincial Congress and the General Court, 1775–76, are published in Force, *American Archives*.

MASSACHUSETTS, REVOLUTION, LETTERS
14 folios, 1775–83.   Force transcripts.

532   Letters to the Massachusetts Board of War, formerly the committee of supply at Watertown, and the Massachusetts Council, primarily concerning the maintenance and supply of the Army. Also includes material on wage and price controls, the handling of loyalists, Burgoyne's Convention Army, lists of prisoners, returns of officers and men, and minor accounts.
     Principal correspondents: John Adams, Jonathan L. Austin, Nathaniel Barber, John Burgoyne, Samuel Brewer, Archibald Campbell, Clarke & Nightingale, Nicholas Cooke, Thomas Crafts, Francis Dana, Timothy Danielson, Asa Douglas, Franklin, William Frost, Horatio Gates, Jonathan Glover, John Hancock, William Heath, Aaron Hobart, Henry Knox, Henry Laurens, Arthur Lee, Charles Lee, Benjamin Lincoln, Abner Livingston, James Lovell, Charles Miller, Hugh Orr, Joseph Otis, Enoch Poor, William Rice, Jr., Philip Schuyler, Dummer Sewall, Alexander Shepard, Jr., William Smith, Joseph Spencer, William Spooner, John Stark, John Sullivan, William Thompson, Jonathan Trumbull, Jonathan Warner, Washington, and Meshech Weare.
     Originals in Massachusetts State Archives.

MASSACHUSETTS, REVOLUTION, MILITARY AFFAIRS
6 folios, 1775–83.   Force transcripts.

533   Militia returns, muster rolls, payrolls, officer lists, draft quotas, and accounts of supplies. Also includes miscellaneous letters, resolves, and records of the Massachusetts Provincial Congress and the committee of safety at Cambridge, and records of a court of inquiry on the failure of the Rhode Island expedition. The volumes are calendared.
        Principal correspondents: William Baylies, David Brewer, David Cobb, Timothy Danielson, Elbridge Gerry, Richard Gridley, Udney Hay, William Heath, Timothy Pickering, Edmund Ridge, Lemuel Robinson, Philip Schuyler, Joseph Spencer, Jonathan Thomas, Jonathan Titcomb, Benjamin Tupper, Joseph Vose, Artemas Ward, and David Wooster.
        Originals in Massachusetts State Archives.

MASSACHUSETTS, TOWNS, RECORDS AND RESOLVES
11 folios, 1765–87.   Force transcripts.

534   Miscellaneous town records including resolutions, official documents, and letters, particularly pertaining to such issues as closing the port of Boston, the Declaration of Independence, the Articles of Confederation, the State constitution, and various political and economic matters. Most of the correspondence and town meeting records concern requests of the committee of supplies and the Board of War for supplies and men. Also includes records of county conventions held to protest economic and governmental conditions in Massachusetts during and after the war, grievance petitions for the years 1784–87, material pertaining to Shays' Rebellion, requisitions, and receipts.
        Originals in Massachusetts State Archives.

MASSACHUSETTS, TOWNS, RECORDS OF VOTES ON INDEPENDENCE
1 folio, 1776.   Force transcripts.

535   Records of resolutions favoring a declaration of independence passed by 19 town meetings at the request of the Massachusetts Provincial Congress, May 10, 1776.
        Originals in Massachusetts State Archives.

MASSACHUSETTS BAY, CONNECTICUT, AND NEW HAMPSHIRE CONVENTION
1 folio, Aug. 1780.   Force transcripts.

536   Minutes of the meeting of delegates providing information on economic and military conditions within New England. Includes resolutions on recruitment, military supplies, the powers of Congress, and State embargoes.
        Originals in Massachusetts State Archives.

MASSACHUSETTS BAY, CONNECTICUT, NEW HAMPSHIRE, RHODE ISLAND, AND PROVIDENCE PLANTATIONS CONVENTION
1 vol., Dec. 1776—Jan. 1777.   Force transcripts.

537   Minutes of one of several wartime meetings called to find ways of restricting emissions of paper money and to enact measures in support of public currencies. The meeting at Providence, R.I., resolved not to emit any more paper money, and recommended setting maximum prices and wages, as well as the establishment of uniform military bounty, pay, ration, and transportation rates.
        Originals in New Hampshire Historical Society.

PHILIP MAZZEI PAPERS
1 box, 1773–1816.   *NUCMC* 71–1382

538   Mazzei (1730–1816): Italian immigrant to Virginia, physician, horticulturist, and author; sent to Europe as agent for Virginia, 1779.
        Four letters from John Adams, 1782–86, concerning the revival of commerce between Europe and America, commercial treaties, Adams' opinion on a proposed history of the

American Revolution by Abbé de Mably, and the geography and history of New England. One letter each from George Webb, 1784, John Blair, 1786, and James Monroe, 1786, and two letters from Edmund Randolph, 1786, concern Mazzei's business affairs. Also includes a printed copy of "A Poem addressed to the Armies of the United States of America," by David Humphreys, 1785, and a memorial signed by John Page, John Cocke, Richard Taliaferro, and others requesting payment of war loans.

PHILIP MAZZEI PAPERS
1 vol., 1780–82.   Force manuscripts.
539   Mazzei (1730–1816): See entry no. 538.

Extracts and copies of letters from public figures in Italy and America, chiefly concerning Mazzei's travels and business affairs as agent for Virginia. Also includes copies of three essays, in Italian: "Ragioni per cui non pero darsi agli stati Americani Lataccia de Ribelli," 1781; "Rifflessioni tendenti a prognosticar L'evento della presente guerra," 1781; and "Istoria del principio, progresso, e fine del denaro, de Carta degli Stati Uniti Americani," 1782.

Principal correspondents: John Adams, Francis Dana, Francesco Favi, Franklin, Jefferson, Mark Lynch, George Mason, Jr., and P. Penet.

RETURN JONATHAN MEIGS FAMILY PAPERS
1 box, 1772–1862.   *NUCMC* 68–2056
540   Meigs (1740–1833): Lt., maj., Connecticut Militia, 1772, 1775; col., 6th Connecticut Regiment, 1778–81; surveyor and settler of the Ohio Company at Marietta, 1788; agent to the Cherokees, 1801.

Includes letters of commendation for Meigs' command of the Sag Harbor raid, May 23, 1777, and his commissions in the militia and Continental Army.

MICHIGAN, MISCELLANY
1 box, 1 vol., 1706–1876.   Part photostats.
541   Includes drawings of Fort Michilimackinac, 1766, and extracts of documents pertaining to its role on the northern frontier, 1715–80, prepared by the Old Forts and Historical Memorial Association of Detroit, Mich.

GARRETT MINOR PAPERS
2 boxes, 1765–98.
542   Minor: Sawmill owner, merchant-storekeeper in Louisa County, Va.; maj., lt. col., Virginia Militia, 1778–79, 1787.

Miscellaneous letters and accounts concerning business and military affairs in Virginia and Georgia. Includes a ledger, 1765–91, recording transactions of Minor's sawmill and store, and his speculation in military certificates and land. The records of the sheriff of Louisa County for 1787–89 are also in the account book. Nearly 50 letters of Charles and Sydnor Crosby and James Tait describe in detail their economic and political activities in Wilkes County, Ga., particularly in land speculation. Several letters by Minor's sons, Peter and Dabney, describe the campaigns against Dunmore, 1776–77, and Cornwallis, 1781, in Virginia.

Miscellaneous Manuscripts

543   JAMES ADAMS
Commission as captain in Col. Frederick Watts' battalion, Pennsylvania Militia, 1777, and two certificates of loyalty, 1779.

544   SAMUEL ADAMS
Three photostats and one facsimile of letters on political and military matters to William Bradford, Artemas Ward, and Elbridge Gerry, 1775, 1789.

545   WILLIAM ALEXANDER (LORD STIRLING)
Typescripts of four military letters to and from Stirling, 1776–78, and a photostat of a document bearing the signatures of 10 men volunteering to patrol the shores of the Raritan River.

546   ALEXANDRIA, VA.
Photostats of the "Proceedings of the Trustees of the town of Alexandria," 1749–67.

547   WILLIAM ALLASON
Lord Dunmore's account with Allason, Dec. 1774—Nov. 1775, and miscellaneous business letters and papers, 1758–93.

548   ETHAN ALLEN
Facsimile of letter to the Albany committee of correspondence on the capture of Ticonderoga, 1775.

549   FISHER AMES
Letter describing a program of taxation being considered in Congress, 1789.

550   JOHN ANDRÉ
Photostats of two letters to Washington concerning André's execution and of the sketch André made of himself the day of his death, Oct. 2, 1780.

551   JOHN ARMSTRONG, JR.
Letter to John Dickinson concerning the discharge of Pennsylvania troops, 1784.

552   BENEDICT ARNOLD
Letter to Col. John Beatie [Beatty], commissary of prisoners, 1778.

553   W. B. BALFOUR
Four letters on military and personal matters from Mrs. Katherine Balfour and Lt. Col. Nesbit Balfour, 1780–81.

554   STEPHEN BALLIET
Letter to Joseph Reed reporting Indian forays in Northampton County, Pa., 1780.

555   THOMAS BARCLAY
Order from Congress to American agents in Europe to close accounts, 1783.

556   SAMUEL BARRINGTON
Personal letter from Barrington containing remarks on an expected attack by Comte d'Estaing, St. Lucia, 1778.

557   THOMAS BEE
Letter to the President of the Virginia House of Delegates, 1777, and letter from the delegates of South Carolina to R. Williams concerning military supplies, 1778.

558   ANDREW BELL
Personal letter to his sister, Cornelia Bell, 1777, and personal letter from Grove Bend, 1784.

559   CLEMENT BIDDLE
Business letter to John Groves, 1786.

560   WILLIAM BINGHAM
Two business letters to Willing & Morris, 1777, a business letter from Jean Holker, 1779, and four letters, three in French, concerning the Continental frigate *Confederacy*, 1780.

561   ARCHIBALD and ROBERT BLAIR
Seven business letters and papers chiefly concerning trade with India, 1786–98.

562   JOHN BLAIR
Letter to Gov. Benjamin Harrison appealing for aid to lunatics, 1782.

563   TIMOTHY BLOODWORTH
Letter concerning problems of State imposts, 1786.

564   "BONHOMME RICHARD"
Photostat of a list of officers serving on the *Bonhomme Richard*, 1779.

565   JAMES BOWDOIN
Letter to Bowdoin concerning British seizures and customs duties at New Brunswick, 1786.

566   JOSEPH BOWNE
Typescripts of three letters to Bowne concerning the business of the quartermaster department, 1781–82.

567   JOHN BRADFORD
Three business letters to Henry Bromfield & Co. and Abraham Dupuis & Co., 1775.

568   JOHN BRADSTREET
Personal letter to J. T. Kempe, 1763.

569   DAVID BREARLEY
Business letter to Gov. William Livingston, 1784.

570   JOHN BROOKS
Business letter to William Syles & Co. of Alexandria, Va., 1786.

571 JOHN BROWNE
Letter to Gen. John Thomas attacking Parliament and encouraging Americans to stand firm in their rights, 1776.

572 EDWARD BURD
Business letter to Edward Shippen, 1769.

573 AEDANUS BURKE
Letter on military matters to Arthur St. Clair, 1781.

574 RICHARD BUTLER
Letter from William Pierce describing action at Hobkirk's Hill, 1781.

575 JOHN CALFE
Letter of invitation from Jacob Cram to pastor of a church at Hempstead, L. I., N. Y.

576 SIR GUY CARLETON
Letter to Lord Sydney concerning a possible attack on British provinces in North America, 1786.

577 WILLIAM CARMICHAEL
Nine personal letters to Richard Harrison, American consul at Cádiz, containing information on diplomatic affairs, 1780–82. Carmichael was secretary to John Jay.

578 SAMUEL CARPENTER
Register of Carpenter's will, Newcastle, Del., 1778.

579 EDWARD CARRINGTON
Letter on military matters to Richard Young, quartermaster at Fredericksburg, Va., 1781.

580 CHARLES CARROLL
Photostat of a letter of recommendation for Daniel Carroll, 1785.

581 DANIEL CARROLL
Photostats of four letters on military and political matters to Gov. Thomas Sim Lee, 1781–82.

582 DEBORAH CHAMPION
Letter describing a trip to Boston to present important dispatches to Washington, 1775.

583 SAMUEL CHASE
Photostat and facsimile copies of two military and political letters, 1776, 1778.

584 PATRICK CHESTER
Photostat of letter in Spanish and English announcing his arrival at Pensacola to assume command of West Florida, 1770.

585 RICHARD CLAIBORNE
Three letters on military matters to Richard Young, quartermaster at Fredericksburg, Va., 1781.

586   GEORGE ROGERS CLARK
Certificate of conduct issued to Joseph Andrews, 1784, and a military pass, 1786.

587   DE WITT CLINTON
Letter to Clinton concerning the U.S. Constitution, 1788.

588   GEORGE CLYMER
Account against the State of Pennsylvania for service in Congress, 1782.

589   JOHN COATES
Letter to Capt. John Kilty concerning the Society of the Cincinnati, 1787.

590   EZRA COLLINS
Facsimile of letter to his brother concerning correspondence from Congress, 1774.

591   STEPHEN COLLINS
Four business letters to Collins, 1776, and a business letter from Samuel Eliot to William Barrell, 1766.

592   PATRICK COLQUHOUN
Two letters on political and business matters to Henry Dundas, Glasgow, 1785, 1789.

593   PETER COLT
Letter from Benjamin Tallmadge concerning naval affairs, 1781.

594   JOHN CONNERY
Receipt for bounty paid for enlisting troops in the 1st Regiment of Light Dragoons, 1780.

595   THOMAS CONWAY
Photostat of a letter to John Hancock concerning military affairs, 1777.

596   GUSTAVUS CONYNGHAM
Account of the sale of the prize snow *Fanny*, 1778.

597   GILBERT COOPER
Orderly books kept at New York, 1776–77. Includes personal accounts and receipts, 1775–90.

598   TENCH COXE
Business letter to John Nicholson, 1786.

599   THOMAS CRESAP
Facsimile of letter to Gov. Horatio Sharpe concerning Indian forays on Maryland's western frontier, 1763, and a typescript of Cresap's last will and testament, 1784.

600   JOHN CROPPER
Photostats of four military commissions, 1775–77.

601   MRS. ARCHIBALD CROSSLEY AUTOGRAPH COLLECTION
Photostats of 15 letters on military, political, and religious matters, 1767–82, by Benedict Arnold, Comte d'Estaing, Franklin, Alexander Hamilton, John Jay, Henry Lee, Peter

Muhlenberg, Lord Stirling, Philip Schuyler, Washington, John Wesley, and William Woodford.

Originals in Princeton University Library.

602 THOMAS CUSHING
Three letters on military and political matters to Elbridge Gerry and John Hancock, 1775–76.

603 WILLIAM DAVIES
Letter to Richard Young, quartermaster at Fredericksburg, Va., concerning military supplies, 1781.

604 COMTE D'ESTAING
Photostats of three letters, two to Washington, concerning the Rhode Island expedition and cooperation between French and American forces.

605 RENÉ-DOMINIQUE DESTOUCHES
Six items—military plans, naval charts, notes on naval affairs, and a letter to Washington, 1784.

606 JOHN DICKINSON
Letter to the speaker of the Delaware Legislative Council concerning steam engines, 1787.

607 JOHN DONELSON
Letter to Gov. Benjamin Harrison concerning Indian affairs, 1782.

608 "ANDREW DORIA"
Page from the journal of the brig *Andrew Doria*, 1776.

609 EDWARD DREW
Certificate attesting to character of George Finwick, 1778.

610 DANIEL DULANY
Letter concerning sale of Negroes in Maryland, 1768.

611 JOHN DUNLAP
Photostats of six letters to Dunlap's brother, 1785–89.

612 PIERRE ÉTIENNE DU PONCEAU
Military and personal letter to Major Walker, 1783.

613 JOSEPH EGGLESTON, JR.
Letter on military matters to Col. Everard Meade, 1781.

614 OLIVER ELLSWORTH
Account for prosecution of several militia for delinquency, 1777–81.

615 JONATHAN ELMER
Typescripts of two political addresses in Cumberland County, Pa., 1774, 1776.

616 ROBERT ERSKINE
Two letter on military matters to Lord Stirling and Washington, 1777, 1779.

617 NICHOLAS EVELEIGH
Personal letter to Peyton Skipwith, 1780.

618 JANE EWING
Photostat of letter to her brother concerning Washington's reception at Trenton en route to inauguration as President of the United States, 1789.

619 WILLIAM FANCITT
Letter to John Calcraft concerning possible recall of Gen. Thomas Gage, 1768.

620 NICHOLAS FISH
Photostats of military papers, including four letters, 1775–84.

621 WILLIAM FITZHUGH
Letter on political matters to Governor Jefferson, 1781.

622 RICHARD FITZPATRICK
Five letters on military matters written from Philadelphia and Staten Island, 1777–78.

623 WILLIAM FLOYD
Facsimile of letter concerning the movements of Generals Clinton and Cornwallis, 1780.

624 SIR JOHN FORBES
Business letter to Luke Gardiner containing remarks on the war, 1778.

625 URIAH FORREST
Letter on political matters to [Benjamin] Stoddert, 1783.

626 BENJAMIN FRANKLIN
Includes seven letters—chiefly photostats—to and from Franklin, on political and scientific matters, 1773–88.

627 THOMAS GAGE
Typescript of letter to Sir William Johnson concerning Indian affairs, 1765.

628 BERNARDO DE GALVEZ
Typescript of tariff schedule in Louisiana, 1777.

629 HORATIO GATES
Photostats of two letters on military matters to Lafayette and Artemas Ward, 1776, 1778.

630 JOHN T. GILMAN
Business letter, Nov. 1780.

631 SAMUEL GIST
Business letter to Garrett Minor, London, 1774.

632 RICHARD GRAHAM
Personal letter to Peter Smith, 1784.

633   **JAMES GRANT**
Claim against the United States for losses suffered during the war, with supporting documents, 1774–97.

634   **NATHANAEL GREENE**
Four letters on military matters to Francis Marion, Henry Lee, Robert Walton, and Nehemiah Hubbard, 1779–81; one letter affirming that Colonel Fenwick of South Carolina was serving as a spy in the British Army, 1782; and photostats of a letter to Moore Furman, 1780.

635   **CYRUS GRIFFIN**
Letter on political and military matters, 1779.

636   **HUGH BLAIR GRIGSBY**
Copy of the "Proceedings of a Meeting of Freeholders of Augusta County, Va.," 1775.

637   **BUTTON GWINNETT**
Facsimile of legal document signed by Gwinnett, 1774.

638   **HADWIN-BRAGG FAMILY**
Business and personal letters and papers, 1774–88.

639   **FREDERICK HALDIMAND**
Photostat of deed for land in Canada given to Indians and displaced loyalists, 1784.

640   **NATHAN HALE**
Typescripts of 16 letters of Col. Nathan Hale of Rindge, N.H., to his wife, Abigail, 1775–80.

641   **JOHN HAMILTON**
Personal letter containing remarks on the Annapolis Convention, 1787.

642   **EDWARD HAND**
Letter of Jasper Yeates on political matters, 1789.

643   **DANIEL HANDS**
Photostat of a payroll for Hands' Connecticut militia company, 1776.

644   **JOSEPH HARDY**
Photostat of a personal letter to W. E. Watson, 1782.

645   **JOHN HARRIS**
Family letter to his mother, 1767.

646   **BENJAMIN HARRISON**
Photostat of certificate honoring Mrs. Martha Gray for care of American prisoners in Philadelphia, 1778.

647   **ROBERT H. HARRISON**
Letter on military matters to Dr. Baylor, 1777.

648 JOHN HART
Facsimile of letter on military matters to Samuel Morris, 1776, and photostat of a document signed by Hart.

649 JASON HAVEN
Personal letter to Stephen Metcalf, 1786.

650 BENJAMIN HAWKINS
Letter on political matters to Richard Caswell, 1787.

651 A. HAWKES HAY
Personal letter to Gov. George Clinton, 1783.

652 ROBERT HAZZARD
Hazzard's will, 1771.

653 WILLIAM HEATH
Photostat of letter on military matters to Washington, 1780.

654 DAVID HENLEY
Letter on political matters, with enclosure, to Samuel Henley, 1788.

655 JOHN HENRY, JR.
Photostats of seven letters on military and political matters to Gov. Thomas Sim Lee of Maryland, 1780.

656 PATRICK HENRY
Land grant to Richard Anderson signed by Henry, 1786.

657 SAMUEL HOLTEN
Photostat of a resolution by the medical committee of Congress, 1777.

658 FRANCIS HOPKINSON
Photostat of two personal letters to and from Washington, 1788–89, and an undated poem.

659 WILLIAM HOUSTOUN
Photostats of a personal letter to his brother, 1777, and three legal papers, 1784 and undated.

660 WILLIAM HOWE
Photostats of a military proclamation, Boston, 1775, and of the first page of the Stamp Act.

661 COUNTESS SELINA HUNTINGDON
Letter concerning Christianizing American Indians, 1784, and an engraving of the countess.

662 JOSEPH HUNTINGTON
Personal letter to Samuel Huntington, 1788.

663 SAMUEL HUNTINGTON
Photostat of account with Benedict Arnold, 1765–67.

664 JOHN IRWIN
Business letter to Messrs. Baynton, Wharton, & Morgan, 1767.

665 RALPH IZARD
Copy of letter thought to be by Dr. Edward Bancroft, 1778.

666 JOSEPH JAMES
List of subscribers for an American edition of Barclay's *Apology* and the *Works of Thomas Chalkey*, 1787.

667 CHARLES JENKINSON
Document received by Jenkinson describing settlements along the coast of West Florida between Pensacola and Louisiana, with references to trade, defenses, climate, soil, rivers, and Indians, 1767.

668 DANIEL JENNINGS
Photostat of petition from disabled veterans of the Massachusetts Continental Line, 1789.

669 THOMAS JOHNSON, JR.
Photostat of letter on political and military matters to Horatio Gates, 1775.

670 GEORGE JOHNSTON
Four letters to Leven Powell concerning activities against Lord Dunmore in Virginia, 1775–76.

671 JOSEPH JONES
Personal and business letter to [James] Wood, 1784.

672 BISHOP OF KILLALOE
Letter on personal and religious matters to Thomas Ashe, 1786.

673 THADDEUS KOSCIUSZKO
Letter, in French, on military matters to Arthur St. Clair, 1777, and photostat of letter to Washington, undated.

674 MARQUIS DE LAFAYETTE
Photostat of letter to William Short acknowledging notice of the death of Washington, 1800.

675 JOHN LAMB
Copy of letter on diplomatic matters to John Adams, 1786, and photostat of a letter on political matters to Nathaniel Peabody, 1788.

676 PETER LANDAIS
Photostats of Landais' account with the United States, Jan. 1782—July 1783; Landais' observations on the account, 1785; and a letter from Joseph Nourse to Rufus King, Register's Office, Mar. 1785.

677 JOHN LANGDON
Letter on political matters to Nicholas Gilman, 1788, and photostat of a letter by the marine committee, 1776.

678   WOODBURY LANGDON
Letter on political matters to Nathaniel Peabody, 1779.

679   WILLIAM LAVENDER
Land warrant signed by Gov. Richard Caswell, 1787.

680   ARTHUR LEE
Includes an unsigned letter from Lee to Richard Henry Lee urging that Congress not abide by the terms of the Saratoga Convention, Paris, Dec. 1777.

681   HANNA P. LEE
Personal letter to relatives in London, 1769.

682   RICHARD HENRY LEE
Typescript, photostat, and original of three letters relating to military affairs, 1777–78.

683   WILLIAM LEE.
Two letters to Robert Carter Nicholas, 1769, concerning the business affairs of William's wife, formerly Hanna P. Ludwell.

684   GOWER LEVESON
Business and personal letter, 1773.

685   BETTY LEWIS
Personal and family letter to Mrs. Washington [1777?].

686   MORGAN LEWIS
Letter on military matters to Benedict Arnold, 1780.

687   BENJAMIN LINCOLN
Letter on military matters to Lieutenant Colonel Williams, 1788.

688   SAMUEL LIVERMORE
Letter on political matters to John Langdon.

689   PHILIP LIVINGSTON
Business letter to Charles Pettit, 1786.

690   ROBERT S. LIVINGSTON
Includes four letters on business and legal matters from Benjamin Harrison to Edmund Randolph, 1770–89.

691   ISAAC LOW
Business letter to John Mitchel, 1774.

692   RAWLINS LOWNDES
Letter to Gov. Richard Caswell concerning Indian affairs, 1778, and a bill for goods shipped to South Carolina, 1779.

693   H. P. LUDWELL
Business letter to Robert Carter Nicholas, 1768.

694 EARL OF MACCLESFIELD
Letter concerning claim of New York loyalist judge Thomas Jones, ca. 1785.

695 ENEAS MACKAY
Two business letters to Barnard & Michael Gratz, 1771, and a letter concerning Indian affairs on the Pennsylvania frontier, 1774.

696 ARCHIBALD MACLAINE
Letter on political matters to James Iredell, 1788.

697 ALEXANDER McDOUGALL
Letter on military matters to Gen. Arthur St. Clair, 1783.

698 LACHLAN McINTOSH
Photostats of two letters on military matters to John Laurens and Washington, 1778.

699 JAMES MADISON
Photostat of personal letter to Jefferson, 1789, and letter from Noah Webster concerning copyright law for Virginia, 1784.

700 MASSACHUSETTS, MISCELLANEOUS
Document concerning Boston public schools, 1767, photostat of the proceedings of a convention held at Concord, 1779, and a letter from John Hancock calling for the election of a representative to Congress, 1788.

701 SAMPSON AND GEORGE MATHEWS
Land warrant, 1771.

702 JOHN MAUNSELL
Business letter to Aaron Burr, 1785.

703 HUGH MAXWELL
Photostats of Maxwell's military commission and a return of casualties at the battles of Ticonderoga and Bennington, 1777.

704 GEORGE MERCER
Two personal and business letters to Captain Rutherford and the committee of the Ohio Company, 1763, 1767.

705 JOHN FRANCIS MERCER
Letter on political matters to Benjamin Harrison, 1784.

706 FORT MIFFLIN
Photostat of map of Fort Mifflin, 1777.

707 THOMAS MIFFLIN
Letter on political matters to Gov. George Clinton, 1783.

708 AMOS MINOR
Personal and family letter to David Minor, 1776, and facsimiles of parts of three other letters by Minor, 1776.

709   LORD CHARLES MONTAGUE
Photostats of two letters on military matters to and from Gen. William Moultrie, 1781.

710   JOHN MONTGOMERY
Letter on political matters to Edward Hand, 1784.

711   SIR HENRY MOORE
Photostat of letter on quartering troops, 1765, and typescript of a letter concerning the New York-Canadian boundary, 1766.

712   CADEO MORRIS
Business letter to his brother Samuel, 1764.

713   GOUVERNEUR MORRIS
Photostat of letter on military matters to Washington, 1778.

714   ROBERT MORRIS
Photostats of three letters to Capt. John Barry concerning naval affairs, 1782.

715   WILLIAM MOULTRIE
Commission as colonel, 2d South Carolina Regiment of Foot, 1775, and misdated letter concerning siege of Savannah, 1779.

716   STEPHEN MOYLAN
Military pass, 1776.

717   FRANCIS NELSON
Commission as 1st lieutenant in the Dutchess County militia, New York, 1781.

718   JOHN PAGE
Personal letter from Philip Mazzei, 1776.

719   MANN PAGE, JR.
Letter on military matters to John Page, 1777.

720   THOMAS PAINE
Letter on political matters to Thomas Walker, 1789.

721   JAMES PARSONS
Political address to the Speaker of the Pennsylvania Assembly, 1776.

722   THEODORE PARSONS
Letter on military matters to Micajah Sawyer, 1776, and an agreement on distribution of prize vessels, 1779.

723   DAVID PARTRIDGE
Personal letter to his sister, 1779.

724   ANDREW PATON
Letter describing voyage to America during which Paton was taken prisoner, 1778.

725   CHARLES PETTIT
Two business letters, 1779, 1786. One is to Jeremiah Wadsworth.

726   ALEXANDER PHILLIPS
Personal letter to Richard Young, quartermaster at Fredericksburg, Va., 1781.

727   TIMOTHY PICKERING
Letter to Col. Walter Stewart concerning military supplies, 1778.

728   WILLIAM PIERCE
Photostat of certificate of membership as a Mason, 1779.

729   THOMAS PINCKNEY
Petition to Governor Pinckney in behalf of a Negro sentenced to death for theft, 1787.

730   THOMAS PITT (BARON CAMELFORD)
Note to John Glover and Henry Laurens concerning lands in South Carolina seized during the Revolution [1784?].

731   THOMAS POWNALL
Personal letter to Benjamin Franklin [1775?].

732   WILLIAM PRICE
Photostat of letter on military matters to James Blake, 1779.

733   ISRAEL PUTNAM
Photostats of two letters on political matters to Col. Beverley Robinson and Washington, 1783.

734   THOMAS QUIGLEY
Bill of sale for the brig *Betsy*, sold at auction, 1782.

735   CHARLES PAUL RAGUETT
Four business letters from James Maxwell of Baltimore, 1782, and single letters from eight other correspondents concerning mercantile matters, 1781–84.

736   JOSEPH REED
Letter on political matters to Elbridge Gerry, 1784.

737   JAMES R. REID
Pay voucher for attendance in Congress, 1788.

738   JAMES RICHIE
Instructions of James Richie & Co. to American agents James Anderson, Thomas Montgomerie, Neil McCoull, and James Dunlop, 1784.

739   MATTHEW RIDLEY
Twelve business letters, chiefly to Thomas Barclay, 1782–85. Includes comments on diplomatic affairs.

740   BARON VON RIEDESEL
Letters on military matters to William Heath, 1778.

741   ABRAHAM RIKER
Photostat of letter on personal and military matters to Mrs. Riker, 1777.

742   JAMES RIVINGTON
Facsimile of letter concerning Indian affairs [1768?].

743   WILLIAM ROBINSON
Four items—accounts and legal papers, 1761–67.

744   COMTE DE ROCHAMBEAU
Photostat of letter to Thomas McKean concerning a resolution of Congress expressing appreciation for the services of Rochambeau, 1781, and two military papers, 1780.

745   ROBERT ROSE
Letter concerning consignment of Continental horses at the end of the war, 1782.

746   JOHN ROSS
Certificate concerning the account of John Ross with the United States, 1780.

747   JAMES RUMSEY
Three letters on personal and scientific matters to [Benjamin] West and Charles Morrow, 1789.

748   BENJAMIN RUSH
Letter on political matters to the President of the Pennsylvania Executive Council, 1776.

749   JAMES RUSSELL
Two photostats and an original of business letters to Thomas Sim Lee, 1769–70.

750   EDWARD RUTLEDGE
Business letter, 1788. Includes personal and family matters.

751   JOHN RUTLEDGE
Letter on military and diplomatic matters to Henry Laurens, 1778.

752   SAMUEL SANDS
Photostat of muster roll for Sands' company in the 3d Pennsylvania Battalion, 1781.

753   THOMAS SAVADGE
Letter to Robert Morris requesting protection of Savadge's Pennsylvania salt works against attacks by Tories, 1777.

754   ALEXANDER SCAMMELL
Personal letter to his brother [1771?].

755   JACOB SCHIEFFELIN
Photostat of James Rivington's *Royal Gazette*, July 1780. Contains narrative of confinement and escape of Henry Hamilton.

756   PHILIP SCHUYLER
Four letters on political matters to Stephen Van Rensselaer, 1787–88.

757   JAMES SEARLE
Business letter to Thomas Fitzsimmons, 1787.

758   HORATIO SHARPE
Eight personal and business letters to his brother Philip, and to John and Samuel Ridout, 1763–84.

759   WILLIAM SHARPE
Account of living expenses in Philadelphia while serving in Congress, 1780, and typescript of a letter on military matters to [Nathanael Greene], 1781.

760   JOHN SHAW
Photostat of letter from Col. Beverley Robinson, authorizing him to recruit a loyalist battalion, 1777.

761   WILLIAM SHEPARD
Photostat of letter on military matters to Washington, 1777.

762   THOMAS SHIPMAN
Business letter to Henry Remson, Jr., 1769.

763   WILLIAM SHIPPEN, JR.
Letter to Nathanael Greene countering accusations of mismanagement, 1780.

764   ISAAC SMITH
Essay entitled "Whether the Bank of North America, as now conducted, is a public Benefit?" 1785.

765   JOHN SMITH
Photostats of six family and business letters to his father, William Smith, 1780–89.

766   JONATHAN BAYARD SMITH
Certificate of appointment as prothonotary of the county of Philadelphia, 1778.

767   WILLIAM LOUGHTON SMITH
Letter on political matters to the "Electors of the Parish of St. Bartholomew" in South Carolina, 1788.

768   WILLIAM SMITHSON
Miscellaneous business papers and accounts, 1784–85.

769   SOCIETY OF THE CINCINNATI
Photostat of a document concerning the establishment of the society, 1783.

770   ALEXANDER SPOTSWOOD
Letter to the President of the Virginia Convention requesting command of a Continental regiment, 1775.

771   ADAM STEPHEN
Photostat of a letter to Angus McDonald asking him to accept a military commission, 1777.

772   FRIEDRICH WILHELM VON STEUBEN
Letter, in French, to Richard Peters, 1785, and a photostat of notes on the organization of the Army, 1782.

773   WALTER STEWART
Letter to Gen. Henry Jackson, concerning safety of people living in New York after the British evacuation, 1783.

774   ROBERT STOBO
Photostats of Stobo's military commission, 1760, a petition to the Earl of Hillsborough for land in America, 1769, and a document showing the distribution of 18 surveys to the Virginia regiment, 1772–73.

775   ISAAC STUART
Photostat of claims for losses in South Carolina during the war, 1784.

776   JAMES SULLIVAN
Two letters on political matters to Elbridge Gerry, 1776, 1789, and a letter to Judge Holten concerning Tory activities east of the Kennebec River.

777   JETHRO SUMNER
Photostat of letter concerning a meeting of the Society of the Cincinnati at Philadelphia, 1784, and typescript of a military letter, 1780.

778   ARCHIBALD SUNTHERLAND
Photostat of letter to Benedict Arnold relating to a flag of truce, 1780.

779   JOHN TAYLOR
Typescript of letter on military matters to William Woodford, 1778, and a document, 1784, certifying clothing purchases made by Taylor in 1776.

780   JEAN BAPTISTE DE TERMANT
Letter to Jacob Read acknowledging his promotion by brevet, 1783.

781   GEORGE THATCHER
Letter to William Taylor concerning impost bill being considered in Congress, 1789.

782   ISAAC THOMPSON
Account with James and Henry Drinker, 1771.

783   ROBERT THOMPSON
Account for grain purchases, 1780.

784   DAVID TILGHMAN
Deed for land in Somerset County, Md., 1783.

785   OLIVER TOWLES
Business letter to Edward Herndon, Jr., of Fredericksburg, Va., 1783.

786   DAVID TRUMBULL
Photostat of letter on military matters to Gov. Jonathan Trumbull, 1777.

787   JONATHAN TRUMBULL
Letter on military matters to Artemas Ward, 1775.

788   JOSEPH TRUMBULL
Letter to Jeremiah Wadsworth authorizing him to sign trade agreements in Trumbull's absence, 1776.

789   TUCKER
Letter relating general war news, 1781.

790   HENRY ST. GEORGE TUCKER
Personal and business letter, 1776.

791   SAMUEL TUCKER
Business letter to Elizabeth Lawrence, 1783.

792   UNITED STATES REVOLUTION
Chiefly letters on military matters and returns, 1777–83. Correspondents include John Van Woert, Richard Peters, David H. Conyngham, Robert Digby, and Walter Stewart.

793   RICHARD VARICK
Typescript of letter to Jane Varick describing Arnold's treason, 1780.

794   "VICTOIRE"
Photostat of port book of the *Victoire*, 1777. Includes information on some of the officers who sailed with Lafayette.

795   BARON DE VIOMÉNIL
Photostats and typescripts of three letters concerning French troops who served in America, 1782–83.

796   FRANCIS WADE
Letter to John Swanwick concerning payment for money lent to Congress for the Army during the Revolution, 1784.

797   BENJAMIN WALKER
Business letter to Steuben, 1785.

798   SAMUEL WARD
Photostats of two letters on personal and political matters to his brother Henry, 1775, and his daughter Kitty, 1773.

799   ANTHONY WAYNE
Typescripts of five letters on military, political, and personal matters to Benjamin Rush, Washington, and James Madison, 1779–89.

800   NOAH WEBSTER
Letter to the Speaker of the Delaware Assembly requesting passage of a copyright law, 1787.

801   ANN WELSH
Application, undated, for relief based on her deceased husband's service in the Revolution.

802   BENJAMIN WEST
Letter on political and personal matters to Charles Willson Peale, 1775.

803   ALEXANDER WHITE
Letter to James Wood on the ratification of the U.S. Constitution, 1788.

804   ANTHONY WALTON WHITE
Two letters on military matters from Charles Stewart and Edward Carrington, 1780, 1782.

805   GEORGE WHITESIDE
Legal papers and accounts between Maurico Griffith and various persons, 1770–76.

806   ELISHA WILDS
Seven personal and family letters written while serving in the Northern Army, on board the ship *Putnam*, and from a British prison, 1776–84. Includes war news.

807   JOHN WILKINS
Letter to George Morgan concerning military affairs in the Illinois country, 1768.

808   HUGH WILLIAMSON
Letter to Samuel Johnston of New York accepting the offer of a public office, 1789.

809   THOMAS WILLING
Letter to William Bingham on the ratification of the U.S. Constitution, 1788.

810   JAMES WILSON
Letter to George Gray involving a case between the State of Pennsylvania and Timothy Matlack, 1784.

811   JOHN WINTHROP
Photostat of letter concerning astronomical observations, 1769.

812   RALPH WORMELEY, JR.
Letter to John Robinson concerning slaves shipped from New York, 1782.

813   JOHN WORTHINGTON
Business letter, 1788.

814   WILLIAM YOUNG
Three letters to Lenard Dorsey concerning commerce and trade regulations, 1778–79.

JAMES MONROE PAPERS
45 vols., 1758–1839.   Part photostats. Microfilm available.   *NUCMC* 60–428
815   Monroe (1758–1831): Lt., 3d Virginia Continental Regiment, 1776–77; aide-de-camp to Lord Stirling, 1777–78; member, Continental Congress, 1783–86, and U.S. Senate, 1790–94; President of the U.S.
Volumes 1 (series one) and 38 (series two) contain over 100 documents from the period of the Revolution, chiefly letters to Monroe from Joseph Jones, Jefferson, William

Grayson, Edward Carrington, and Beverley Randolph, including a few letters written during the war. Letters Monroe received while he was in the Continental Congress and during the late Confederation period concern State and National politics, foreign affairs, and Monroe's personal and business affairs.

See the published *Index to the James Monroe Papers* (Washington, D.C., 1963), and S. M. Hamilton, ed., *The Writings of James Monroe*, 7 vols. (New York, 1898–1903). See also the James Monroe Ephemera (recent acquisitions) for three Monroe letters concerning political affairs, 1783–85.

GEORGE MORGAN PAPERS
1 vol., 1775–1822.

816   Morgan (1743–1810): Philadelphia merchant and speculator; U.S. Indian agent and deputy commissary of purchases, Fort Pitt, 1776–79.

Chiefly correspondence pertaining to Indian affairs on the western frontier and the supply of soldiers and citizens in the Fort Pitt area. Also includes a description of conditions in an early settlement on the Mississippi River below Natchez, 1775; two letters to the Spanish Governor of Louisiana, 1777–78; and two letters concerning Morgan's scientific activities and his election to the South Carolina Society for Promoting and Improving Agriculture, 1785, 1787. Four letters between Dr. John Morgan, brother of George, and Aaron Burr concern Burr's handling of Dr. Morgan's legal affairs in New York.

Principal correspondents: Board of War, committee of Congress on Indian affairs, Daniel Clark, William Drayton, Josiah Harmar, Patrick Henry, Thomas Hutchins, and Charles Thomson.

J. P. MORGAN COLLECTION: SIGNERS OF THE DECLARATION OF INDEPENDENCE
1 vol., 1761–1803.

817   An autograph collection containing miscellaneous letters and political, economic, military, legal, and social documents. Includes such items as a letter from Stephen Hopkins, 1769, describing the purpose of Rhode Island College; a Richard Henry Lee letter assessing the military and political situation, 1777; a Samuel Adams letter to Peyton Randolph explaining the Coercive Acts; a receipt bearing the signature of Button Gwinnett; and engraved portraits of the signers of the Declaration.

GOUVERNEUR MORRIS PAPERS
24 boxes, 1771–1834.   Finding aid available.

818   Morris (1752–1816): New York lawyer, politician; member, Continental Congress, 1778–79, and Constitutional Convention, 1787; U.S. commissioner to England, 1790–91; U.S. minister to France, 1792–94; member, U.S. Senate, 1800–1803.

Contains legal notes, a personal docket book, and material pertaining to the New York courts, 1771–75. Also includes Morris' bankbook for the Bank of North America, 1782–88, and ledgers and daybooks for Morrisania, 1788–92. A journal for the period Sept.—Nov. 1788 contains personal and Morrisania accounts.

ROBERT MORRIS PAPERS
18 vols., 4 boxes, 2 folios, 1775–1829.   Finding aid available.

819   Morris (1743–1806): Philadelphia, Pa., merchant; member, Continental Congress, 1776–78; superintendent of finance, 1781–84.

About two-thirds of the collection consists of Morris' official correspondence and papers as superintendent of finance. These include seven letterbooks, a three-volume "diary," and two volumes of Congressional proceedings pertaining to the Office of Finance, 1782–84. The diary, Feb. 1781–Sept. 1784, contains records of conferences and interviews with military and commercial leaders and public officials. Most correspondence to and from the superintendent concerns contracting for loans and supplies, and military pay. Also in the collection are letters concerning Morris' work on the secret committee of correspondence and his involvement in the controversial sale of cargo seized on the *Victorious*, as well as correspondence with various business associates and contractors whose dealings involved Morris in both a public and a private capacity.

Principal correspondents: John Barry, Samuel Bean, John Bradford, Thomas Burke, William Carmichael, Daniel Clarke, Silas Deane, John Deas, William Duer, John Eustace, Albert Gallatin, Conrad Alexandre Gérard, Elbridge Gerry, Benjamin Harrison, Benjamin Harrison, Jr., Jonathan Hudson, Samuel Inglis, John Jay, Daniel of St. Thomas Jenifer, John Paul Jones, Lafayette, Henry Laurens, Bernard Lavaud, Charles Lee, Thomas Morris, Jacques Necker, Edmund Pendleton, Richard Peters, Samuel Purviance, Joseph Reed, Matthew Ridley, Marquis de la Rouerie (Armand-Charles), Richard Rush, Thomas Russell, Comfort Sands, John Schweighauser, Haym Solomon, Stephen Steward, David Stewart, Stephen Stuart, Charles Thomson, Tench Tilghman, Thomas Wharton, Jr., Peter Whiteside, Jonathan Williams, and Jacob Winey, and the firms William Alexander & Co., Tench Francis & Co., Fizeau, Grand & Co., Hazelwood & Blackiston, Le Couteulx & Co., Jonathan Nesbitt & Co., Ridley & Pringle, David Ross & Co., William Turnbull & Co., and Wilhem Willink & Co.

See also Constable, Rucker & Co., entry no. 207, and Morris-Croxall Collection, entry no. 820.

Morris–Croxall Collection
1 box, 1767–1895.
820   Robert Morris: See entry no. 819.
Includes an "inventory" of the Morris Eden Park estate, 1781, and two letters of Gouverneur Morris, 1784 and 1809.

Morris–Popham Papers
4 boxes, 1669–1892.
821   Lewis Morris (1726–98): Morrisania, N.Y., gentleman farmer; gen., New York Militia; member Continental Congress, 1775–77. Richard Morris (1730–1810): Lawyer; judge, Vice-Admiralty Court, 1762–75; justice, New York Superior Court, 1799–90.
Chiefly miscellaneous deeds, leases, and plats for land in New York, New Jersey, and Virginia, but contains 16 letters of the Morris family concerning personal and business affairs. Includes Lewis Morris' chancery court records for 1767, and minor papers of Richard Morris when he was on the superior court.
Principal correspondents: George Clinton, John Jay, John Livingston, Henry B. Ludlow, Gouverneur Morris, Robert Morris, Robert H. Morris, Samuel Ogden, and Sarah Robinson.
See also Gouverneur Morris Papers, entry no. 818.

Anthony Mullins Papers
1 box, 1772–88.
822   Mullins: Virginia overseer; employed on Archibald Cary's Willis Creek plantation.
Correspondence concerning crops, livestock, and the care of slaves on the Willis Creek plantation. Includes a list of slaves, 1787, and records on the tobacco crop for the years 1782, 1783, and 1786.
Principal correspondents: Archibald Cary and Carter Page.

William Vans Murray Papers
2 boxes, 1 folio, 1784–1805.
823   Murray (1760–1803): Maryland lawyer; member, U.S. House of Representatives, 1791–97; diplomat.
Includes seven letters written while Murray was a student at the Middle Temple in London, including descriptions of places of interest in England and on the Continent and

comments on news from America, political affairs in England, and London styles and manners.

MUSIC MISCELLANY, AMERICAN HYMNBOOKS

824
Several hymnbooks in the collections of the Music Division contain manuscript music, lyrics, and miscellaneous entries from the period of the Revolution. See select copies of William Billings, *The Singing Master's Assistant*; . . . (Boston, 1778); Thomas Walter, *The Grounds and Rules of Musick Explained*: . . . (Boston, 1746), and other editions; and Nahum Tate and Nicholas Brady, *A New Version of the Psalms of David* (London, n.d.).

See also the "Manuscript Hymn-Tune Book," Music Division.

MUSTER ROLLS MISCELLANY
1 folio, 1777–83.

825
Includes original and contemporary copies of muster rolls for the following units: Capt. Thomas Massie's company, 6th Virginia Regiment; Maj. Henry Lee's "Partizan Corps"; Capt. John Rogers' Light Dragoons; 1st and 2d Virginia State Regiments; Capt. Isaac Warren's company, 2d Massachusetts Regiment; Virginia State Artillery; Col. Francis Taylor's Virginia Convention Guards; Col. Joseph Crockett's 5th Virginia Regiment. Also includes lists of officers and payrolls.

JOHN DE NEUFVILLE PAPERS
1 vol., 1 box, 1780–89.

826
Neufville: Amsterdam, Holland, merchant.

A letterbook, 1781–85, contains business correspondence with merchants in America. Loose correspondence includes letters between Neufville and John Lewis Gervais, Christopher Gadsden, and Alexander Gillon concerning business matters, particularly Neufville's accounts with the State of South Carolina. Miscellaneous items include an invoice of goods shipped to South Carolina, and an invoice for goods ordered for "the honorable Lady Adams, in Braintree. . . ."

Principal correspondents: Elias Boudinot, James Bowdoin, Thomas Cushing, Tristram Dalton, Barnabas Deane, William Lee, George Mason, Isaac Sears, and Samuel Smith.

NEW EBENEZER, GEORGIA, JERUSALEM LUTHERAN CHURCH RECORDS
1 box, 4 folios, 1 vol., 1754–1820.

827
Miscellaneous letters and documents. Includes letters, in German, between Rev. Henry Muhlenberg and Jacob Waldhauer, 1783–84; letters between members of the Jerusalem Church and friends in Augsburg, Germany, 1773–86; an account for the estate of Thomas Sweighoffer, 1773–79; extracts from church conference minutes, Nov. 1774; a church minute book, 1784–87; and a bound church register, 1756–1800.

NEW HAMPSHIRE, LIVIUS CONTROVERSY
1 vol., 1772–74.   Force transcripts.

828
Memorials, depositions, and letters pertaining to the Livius affair, in which Peter Livius, member of the New Hampshire Governor's Council and later chief justice of Quebec, accused Gov. John Wentworth of illegally granting crown lands and was removed by Wentworth from the council.

Principal correspondents: Theodore Atkinson and Lord Hillsborough.

Published in New Hampshire Historical Society, *Collections*, vol. 9 (1889), 304–63. Originals in New Hampshire Historical Society.

NEW HAMPSHIRE, MISCELLANY
3 boxes, 1652–1792.

829   Contains material concerning the conflict between New Hampshire and Vermont over the New Hampshire Grants, including proclamations, orders in council, assembly reports and resolves, and letters. Also includes documents pertaining to military preparations, taxation, price setting, instructions from the towns for voting on the Articles of Confederation, records of attendance at committee of safety meetings, and proceedings of the Federal Constitutional Convention.

Principal correspondents: Jacob Bayley, Benjamin Bellows, Thomas Chittenden, Cadwallader Colden, Enoch Poor, John Sullivan, William Tryon, Benning Wentworth, and John Wentworth.

NEW HAMPSHIRE, PROVINCIAL CONGRESS RECORDS
1 vol., May 25—Sept. 2, 1775.   Force transcripts.

830   A journal revealing the provincial congress' concern with the raising and provisioning of a military force for the defense of New Hampshire and for use in Massachusetts.

NEW HAMPSHIRE, RECORDS, ASSEMBLY
15 folios, 1716–90.   Force transcripts.

831   Journals of the assembly providing a detailed record of the legislative branch of government under royal and republican rule.

Journals for the years 1716–81 published in Nathaniel Bouton, ed., *Documents and Records Relating to the Province of New Hampshire*, vols. 3-8 (Concord, N. H., 1869–74); for the years 1781–90, published in Albert S. Batchellor, ed., *Early State Papers of New Hampshire*, vols. 20-21 (Manchester, N. H., 1891, Concord, N. H., 1892).

NEW HAMPSHIRE, RECORDS, COMMITTEE OF SAFETY
3 folios, 1775–84.   Force transcripts.

832   Committee orders, correspondence, petitions, warrants, and committee journal recording the events of the Revolution affecting New Hampshire residents: the appointment and maintenance of military units, frontier defense, the New Hampshire Grants, internal police power, and the control of vital supplies. Minutes provide information on committee actions, letters sent, and petitions and letters received for the years 1775–84.

Principal correspondents: Robert Fulton, William Gardner, Nathaniel Peabody, Enoch Poor, and John Stark.

Published in New Hampshire Historical Society, *Collections*, vol. 7 (1863), p. iii-xxviii, 1-340.

NEW HAMPSHIRE, RECORDS, COUNCIL
11 folios, 1777–88.   Force transcripts.

833   Letters to and from the council concerning the war in the Northern Department, particularly the Burgoyne invasion, Rhode Island campaign, and Indian raids. Letters of delegates to the Continental Congress discuss national issues. Also includes a 1778 list of American naval prisoners exchanged at Rhode Island, and postwar letters of members of the Confederation Congress.

Principal correspondents: Ephraim Blaine, Jonathan Blanchard, Nicholas Cooke, Nathaniel Folsom, Abiel Foster, Franklin, Horatio Gates, John T. Gilman, Nicholas Gilman, Enoch Hale, John Hancock, John Hanson, William Heath, Samuel Huntington, John Jay, John Paul Jones, John Langdon, Heny Laurens, Richard Lee, Samuel Livermore, Robert R. Livingston, Pierse Long, Thomas McKean, Robert Morris, Alexander Scammell, Philip Schuyler, John Stark, John Sullivan, Thomas Thompson, Charles Thomson, Jonathan Trumbull, Artemas Ward, Washington, Anthony Wayne, John Wentworth, William Whipple, and Paine Wingate.

Originals in New Hampshire State Archives.

NEW HAMPSHIRE, RECORDS, GOVERNOR
5 folios, 1697–1787.   Force transcripts.

834   Contains messages of the Governor to the legislature, petitions to the Governor, and instructions from Great Britain to the Governor for the period before the war, centering on the themes of opposition to crown officials and the New Hampshire Grants. Also includes summary accounts for military expenses, 1775–87.
Originals in New Hampshire State Archives.

NEW HAMPSHIRE, RECORDS, MISCELLANEOUS
4 folios, 1652–1792.   Force transcripts.

835   Resolves, memorials to, and correspondence of the New Hampshire Council, Assembly, and Governor pertain to the military aspects of the Revolution, land grants, the conflict over the New Hampshire Grants, and the Articles of Confederation. Also includes town instructions on the Articles of Confederation; records of the New Hampshire Federal Constitutional Convention; State treasury accounts, 1765; valuations in kind for taxes, 1765–66; and William Priest's testimony of Mar. 1765 on the slave revolt aboard the brigantine *Hope*, from New London, Conn., published in large part in Isaac Hammond, ed., *New Hampshire State Papers*, vols. 7-8 (Manchester, N. H., 1889, 1890).
Principal correspondents: Jacob Bayley, Benjamin Bellows, Elias Boudinot, Thomas Chittenden, Cadwallader Colden, Enoch Poor, Alexander Scammell, John Sullivan, Benning Wentworth, and John Wentworth.
Originals in New Hampshire State Archives.

NEW HAMPSHIRE COLLECTION
1 box, 1682–1936.

836   Contains the minutes of the Portsmouth town meeting, Apr. 20, 1775, a letter by the New Hampshire committee of safety, 1777, concerning recruitment and military stores, and a folio on the "State of Land Titles of Old Grantees Between 1767 and 1772," describing the action taken against 28 towns whose grants lapsed because of nonsettlement.

NEW HAMPSHIRE GRANTS COLLECTION
1 box, 1770–84.   Force transcripts.

837   Documents and correspondence concerning the controversy between New York, New Hampshire, and the inhabitants of the New Hampshire Grants over the jurisdiction of the present State of Vermont. Includes related papers of the Continental Congress, New Hampshire Assembly, Vermont Assembly, New York committee of safety, New Hampshire committee of safety, and Vermont committee of safety.
Principal correspondents: Ebenezer Allen, Ethan Allen, Ira Allen, Jacob Bayley, Benjamin Bellows, Thomas Chittenden, Joseph Fay, John T. Gilman, Enoch Hale, Woodbury Langdon, Samuel Livermore, Elisha Payne, John Sullivan, William Tryon, and Meshech Weare.
Originals at New Hampshire State House.

NEW JERSEY, LOYALIST MUSTER ROLLS
1 box, 1777–82.   Photostats.

838   Consists of muster rolls of 1st, 3d, 4th, 5th, and 6th Battalions of New Jersey Volunteers, 1777–81. Returns for the Nova Scotia Volunteers, Orange Rangers, and King's Rangers reveal the strength and distribution of loyalist forces in Nova Scotia, 1781. Also contains lists of provincial troops at Philadelphia, 1777, New York, 1778, and Charleston, S. C., 1781, and miscellaneous sick lists and petitions of prisoners.

NEW JERSEY, MISCELLANY
7 boxes, 5 vols., 1664–1890.

839   Contains New Jersey laws, 1776–81, regulating troop induction, behavior, pay, etc.,

and payrolls for the New Jersey Continental Line through May 1784. Also records and accounts of the East New Jersey proprietors, 1771–1843, including a list of certificates of mislocation of tenants, 1789–1842; letters of Robert Morris and George Weedon describing the trial and incarceration of Tories, 1777; and miscellaneous indentures, marriage licenses, and petitions from the Revolutionary era.

NEW JERSEY PAPERS
1 folio, 1776–81.   Force transcripts.

840   Contains letters concerning the formation of the Continental Line, the situation of Lake Champlain and Lake George, the defense of Philadelphia, the mutiny of the Pennsylvania and New Jersey Lines, and the need for supplies.

Principal correspondents: Philemon Dickinson, Frederick Frelinghuysen, Nathanael Greene, John Hancock, Arthur St. Clair, and Washington.

NEW JERSEY (EAST), RAMAPOCK PATENT
1 vol., 1787–91.

841   Records of Ramapock patent kept by Cornelius Haring, agent for the proprietors of East New Jersey, contain a tenant rent list, 1787; a list of 206 lots with names of holders, terms of rental, valuation, and other miscellaneous remarks, to 1787; and accounts of land sales at Ramapock, 1787–91.

NEW YORK, COMMITTEE OF OBSERVATION
1 vol., 1775–76.   Force manuscripts.

842   Minutes of the New York committee of observation, May 1, 1775—Jan. 16, 1776. Includes a list of members of the committee, a record of letters received. The minutes reflect the efforts of the committee to enforce restrictions on trade.

NEW YORK, FRANCIS NELSON COMMISSION
1 folio, 1781.

843   Commission of Francis Nelson, 1st lieutenant in John Freer's regiment, New York Militia, Nov. 6, 1781.

NEW YORK, MISCELLANY
2 boxes, 4 vols., 2 folios, 1625–1915.

844   Scattered items include a lawyer's commonplace book, 1752–1804, containing copies of laws, declarations, pleas, writ forms, the 1752 rules of the court, and New York Supreme Court decisions; half-pay claims for widows and orphans of Continental Army men, filed as part of the New York claims against the U.S., Oct. 1788; and accounts for the Genesee Company, 1787–94, providing information on land speculation and settlement in western New York. Military activities in New York are discussed in letters and reports to the assembly. Also includes an account of prize agents for the State of New York, 1777.

Principal correspondents: Alexander Colden, Cadwallader Colden, Isaac Ledyard, Alexander McDougall, and Henry Van Schaack.

NEW YORK, RECORDS, ASSOCIATION TO SUSTAIN THE CONTINENTAL CONGRESS
AND THE PROVINCIAL CONGRESS
1 folio, 1777.   Force transcripts.

845   Miscellaneous collection of resolves, letters, lists of associators and Tories, attendance records of convention delegates, petitions and reports on the New Hampshire Grants, supply inventories, and militia regulations.

Originals in Office of Secretary of State in Albany, N.Y. Calendared in *Calendar of Historical Manuscripts Relating to the War of the Revolution, in the Office of the Secretary of State, Albany, N.Y.*, 2 vols. (Albany, 1866).

NEW YORK, RECORDS, COMMITTEE ON CONSPIRACIES
2 folios, 1776–78.   Force transcripts.

846   Committee testimony includes material pertaining to hearings, trials, and investigations of suspected loyalists and spies. Also minutes of the "Proceedings of the Committee for Inquiring Into, Detecting, and Defeating all Conspiracies which may Be Formed in the State of New York Against the Liberties of America."
      Originals in New York Historical Society. Published in its *Collections*, vols. 57–58 (1924, 1925).

NEW YORK, RECORDS, CONVENTION AND COUNCIL OF SAFETY
11 folios, 1776–78.   Force transcripts.

847   Consists of minutes of meetings of New York committee of safety and convention, which later became the council of safety. Correspondence of the committee includes several unpublished letters from members of the Continental Congress concerning maintenance of the Army, civilian control, and British invasions. Also includes court-martial proceedings for New York officers, and records and resolves of the New York Assembly.
      Principal correspondents: John Barclay, George Clinton, Cadwallader Colden, James Duane, William Duer, John Hancock, William Heath, John Henry, Francis Lewis, Peter R. Livingston, Philip Livingston, Alexander McDougall, Gouverneur Morris, Israel Putnam, Philip Schuyler, and Washington.
      Extracts have been published in the *Journals of the Provincial Congress* . . . (Albany, 1848). Originals in State Department, Albany, N.Y.

NEW YORK, RECORDS, LETTERS
8 folios, 1776–79.   Force transcripts.

848   Military, political, economic, and social affairs are discussed in letters to the New York council of safety, including several unpublished letters of members of the Continental Congress. Some letters duplicate those in the minutes of the council of safety. Also contains returns for militia units, fort garrisons, and ranger companies and lists of loyalist troops and those suspected of having joined the British Army.
      Principal correspondents: Albany committee of safety, John Barclay, Egbert Benson, Elias Boudinot, George Clinton, Cadwallader Colden, Philip Cortlandt, James Duane, William Duer, William Floyd, Alexander Hamilton, John Hancock, John Henry, Francis Lewis, Henry B. Livingston, Philip Livingston, Robert Livingston, Robert R. Livingston, Alexander McDougall, Gouverneur Morris, Zephaniah Platt, Arthur St. Clair, Philip Schuyler, Melancton Smith, Jonathan Trumbull, Washington, and Marinus Willett.
      Originals in State Department, Albany, N.Y.

NEW YORK, RECORDS, MILITARY COMMITTEE AND MILITARY RETURNS
2 folios, 1775–78.   Force transcripts.

849   Troop rosters, officer lists, returns, supply inventories, and other records of the New York Militia. Also includes resolutions and instructions from the provincial congress and convention and its military committee, and lists of New York City retailers and taverns, 1776. The folios are indexed.
      Originals in State Department, Albany, N. Y. Calendared in *Calendar of Historical Manuscripts* (Albany, 1866).

NEW YORK, RECORDS, MISCELLANEOUS PAPERS AND PETITIONS
13 folios, 1775–78.   Force transcripts.

850   Consists of letters, resolves, court-martial records, reports of State and local councils of safety, and minutes of the meetings of the committee on government, 1776–77, appointed to write a new State constitution and secure its ratification. Topics include Vermont, the military situation, Tory plots, mining possibilities in the State, supplies, and officer and troop arrangements. Also includes accounts for prisoners of war, regulations for draft

and militia exemptions, prisoner lists, records of meetings to establish economic policy, and petitions to the council of safety, the Convention of New York, and the Continental Congress, 1776–77.

Principal correspondents: Jacob Bayley, George Clinton, Cadwallader Colden, William Ellsworth, William Floyd, Nathanael Greene, William Heath, John Henry, John Inglis, John Jay, Francis Lewis, Henry B. Livingston, John McDonald, Alexander McDougall, Gouverneur Morris, Richard Morris, Pliarne, Penet & Co., Comfort Sands, Jonathan Trumbull, Washington, Henry Wisner, and Robert Yates.

Originals in the State Department, Albany, N.Y. Calendared in *Calendar of Historical Manuscripts* (Albany, 1866).

NEW YORK, SUPERIOR COURT OF JUDICATURE, MINUTE BOOK
7 reels microfilm, 1704–76.

851   Contains a list of court cases, records of motions, evidence, decisions, and lists of judges and juries.

NEW YORK, VICE-ADMIRALTY COURT
4 boxes, 1715–74.   Photostats.

852   Records of the British Vice-Admiralty Court sitting at New York concerning court proceedings, problems of the shipping industry, insurance claims, and relations between the British and Colonial governments. The court entries contain charges of the judges, motions, and dispositions of cases.

Originals in U.S. Attorney's Office, New York, N.Y.

NEW YORK CITY, TAX LIST
1 reel microfilm, 1789.

853   Tax list for the East, South, North, West, Montgomery, and "out wards," and the Harlem division, showing names of proprietors and tenants, addresses, and assessments.

WILSON CARY NICHOLAS PAPERS
7 vols., 2 folios, 1765–1831.

854   Nicholas (1761–1820): Virginia lawyer and statesman; member, U.S. Senate, 1799–1804; gov., Virginia, 1814–17.

Includes business and legal correspondence with merchants at Glasgow and London concerning the collection of debts, 1765–74. Also responses to Nicholas' demands for payment by merchants in Virginia.

NORTH CAROLINA, CONVENTION
1 vol., 1788.   Force manuscripts.

855   Includes a typescript of a letter from John Swann to James Iredell concerning the fight over ratification of the U.S. Constitution in North Carolina, and a letter from Hugh Williamson and John Swann to Samuel Johnston, New York, July 1788, concerning the ratification controversy.

NORTH CAROLINA, MISCELLANY
3 boxes, 1668–1948.   Part photostats.

856   Includes letters and documents concerning military affairs in North Carolina, 1777–82, chiefly maneuvers, supplies, and recruits. Also a letter from David Ramsay to the Governor, Jan. 1786, concerning the attendance of North Carolina delegates in Congress; a 1787 letter from William Blount and Benjamin Hawkins to Gov. Richard Caswell concerning the tobacco market; and a typescript of an orderly book kept by an officer in the North Carolina Continental Line, 1777.

Principal correspondents: John Ashe, Thomas Burke, Arthur Campbell, William R.

Davie, John Donaldson, Horatio Gates, Nathanael Greene, Baron de Kalb, Alexander Lillington, Marquis de Malmady, Abner Nash, Griffith Rutherford, William Sharpe, Jethro Sumner, and John Williams.

NORTH CAROLINA PAPERS
1 vol., 1767–1874.   Draper Mss., series KK, WHi. 1 reel microfilm.

857   Contains papers of Waighstill Avery (1743–1821) and Silas McDowell (1793–1877), and miscellaneous documents. The Avery papers consist of both original documents and Draper transcripts, 1769–82, concerning frontier developments and Indian affairs during the war. Includes a 69-page manuscript journal, Jan. 1769—Jan. 1770, describing Avery's travels in North Carolina, where he settled after former residence in Connecticut and Maryland. The McDowell papers date from the 1870's and reflect Draper's efforts to collect information on the Cherokee campaign of 1776.
       See Thwaites, *Descriptive List of Manuscript Collections*, p. 50-51.

NORTHWEST TERRITORY COLLECTION
1 box, 1 folio, 1773–1872.

858   Contains a few items pertaining to early settlement of the Northwest Territory, including lists of 22 proprietors of the Illinois Land Company, 1773, and 20 proprietors of the Wabash Land Company, 1775; the commission of Thomas Lord as justice of the peace for Washington County, Northwest Territory, 1788; and a letter of instruction to a riverboat captain named Andross, 1787.

WILLIAM A. OLDRIDGE COLLECTION
9 vols., 1 box, 1 folio, 1775–83.   Transcripts and photostats.

859   Oldridge: Collector.
       Typescripts of "Official writings of Washington's Headquarters Staff" and photostats of letters of Joseph Reed, Alexander Hamilton, Tench Tilghman, Caleb Gibbs, John Laurens, James McHenry, John Beatty, Alexander Scammell, Robert H. Harrison, Richard Kidder Meade, Stephen Moylan, William DeHart, David Humphreys, and Edward Hand.

FREDERICK LAW OLMSTED PAPERS
50 boxes, 1777–1928.   Finding aid available.   *NUCMC* 62–4663

860   Olmsted (1822–1903): Architectural engineer; author.
       Contains a journal, Dec. 19, 1777—Dec. 18, 1778, written by Gideon Olmsted, a merchant seaman, describing adventures leading up to his seizure of the British sloop *Active*. Purchased by Gen. Benedict Arnold, Olmsted's claim on the *Active* provided the basis for an early legal case involving a conflict between State and Federal authority. Also includes printed documents relating to the Olmsted case, 1778 and forward, and several letters of Charles Moore, a Philadelphia doctor, concerning Pennsylvania politics, efforts to organize a silk culture business, and the first Continental Congress.

Orderly Books: American

EBENEZER ADAMS: Attached to Col. John Durkee's 20th Continental Infantry, Connecticut.
1 vol., July 15—Oct. 12, 1776.

861   General and regimental orders: New York, Harlem, and White Plains, N.Y., Paulus Hook, N. J. Includes miscellaneous private accounts kept during and after the war.

NICHOLAS ALGER: Sgt., Col. John Topham's Rhode Island State Regiment.
1 vol., May 10—Nov. 26, 1779.

862   General orders: Newport, Providence, and Tiverton, R. I. Includes weekly returns and miscellaneous accounts.

CALEB BOYNTON, JR.: Pvt., Capt. Thomas Williams' company, Massachusetts Militia, 1775; Capt. David Batcheller's company, 1778.
2 vols., Sept. 5—Nov. 12, 1775; July 16—Aug. 17, 1778.

863   General, brigade, and regimental orders: Cambridge and White Plains, N. Y. Includes a return of Col. Ezra Woods' regiment, July 1778, and a reference to the erection of a stone monument at White Plains.

JAMES BRIGGS: Capt., Col. John Bailey's regiment, Massachusetts Militia.
1 vol., Dec. 14, 1775—Jan. 13, 1776.

864   General and regimental orders: Roxbury, Mass. Includes a return of Briggs' company by towns represented, Dec. 1775.

JOHN BROWN: Capt., 1st North Carolina Continental Regiment.
1 vol., May 21, 1777—Jan. 3, 1778.

865   General and regimental orders: Issued on march between North Carolina and New Jersey. Includes military accounts, medical remedies, and postwar court records for Bladen County, N. C.

ROBERT BROWN: Capt., Col. William Douglas' Connecticut State Regiment.
1 vol., Aug. 16—Sept. 14, 1776.

866   Division, brigade, and regimental orders: New York. Includes receipts for wages and supplies.

RICHARD BUCKMASTER: Lt., adjutant, 6th Massachusetts Continental Regiment.
1 vol., Aug. 7, 1778—Feb. 1, 1779.

867   General, brigade, and regimental orders: Connecticut and New York.

JOHN BURNHAM: Capt., 8th Massachusetts Continental Regiment.
1 vol., Jan. 15—Feb. 25, 1777.

868   General and brigade orders: Tarrytown, N. Y., to Morristown, N. J., encampment. Includes Gen. Benjamin Lincoln's standing orders for his division.

SHEREBIAH BUTTS: Capt., Col. John Douglas' regiment, Connecticut Militia.
1 vol., Sept. 19—Nov. 8, 1776.

869   General, division, and regimental orders: Harlem Heights, Westchester, White Plains, and North Castle, N. Y. Includes a list of captains in the regiment.

CALEB CLAP: Lt., adjutant, 9th Massachusetts Continental Regiment.
1 vol., Sept. 24, 1778—July 9, 1779.

870   General, brigade, and regimental orders: Danbury and Hartford, Conn.; Middlebrook, N. J.; Peekskill, Fishkill, West Point, and New Windsor, N. Y. Includes returns for the 8th Massachusetts, Oct. 1778 and Apr. 1779.

LEMUEL CLIFT: Capt., 1st Connecticut Continental Regiment.
1 vol., May 10—Sept. 20, 1782.   Force manuscripts.

871   Division, brigade, and regimental orders: Newburgh, N. Y., and vicinity.

JAMES CLINTON: Brig. gen., Continental Army.
1 vol., May 4—Aug. 23, 1779.

872   Chiefly orders issued by Clinton during the expedition against the Iroquois, 1779: Albany and the western frontier of New York. Kept by Clinton's brigade major, Leonard Bleeker. Includes an organizational plan for the inspector general's office, Feb. 1779.

THOMAS COLE: Sgt., Col. Jacob Gerrish's regiment of guards, Massachusetts Militia.
1 vol., July 1—Oct. 1, 1778.

873   General and regimental orders: Boston. Includes a copy of a return of American prisoners captured in the 1776 campaign, a return of German prisoners drawing provisions at Winter Hill, a return of British prisoners at Prospect Hill, and miscellaneous poems and songs.

JOHN SINGER DEXTER: Maj., assistant to the adjutant general.
2 vols., Apr. 22—Aug. 2, 1781; Nov. 26, 1782—Jan. 17, 1783.   Force manuscripts.

874   General orders: New Windsor, Peekskill, Dobbs' Ferry, Tarrytown, Phillipsburg, and Newburgh, N. Y., and vicinity. Includes a copy of a letter (translated) from La Luzerne to Washington, Jan. 1783.

PETER DOLSON: Sgt., 3d New York Continental Regiment.
1 vol., July 29—Sept. 12, 1776.

875   General, brigade, and regimental orders: New York and vicinity. Includes a return for the company of Capt. Daniel Denton, July 1776.

WILLIAM DOUGLAS: Col., Connecticut State Regiment.
1 vol., July 10—Dec. 13, 1776.   Force manuscripts.

876   Brigade and regimental orders: New York, Harlem Heights, and White Plains, N. Y. Includes a return of Douglas' regiments by companies. The second half of Andrew Ward's orderly book.

JONATHAN EDDY: Col., Massachusetts Militia.
1 vol., Aug. 1—25, 1777.

877   Regimental orders: Machias, Maine. Includes a list of officers in the regiment, returns of provisions for McCobb's and Eddy's regiments, Aug. 18—25, 1777, and miscellaneous accounts and notes.

JOHN FENNO: Secretary to Gen. Artemas Ward, Massachusetts Militia.
1 vol., Apr. 20—Sept. 6, 1775.

878   General and division orders: Cambridge, Mass.
Original in Massachusetts Historical Society.

NATHAN GALLUP: Lt. col., Connecticut Militia.
1 vol., July 16—Aug. 22, 1779.   Force transcripts.

879   General and regimental orders: New London and Groton, Conn.

HORATIO GATES: Maj. gen., Continental Army.
1 vol., July 20—Nov. 18, 1776.   Force transcripts.

880   General orders: Ticonderoga, Lake Champlain, and vicinity. Includes some returns.
See also Horatio Gates Papers, entry no. 286.

GERMAN REGIMENT: Pennsylvania.
2 pages.   Photostats.

881   Washington's orders for the organization of the Army at the start of the Princeton campaign, Dec. 30, 1776.
Original in Historical Society of Pennsylvania.

JOHN GLOVER: Brig. gen., Continental Army.
1 vol., Aug. 24, 1777—Jan. 18, 1778.

882   General, brigade, and regimental orders: Stillwater, Albany, and Saratoga, N. Y., White Marsh and Valley Forge, Pa.

JAMES GREGG: Capt., 3d New York Continental Regiment.
1 vol., Apr. 24—Oct. 14, 1779.

883   General and regimental orders: Middlebrook, N. J., Albany, Lake Oswego, and Fort Sullivan, N. Y. Includes returns of supplies and munitions and a list of deserters.

THOMAS GROSVENOR: Lt., Connecticut Militia.
1 vol., July 3—Dec. 30, 1775.   Force transcripts.

884   General, brigade, and regimental orders: Cambridge, Mass.

MOSES HAZEN: Col., 2d Canadian Regiment, Continental.
1 vol., Jan. 1—Apr. 27, 1780.   Force manuscripts.

885   General, division, and regimental orders: Morristown, N.J., and vicinity.

WILLIAM HEATH: Brig. and maj. gen., Continental Army.
1 vol., Mar. 31—Aug. 13, 1776.

886   General and brigade orders: New York. Includes a list of officers in the 3d and 7th Continental Infantry, Massachusetts, and numerous pay warrants.

ROBERT HOWE: Brig. and maj. gen., Continental Army.
1 vol., June 15, 1776—July 14, 1778.   Microfilm.

887   General, brigade, and regimental orders: Charleston, S. C., Savannah, Ga., East Florida, and various locations in the Southern Department.
Original owned by Justin G. Turner.

ADAM HUBLEY: Capt., 1st Pennsylvania Battalion.
1 vol., May 11—June 10, 1776.   Force manuscripts.

888   General orders: Fort Chambly and Sorel River, Canada. Entries are in irregular order.

EBENEZER HUNTINGTON: Maj., lt. col., Col. Samuel Webb's regiment, 1777–80; 3d Connecticut, 1781–83; 1st Connecticut, 1783.
1 folio, Sept. 7, 1778—Oct. 8, 1783.   Force transcripts.

889   Regimental orders: Tiverton, R. I., Warren, Conn., West Point and vicinity. Includes the arrangement of the Connecticut Continental Line, Nov. 1782.

JOHN HYATT: Capt., 3d regiment, New York Militia.
1 vol., May 14—June 24, 1776.

890   General, brigade, and regimental orders: New York.

OBADIAH JOHNSON: Maj., 3d Connecticut Continental Regiment.
5 pages, July 22–23; Sept. 22, 1775.   Force transcripts.

891   General orders: Cambridge, Mass.

OBADIAH JOHNSON: Lt. col., Col. Andrew Ward's Connecticut State Regiment.
23 pages, Nov. 3–27, 1776; Feb. 9—Mar. 18, 1777.   Force transcripts.
892   General, division, and regimental orders: New York and New Jersey.

ROBERT KIRKWOOD: 1st lt., capt., Delaware Regiment.
1 vol., Mar. 1—Dec. 21, 1777.
893   General and regimental orders: New Jersey and New York. Includes miscellaneous returns and lists of officers. Also includes Capt. Kirkwood's military journal, Apr. 13—May 11, 1780; Jan. 17—Apr. 17, 1782.
        Printed in the *Papers of the Historical Society of Delaware*, vol. 26 (1910). Reissued in 1970 by the Kennikat Press, Port Washington, N. Y.

CHARLES LEE: Maj. gen., Continental Army.
1 vol., Jan. 26—Nov. 17, 1775; Mar. 30—Aug. 6, 1776; Oct. 12—Nov. 17, 1776.
894   General, division, and regimental orders: New York and vicinity, Williamsburg, Va., Charleston, S. C., Elizabethtown, N. J., and North Castle, N. Y.

JOHN LINING: Capt., South Carolina Militia.
1 vol., Apr. 2–30, 1776.
895   General and regimental orders: Charleston, S. C. Includes accounts of provisions seized by Capt. Lining, returns, and lists of soldiers and officers in several South Carolina militia companies.

ROBERT McCREADY: Sgt., adjutant, Col. Jonathan Stephenson's regiment, Pennsylvania Militia.
2 vols., Oct. 17—Dec. 8, 1778.
896   Brigade orders: Fort McIntosh, Pa. Includes a return of troops at Fort McIntosh, Oct. 1778.

JAMES McLEAN: Adjutant, 10th Pennsylvania Continental Regiment.
1 vol., July 24—Aug. 23, 1780.
897   General, division, brigade, and regimental orders: Preakness and Totowa, N. J., Orangetown and Peekskill, N. Y., and vicinity.

JAMES MAYSON: Lt. col., unit unknown.
1 vol., June 23, 1778—May 1, 1779.
898   General and regimental orders: Charleston, Orangeburg, and Prysburg, S. C. Includes a muster roll for Capt. Richard Brown's company, 1778, and Capt. George Lidell's company, 1779.

JAMES MILLER: Lt., 1st Rhode Island State Regiment.
1 vol., Mar. 17, 1779—Mar. 1, 1780.
899   Regimental orders: Providence, Tiverton, Newport, R. I., and vicinity.

RICHARD MONTGOMERY: Brig. and maj. gen., Continental Army.
1 vol., June 5—Oct. 6, 1775.   Force manuscripts.
900   Orders issued by Gen. Philip Schuyler during the early part of the Canadian expedition. Kept by Jonas Prentice, adjutant, and John McPherson, aide-de-camp.

BENJAMIN MOOERS: Lt., adjutant, 2d Canadian Regiment.
1 vol., Sept. 16—Nov. 19, 1780.
901   General, division, brigade, and regimental orders: Orangetown, West Point, Tappan, N. Y., and vicinity.

DANIEL MORGAN: Col., 11th Virginia Continental Regiment.
1 vol., May 15—July 1, 1777.   Force transcripts.
902   General, division, brigade, and regimental orders: Middlebrook, N. J.

PETER MUHLENBERG: Maj. gen., Continental Army.
1 vol., Oct. 25, 1780—Apr. 18, 1781.
903   General orders: Virginia campaign.

CHRISTIAN MYERS: Capt., German regiment of Pennsylvania.
1 vol., June 1779—Mar. 1780.
904   General and brigade orders: Pennsylvania and New York. Also garrison orders: Fort Sullivan. Provides a record of activities in the American camp during Sullivan's expedition against the Iroquois and movements of Sullivan's division immediately following the battle of Monmouth. Includes accounts, sketches, charts, orders of march and battle, intelligence, and memoranda. Entries are in irregular order, separated by selections of political, romantic, and sentimental poetry.

JEREMIAH NILES: Adjutant, Col. Richard Gridley's artillery regiment, 1775; Col. Henry Knox's artillery regiment, 1775–76.
2 vols., Aug. 10—Nov. 15, 1775; Nov. 18, 1775—Jan. 5, 1776.
905   General and regimental orders: Cambridge, Mass.

ORDERLY BOOK: 6th Connecticut Regiment.
1 vol., June 3—Aug. 25, 1775.
906   General and division orders: Roxbury, Mass.

ORDERLY BOOK: Col. Adam Stephen, 4th and 5th Virginia Regiments.
1 vol., May 13—Sept. 20, 1776.   Force manuscripts.
907   General and regimental orders: Norfolk, Va., and vicinity.

ORDERLY BOOK
1 vol., May 19—Aug. 5, 1776.   Force transcripts.
908   General orders: New York.

ORDERLY BOOK
1 vol., Aug. 30—Oct. 4, 1776.   Force transcripts.
909   General orders: New York City.

ORDERLY BOOK
1 vol., Aug. 30—Oct. 4, 1776.   Force transcripts.
910   General orders: New York City and vicinity.

ORDERLY BOOK
1 vol., Sept. 8–21, 1776.   Force manuscripts.
911   General orders: Harlem Heights, N. Y.

ORDERLY BOOK: Pennsylvania Militia.
1 vol., June 18—July 20, 1777.   Force manuscripts.
912   General orders: Coryell's Ferry and Chester, Pa. Includes a list of detachments en route to join the Army under Washington.

ORDERLY BOOK
1 vol., Jan. 1—Apr. 23, 1778.   Force transcripts.
913   General orders: Valley Forge, Pa.

ORDERLY BOOK
1 vol., Aug. 15—Dec. 24, 1779.   Force manuscripts.
914   General, brigade, and regimental orders: Morristown, N. J., and New York highlands. Appears to have belonged to Col. Otho H. Williams' 6th Maryland Continental Regiment.

ORDERLY BOOK
1 vol., Sept. 18—Oct. 14, 1779.
915   General orders: Seige of Savannah. Includes a plan of attack and retreat and scattered returns.

ORDERLY BOOK: 6th Maryland Regiment.
1 vol., Apr. 4—Aug. 11, 1780.
916   General, division, brigade, and regimental orders: Morristown and Trenton, N. J., and march through Virginia and North Carolina.

ORDERLY BOOK: 4th Pennsylvania Continental Regiment.
1 vol., Apr. 7—June 6, 1780.   Force manuscripts.
917   General, division, brigade, and regimental orders: Morristown, N. J. Includes miscellaneous returns of clothing and supplies.

ORDERLY BOOK: 2d (4th?) New York Continental Regiment.
1 vol., July 8—Oct. 12, 1780.   Force manuscripts.
918   General, brigade, and regimental orders: New York highlands.

ORDERLY BOOK
7 pages, Sept. 24—Oct. 1, 1781.   Photostat.
919   General orders: Orangetown, N. Y.

SAMUEL H. PARSONS: Brig. and maj. gen., Continental Army.
2 vols., Apr. 18—July 16, 1778; July 31—Sept. 15, 1778.   Force transcripts.
920   General and division orders: Fort Arnold, White Plains, N. Y., and vicinity.

JOHN PATTERSON: Col., Massachusetts Militia.
1 vol., July 19—Sept. 22, 1775.
921   General, division, and regimental orders: Cambridge, Mass.

NATHANIEL PENDLETON: Aide-de-camp to Maj. Gen. Nathanael Greene.
1 vol., July 28, 1781—Jan. 1, 1782.
922   General orders: southern campaign.

JOHN PIPER: Adjutant, Virginia Militia.
1 vol., Mar. 4—Apr. 1, 1781.
923   General orders: Fredericksburg, Williamsburg, Va., and vicinity. Chiefly orders issued by Gen. George Weedon during the Virginia campaign.

WILLIAM REED: Capt., Col. John Thomas' regiment, Massachusetts Militia.
1 vol., May 12—Aug. 25, 1775.

924   General, brigade, and regimental orders: Roxbury, Mass. Includes periodic returns and lists of officers in Reed's company.

ENOS REEVES: Quartermaster, adjutant, 10th Pennsylvania Continental Regiment.
3 vols., July 7–20, 1780; Aug. 25—Oct. 10, 1780; Oct. 14—Nov. 23, 1780.

925   General, division, brigade, and regimental orders: Preakness, Totowa, Passaic Falls, N. J., Haverstraw, N. Y.

JAMES ROBERTS: Lt. col., Col. Edward Wiggleworth's regiment, Massachusetts Militia.
1 vol., July 30—Nov. 24, 1776.

926   General, brigade, and regimental orders: Charleston, N. Y., and Ticonderoga and vicinity. Includes regimental accounts and returns.

PHILIP SCHUYLER: Maj. gen., Continental Army.
1 vol., Sept. 22, 1775—Oct. 6, 1776.

927   General, division, brigade, and regimental orders: Albany, Ticonderoga, Fort George, Tarrytown, and Kingsbridge, N. Y. Entries are irregular.

ABRAHAM SCRANTON: Capt., sgt., Capt. Josiah Baldwin's company, Connecticut Militia.
16 pages, Sept. 8–20, 1778.

928   General and brigade orders: Providence, R. I.

WILLIAM SHEPARD: Col., 4th Massachusetts Continental Regiment.
1 vol., Sept. 1, 1779—Jan. 16, 1780.   Transcript.

929   General, brigade, and regimental orders: Salem, Mass., West Point, N. Y., and vicinity. The first half of Ebenezer Sprout's orderly book.

PETER SIMMONS: Col., South Carolina Militia.
1 vol., June 13—Aug. 1, 1776.

930   General and regimental orders: Charleston, S. C. Includes miscellaneous personal accounts, 1781–82.

WILLIAM SMALLWOOD: Brig. and maj. gen., Continental Army.
1 vol., July 3—Oct. 2, 1780.   Force manuscripts.

931   General, division, and brigade orders: Chatham County, N. C. Orders issued by Generals Baron de Kalb and Horatio Gates. Includes a return on the arrangement of Maryland and Delaware troops, July 1780.

JOHN SMITH: Lt., Capt. Robert Walker's company, 2d Artillery Regiment, New York.
1 vol., Oct. 18—Nov. 9, 1780.

932   Division, brigade, and regimental orders: New Jersey highlands. Includes a return of Walker's company, Oct. 1780, and a return of horses and gear, Nov. 1780.

JOSEPH SPENCER: Maj. gen., Continental Army.
1 vol., Oct. 19–27, 1777.

933   General and brigade orders: Tiverton, R. I. Includes returns of troops and equipment and copies of letters from Brig. Gen. Joseph Palmer to Spencer, Brig. Gen. John Nixon, and Jeremiah Powell.

EBENEZER SPROUT: Lt. col., 12th Massachusetts Continental Regiment.
1 vol., Jan. 17—Feb. 13, 1780.   Transcript.

934   General, brigade, and regimental orders: New York highlands. The second half of William Shepard's orderly book.

THOMAS THOMAS: Col., New York Militia.
1vol., Aug. 17—Oct. 5, 1776.

935   General, brigade, and regimental orders: Kingsbridge, N. Y. Includes several returns on troops under Thomas' command.

WILLIAM TORREY: Adjutant, 2d Massachusetts Regiment.
24 vols., Sept. 6, 1777—May 31, 1783.

936   General, division, brigade, and regimental orders: Danbury and Hartford, Conn., Middlebrook, N. J., Saratoga, White Plains, West Point, and New Windsor, N. Y. Includes lists of officers and returns for the 2d Massachusetts.

FRANCIS TUFTS: Lt., adjutant, 8th Massachusetts Regiment.
1 vol., Jan. 10—Apr. 8, 1782.

937   General, brigade, and regimental orders: New York highlands.

ROBERT WALKER: Capt., 2d Artillery Regiment, New York.
2 vols., July 12, 1777—June 4, 1778; Sept. 13—Nov. 24, 1778.

938   General, division, brigade, regimental, and company orders: Peekskill, Fredericksburg, and Fort Arnold, N. Y. Includes several weekly returns for Walker's company, 1777 and the arrangement of officers in the 2d Artillery Regiment, 1778.

WILLIAM WALKER: Adjutant, Col. John Paterson's regiment, Massachusetts Militia.
1 vol., July 8—Oct. 9, 1775.

939   General and division orders: Charlestown, Mass.

WILLIAM WALTON: Sgt., Capt. John Henderson's company, New Jersey Militia.
1 vol., July 10–18, 1776.

940   General orders: Long Island, N. Y. Includes miscellaneous personal accounts.

ANDREW WARD: Lt. col., Connecticut Militia.
1 vol., Feb. 22—Mar. 23, 1776.   Force manuscripts.

941   General and regimental orders: New York City, Turtle Bay, Harlem Heights, White Plains, North Castle, and Phillipsburg, N. Y. Includes lists of officers in the Connecticut Militia and general and regimental returns. Second half of this volume contains the orderly book of William Douglas.

ARTEMAS WARD: Maj. gen., Continental Army.
1 vol., June 7—Aug. 1, 1775.   Force transcripts.

942   General, division, and regimental orders: Roxbury and Cambridge, Mass.
See also Artemas Ward Papers, entry no. 1111.

DANIEL WARNER: Capt., Col. Jonathan Holman's regiment, Massachusetts Militia.
1 vol., July 30—Oct. 16, 1776.

943   General, brigade, and regimental orders: New York City and vicinity. Includes company and regimental returns and miscellaneous personal accounts.

WASHINGTON'S ORDERS
2 pages, Nov. 1, 1780.   Force transcripts.
944   Concerns the new organization of the Continental Army.

DAVID WATERBURY: Col., 5th Connecticut Regiment; brig. gen., Connecticut State Line.
1 vol., June 6–22, 1775; Sept. 25—Oct. 7, 1775; May 26—July 26, 1781.   Transcript.
945   General, brigade, and regimental orders: march from Stamford, Conn., to St. Johns, Canada, Connecticut coast, White Plains, N.Y., and vicinity. Includes a return of the 5th Connecticut, Sept. 1775.

FREDERICK WEISSENFELS: Brigade maj., 5th Connecticut Regiment.
1 vol., Nov. 8, 1775—Feb. 26, 1776.
946   Brigade and regimental orders: siege of Quebec.

JAMES WILSON: Capt., 1st Pennsylvania Continental Regiment.
1 vol., Aug. 14—Sept. 23, 1780.
947   General, brigade, and regimental orders: Orangetown, N. J., and vicinity.

NATHANIEL YOUNG: 2d lt., 1st New York Continental Regiment.
1 vol., Feb. 23—May 28, 1780.   Microfilm available.
948   General, brigade, and regimental orders: West Point and vicinity.

Orderly Books: British

FREDERICK BAUM: Lt. col., Hessian troops.
1 vol., May 29—June 28, 1777.
949   General orders: Issued by Gen. John Burgoyne during march from Montreal to Crown Point.

BEAMSLEY GLAZIER: Capt., 2d Battalion, 60th Regiment.
1 vol., Nov. 4, 1771—Mar. 13, 1773.   Force manuscripts.
950   General and regimental orders: Niagara, La Prairie, and New York, N.Y., Antigua and Chatteau Bellair, West Indies.

JOHN HATFIELD: Capt., 43d Regiment.
1 vol., Feb. 7—Mar. 14, 1776.   Force manuscripts.
951   General and battalion orders: Boston.

ORDERLY BOOK
4 pages, Sept. 11, 1777.
952   Orders of march issued by Lord Cornwallis on the approach to Brandywine.

ORDERLY BOOK
1 vol., July 2—Oct. 2, 1779.
953   General orders: siege of Savannah. Also includes a list of provincial promotions and a list of sick soldiers to be returned to New York.

ORDERLY BOOK
2 vols., May 23—Oct. 22, 1781.
954   General and brigade orders: Virginia and Yorktown campaigns.

THOMAS PAINE PAPERS
1 vol., 1774–1801.

955   Paine: Truro and Ipswich, Mass., physician.

Four letters from Dr. Samuel Adams of Ipswich, Mass., reveal his attitude toward Tories, 1774–83. A letter of Mar. 5, 1783, contains comments on prospects for peace.

PALMER–LOPER PAPERS
11 boxes, 2 vols., 1767–1900.   *NUCMC* 64–1578

956   Nathaniel B. Palmer (1799–1877); Alexander S. Palmer (1806–90); Richard F. Loper (1800–81).

Includes a logbook from the *Yarmouth* kept by Peleg Brown on a voyage between Rhode Island and the West Indies, Dec. 1767—July 1768. Entries are routine, giving course, location, weather, cargo, and ships sighted.

MOSES PARSONS FAMILY PAPERS
1 box, 1783–1899.

957   Parsons (d. 1783): Byfield, Mass., Congregational minister.

Items from the Revolutionary era include six undated sermons on obedience and a few personal letters.

Principal correspondent: Judith Parsons.

SAMUEL H. PARSONS PAPERS
1 box, 1769–1871.

958   Parsons (1737–89): Col., Connecticut Militia, 1775–76; brig. and maj. gen., Continental Army, 1776–82; Indian commissioner, Northwest Territory, 1785; promoter and director of the Ohio Company, 1787–89.

Chiefly correspondence concerning land speculation in the Ohio Valley, 1785–89. Includes a 1778 letter from Parsons to loyalist William Walter regarding possibilities for peace and an Israel Putnam letter on the disposition of troops in New York.

Principal correspondents: Benjamin Huntington and Jonathan Parsons.

WILLIAM PATERSON PAPERS
1 box, 1760–1806.   Part photostats.   *NUCMC* 71–1394

959   Paterson (1745–1806): New Jersey lawyer and political leader; attorney general, 1776–83; member, Constitutional Convention, 1787, U.S. Senate, 1789–90; gov., 1790–93; justice, U.S. Supreme Court, 1793–1806.

Pertinent material includes several literary exercises and essays Paterson wrote as a young man, probably while a student at Princeton; two essays from his adult years; and letters from Paterson to Cornelia Bell, 1777–82, whom he married in 1779. Also several miscellaneous manuscripts bearing on Paterson's legal practice, 1772–86; personal and business correspondence, 1782, 1806; and notes of debates and resolutions from the Federal Constitutional Convention, 1787.

Documents relating to the Constitutional Convention are published in *The American Historical Review*, vol. 9 (Jan., 1904), p. 310–40. See also Max Farrand, ed., *The Records of the Federal Convention of 1787* (New Haven, Conn., 1911), vol. 1, p. 242–45; vol. 3, p. 611–16.

ROBERT PATTERSON PAPERS
3 vols., 1758–1812.   Draper Mss., series MM, WHi. Microfilm, 1 reel.
960   Patterson (1753–1827): Pennsylvania and Kentucky pioneer settler, soldier, and public official.
Contains original papers concerning land claims, the early settlement of Lexington, 1779, the defense of the frontier, and the exchange of white and Indian prisoners. Also includes survey books, muster rolls, 1780–89, and personal and family correspondence.
Principal correspondents: Mathias Dinman, William Finney, Christopher Greenup, James Henry, John May, Elizabeth Patterson, William Russell, and Levi Todd.
See Thwaites, *Descriptive List of Manuscript Collections*, p. 51–53.

THOMAS PENN LETTERS
1 vol., 1748–70.   Force transcripts.
961   Penn (1702–75): Pennsylvania proprietor.
Letters from Penn in London to James Hamilton, Lieutenant Governor, council president, and Acting Governor of Pennsylvania, Feb. 1748—Mar. 1770. A few letters dated after 1763 contain information on Penn's reaction to news of conditions on the Pennsylvania frontier and relations with the Indians, of efforts to tax proprietary lands, and of measures under consideration in Parliament affecting the American Colonies.

PENNSYLVANIA, CONTINENTAL LOAN OFFICE RECEIPT BOOKS
1 vol., 1786–91.   Force manuscripts.
962   Three receipt books, bound into a single volume, belonging to Thomas Smith, Continental loan officer in the State of Pennsylvania. Contain signatures of holders of loan office certificates, a record of the value of securities owned, and interest payments received by each holder.

PENNSYLVANIA, MISCELLANY
1 vol., 4 boxes, 2 folios, 1680–1887.
963   Documents from the period of the Revolution, chiefly letters, deeds, petitions, commissions, etc., concern the Virginia–Pennsylvania boundary and Indian affairs on the western frontiers of both provinces. Also includes designs of a proposed new exchange, coffeehouse, and tavern for the Philadelphia dock area and accounts of Col. Thomas Proctor's 4th Pennsylvania Artillery Regiment, 1776–81. Individual items relate to George Bryan, Richard Butler, James Chrystie, George Croghan, Lord Hillsborough, John Hubley, Robert Milligan, Robert Morris, Lewis Nicola, Timothy Pickering, Joseph Reed, and Arthur St. Clair.

PENNSYLVANIA, RECORDS OF THE COURT OF QUARTER SESSIONS OF LANCASTER COUNTY
3 reels microfilm, 1729–1801.
964   Transcripts of an original court docket. Includes lists of constables and jurors, indictments, petitions, and court decisions. Also material concerning indentured servants, road construction, and the licensing of attorneys.

PENNSYLVANIA, VICE-ADMIRALTY COURT
2 boxes, 1735–76.   Photostats.
965   Chiefly British Vice-Admiralty Court records to 1759, but contains records of the Pennsylvania Court of Admiralty, Apr.—Dec. 1776. Includes testimonies, documentary evidence, and decisions in cases before Judge George Ross, involving American Captains John Barry, Charles Alexander, George McAvoy, Lambert Wicks, John Adams, and John Craig.
Originals in the office of the clerk of the U.S. District Court, Philadelphia.

PENNSYLVANIA ABOLITIONIST SOCIETY
5 reels microfilm, 1748–1916.

966   The collection virtually begins in 1775, the year the society was organized, but since meetings were not held during the war, there are no materials for the period 1776–83. Postwar materials comprise official correspondence, minutes of meetings, petitions, indentures, committee minutes, copies of State laws affecting Negroes, receipts, sermons, and various legal documents.

Principal correspondents: George Churchman, George Clinton, John Collins, David Cooper, Tench Coxe, John Skey Eustave, Benjamin Franklin, Enos Hitchcock, Samuel Hoare, John Hopkins, Samuel Hopkins, Samuel Huntington, Isaac Lane, John Langdon, James Pemberton, James Phillips, Robert Pleasants, Beverley Randolph, Edmund Randolph, Thomas Robinson, Benjamin Rush, Granville Sharp, and Noah Webster.

Originals in Historical Society of Pennsylvania.

PENNSYLVANIA PROVINCIAL COUNCIL, MINUTES
1 folder, 1773–75.   Force transcripts.

967   Contains a portion of the minutes of the Pennsylvania Council, Dec. 1773—Dec. 1775. Published in *Minutes of the Provincial Council of Pennsylvania*, vol. 10 (Harrisburg, Pa., 1852).

PHILADELPHIA CALENDAR
1 vol., 1775.   Force manuscripts.

968   Consists of a printed almanac for the year 1775 with diarylike entries in German script by Friederick Ernst, who apparently emigrated from Strasbourg in 1764. Ernst records weather conditions and memorable events in his family, church, and city. His "Diary of the Soul," a kind of religious self-analysis, is appended to several of the monthly entries.

SIR THOMAS PHILLIPPS COLLECTION
66 vols., 1524–1847.   Finding aid available.

969   Phillipps (1792–1872): Collector.

Contains four indexed letterbooks of the Grenadines and Tobago, Feb. 1777—June 1779; a lawyer's form book containing examples of official forms and a section on "The Manner and Method of Proceedings in the Several Courts of Common Pleas in . . . Barbados," ca. 1773; returns of ordnance and stores for St. Augustine, 1763–66; depositions of Samuel Little, Rev. Stephen Peabody, Ichabod Shaw, Nathaniel Track, and John Webster pertaining to land cases in New Hampshire, 1773; and legal documents concerning a 1773 North Carolina land case between William Adair and Henry McCulloch. A volume of accounts pertains to the British Army in North America, 1738–75, and includes bills of the commander in chief in America and miscellaneous papers relating to Indian affairs, expenses, and the maintenance of frontier outposts. Additional legal material includes papers concerning a 1769 Virginia case between Edward and Thomas Hunt and the estate of Robert Tucker, and correspondence continuing up to 1766 pertaining to a case argued in Massachusetts in 1751–52. Also contains 11 letters to William Bentinck, 3d Duke of Portland, from Lord North, 1783; an extract of a letter from New York Lt. Gov. Cadwallader Colden to Secretary of State Conway, with a 15-page "State of the Province of New York," Dec. 1765; and a letter from Thomas Pownall to George Grenville, Feb. 1765, concerning the printing of paper money.

TIMOTHY PICKERING PAPERS
69 reels microfilm, 1756–1829.   *NUCMC* 68–761

970   Pickering (1745–1829): Massachusetts and Pennsylvania lawyer, judge, and statesman; quartermaster general, 1780–85; postmaster general, 1791–95; secretary of war, 1795;

secretary of state, 1795–1800; member, U.S. Senate, 1803–11, U.S. House of Representatives, 1813–17.

Contains private and family correspondence, 1775–1827, chiefly between Pickering, his wife Rebecca, and his eldest son, John Pickering (1775–1829). Also correspondence with military officers, State officials, private citizens, and members of Congress concerning the organization and supply of the Army, political and diplomatic affairs, the progress of the war, particularly during the Yorktown campaign, and personal matters. Letters Pickering wrote to his wife in the postwar period concern Pennsylvania politics and land speculation in the Wyoming Valley. Miscellaneous items include requisition lists, pay receipts, bills of lading, vouchers, and accounts, as well as pamphlets, newspaper clippings, and legal papers.

The collection was filmed under the auspices of the National Historical Publications Commission. Material from the Revolutionary era appears on reels 1–6, 17–19, 33–35, 39–40, 45–47, 50–53, 56–59, 63, and 67–68. Reel 69 contains an index of correspondents in reels 1–4 and 63–68, and an index of names appearing in reels 5–62.

A complete index for material on reels 5–62 is published in Massachusetts Historical Society, *Collections*, 6th ser., vol. 8, (1896). For additional information see Frederick S. Allis, Jr., and Roy Bartolomei, *Guide to the Microfilm Edition of the Timothy Pickering Papers* (Boston, 1966).

CHARLES COTESWORTH PINCKNEY FAMILY PAPERS
36 units, 1694–1886.   Microfilm calendar available, 1 reel.

971   Pinckney (1746–1825): South Carolina soldier, statesman, and diplomat; served as Washington's aide-de-camp during the battles of Brandywine and Germantown; captured at Charleston, S.C., 1780; exchanged, 1782.

Letters, deeds, accounts, surveys, receipts, and miscellaneous documents relating to the Pinckney family of South Carolina. Includes numerous letters from the Revolutionary era between Charles Cotesworth Pinckney, his brother Thomas (1750–1828), his mother, Mrs. Eliza Lucas Pinckney, and his sister Harriet, wife of Daniel Horry. Most of the letters concern family matters and political and military affairs, particularly during the southern campaigns of Generals Lincoln, Gates, and Greene. Also includes an account book of expenditures on the Charles C. Pinckney plantation, 1785–87, and a letterbook containing correspondence of Thomas Pinckney during the period he served as Governor of South Carolina, 1787–89.

Principal correspondents: Ann Clay, Daniel Horry, Arthur Lee, Alexander Leslie, Benjamin Lincoln, William Moultrie, and Banastre Tarleton.

THOMAS PINCKNEY PAPERS
1 vol., 1751–1831.

972   Pinckney (1750–1828): South Carolina lawyer, gov., 1787–89; U.S. minister to Great Britain, 1792–96; U.S. envoy extraordinary to Spain, 1794–95; member, U.S. Congress, 1797–1801.

Miscellaneous collection of deeds, bonds, and letters, most of which are post-1790. Includes a list of bonds and notes belonging to the estate of Jacob Motte, 1773, and a list of slaves in his estate stating their age, sex, trade, and place of residence, 1777. Also contains family letters and an Andrew Pickens letter, 1787, reporting on frontier conditions and the state of the military.

Principal correspondents: Andrew Pickens, Charles C. Pinckney, and Eliza Lucas Pinckney.

CHARLES PINFOLD PAPERS
11 vols., 1735–67.

973   Pinfold: Gov., Barbados, 1756–66.

Consists of letterbooks; transcripts of legislative journals, council minutes, and acts of assembly; broadsides; and a few original papers. The only items directly concerning America are entries in the minutes of the council describing the Barbadian response to the Stamp Act. Letterbooks contain correspondence of Pinfold with the colony's agents and various officials in England, 1756–66.

PITTSBURGH AND NORTHWEST VIRGINIA MANUSCRIPTS
10 vols., 1760–1854.   Draper Mss., series NN, WHi. Microfilm, 2 reels.

974   Miscellaneous collection of original papers and transcripts concerning military commanders and popular heroes of the Fort Pitt region. Transcribed materials include a Daniel Brodhead letterbook, 1779–81; personal letters from Lt. Col. Antoine Felix Wuibert and Baron Gustavus Henri de Rosenthal, a Russian nobleman known in America as John Rose, to Gen. William Irvine, 1783–1830; letters of Edward Hand written from Fort Pitt and Albany, N.Y., 1775–78; and an orderly book of the 8th Pennsylvania Regiment containing the orders of three commandants at Fort Pitt—Gen. Lachlan McIntosh, 1778–79, Col. Daniel Brodhead, 1779–81, and William Irvine, 1781–83. Original materials include the papers of William Harrod (1737–1801)—largely family records, military commissions, accounts, warrants, certificates, and muster rolls and payrolls, 1760–91; and the papers of John McCulloch, Sr., and John McCulloch, Jr.—commissions, military returns, receipts, accounts, and business papers. Also includes letters of Matthew Arbuckle, Benjamin Biggs, Samuel Brady, David Chambers, George Rogers Clark, William Crawford, John Gibson, Archibald Lochry, David Shepherd, David Williamson, and James Willing.
See also Thwaites, *Descriptive List of Manuscript Collections*, p. 53–58.

ROBERT PLEASANTS LETTERBOOK
1 vol., 1771–81.   Photostats.

975   Pleasants (b. 1722): Virginia Quaker; planter, emancipator.
Contains letters written from Pleasants' Curles Neck plantation along the upper James River to relatives, friends, and business associates in England and America. Includes his protest of the confinement of several members of the Society of Friends and persuasive arguments for religious toleration, 1773; a letter to Charles Pleasants of Dublin, Ireland, describing the impending crisis in America, 1774, and letters discussing the invasion of Virginia by Generals Benedict Arnold, William Phillips, and Cornwallis, 1781. Also includes letters to Anthony Benezet concerning slavery and the slave trade, and miscellaneous accounts, invoices, and commercial orders.
Published in part in *William and Mary Quarterly*, 2d ser., vols. 1–2, (Oct. 1921, Apr. 1922), p. 257–75; p. 107–13. Originals in the possession of the Baltimore Orthodox Friends.

WILLIAM PLUMER PAPERS
20 vols., 1774–1845.   Part transcripts.   *NUCMC* 60–28

976   Plumer (1759–1850): Lawyer; itinerant Baptist preacher, 1779–82; member, New Hampshire Assembly, 1785–86, 1788, 1790–91, 1797 1800, U.S. Senate, 1802–7; gov., New Hampshire, 1812, 1816–19.
Includes several letters by Plumer written during the 1780's concerning political unrest in New Hampshire and religious matters, particularly Shaker beliefs and activities. Also copies and extracts of letters between the Continental Congress, Jonathan Trumbull, and Thomas Gage relating to the Coercive Acts; extracts from the journals of the Continental Congress, 1774–90; an essay attacking religious qualifications for holding office under the New Hampshire constitution, 1782; and Plumer's manuscript autobiography.
Principal correspondents: William Coleman, John Hale, Jesse Johnson, Jr., Moses Neal, Samuel Plumer, Samuel Shepard, and John Sullivan.

JAMES K. POLK PAPERS
176 units, 1775–1891.   Microfilm available.

977 Polk (1795–1849): Tennessee lawyer; member, U.S. Congress, 1825–39; President of the U.S.

Includes a 1775 will of James Terry; a deed for land, 1789; a certificate of service for Pvt. Thomas Gore of the 3d South Carolina Regiment, 1777; a return for Capt. Hugh Beatey's militia company, 1781; copies of two Washington letters, 1783 and 1784; and a copy of an address to George III by Patience Brayton, 1787.

POLK FAMILY PAPERS
2 vols., 1767–1859.

978 Thomas Polk (1732–94): Mecklenberg County, N.C., planter and statesman; col., 4th North Carolina Regiment, 1776–78; state commissary of supplies, 1780; councillor of state, 1783–84.

Includes two deeds of Henry E. McCulloch, 1767; a petition from the District of Salisbury officers to Nathanael Greene asking for the appointment of Thomas Polk as brigadier general; and Polk's commission as brigadier general of Salisbury militia, 1781.

OLIVER POLLOCK PAPERS
2 vols., 1767–88.   Force manuscripts.

979 Pollock (1737–1823): Pennsylvania merchant, planter, financier; U.S. agent at New Orleans, La., 1777–82, and Havana, Cuba, 1783–91.

Chiefly letters to Pollock and miscellaneous accounts and receipts concerning the management of his Louisiana plantation, the slave trade, commercial affairs with merchants in Philadelphia, Pensacola, Richmond, and Natchez, and family matters.

Principal correspondents: William Blount, William Constable, Robert Dow, William Dunbar, Jeremiah German, James Hamilton, David Hodge, George Meade, Charles Pollock, Nancy Pollock, James Rumsey, and George Urquhart.

RALPH POMEROY PAPERS
1 folio, 1777–82.

980 Pomeroy: Commissioner of clothing accounts, 1777–78; deputy quartermaster general for Connecticut, 1781–82.

Materials concerning supplies, shipment of recruits, hiring of ox teams, clothing supply, and military operations particularly in the New York theater.

Principal correspondents: Jedediah Huntington, Henry Knox, Samuel H. Parsons, Timothy Pickering, Peter Robertson, Jonathan Trumbull, and Washington.

POTTER FAMILY PAPERS
1 vol., 1747–1807.   Draper Mss., series PP, WHi. Microfilm, 1 reel.

981 Potter: Central Pennsylvania family.

Includes military orders and accounts, addresses from various bodies of militia, and a few letters concerning military and political affairs, 1775–86.

Principal correspondents: Samuel Hunter, William Maclay, William Maxwell, Timothy Pickering, and Joseph Reed.

See Thwaites, *Descriptive List of Manuscript Collections*, p. 59–60.

JONATHAN POTTS PAPERS
1 vol., 1775–80.

982 Potts (1745–81): Pennsylvania physician; member, Pennsylvania Provincial Congress, 1775; deputy director general of hospitals, Northern Department, 1777, Middle Department, 1778–80.

Correspondence and papers concerning Potts' management of hospital affairs. Includes letters from the medical committee of Congress and the Treasury Board. Also a letter of Edward Biddle, Speaker of the Pennsylvania Assembly, concerning Pennsylvania's response to the First Continental Congress and efforts in the assembly to defeat conservative maneuvers toward conciliation.

Principal correspondents: Thomas Bond, James Craik, Robert Morris, Friedrich Augustus Muhlenberg, and Thomas Wharton.

MARY E. POWEL COLLECTION
63 boxes, 1745–1922.   *NUCMC* 69-2047

983   Powel (1846–1931): Author and collector.

Contains letters, autographs, newspaper clippings, illustrations, pamphlets and notes on American and foreign naval officers and navies, and miscellaneous secondary source material concerning Franklin and John Paul Jones, including a copy of Pierre Landais' journal entries for the battle of the *Serapis* and *Bonhomme Richard*. Also manuscript commissions of British naval officers for the Revolutionary era.

In Naval Historical Foundation Collection.

LEVEN POWELL PAPERS
1 vol., 1775–1827.

984   Powell (1737–1810): Virginia planter; delegate, Virginia Convention, July 1776; maj., Virginia Militia, 1775–76; lt. col., William Grayson's Continental Regiment, 1777–78.

Chiefly correspondence to Powell, 1775–85, concerning military affairs—supply, recruiting, campaigns, and Indian uprisings. Five letters written between 1775 and 1785 concern Powell's personal and business affairs.

Principal correspondents: Thomas Davis, William Grayson, David Griffith, Benjamin (Burr) Harrison, James Hendricks, Joseph Hite, George Johnston, John Marshall, John Page, William Pope, Sarah Powell, and Simon Triplett.

Printed in part in Robert C. Powell, *A Biographical Sketch of Col. Leven Powell* (Alexandria, Va., 1877).

EDWARD PREBLE PAPERS
58 vols., 1680–1807.   *NUCMC* 60–11

985   Preble (1761–1807): Falmouth, Maine, merchant; son-in-law of Nathaniel Deering; midshipman, lt., Massachusetts navy, 1779–81; lt. comdr., U.S. Navy, 1798–1806.

Correspondence of Nathaniel Deering concerning mercantile activities during the Revolutionary era, particularly the problems associated with multiple ownership of trading vessels. Also includes descriptions by Moses Little of the best routes and cargoes for vessels sailing to Martinique, 1778; correspondence concerning business in the post war period, and several leases for property owned by Deering in Falmouth, 1785–89.

Principal correspondents: Samuel Eaton, William Gray, Joseph Ingraham, Robert Jenkins, Moses Little, and Moses Shattuck.

WILLIAM PRESTON PAPERS
6 vols., 1731–91.   Draper Mss., series QQ, WHi. Microfilm, 2 reels.

986   Preston (1729–83): Fincastle County, Va.; militia officer and county lieutenant.

Correspondence concerning Indian warfare along the western frontier during Pontiac's Conspiracy, 1763–64, Dunmore's War, 1774, and the Revolutionary War. Also letters and papers on negotiations with the Cherokees and efforts to suppress loyalists operating in western Virginia, as well as official correspondence from Governor Jefferson concerning frontier defense. Miscellaneous documents include military accounts, returns, pay receipts, land warrants, surveys, and petitions.

Principal correspondents: John Blair, Anthony Bledsoe, John Brown, Arthur Campbell, William Campbell, Archibald Cary, William Christian, Lord Dunmore, William Fleming, John Floyd, Patrick Henry, Andrew Lewis, Charles Lewis, Hugh Mercer, Robert Carter Nicholas, William Peachey, Edmund Pendleton, William Russell, and Thomas Walker.

Calendared in *The Preston and Virginia Papers of the Draper Collection of Manuscripts* (Madison, Wis., 1915). See also Thwaites, *Descriptive List of Manuscript Collections*, p. 60–64.

WILLIAM C. PRESTON FAMILY
1 vol., 1779–1840.
987   Preston: Virginia family.
Includes a letter from Edmund Pendleton to William Preston, June 1779, concerning the sale of land in southwest Virginia and eastern Kentucky; and a letter from Granville Smith to William Preston, Nov. 1779, describing his experiences as a prisoner of war in New York City.

PRESTON FAMILY PAPERS
15 reels microfilm, 1727–1896.   *NUCMC* 65–971 and 70–449
988   Preston: Virginia family.
Letters and copies of letters to William Preston (1729–83) concerning personal and family matters and military and political affairs in Virginia, 1767–82. Miscellaneous documents include accounts, memoranda, bonds, receipts, bills, inventories, military orders, land warrants, estate records, petitions, surveys, and legal papers. Also the "Virginia Carrington Scrapbook," 1748–1929, containing correspondence to William Campbell and others, 1775–81.
Principal correspondents: Arthur Campbell, Archibald Cary, William Christian, Dudley Digges, William Fleming, Benjamin Harrison, Patrick Henry, Thomas Jefferson, Thomas Lewis, James Madison, Thomas Madison, Peter Muhlenberg, John Page, William Peachey, Robert Preston, William Rind, Robert Rutherford, Charles Simms, Granville Smith, and John Todd.
Originals in Virginia Historical Society.

PRIVATEERS IN THE REVOLUTION
1 vol., 1777–82.
989   Alphabetical list of privateers, with names of commanders and officers and dates of bonds for commissions.

"PROCEEDINGS OF A TOWN MEETING"
1 folio, ca. 1778.   Force manuscripts.
990   Anonymous poem in two cantos satirizing the patriot militia and the treatment of Tories.

RUFUS PUTNAM
1 vol., 1781–83.
991   Putnam (1738–1824): Col., 5th Massachusetts Regiment, 1776–82; brig. gen., Continental Army, 1783.
Weekly returns of the 5th Massachusetts, Jan. 1781—Apr. 1783.

PAUL QUATTLEBAUM COLLECTION
1 box, 1787–1947.
992   Petition of 15 German Protestant churches in South Carolina for a charter recognizing their ecclesiastical union in 1787, with about 300 signatures of church members in the Orangeburgh District.
Published in *South Carolina Historical and Genealogical Magazine*, vol. 47 (Oct. 1946), p. 195–204.

CHARLES PAUL RAGUETT PAPERS
12 items, 1781–84.

993   Raguett: French merchant in Philadelphia, Pa.

Consists of four letters from James Maxwell of Baltimore, who sold goods in Maryland and Virginia imported by Raguett and business letters from eight other correspondents.

WILLIAM B. RANDOLPH PAPERS
14 boxes, 1696–1884.   Finding aid available.   *NUCMC* 71–1403

994   Randolph (b. 1793): Henrico County, Va., planter.

Revolutionary material consists largely of business correspondence between Peter Skipwith Randolph and Beverley Randolph, executor for the estate of Peter's father, William Randolph, and various persons holding claims against the estate. Also includes a copy of Peter Randolph's account with Francis Goode, 1788–92; a copy of the will of Thacher Burnett, 1780; personal correspondence from Mary Meade and Ann Randolph Meade to Peter Randolph; and miscellaneous receipts, bills, deeds, and accounts.

JACOB READ PAPERS
1 box, 1778–1813.

995   Read (1752–1816): South Carolina lawyer; member, Continental Congress, 1783–85; speaker, South Carolina House of Representatives, 1787–94; member, U.S. Senate, 1795–1801.

Correspondence from the period of Read's service in Congress, mostly personal letters soliciting support or recommending friends. A letter from Richard Peters, Feb. 1784, assesses national political conditions.

Two letters from Read to Governor Guerard of South Carolina are published in Burnett's *Letters of Members of Congress.*

READ FAMILY PAPERS
6 vols., 4 boxes, 1735–1906.

996   George Read (1733–98): Delaware lawyer; signer of the Declaration of Independence.

Consists of about 40 letters from the Revolutionary era, including those to and from Read pertaining to his law practice, personal life, and Revolutionary activities and a few miscellaneous accounts. Approximately half of the correspondence is between his three sons, John (1769–1854), William, and George Read, Jr.

Principal correspondents: John Dickinson, Philemon Dickinson, Tench Tilghman, James Wilson, and John Witherspoon.

WILLIAM REYNOLDS LETTERBOOK
1 vol., 1771–96.

997   Reynolds (d. 1802): Virginia merchant.

Two letterbooks, bound together, Apr. 1771—Aug. 1779 and Aug. 1772—Aug. 1783, containing letters written by Reynolds from London, Annapolis, Yorktown, and Philadelphia, concerning business and family matters. Letters written during the war reflect Reynolds' involvement in the supply of Continental troops and include accounts of skirmishes and news on the progress of the war.

A few letters are printed in Frances N. Mason, ed., *John Norton & Sons, Merchants of London and Virginia* (New York, 1968).

RHODE ISLAND COLLECTION
7 boxes, 2 vols., 2 folios, 1653–1841.

998   Contains a few Revolutionary documents, including a 1775 commission of Maj. John Crane and a letter from Gov. Nicholas Cooke to Stephen Hopkins and Samuel Ward, delegates to Congress, concerning money due Rhode Island and the failure of the State's recruiting program, Dec. 1775.

RHODES FAMILY PAPERS
1 box, 1763–1858.

999   Joseph Rhodes: Portsmouth, R.I., teacher, 1774–82; tutor, Hampton, Va., 1783–86.
Letters and contracts of Joseph Rhodes provide information on teaching in Rhode Island and Virginia. Also includes probate records for Rhodes' estate and miscellaneous family correspondence.

    Principal correspondents: Mary Bagnall, Robert Bagnall, Edward Rhodes, and William Rhodes.

HENRY RIDGELY NOTEBOOK
1 vol., 1784.

1000   Ridgely (d. 1812): Anne Arundel County, Md., planter; 1775 graduate, University of Pennsylvania.

    A law notebook consisting chiefly of index entries to legal works, which is organized by categories, such as indictment, legacy, pleas, wills, and witnesses. Ridgely probably used it as a reference guide in preparing legal briefs.

    Law Library.

BARON FRIEDRICH ADOLPH VON RIEDESEL
1 vol., 1778.   Force manuscripts.

1001   Riedesel (1738–1800): Maj. gen., British Army; commanded the Brunswick troops in North America; prisoner of war, 1777–80.

    Manuscript treatise on the organization of the Prussian Army before 1776, written in 1778 while Riedesel was a prisoner at Cambridge, Mass. The treatise was intended for use by Maj. Gen. William Phillips, senior officer of the Convention Army after the departure of Gen. John Burgoyne. Included are descriptions of battle tactics and plans of Frederick the Great, with specific reference to important campaigns of the Seven Years' War, as well as organizational charts, and sketches of battle formations.

BARON FRIEDRICH ADOLPH VON RIEDESEL PAPERS
2 folios, 1776–83.

1002   Riedesel: See entry no. 1001.

    Includes copies of 13 letters between Major General Riedesel and various officers in the British Army, 1776–83; a letter from Riedesel to Maj. Gen. William Heath, Jan. 1778, concerning the exchange of Captain Willoe of the 8th Regiment of Foot; and a 26-page "Abstract from a Military Memoir concerning the campaign of 1777."

JAMES RITCHIE & COMPANY PAPERS
2 boxes, 1761–1813.

1003   James Ritchie & Company: Glasgow mercantile firm operating stores in Essex County, Va., before 1776.

    Consists of lists of debts due, inventories, receipts, and fragments of daybooks and ledgers, apparently compiled and preserved for the purpose of recovering debts contracted by Virginians at the company's two Rappahannock stores. Some of the lists were compiled by William Woddrop, a company employee who became "an attorney in fact" to protect the company's interests. Instructions to Col. Abraham Maury for the collection of debts due James Ritchie & Co. were issued Nov. 1789. Among the miscellaneous papers is a letter from John Taylor of Caroline County, Va., to Robert Ritchie of Fredericksburg, May 1789, discussing uses of bills of exchange in Virginia in 1784.

WILLIAM CABELL RIVES PAPERS
167 boxes, 1674–1939.   Partial index available.   *NUCMC* 71–1406

1004   Rives (1793–1868): Virginia statesman, minister to France. Francis Walker (1764–1806): Father of Judith Page Walker who married William Rives; lawyer, land agent, and statesman; member, Virginia House of Delegates, 1788–91, 1797–1801, U.S. House of Representatives, 1793–95. Thomas Walker (1715–94): Father of Francis; doctor and merchant of "Castle Hill," near Cobham, Va.; member, House of Burgesses, 1752, 1756–61, and Virginia committee of safety; served on a special commission to the Indians, 1775.

Rives' papers contain a large body of material, chiefly transcripts, pertaining to the War of Independence, most of which he collected for a biography of James Madison. The incomplete draft of the biography is in the collection. Included are numerous Richard Henry Lee letters, chiefly to Patrick Henry, pertaining to political and military affairs, 1776–79, 1789, and letters from other prominent Revolutionary figures concerning military supplies, levies, prisoners of war, foreign alliances, war debts, trade, western lands, taxation, and a variety of other subjects.

The Walker papers contain nearly 100 letters from the Revolutionary era, most of which are to Thomas Walker from merchants in England, and friends and business associates in America. They concern tobacco and land sales, loans, accounts, and Walker's legal and personal affairs. Also included are a receipt book, 1786–89, and a memorandum book, 1784–89.

Principal correspondents: Tench Coxe, Silas Deane, Mathew Gale, Horatio Gates, Samuel Gist, William Grayson, Edward Harford, Patrick Henry, David Hoops, James Innes, Lafayette, Andrew Lewis, George Mason, James Maury, Philip Mazzei, James Mercer, James Monroe, John Norton, James Tayloe, John Walker, and the firms Dobson, Daltera & Walker and Farch & Jones.

COMTE DE ROCHAMBEAU PAPERS
16 vols., 1 folio, 1763–94.

1005   Jean Baptiste Donatien de Vimeur, Comte de Rochambeau (1725–1807): Lt. gen., French Army; commanded the French expeditionary force in America, 1780–83.

Letterbooks (nine volumes) and original correspondence and papers concerning the French expeditionary army in America. Most of correspondence for 1781 pertains to the Yorktown campaign. Letters for 1782–83 concern the southern campaigns of Gen. Nathanael Greene and French efforts to withdraw from North America to the West Indies. In addition to correspondence, the letterbooks contain notes on councils of war, orders of march, lists of officers and men, supply accounts, and instructions and memoranda. Also in the collection are muster rolls, supply requisitions, accounts, and ordnance lists, a few papers concerning the Society of the Cincinnati in France, and a manuscript copy of Rochambeau's *Mémoire de la Guerre En Amérique en 1780 & Histoire de L'Origine et Progress de la Guerre 1763–1780.*

Principal correspondents: Conde de Aranda, Comte de Barras, Guy Carleton, Marquis de Castries, Henry Clinton, Chevalier Destouches, Lord George Germain, Comte de Grasse, Nathanael Greene, Lafayette, La Luzerne, Comte de Laperouse, Prince de Montbarey, Marquis de Ségur, Benjamin Tallmadge, Marquis de Vaudreuil, Baron de Vioménil, and Washington.

The original Rochambeau memoir is in the Archives de la Guerre at Vincennes, (ser. A1, vol. 3732).

See also Claude C. Sturgill, ed., "Rochambeau's Memoire De La Guerre En Amerique," *Virginia Magazine of History and Biography*, vol. 78 (Jan. 1970), p. 34–64.

RODGERS FAMILY PAPERS
35 boxes, 32 vols., 1740–1953.   Finding aid available.

1006   John Rodgers (1773–1838); John N. Macomb (1774–1810); and others.

Miscellaneous documents in series two include a land grant to Alexander Macomb, 1787, and a copy of a treaty between the State of Georgia and the Creek Indians, 1785.

RODNEY FAMILY PAPERS
9 vols., 2 boxes, 1771–1824.   *NUCMC* 68–2065

1007   Caesar Rodney (1728–84): Revolutionary statesman; pres., Delaware; member, Continental Congress, 1774–76. Thomas Rodney (1744–1811): Brother of Caesar; planter, soldier; member, Continental Congress, 1781–82, 1786. Caesar Augustus Rodney (1772–1824): Son of Thomas; Delaware lawyer.

Contains two diaries of Thomas Rodney, one written Dec. 1776—Jan. 1777 describing his participation in the Trenton and Princeton campaigns, the other written in 1781 and 1786 while he was a member of Congress. Includes correspondence between Caesar and Thomas Rodney and political and military figures, 1770–89, concerning such topics as the Confederation, military recruiting and supply, and Thomas Rodney's business activities, especially his Poplar Grove plantation. Several letters from Thomas to his son Caesar Augustus reflect the former's interest in science and ancient history. Also includes miscellaneous accounts of Thomas Rodney, 1780–83, and his account book as clothier and agent for the Delaware Regiment, Apr. 1778—Jan. 1779.

Principal correspondents: Ephraim Blaine, John Dickinson, Henry Laurens, Robert Morris, Samuel Patterson, John Vining, and Washington.

The second diary has been published in Burnett, *Letters of Members of Congress.*

RUMSEY FAMILY PAPERS
7 boxes, 1662–1870.

1008   Rumsey: Bohemia Manor, Cecil County, Md., family. Benjamin Rumsey (1734–1808): Maryland legislator; member, Continental Congress, 1776–77. William Rumsey (1730–77): Brother of Benjamin.

Contains letters to William Rumsey from his brother Benjamin concerning Maryland politics, Nov. 1775—June 1776. Also letters from Benjamin's son Nathan, who was sent to France in 1776 as agent for Hodge, Bayard & Company concerning trade with France. A long letter from David Ramsay in Charleston to Nathan Rumsey, Mar. 15, 1777, discusses America's military situation, recent political developments, and prospects for independence after the forthcoming campaign.

BENJAMIN RUSH PAPERS
4 boxes, 1 folio, 1779–1812.   Part photostats.

1009   Rush (1745?–1813): Pennsylvania physician and statesman; member, Continental Congress, 1776–77; surgeon general, Continental Army, 1777; professor, University of Pennsylvania, 1789–97; U.S. treasurer, 1797–1813.

Contains photostats of John Adams—Rush correspondence, 1779–1812. Manuscript material includes a letter each from William Bingham, 1783, and Rev. Henry Muhlenberg, 1788; and 26 letters from William Maclay, 1789–90.

THOMAS RUSTON PAPERS
1 box, 1762–92.   *NUCMC* 70–971

1010   Ruston (1739–1804): Philadelphia physician; graduate, College of New Jersey, 1762, and Edinburgh, 1765; resided in England, 1765–85; practicing physician at Devon, England, 1782–84.

Two small journals describe Ruston's student years at Edinburgh, 1762–65, and a trip to France, Mar.—May 1785. Also includes correspondence, miscellaneous accounts, and copies of Ruston's medical degrees. Letters by Ruston, chiefly to his father, Job Ruston, of Chester County, Pa., 1764–83, comment on the social life of the period and the impact of the Revolution abroad.

JOHN RUTLEDGE PAPERS
2 reels microfilm, 1782–1872.

1011   John Rutledge (1739–1800): Member, Continental Congress, 1774–75, 1782–83; pres.

and gov., South Carolina. John Rutledge (1766–1819): South Carolina lawyer; son of Governor Rutledge; often referred to as Gen. John Rutledge to distinguish him from his father.

Revolutionary items primarily consist of letters to Gen. John Rutledge while he was in Europe, 1787–90, concerning social and political affairs in Charleston, S.C., and London, the ratification of the U.S. Constitution, the trial of Warren Hastings, and Indian affairs in Georgia and South Carolina.

Principal correspondents: John Brown Cutting, Thomas Jefferson, Francis Kinloch, Richard Pigot, Edward Rutledge, Thomas Lee Shippen, William Short, de Tournay, and John Wilmot.

Filmed under the auspices of the National Historical Publications Commission. Originals in the Southern Collection, University of North Carolina.

ARTHUR ST. CLAIR PAPERS

3 folios, 1772–93. Force transcripts. *NUCMC* 61–1748

1012 St. Clair (1734–1818): Maj. gen., Continental Army, 1777–83; member, Continental Congress, 1785–87; gov., Northwest Territory, 1789–1802.

Includes letters written during the war concerning military intelligence, plans, maneuvers, supply, and reinforcements during the campaigns in New York, New Jersey, Pennsylvania, and the Southern States. Also payrolls and returns for the 2d Pennsylvania Battalion, July 1776. Several letters to St. Clair from friends in Pennsylvania contain political and family news.

Principal correspondents: Elias Boudinot, Richard Butler, George Croghan, James Gardoqui, Nathanael Greene, John Hancock, Robert L. Hooper, William Irvine, John Jay, John Paul Jones, Henry Knox, Lafayette, Benjamin Lincoln, Pierse Long, Eneas McKay, Samuel H. Parsons, John Penn, Richard Peters, Joseph Reed, Winthrop Sargeant, Thomas Smith, Baron von Steuben, William Thompson, Washington, Anthony Wayne, and James Wilson.

Originals in Ohio State Library.

ARTHUR ST. CLAIR PAPERS

1 box, 1778. Force manuscripts.

1013 St. Clair (1734–1818): See entry no. 1012.

Pamphlet of proceedings of a general court-martial held at White Plains, N.Y., for the trial of Maj. Gen. St. Clair, Aug. 26, 1778.

ST. JOHN'S AND MICKMAC INDIANS

1 vol., 1776. Force transcripts.

1014 Minutes of a conference between the St. John's and Mickmac Indians and the Massachusetts Bay Council at Watertown, Mass., July 10–17, 1776. A treaty of alliance was drawn up providing for formation of a combined Massachusetts–Indian regiment.

RICHARD SALTER PAPERS

1 vol., 1768–77.

1015 Salter (1721–87): Boston native, Harvard graduate, 1739; Mansfield, Conn., minister, 1744–87.

Contains three sermons delivered by Salter, 1768, 1774, and 1777.

SCHENECTADY, NEW YORK, MINUTES OF THE COMMITTEE OF SAFETY

1 vol., Jan. 1777—Feb. 1778. Force manuscripts.

1016 Records and corrsepondence concern efforts to secure supplies and men for the Northern Army under Generals Schuyler and Gates and to maintain order in the committee's district. The minutes of meetings include lists of members present, hearings pertaining to Tories, and orders for the control of loyalists, Indians, and Negroes. Also contains information on the movements of various militia units and the activities of the Albany committee of safety.

Published as an addendum to *Minutes of the Albany Committee of Correspondence, 1775–1778*, vol. 2 (Albany, N. Y., 1925), Alexander C. Flick, ed.

1017   HENRY R. SCHOOLCRAFT COLLECTION
91 vols. and boxes, 1782–1878.   Finding aid available.

Schoolcraft (1793–1864): Author, collector, explorer, and Indian agent.

Contains two manuscript drafts of "Stanwix," a Revolutionary chant of 1777; a poem dated 1788, written by Jane Johnston, later the wife of Schoolcraft; and "Poetic Remains of John Johnston, Esq.," a scrapbook compiled 1782–1827, which includes sonnets, allegories, elegies, and odes written in the 1780's.

PHILIP J. SCHUYLER PAPERS
2 boxes, 1776–87.

1018   Schuyler (1733–1804): New York merchant and land baron; maj. gen., Continental Army, 1775–79; commander in chief, Northern Department, 1775–77; member, Continental Congress, 1775, 1779–80, State legislature, 1780–84, 1786–90, and 1792–97, U.S. Senate, 1789–91 and 1797–98.

Includes two detailed memorandum books. The first chronicles problems of supply, reinforcements, tactics, and strategy which Schuyler encountered as major general from early 1776 to mid-1779. The second, Apr. 1783—July 1787, contains a daily account of personal expenditures for food, clothing, and professional services.

SCIENCE IN THE COLONIES, RELATED PAPERS
1 folio, 1678–1766.   Photostats.

1019   Includes two James Bowdoin letters, 1763–64, concerning construction of telescopes, and a 1765 Ezra Stiles letter discussing guidelines for an American Academy of Science modeled on the Royal Society.

Originals in Massachusetts Historical Society.

SÉGUR PAPERS
3 vols., 1781–88.

1020   Philippe Henri Ségur (1724–1801): Marechal de camp; French minister of war during the last three years of the American Revolution; reorganized the supply and hospital systems of the French Army.

Papers concerning the administration of the French Army—troop assignments, supply allocations, and rewards for officers and men, 1781–83. Correspondence focuses on the commands of Comte de Langeron, marechal de camp and commandant at Brest, and Comte de Coigny, marechal de camp and inspector of French infantry.

LEMUEL SHAW PAPERS
61 reels microfilm, 1648–1920.   *NUCMC* 65–186

1021   Shaw (1781–1861): Massachusetts lawyer, chief justice, State supreme court, 1830–61.

Miscellaneous material concerning the Savage, Shaw, and Melville families, 1763–89, includes letters of Susanna Hayward Shaw, mother of Lemuel, containing information on events in Barnstable during the Revolutionary War. Letters and receipts of Oakes Shaw, Lemuel's father, describe a financial struggle with his parish at Barnstable; an account book, 1787–1807, contains detailed information on his household and personal expenses. Correspondence of Henry Bass and George Thatcher and miscellaneous accounts of Samuel P. Savage pertain to the business activities of Savage, a Weston, Mass., merchant. Letters of Henry Savage to his father discuss the Army in New York City, 1776, and at Saratoga, 1777. Also includes records of meetings, accounts, petitions for aid, and membership lists for the Scottish Charitable Society of Boston, to 1770, and deeds, indentures, receipts, and minor accounts of the Savage and Shaw families.

Originals in Massachusetts Historical Society and Social Law Library of Boston. National Historical Publications Commission guide available.

NATHANIEL SHAW PAPERS

1 vol., 1775–82.   Force transcripts.

1022   Shaw (1735–82): Naval agent for Connecticut and the Continental Congress.

Correspondence of the Navy Board of the Eastern Department pertaining to Connecticut privateers and naval prisoners. Includes ship inventories; information on ship departures, cargoes, and losses; material concerning payments in support of American seamen held prisoner by the British; and a petition of the inhabitants of New London asking for stronger fortifications, 1782.

Principal correspondents: John Brown, Thomas Cable, John Deshon, Andrew Huntington, John Kerr, Jonathan McCurdy, Samuel H. Parsons, David Phipps, Nathaniel Saltonstall, Isaac Sears, Thomas Shaw, and William Vernon.

SHAW FAMILY PAPERS

2 boxes, 1636–1892.

1023   Elizabeth S. Shaw (1750–1815): Sister of Abigail Adams and wife of (1) John Shaw of Haverhill, Mass., and (2) the Rev. Stephen Peabody of Atkinson, N.H. Abigail Adams (1744–1818): Wife of John Adams.

Over 100 letters from Abigail Adams to Elizabeth Shaw discussing European society, the reaction of Englishmen to American independence, U.S. diplomatic efforts, and family affairs. Letters of Elizabeth Shaw comment on literature, philosophy, politics, and personal matters. Also includes miscellaneous transcripts from early Massachusetts records, 1784–89, copied by Joseph B. Felt; vouchers signed by Jonathan Harris, a Boston storekeeper, 1776–79; and a census for Salem, 1784–85.

Principal correspondents: John Adams, Mary Cranch, and Mrs. Isaac Smith.

ISAAC SHELBY

1 vol., 1780.

1024   Shelby (1750–1826): Virginia and North Carolina militia officer; gov., Kentucky, 1792–97, 1812–16.

Manuscript copy of Shelby's narrative of the battle of King's Mountain, Oct. 1780, including copies of supporting letters and documents.

SHELBY FAMILY PAPERS

9 vols., 1738–1916.   Finding aid available.   *NUCMC* 60–1698

1025   Evan Shelby: Western Virginia trader and land speculator; father of Isaac. Isaac Shelby (1750–1826): See entry no. 1024.

Papers from the period of the Revolution chiefly concern defensive operations and political and economic development along the western frontiers of North Carolina, Virginia, Maryland, and Pennsylvania. Postwar materials relate to the organization of the State of Franklin and Isaac Shelby's career as a land agent and surveyor in Kentucky. Includes miscellaneous business and personal accounts, genealogical data, deeds, indentures, bills of exchange, contracts, and other legal papers.

Principal correspondents: Abram Barnes, Arthur Campbell, George Croghan, Moses McLean, Edmond Moran, John Taylor, George Thompson, Robert Todd, Jr., Robert Tuckness, and Stephen West.

WILLIAM SHEPARD

1 vol., 1781–83.

1026   Shepard (d. 1817): Col., 4th Massachusetts Continental Regiment, 1777–83.

Weekly returns for the 4th Massachusetts, West Point and vicinity, Jan. 1781—Feb. 1783.

DAVID SHEPHERD PAPERS

5 vols., 1755–94.   Draper Mss., series SS, WHi. Microfilm, 1 reel.

1027   Shepherd (1734–95): Virginia pioneer; commander at Fort Henry during the siege of 1777; county lieutenant of Ohio; served under Col. Daniel Brodhead in an expedition against Indians in the Northwest Territory, 1781.

Papers and correspondence concerning the supply and maintenance of troops stationed around Wheeling, including numerous letters from Shepherd's brother, Abraham, who attempted to provide information on prices of supplies and goods available in Virginia. A memorandum book kept by David Shepherd, 1777–90, contains entries for rations and ammunition supplied to his troops, drafts and tithables for 1778, a list of articles belonging to the State of Virginia, and miscellaneous private accounts.

Principal correspondents: Daniel Brodhead, George Rogers Clark, John Gibson, Edward Hand, Patrick Henry, Jefferson, Lachlan McIntosh, George Morgan, Beverley Randolph, and Edmund Randolph.

See also Thwaites, *Descriptive List of Manuscript Collections*, p. 66.

SAMUEL SHERBURNE PAPERS

1 folio, 1778–1812.   Force manuscripts.

1028   Sherburne (d. 1830): New Hampshire merchant; brigade-major, William Whipple's brigade, New Hampshire Militia, 1778.

Chiefly letters between Sherburne and Benjamin Austin of Boston concerning Sherburne's dry goods business. Includes notes of condolence to Sherburne upon the loss of his leg, 1778.

ROGER SHERMAN PAPERS

2 vols., 2 boxes, 1746–1810.   Part photostats.

1029   Sherman (1721–93): Connecticut lawyer; member, Continental Congress, 1774–81, 1783–84, U.S. Senate, 1791–93.

Two small notebooks contain accounts of monies loaned the United States between Sept. 1777 and Aug. 1780, Sherman's expenses while attending Congress, June 7—Oct. 2, 1780, the British national debt, 1740–75, and extracts from the writings of Rousseau. Also a 1776 almanac signed by Sherman containing personal accounts, 1775–76; a letter to William Williams, Aug. 1777, regarding the appointment of Gen. Horatio Gates to the Northern Department; and copies of five letters between Sherman and John Adams concerning ratification of the Constitution, July 1789.

JOSEPH SHIPPEN PAPERS

1 vol., 1727–95.   Force manuscripts.

1030   Shippen (1732–1810): Secretary of the province of Pennsylvania after 1762; son of Edward Shippen (1703–81) of Lancaster, Pa.

Contains letters of Edward and Joseph Shippen concerning the massacre of Indians at Carlisle, 1763, and the subsequent political turmoil in Pennsylvania, and correspondence on boundary disputes with Maryland, Virginia, and Connecticut. Also includes correspondence of Thomas Penn with Joseph Shippen regarding the latter's duties as secretary of the province, letters from Joseph to his father, and letters between Joseph Shippen and Gov. John Penn. Shippen's letter to Penn pertain to political issues and the social life and personal concerns of some of Pennsylvania's leading families. Penn's letters, written from England, 1771–73, contain comments on the degeneracy of English life, the alarming British ignorance of America, and his desire to return to Pennsylvania.

Principal correspondents: John Armstrong, Edward Burd, Charles Mason, Jeremiah Dixon, Timothy Matlack, Samuel Postlethwait, Arthur St. Clair, William Shippen, James Tilghman, and Henry Wilmot.

SHIPPEN FAMILY PAPERS
28 boxes, 1671–1936.   Finding aid available.

1031   William Shippen, Jr. (1736–1808): Philadelphia, Pa., physician; director general, Continental Army hospitals, 1777–81; brother-in-law of Richard Henry Lee. Ann Hume Shippen (1763–1841): Daughter of William Shippen, Jr.; married Henry Beekman Livingston. Thomas Lee Shippen (1765–98): Son of William Shippen, Jr.; married Elizabeth Carter Byrd of Westover, Va., 1791.

Chiefly personal and family correspondence between Dr. Shippen and his children, Ann Hume and Thomas Lee Shippen. Ann's correspondence, written after her marriage, includes letters from the Lees of Virginia and letterbooks containing her replies to correspondence which does not survive. Letters from Dr. Shippen to his son Thomas, a law student in England, 1786–89, contain observations on political developments in the United States. In numerous letters to his father and sister, and to Americans abroad, Thomas describes his life as a student in London, 1786–88, and his European travels, 1788–89. Also in the collection are diaries Thomas Shippen maintained in Europe; a ledger, 1775–94, and a daybook, 1763–76, containing records of Dr. Shippen's medical practice; and a ledger, 1759–65, containing transactions of a Pennsylvania ironworks and a store in which Dr. William Shippen, Sr. apparently had an interest.

Principal correspondents: John Banister, John Brown Cutting, William Gordon, Jefferson, Arthur Lee, Francis Lightfoot Lee, Ludwell Lee, Richard Henry Lee, Henry B. Livingston, Margaret Livingston, Lord Shelburne, William Short, Bushrod Washington, and Washington.

JOHN CLEVES SHORT FAMILY PAPERS
61 units, 1761–1901.

1032   Short family: Virginia and Kentucky lawyers, planters, and statesmen.

Pertinent materials include personal and family correspondence and documents relating to the settlement of the Kentucky district of Virginia. Letters from William Short to his brother, Peyton, 1783–84, concern the latter's legal studies at the College of William and Mary. Also includes land warrants for John Cleves Symmes, 1787–88, William Short's expense account for European travel beginning in 1789, and a record of American ship arrivals in France, Feb.—Sept. 1789.

Principal correspondents: George Rogers Clark, Harry Innes, J. M. T. Legra, John May, John Overton, Benjamin Skipwith, and Benjamin Stiles.

WILLIAM SHORT PAPERS
53 vols., 3 boxes, 1 folio, 1778–1849.

1033   Short (1759–1849): Diplomat; member, Executive Council of Virginia, 1783–84; Jefferson's private secretary in Paris, 1785–89; American negotiator in Amsterdam; chargé d'affaires in Paris; and minister to The Hague.

Chiefly letters and abstracts and copies of letters of Short and various correspondents in France and America. Topics discussed in letters written during the Revolutionary era range from the adventures of young Americans on tour in Europe to the difficulties of negotiating loans to support American credit abroad. Many letters from friends and relations in Virginia provide detailed accounts of political and social affairs, the struggle over ratification of the Federal Constitution, and business matters.

Principal correspondents: John Adams, John Banister, John Brown Cutting, C. W. F. Dumas, William Grayson, Jefferson, James Madison, Philip Mazzei, James Monroe, William Nelson, Jr., John Rutledge, Jr., Thomas Lee Shippen, Fulwar Skipwith, Peyton Skipwith, and William S. Smith.

RICHARD SHUCKBURGH PAPERS
1 box, 1745–73.   Typescripts.

1034   Shuckburgh (d. 1773): Surgeon, 17th Regiment of Foot, 1763–67; secretary to Sir William Johnson, 1767–73.

Most of the material pertains to Shuckburgh's appointment as secretary to Sir William Johnson, Superintendent of Indian Affairs.

Originals in New York State Library.

CHARLES SIMMS PAPERS
7 vols., 1731–1822.   Force manuscripts.

1035   Simms (1755–1819): Virginia lawyer; maj., 12th Virginia Continental Regiment, 1776; lt. col., 6th Virginia, 1777, and 2d Virginia, 1778–79.

Includes 132 items from the period of the Revolution, chiefly legal papers and documents: promissory notes, deeds, indentures, surveys, bills of sale, depositions, wills, accounts, notes on court proceedings, and a power of attorney. Correspondence consists mostly of letters to Simms regarding legal matters but includes three letters from Simms to Miss Nancy Douglass, 1778, a letter from William Douglass to his daughter Nancy, 1783, written after her marriage to Simms, and a 1784 letter from John Marshall to Simms.

Principal correspondents: William T. Alexander, William Brent, Charles Carter, Christopher Greenup, C. H. Harrison, John Harvie, John Mason, Daniel Morgan, William Nelson, Jr., John Peyton, Benjamin Philpott, Edmund Randolph, Samuel Rogers, William Smallwood, John Stuart, John Taliaferro, and John Witherspoon.

SLAVES, MISCELLANY
2 boxes, 7 folios, 1719–1869.

1036   Contains appraisals of the estates of Adam Capentin, 1783, Nathan Lynn, 1784, and Stephen Glad, 1789; a mortgage, in Spanish, on two slaves, Natchez, Feb. 1786; a legal certificate allotting several slaves to the widow of John Gibson, 1787; and a copy of a bill of sale, in Spanish, for two Guinea Negroes, 1789. Also includes a bill of sale for a slave, Nov. 1789, and photostats of a poem, "An Essay on Slavery, with submission to Divine providence, knowing that God Rules over all things," by Jupiter Hammon, a slave belonging to John Lloyd of Queens Village, Long Island, N.Y., Nov. 1786.

Original Hammon poem is in Yale University Library.

HEZEKIAH SMITH PAPERS
1 box, 1762–1805.

1037   Smith (1737–1805): Pastor, First Baptist Church of Haverhill, Mass., 1766–1805; chaplain, Col. John Nixon's Massachusetts Regiment, 1775, the 4th Continental Infantry, 1776, and the 6th Massachusetts Regiment, 1777; brigade chaplain, 1778–80.

Eleven diaries, 1762–1805, describe Smith's work as pastor of the Haverhill Baptist Church and part-time evangelist. Entries record sermon texts, public responses, personal observations, and pastoral experiences. There are also brief references to Smith's work on the board of Rhode Island College (Brown University), of which he was a cofounder. Fifteen letters Smith wrote to his wife during the war deal with general war news, specific events leading up to the surrender of Gen. John Burgoyne's army at Saratoga, and personal matters. Miscellaneous documents include lists of officers, copies of Gen. Horatio Gates' orders, and returns of British troops captured at Saratoga.

JOHN R. SMITH COLLECTION
1 box, 1783–1809.   Force manuscripts.

1038   Smith: Graduate, College of New Jersey, 1787; Philadelphia, Pa., lawyer after 1791.

Contains four letters to Smith from his brother Samuel, Oct. 1785—Mar. 1786, concerning family matters and Pennsylvania politics. Includes a book of poetry, ca. 1787–93, and a geometry copybook.

JONATHAN BAYARD SMITH FAMILY PAPERS
5 vols., 1 box, 1686–1903.

1039   Jonathan B. Smith (1742–1812): Philadelphia, Pa., merchant; secretary, Pennsylvania provincial conventions, 1774–76; member, Continental Congress, 1777–78; justice, Philadelphia court of common pleas, 1778; alderman, 1792; auditor general of Pennsylvania, 1794.

Jonathan B. Smith materials include letters from Benjamin Rush in Edinburgh, 1767–68; letters from Joseph Reed concerning the crisis in the American Army during the winter of 1777–78; miscellaneous items concerning military supply and the defense of Pennsylvania and New Jersey, 1776–78; and commissions and letters of appointment to various offices, 1775–94. Other Smith family items include wills; a Samuel and Jonathan Smith mercantile letterbook, 1765–70, containing routine business correspondence—prices, market conditions, remittances, etc.; and documents pertaining to Thomas Smith's position as commissioner of the Loan Office. Also contains copies of an unpublished Washington letter to Tobias Lear, June 29, 1778; a June 18, 1775, letter from Washington to his wife; and a brief note by John Hancock, Dec. 1775.

Principal correspondents: Thomas Amory, Thomas Boylston, Billings Bradish, Nathaniel Cary, Richard Clarke, Isaac Codman, Lewis Gray, Thomas Hickling, Alexander Hill, Nathan Holmes, John Hurd, Clement Jackson, Gabriel Johonnot, William Kettle, Moses Little, Samuel Orne, Samuel A. Otis, Jacob Rivera, Jacob Sheafe, John Soley, Arnold Wells, Jonathan Williams, and Isaac Winslow, and the firms Michael & Tristram Dalton, Jackson & Bromfield, John Leverett & Co., March & Treadwell, Joseph Rotch & Co., and Samuel Starbuck & Co.

SAMUEL SMITH PAPERS
18 boxes, 1 vol., 1772–1869.

1040   Smith (1752–1839): Baltimore, Md., merchant; maj., lt. col., 4th Maryland Regiment, 1776–79; member, U.S. House of Representatives, 1792–1803, 1816–22, U.S. Senate, 1803–15, 1822–33.

Contains a few returns, receipts, and clothing accounts relating to Smith's military service, 1777–78; transcripts of correspondence between Washington and Smith concerning the defense of Fort Mifflin, Sept.—Oct. 1777; and 32 mercantile letters from Robert Morris to Samuel and John Smith, 1786–87. The volume, a letterbook, 1772–74, which Smith maintained while visiting foreign correspondents of his father's firm, contains a full record of his activities as well as evaluations of commercial opportunities in London, Bristol, Venice, Rome, Leghorn, Genoa, Marseilles, Barcelona, Alicante, Málaga, Gibraltar, Cádiz, Lisbon, and Plymouth. Several pages written years later contain a list of prices current in 1782.

See also Dutilh and Wachsmuth Collection, entry no. 250.

SAMUEL HARRISON SMITH
1 vol., 1787.   Force manuscripts.

1041   Smith (1772–1845): Philadelphia, Pa., author, editor, and banker.

Consists of a student's exercise book containing an essay on logic, apparently based on college lectures and reading, written while Smith was a student at the University of Pennsylvania.

WILLIAM SMITH, WILLIAM R. LEE, AND HENRY JACKSON PAPERS
1 vol., 1777–81.

1042   Smith, Lee, and Jackson: Massachusetts Continental officers.

Regular returns for one of the 16 additional Continental regiments. The regiment was commanded by Col. William R. Lee until Apr. 1779, when it was consolidated with Jackson's regiment. Lt. Col. William R. Smith served under both Lee and Jackson.

SOUTH CAROLINA, MISCELLANY
1 box, 1683–1886.

1043   Contains a few brief extracts of tax returns for two South Carolina parishes, 1777–78; extracts of various ordinances of the assembly, 1776–77; and a copy of an appraisal of sundries belonging to the estate of Alexander Russell (d. 1771).

SOUTH CAROLINA, NAVY BOARD
1 folio, 1777–79.   Force transcripts.

1044   Minutes of the Navy Board of South Carolina, Jan. 1777—Mar. 1779. Originals in New York State Library.

SOUTH CAROLINA, PROVINCIAL CONGRESS
1 folio, 1774–76.   Force transcripts.

1045   Letters, memorials, petitions, reports, and accounts addressed to the Provincial Congress of South Carolina and to its presidents Henry Laurens and William Henry Drayton. Consists of pleas of settlers on the western frontier for military support, requests for military commissions, charges of abuse by military officers, and complaints of displaced ministers.

SOUTH CAROLINA COLLECTION
2 folios, 1780–82.   Force transcripts.

1046   Military correspondence, orders, proclamations, and miscellaneous papers pertaining to the southern campaign, particularly the supply, treatment, and exchange of American soldiers captured at Charleston, May 12, 1780. Transcribed from Banastre Tarleton, *A History of the Campaigns of 1780 and 1781 . . .* (London, 1787), David Ramsay, *History of South Carolina . . .*, 2 vols. (Charleston, S.C., 1809), and the South Carolina *Royal Gazette*.
    Principal correspondents: Henry Clinton, Cornwallis, John Cruden, Nathanael Greene, William Moultrie, Henry Pendleton, Lord Rawdon, John Rutledge, and Patrick Tonyn.

JARED SPARKS PAPERS
1 reel microfilm, 1776–80.

1047   Sparks (1798–1866): Editor and historian.
    Transcripts and extracts of official correspondence of Sir Joseph Yorke, British ambassador to the Netherlands, with Secretaries Eden, Suffolk, Stormont, and Weymouth, concerning American trade with Holland and France, diplomatic affairs, privateers and ships of war operating off the English coast, and the exchange of English seamen held prisoner in Dutch ports.

WILLIAM B. SPRAGUE COLLECTION
9 folios, 1702–83.   Force transcripts.

1048   Sprague (1795–1876): Massachusetts and New York antiquarian, clergyman, and autograph collector.
    Correspondence concerning military supply, Indian affairs on the northern frontier, and political affairs in New York, Pennsylvania, and Delaware. Includes letters pertaining to prewar Indian programs, riots in the New Hampshire Grants against the extension of authority from New York, the Boston Sons of Liberty, and unpublished letters of members of the Continental Congress.
    Principal correspondents: Samuel Adams, Jeffery Amherst, Josiah Bartlett, John Bradstreet, Aaron Burr, Thomas Gamble, Henry Glen, John Hancock, Sir William Johnson, William Malcom, New York committee of safety, George Partridge, Nathaniel Peabody, John Reid, Caesar Rodney, Thomas Rodney, Roger Sherman, Samuel Ward, and Oliver Wolcott.

CALEB STARK COLLECTION

1 folio, 1778–1860.   Force transcripts.

1049   Stark (1804–64): Author; grandson of Gen. John Stark (see entry no. 1050).

Contains unpublished correspondence of General Stark concerning military activities in northern New York and American prisoners of war in Canada, 1776. A letter to Gov. Thomas Chittenden, of Vermont, warns against private negotiations with the enemy, 1778. Also includes a petition, 1786, by Caleb Stark (1759–1833) concerning money owed to his father, John Stark, for service during the Revolutionary War.

See Caleb Stark, ed., *Memoir and Official Correspondence of Gen. John Stark* . . . (Concord, N.H., 1860).

JOHN STARK PAPERS

1 box, 1 vol., 1775–81.   Force manuscripts and transcripts.

1050   Stark (1728–1822): New Hampshire farmer, mill owner; col., 1st New Hampshire Regiment, Apr. 1775, and 5th Continental Infantry, Jan. 1776; brig. gen., Continental Army, Oct. 1777–83.

Contains 10 manuscript items, including a description of the battle of Bennington. Transcripts concern the problems of defense in the Northern Department against British, Tory, and Indian forces. Also includes trial records of accused spies and persons accused of treason.

Principal correspondents: William Alexander, Thomas Chittenden, George Clinton, Horatio Gates, William Heath, Philip Schuyler, John Sullivan, Washington, Meshech Weare, and Marinus Willett.

ADAM STEPHEN PAPERS

1 vol., 1750–1834.

1051   Stephen (ca. 1730–91): Virginia Militia officer; col., 4th Virginia Continental Regiment, Feb. 1776; brig. and maj. gen., Continental Army, Sept. 1776–Nov. 1777; cashiered for conduct unbecoming an officer.

Material from the period of the Revolution primarily concerns Indian affairs of the western frontier and Stephen's personal business activities. Miscellaneous papers include accounts, advertisements, indentures, and surveys.

Principal correspondents: James Adam, Francis Fauquier, William Green, Enoch Innis, William Maxwell, James Mercer, Anthony Noble, Alexander Stephen, and Washington.

BARON VON STEUBEN PAPERS

4 items, 1778–84.   Photostats.   *NUCMC* 60–2923

1052   Friedrich Wilhelm Ludolf Gerhard Augustin von Steuben (1730–94): Prussian officer; volunteer inspector general, Continental Army, 1778; maj. gen., 1778–84.

Comprises essays and reports to the Continental Congress, including Steuben's "Sentiments on a peace establishment," which Washington forwarded to Congress, May 1783; his recommendations to a committee of Congress on "Military academies and manufactures," 1783; "Thoughts on a national militia"; and "Answer to the questions respecting the Swiss Militia," forwarded to Congress from Paris by Arthur Lee, July 1778.

Originals in New York Historical Society.

BENJAMIN FRANKLIN STEVENS'S CATALOGUE INDEX OF MANUSCRIPTS IN ARCHIVES OF ENGLAND, FRANCE, HOLLAND & SPAIN RELATING TO AMERICA, *1763–1783*.

183 vols.

1053   A comprehensive manuscript index to 161,000 manuscripts examined during compilation of B. F. Stevens's *Facsimiles of Manuscripts in European Archives Relating to America, 1773–83*, 25 vols. (London, 1889–98). The index is organized into three basic

171

divisions: "The Catalogue," 50 vols., in which documents are cited according to location —British Public Record Office, French Archives Nationales, Dutch Rijks and Huis Archives, and private collections of Carlisle, Dartmouth, and Germain; a "Chronological Index," which includes an abstract in English of the contents of each document and a list of enclosures and endorsements; and an "Alphabetical Index," arranged according to author and recipient or, where such information is lacking, by subject matter.

A separate volume containing a transcriber's guide to altered locations of P.R.O. collections is published in Charles M. Andrews, *Guide to the Materials for American History, to 1783, in the Public Record Office of Great Britain*, vol. 1 (Washington, D.C., 1912), p. 279–307. Two additional volumes contain incomplete indexes to manuscripts in European archives relating to peace negotiations in Paris, 1782–84, documents pertaining to the French Alliance, 1778–84, and a list of the correspondence between the French Government and French Ministers in America, 1779–84.

CHARLES STEWART PAPERS
1 vol., 1777–82.   Force transcripts.

1054   Stewart (1729–1800): Col., New Jersey Militia, 1775–76; commissary general of issues, 1777–82.

Chiefly letters concerning the acquisition and distribution of military supplies and the settlement of accounts.

Principal correspondents: Ephraim Blaine, Samuel Gray, David Humphreys, Charles Lee, James Millegan, Robert Morris, Robert Troup, and Washington.

WALTER STEWART PAPERS
1 vol., 1776–83.   Force transcripts.

1055   Stewart (ca. 1756–96): Col., Pennsylvania State Regiment, 1777; 13th Pennsylvania Continental Regiment, Nov. 1777; 2d Pennsylvania, 1778.

Correspondence with various Continental officers concerning battles, military stores and supplies, and personal and business affairs. Also includes reports from Stewart while serving as inspector general of the Northern Army, 1782, and Baron von Steuben's plan for reorganization of the Army, 1781.

Principal correspondents: Samuel Adams, Burgess Ball, Benjamin Bartlett, Joseph Brown, Sir Guy Carleton, Horatio Gates, William Irvine, Lafayette, Alexander Nesbitt, Joseph Reed, Philip Schuyler, Alexander Spotswood, Joseph Spencer, Washington, and George Weedon.

THOMAS STOCKTON PAPERS
3 vols., 1783–1829.

1056   Stockton (d. 1846): Officer, U.S. Army; gov., Delaware, 1845–46.

Includes Isaac Carvel's commission, 1785; prisoner of war documents of Jeremiah Wilkey and Paul Brown, 1783; pension papers concerning payments to Thomas Shervin and Thomas Wells, 1776, 1785; and discharge records for Thomas Holdson and John Clifton.

BENJAMIN STODDERT PAPERS
1 vol., 1784–1812.

1057   Stoddert (1751–1813): Capt., Pennsylvania Line, 1777–79; clerk, Board of War, 1779–81; entered mercantile firm, Forrest, Stoddert, and Murdock, Georgetown, Md., 1782; first secretary of the navy, 1798–1801.

Includes 11 business letters from Stoddert to the firm of Washington, Butler, and Levinson at Leeds, Va., 1784–89.

REBECCA L. STODDERT PAPERS
1 box, 1776–1800.

1058   Stoddert (d. 1800): Daughter of Christopher Lowndes, Bladensburg, Md., merchant; wife of Benjamin Stoddert (1751–1813).

Includes a few miscellaneous deeds and a letter of E. Lowndes to Mrs. Robert Carter, Apr. 1777, concerning the disposition of family lands in Virginia.

STONE FAMILY OF MARYLAND
1 vol., 1 folio, 1730–1863.

1059   Walter Stone (d. 1790): Port Tobacco, Md., resident; brother of Thomas Stone (1743–87), a signer of the Declaration of Independence, Michael Jenifer Stone, and John Hoskins Stone.

Principally letters to Walter Stone, including 10 from Thomas Stone, and miscellaneous receipts and business accounts. Several of the letters were written while Walter was employed in the Office of Finance, 1782, and in the Office of Foreign Affairs, 1783. The collection also contains a few letters of prominent Revolutionary leaders of Maryland: Daniel of St. Thomas Jenifer, Charles Carroll of Carrollton, James McHenry, and James Hindman. An eight-page letter from Thomas Stone to [James Hollyday?], May 1776, contains information on the movement toward independence in Congress and Revolutionary activities in Maryland.

SARAH STONE AUTOGRAPH COLLECTION
200 items, 1720–1962.

1060   Miscellaneous letters include: Edward Holyoke to Francis Bernard, Feb. 1766; Marinus Willett to [Barnabas?] Deane, May 1778; George Washington to Benjamin Lincoln, May 1777; Andre Prevost to Benjamin Lincoln, Jan. 1780; Henry Lee to John Fitzgerald, June 1782; and Francis Barber to Gen. Jonathan Dayton, Jan. 1783.

Other correspondents: Thomas Fitzsimmons, Peter R. Livingston, and Richard Peters.

SIR HENRY STRACHEY PAPERS
1 vol., 1776–83.

1061   Strachey (1737–1810): Secretary to the Howe Peace Commission, 1776–78; clerk of deliveries, British Ordnance Office, 1778–80, 1783; chief storekeeper, 1780–82; under secretary of state for home affairs, 1782–83.

Chiefly correspondence to Strachey concerning British military policy in America, the progress of the southern campaign, disloyalty to the Crown among South Carolinians, and conditions at St. Augustine in 1777. A letter from Benjamin Vaughan to Strachey, Nov. 1782, contains reflections on peace and diplomatic affairs. A single letter from Strachey to [Christian D'Oyly?], Aug. 1776, concerns American independence, the strength of the peace element in America, and the frustrations of the Howe Peace Commission.

Principal correspondents: Nesbit Balfour, George Clerk, Alleyne Fitzherbert, John Fothergill, Arthur Gordon, William Howe, Lord Shelburne, Patrick Tonyn, and Thomas Townshend.

JOHN SULLIVAN PAPERS
4 vols., 1775–89.   Force transcripts and manuscripts.   *NUCMC* 66–1462

1062   Sullivan (1740–95): New Hampshire lawyer; member, Continental Congress, 1774–75, 1780–81; brig. and maj. gen., Continental Army, 1775–79; commanded American forces in the Canadian, Rhode Island, and Iroquois expeditions; New Hampshire attorney general, 1782–86, assemblyman, 1782–86, and pres., 1786–87, 1789.

Comprises three volumes of transcripts and one volume of manuscripts dealing with nearly every phase of Sullivan's military career, particularly the siege of Boston and campaigns in New York, New Jersey, Pennsylvania, and Rhode Island. Includes proceedings of the court of inquiry into Sullivan's Staten Island expedition and letters of testimony sustaining his conduct at Staten Island and Brandywine. Original documents include returns of Gen. Israel Putnam's division, May 1777, Sullivan's division, June 1777, and American forces in Rhode Island, Jan. 1779. Scattered letters for the postwar period include several by Henry Knox commenting on the Federal Constitution.

Principal correspondents: Benedict Arnold, Comte d'Estaing, Horatio Gates, Nathanael Greene, John Hancock, William Heath, Henry Knox, Robert Pigot, Philip Schuyler, John Stark, J. M. Varnum, and Washington.

Most of the letters in volumes 1 and 3 are published in Otis G. Hammond, ed., *Letters and Papers of Major-General John Sullivan, Continental Army* (Concord, N. H., 1930–39).

THOMAS SUMTER PAPERS
24 vols., 1780–1832.   Draper Mss., series VV, WHi. Microfilm, 7 reels.
1063   Sumter (1734–1832): Lt. col., 2d South Carolina Rifle Regiment, 1776; col. and brig. gen., South Carolina Militia, 1780–82.

Original correspondence, transcripts, and miscellaneous papers concerning the Revolutionary career of Sumter. Includes instructions from the Governor of South Carolina, John Rutledge, regarding military supplies and recruiting; intelligence reports on the strength and movements of enemy forces in the area; reports on enemy activities in Virginia and several of the Northern States; extracts from 18th-century newspapers and magazines; and Col. William Hill's narrative of the campaign of 1780 in South Carolina, published in A. S. Salley, ed., *Col. William Hill's Memoirs of the Revolution* (Columbia, S.C., 1921). Also includes transcripts of the personal papers of William Gilmore Simms; Sumter's correspondence with various officers in the Southern Department; and miscellaneous accounts, returns, indentures, and orders.

Principal correspondents: Thomas Brandon, William Candler, John S. Dart, William Davidson, Nathanael Greene, Isaac Huger, Edward Hyrne, Francis Marion, John Mathews, Charles Middleton, Nathaniel Pendleton, Andrew Pickens, William Pierce, John Rutledge, William Smallwood, and Otho H. Williams.

JOHN CLEVES SYMMES PAPERS
3 vols., 1787–1827.   Draper Mss., series WW, WHi. Microfilm, 1 reel.
1064   Symmes (1742–1814): New Jersey soldier and statesman; member, Continental Congress, 1785–86; appointed judge of the Northwest Territory, 1788.

Contains extracts of letters pertaining to Symmes' interests in the Miami Purchase, 1787–96, including correspondence with Jonathan Dayton, Elias Boudinot, the treasury commissioners, and members of the Miami Company.

The Library also has another set of transcripts of the same correspondence containing 17 letters dated before 1790. Available on microfilm, these letters are apparently complete copies rather than extracts.

See also Beverley W. Bond, Jr., ed., *The Correspondence of John Cleves Symmes . . .* (New York, 1926), and Thwaites, *Descriptive List of Manuscript Collections*, p. 79–81.

HUGH T. TAGGART COLLECTION
18 boxes, 1751–1889.   Finding aid available.
1065   Taggart: Collector.

Includes the daybook of Charles Beatty of Georgetown, 1771–72, containing records of business activities with William Molleson of London; records of additions to Georgetown laid off in 1769 for Beatty and George F. Hawkins, including lot plats; a list of land holdings included in the District of Columbia; a letterbook, 1787–99, and correspondence, 1773–89, of Daniel Carroll of Duddington pertaining to the sale of pig iron and the difficulties of conducting business during the Revolution. One volume, the "Georgetown Commission, 1751–89," contains information described separately under Georgetown, Maryland, journal, entry no. 401.

BENJAMIN TALLMADGE PAPERS
1 reel microfilm, 1773–1917.

1066   Tallmadge (1754–1835): Wethersfield, Conn., teacher; Capt. maj., 2d Regiment of Continental Light Dragoons, 1776–83; organized spy activities for Washington; merchant; member, U.S. House of Representatives, 1801–17.

Most of the pertinent material consists of Tallmadge's letters and reports to Washington after 1778, which contain information on the spy network around New York and Long Island. Miscellaneous items include poetical letters from Tallmadge to his friends, 1774–75, his Yale diploma, and plans for raids on Long Island, 1780–82.

Originals privately owned.

WILLIAM TAPPAN AUTOGRAPH COLLECTION
2 boxes, 1640–1939.   *NUCMC* 71–1422

1067   Tappan (b. 1863): Collector.

Includes miscellaneous receipts, memoranda, legal papers, and correspondence for the period 1763–89. Letters written during the active part of the war concern the purchase of military supplies, recruits, and the arrangement of officers in the Baltimore Town Battalion of Militia.

Principal correspondents: William Bell, James Brice, Robert Gilmor, Philip Key, John Moale, David Poe, John Purviance, Robert Purviance, and Samuel Purviance.

WILLIAM TAYLOR PAPERS
67 vols., 29 boxes, 3 bundles, 1775–1858.

1068   Taylor: Baltimore, Md., merchant.

Contains letters to the Boston firm Sears and Smith; a list of prices current in Boston, 1783; undated Admiralty Court papers, a list of debtors, accounts of goods, inventories, and Amsterdam book prices; and business receipts for 1777–83.

TENNESSEE MANUSCRIPTS
4 vols., 1771–1854.   Draper Mss., series XX, WHi. Microfilm, 3 reels.

1069   Contains correspondence and papers of Joseph Martin (1740–1808), an Indian agent, soldier, and land promoter on the Virginia-Carolina frontier. Also includes papers of Daniel Robertson (1742–1814), an early Watauga settler; William Blount (1744–1800), a land speculator; and Daniel Smith (1748–1818), a Virginia surveyor and militia officer. Material from the period of the Revolution pertains to the early development of Tennessee.

Principal correspondents: Benjamin Harrison, Alexander Martin, Edmund Randolph, Isaac Shelby, and Hugh Williamson.

See also Thwaites, *Descriptive List of Manuscript Collections*, p. 82–86.

BARTHÉLEMY TERRASSON PAPERS
1 box, 1773–1807.

1070   Terrasson: French merchant residing in Baltimore, Md., 1778–81, and in Philadelphia, Pa., 1781–90.

Consists chiefly of commercial correspondence between Terrasson and various merchants in the United States, West Indies, France, and Spain. Includes letters addressed to Terrasson in Baltimore and Philadelphia, and six letters antedating his arrival in America, four of which are from Terrasson to his son. Letters are primarily in French.

See also Jean Holker Papers, entry no. 339, and the John de Neufville and Son, account book, entry no. 36.

JAMES THACHER PAPERS
32 items, 1780–1842.   Photostats.

1071   Thacher (1754–1844): Massachusetts doctor; surgeon's mate, Cambridge Military

Hospital, 1775; surgeon, Albany Military Hospital, 1777; surgeon, Col. Henry Jackson's Continental Regiment, 1778–83.

Consists of correspondence to Dr. James Thacher, including seven letters written during the period of the Revolution by Massachusetts doctors Samuel Prescott, Samuel Finley, William Eustis, and Daniel Shute concerning the problems of the medical department of the Continental Army, 1780–83.

CHARLES THOMSON PAPERS
6 vols., 1765–1845.   Part photostats.

1072   Thomson (1729–1824): Pennsylvania politician and merchant; secretary, Continental Congress, 1774–89; Biblical scholar and gentleman farmer in retirement.

Consists chiefly of Thomson's correspondence while he was secretary to Congress. Correspondence with Franklin and Jefferson pertains to foreign affairs and reflects Thomson's scientific and scholarly interests; letters from Jay reveal Thomson's extensive knowledge of the events of the Revolutionary era. Also includes Henry Laurens' charges against Thomson, Sept. 1779, and Thomson's 10-page defense. Contains notes on Charles Pinckney's speech of Aug. 10, 1786; notes on debates in Congress, July 24–26, 1777, and Aug. 16–22, 1786; Thomson's evaluation of David Ramsay's *History of the American Revolution* (Philadelphia, 1789), including an account of the achievement of American unity in the aftermath of the Boston Port Bill; a 50-page fragment of Thomson's translation of the Septuagint; and photostats of his nearly complete extract of the Stamp Act Congress' proceedings copied from the *Proceedings of the Congress at New York* (Annapolis, Md., 1766).

Principal correspondents: Elias Boudinot, Robert Clenachan, George Clymer, W. H. Drayton, Rev. John Ettwein, Robert R. Livingston, James Lovell, Jonathan Mifflin, James Monroe, George Morgan, Cadwalader Morris, Gouverneur Morris, Robert Morris, Isaac Norris, William Paca, Richard Peters, Jacob Read, Joseph Reed, John C. Symmes, Washington, and Peter Whiteside.

See *NUCMC* 61–130.

A number of the documents are printed in *Collections of the New York Historical Society (1878)*.

WILLIAM THORNTON PAPERS
18 vols., 5 boxes, 1741–1858.

1073   Thornton (1759–1828): Physician; architect; inventor.

Volume 1 contains 20 letters from the Revolutionary era. The earliest correspondence pertains to Thornton's student days at Edinburgh; eight letters, 1786–89, from Joseph Banks, J. C. Lettsom, and Jean Pierre Brissot de Warville concern Thornton's scientific pursuits and the emancipation and colonization of Negroes in Sierra Leone. Six small notebooks contain Thornton's diary, May 1777—June 1782, the period of his medical apprenticeship with Dr. Fell of Ulverstone and his studies at Edinburgh. Diary entries describe his life with Quaker relatives and acquaintances in Britain.

TENCH TILGHMAN PAPERS
1 box, 1775–86.   Part photostats.

1074   Tilghman (1744–86): Philadelphia, Pa., and Baltimore, Md., merchant; secretary to the commissioners to the Iroquois, 1775; aide-de-camp to Washington, 1776-83.

Business correspondence from William Hemsley to Messrs. Tench Tilghman and Co., 1784–86, concerns the tobacco and wheat trade, with particular reference to Kent Island and the Eastern Shore of Maryland. Robert Morris, Tilghman's business partner, is mentioned in some of the correspondence. Also includes copies of Hemsley's account with Tilghman and Co., Apr.—Nov. 1785, and Tilghman's account with Messrs. Willing, Morris and Swanwick of Philadelphia and Baltimore, Apr.—July 1784. Two diaries kept by Tilghman during the expedition to the Iroquois, Aug.—Sept. 1775, and the siege of

Yorktown, 1781, contain information on Indian culture and on military strategy in the Yorktown campaign.

Both diaries are printed in Samuel A. Harrison, *Memoir of Lt. Col. Tench Tilghman* ... (Albany, N.Y., 1876).

GASTON TISSANDIER COLLECTION

34 boxes, 1776–1914.   Finding aid available.   *NUCMC* 62–4888

1075   Tissandier: Collector.

Papers, news clippings, photographs, drawings, maps, charts, notes, and letters on early aeronautical engineering and aeronauts, collected by Gaston and Albert Tissandier. Most of the pertinent material concerns the career of the European balloonist, François Blanchard.

TONER COLLECTION

282 boxes and vols., 1688–1902.   Part transcripts. Finding aid available.

NUCMC 67-634.

1076   Joseph Meredith Toner (1825–96): District of Columbia physician and amateur historian.

The medical papers, boxes 64–184, contain several letters of Revolutionary era physicians concerning scientific and agricultural experiments, the wartime economy, delayed shipments of medical supplies, and other varied topics. Also a translation of Dr. Johann D. Shoepf's *Materia Medica Americana* ... (Er langae, 1787); articles by Henry Ellis and John Kearsley, Jr.; and letters, testimony, and articles regarding the controversy between John Morgan and William Shippen over management of the medical department of the Revolutionary Army. Numerous indexes include medical men and subjects mentioned in the journals of the Continental Congress, 1774–88; physicians in Peter Force's *American Archives;* medical articles in the *Pennsylvania Gazette* to 1800; and physicians in the *Pennsylvania Archives,* 1st ser. Toner also compiled a bibliography of medical work and theses, 1750–1800; arranged references to medical items in American periodicals and newspapers before 1800; listed American graduates in medicine from the University of Edinburgh and St. Andrews University, 1705–1800; and noted early public health laws, 18th-century medical societies, Virginia physicians who served in the Revolutionary War, and surgeons and surgeon's mates who died in the war.

Washingtoniana, boxes 185–256, primarily consists of transcripts and printed copies of George Washington and Washington family material, including journals, diaries, correspondence, surveys, financial papers, documents concerning Mount Vernon, military records, family genealogy, and miscellaneous papers. Many of the items have been annotated by Toner. Not duplicated in the Library's Washington papers are letters written for Washington by various aides; nearly 100 letters from Lund Washington, the manager of Washington's estates during the Revolution; an account book of Thomas Davis, an Alexandria, Va., weaver, 1767–71; and records of Washington's mill, 1777–85; as well as the "Mount Vernon Store Book," 1787, concerning supplies received and dispensed at the plantation; and "Rolls of Polls" for Frederick and Fairfax Counties, 1758–68. Also the journal of Robert Lewis, who accompanied Martha Washington from Virginia to New York, 1789; the names of officers from pension lists; wills of members of the Washington family; and a descriptive list of forts, blockhouses, and stockades built in America, 1607–1897.

Collected material, boxes 257–282, includes an autograph collection containing 21 letters and documents from the Revolutionary period, among them letters of Lord Dunmore, 1776, Arthur Lee, 1789, Richard Henry Lee, 1784 and 1786, and Lord North, 1780. Other items include miscellaneous deeds and military returns, a series of letters to Capt. Allen McLane concerning the conduct of the war, and documents pertaining to the court-martial of Capt. Richard Lippincott in 1782. Also John Murray's "Mathematical School Book for 1789"; notes in German on Ludwig T. Spitter's "Lectures on

Universal History," 1787–88; and a protest of the committee of safety for Botetourt County addressed to the Virginia Convention, June 1776. The papers of William Douglas, a Scottish emigrant, minister, and tutor in Virginia, contain accounts, surveys, contracts, lists of slaves, and a few letters, 1751–93. Also the journal of John Barr of the 4th New York Militia Regiment, June 1779—Jan. 1781, May—Oct. 1782, including a record of daily expenses; an Aquia, Va., merchant's daybook with a list prepared by Toner of the persons and firms dealing with this merchant; *Musqueto* accounts, 1779–80, concerning the activities of the British privateer; and the orderly books of Edward Burd, July 3—Sept. 24, 1775, Elihu Lyman, Jan. 5—Oct. 4, 1776, and Henry Knox, May 18—June 11, 1778.

THOMAS TOWNSHEND PAPERS
1 box, 1782.

1077   Townshend (1733–1800): 1st Viscount Sydney; member, Parliament, 1754–83; secretary at war, 1782; secretary of state for home affairs, 1782–89.

Three letters between Townshend and Lord Shelburne discuss the granting of independence to America, the safety of loyalists in New York, the appearance of William Franklin in London, and peace negotiations.

JARED TRACY PAPERS
1 folio, 1777–78.   Force transcripts.

1078   Tracy (b. 1741): Norwich, Conn., merchant.

Tracy's correspondence primarily concerns the shipment of flour from Virginia to Boston for the Continental Army and its distribution to storage points throughout Massachusetts.

Principal correspondents: William Aylett, Jedediah Huntington, Aaron Riggs, Jacob Taylor, and Joseph Trumbull.

ROBERT TROUP PAPERS
1 box, 1780–1820.

1079   Troup (1757–1832): Aide-de-camp to Gens. Timothy Woodhull and Horatio Gates; secretary to the Board of War, 1778–79; secretary to the Board of Treasury, 1779–80; New York lawyer and judge.

Five letters between Aaron Burr and Troup, 1780, reveal the thoughts and activities of a young law student and former Army officer.

JOHN TRUMBULL PAPERS
2 boxes, 2 vols., 1786–1841.

1080   Trumbull (1756–1843): Artist; aide to Gens. George Washington and Horatio Gates, 1775–78; studied painting in London, 1780; returned to the U.S. in 1815.

Contains several items pertaining to Trumbull's artistic career during the Revolutionary era. Also a 1786 journal of a trip through France, Germany, and Flanders describing architecture, sculpture, and paintings; and a memo book, 1789, recording income, expenditures, and subscription lists for engravings of his paintings.

JONATHAN TRUMBULL PAPERS
12 boxes, 1774–96.   Force transcripts.   *NUCMC* 61–2783

1081   Trumbull (1710–85): Connecticut merchant; gov., 1769–84.

Chiefly letterbooks and correspondence of Trumbull, 1776–81, discussing Connecticut politics, the Continental Congress, the organization of the Army, frontier defense, the Articles of Confederation, and economic conditions. Also the campaign of 1776 in New York, the Burgoyne invasion, 1777, Connecticut's Susquehanna claims, naval prisoners, and the Connecticut and Continental navies. Also contains numerous military returns, financial reports, and proclamations. An index is available for most of the collection.

Principal correspondents: Andrew Adams, Benedict Arnold, Ephraim Blaine, John Burgoyne, Thaddeus Burr, George Clinton, Nicholas Cooke, Pierre Van Cortlandt, Eliphalet Dyer, Oliver Ellsworth, Horatio Gates, Jonathan Glover, Nathanael Greene, William Greene, Mathew Griswold, John Hancock, Titus Hosmer, Benjamin Huntington, Jabez Huntington, Jedediah Huntington, Samuel Huntington, John Jay, La Luzerne, Henry Laurens, William Ledyard, Henry B. Livingston, Thomas Mumford, Samuel H. Parsons, John Penn, George Pitkin, Israel Putnam, Rochambeau, Jesse Root, Philip Schuyler, Thomas Seymour, Nathaniel Shaw, Thomas Shaw, Roger Sherman, Gold Selleck Silliman, Joseph Spencer, David Sproat, Duncan Stewart, John Sullivan, Joseph Trumbull, Jonathan Tyler, Vergennes, James Wadsworth, Andrew Ward, Washington, and Oliver Wolcott.

Many of the letters are published in the Massachusetts Historical Society, *Collections*, 5th ser., vols. 9-10 (1885, 1888); 7th ser., vols. 2-3 (1902). Originals in the Connecticut Historical Society, the Massachusetts Historical Society, and private collections of Leonard Hebert, Henry Stevens, and John McClellan.

TRURO PARISH, VIRGINIA, VESTRY BOOK
1 vol., 1732–1802.

1082   Entries concern routine vestry matters, such as the building of a new church and the care of orphans and other parish dependents. Also contains lists of vestrymen, including Washington, George Mason, and George William Fairfax.

ST. GEORGE TUCKER PAPERS
1 vol., 1788–1801.

1083   Tucker (1752–1827): Virginia lawyer, professor, and judge.

Contains correspondence between John Randolph of Roanoke and Tucker, his stepfather, concerning Randolph's education and other personal matters.

SAMUEL TUCKER PAPERS
1 vol., 1777–81.   Force transcripts.

1084   Tucker (1747–1833): Marblehead, Mass., naval officer; captain of schooners *Franklin* and *Hancock*, and frigate *Boston*, 1776–80.

Correspondence with the marine committee and the Navy Board of the Eastern Department concerning cruises in American and European waters and the capture and disposal of prize vessels. Also includes instructions to and correspondence from American Ministers in France, descriptions of two cruises, Tucker's opinion on the defense of Charleston harbor, 1780, and miscellaneous documents.

Principal correspondents: John Adams, John Bondfield, John Deshon, Franklin, Arthur Lee, Benjamin Lincoln, Duncan MacPherson, Peter McIntosh, George Mitchell, William Moultrie, Mark Pringle, Joseph Reed, John Rutledge, John Selby, Richard Smith, William Vernon, Abraham Whipple, and William Whipple.

Published in part in John H. Sheppard, *Life of Samuel Tucker* . . . (Boston, 1868). Originals in Harvard University Library.

LEWIS M. TURNER WATERMARK COLLECTION
4 boxes, 1769–1934.

1085   Turner: Collector.

Revolutionary era material consists of miscellaneous writs, appointments, bail bonds, and complaints issued in Frederick and Washington Counties, Md., 1769–86.

PETER TURNER PAPERS
1 box, 1772–1889.   *NUCMC* 70–982

1086   Turner (1751–1822): Surgeon, 1st Rhode Island Regiment, 1777–81; Greenwich, R.I., doctor after 1783; brother-in-law of Gen. James Varnum.

Contains material concerning medical treatment in the late 18th century. Turner's day-book, Jan. 1782—Aug. 1783, lists patients, illnesses, and treatments. Also includes letters asking medical advice, detailed descriptions of unusual cases, and miscellaneous accounts and receipts.

Principal correspondents: Gabriel Allen, George Bowen, Jabez Campfield, John Parrish, and Samuel Tenny.

JOHN TYLER PAPERS
8 vols., 1691–1918.   Microfilm available.   *NUCMC* 60–430
1087   Tyler (1790–1862): Virginia lawyer, President of the U.S.
Documents from the Revolutionary era include a manuscript volume of verse written in part by Tyler's father, Judge John Tyler of Greenway, Va., 1772–1802; an account for the sale of two Negroes to John Carter, 1783; and a letter from Judge Tyler to Henry Tazewell, 1782, concerning a legal matter.

UNITED STATES, MORRISTOWN NATIONAL HISTORICAL PARK MANUSCRIPT COLLECTION
69 reels microfilm, 16th to 20th centuries.   Finding aid available. *NUCMC* 61-1156
1088   Contains many Washington items, including account books, journals, orderly books, and correspondence. Also papers pertaining to Morris County, N. J., and Washington's headquarters there, the Continental Congress, the American and British Armies during the war, and a wide variety of prominent Revolutionary era figures. Includes an Alexander Hamilton letter of Feb. 18, 1781, explaining his break with Washington; Sir William Howe's orderly book, 1776; the diary of an American prisoner of war, 1781; memorandum books of Andrew Bell, 1789–90, and Lord Stirling, 1765–66; Aaron Burr's bankbook for the Bank of North America, 1785–93; James Abeel receipt books, 1778–80; and documents from the colonial assemblies, councils and committees of safety, courts, and militias.

The collection was microfilmed under the auspices of the National Historical Publications Commission. The finding aid, *A Guide to the Manuscripts Collection, Morristown National Historical Park* (n.d.), contains an introduction, information on the provenance of the collection, a comprehensive list of correspondents, and a selected list of recipients.

Principal correspondents: John Adams, Ethan Allen, Jeffery Amherst, Burgoyne, Gov. Peter Chester, Cornwallis, Franklin, Germain, Jefferson, Henry Knox, Lafayette, Henry Laurens, Richard Henry Lee, Robert Livingston, Alexander McDougall, Madison, Gouverneur Morris, Robert Morris, John Sullivan, and Charles Thomson.

UNITED STATES CONSTITUTION
1 folio, 1787.   Force manuscripts.
1089   Federal Convention imprint of the *Report of the Committee on Detail*, Aug. 6, 1787, annotated by William Samuel Johnson and William Jackson.

UNITED STATES CONSTITUTION, ANNOTATED IMPRINTS
9 items, 1787.   Photostats.
1090   Includes copies of the *Report of the Committee on Detail*, Aug. 6, 1787, owned by David Brearley, Nicholas Gilman, and James Madison; copies of the *Report of the Committee of Style*, Sept. 12, 1787, owned by Rufus King, Abraham Baldwin, James Madison, and Washington; and copies of the Constitution as finally submitted by the convention, Sept. 17, 1787, owned by James Madison and Edmund Pendleton.

UNITED STATES CONSTITUTION, MISCELLANY
12 folios, 1 box, 1787–90.   Part photostats.
1091   Includes copies of the Constitution, the resolution of transmittal to the various State legislatures, and miscellaneous related documents.

UNITED STATES NAVY, MISCELLANY
1 box, 1776–1909.

1092   Contains three vendue books for captured naval goods and vessels sold at auction, 1776–81.

UNITED STATES NAVY, PRIZES AND CAPTURES
1 vol., 1775–76.

1093   Chiefly receipts for naval supplies received at Beverly, Mass., by William Bartlett. Also portage bills, contracts, miscellaneous accounts, an inventory of stores aboard the schooner *Harrison*, 1776, and a list of officers and men on the schooner *Warren*.

UNITED STATES REVOLUTION, AUTOGRAPH DOCUMENTS
1 vol., 1766–91.

1094   Miscellaneous letters and documents chiefly pertaining to military affairs, including signatures of Henry Knox, Richard Henry Lee, Isaac Sears, François de Barbé-Marbois, and Jeremiah Wadsworth.

UNITED STATES REVOLUTION, MISCELLANY
7 boxes, 1774–83.   Part photostats and transcripts.

1095   Includes military and political correspondence; receipts, bills, and accounts; and troop returns, discharges, contracts, payrolls, and muster rolls; proclamations; a satire on George III's speech to Parliament, 1774, attributed to Benjamin Franklin; an account of the battle of Bunker Hill by Elijah Hyde; petitions; signed oaths of allegiance; an orderly book, Mar. 23–24, 1778; an entry from the diary of Samuel Miles, Nov. 17, 1776; naval accounts; and an extract from the journal of Christian Senff, Camden, S.C., Aug. 16, 1780.

Principal correspondents: Benedict Arnold, William Barber, John Beatty, Peter Bellinger, John Bigelow, Daniel Brodhead, Henry Brodrick, Thomas Burke, Richard Butler, Edward Carrington, William Christy, John Cochran, Edward Cook, John Cropp, William Davidson, Henry Dixon, John Dooly, Lord Dunmore, David Fanning, Benjamin Ford, William Franklin, Elbridge Gerry, Nathanael Greene, Dr. David Griffith, James Hamilton, Edward Hand, Robert H. Harrison, John Hart, William Heath, Thomas Hincks, James Houstoun, Robert Howe, Edmund Hyrne, Samuel Johnston, Willie Jones, William Kelly, Lafayette, La Luzerne, Henry Lee, Jr., Benjamin Lincoln, Walter Livingston, Alexander Lochry, Alexander McDougall, James McHenry, Marquis de Malmady, Jonathan Mifflin, John Mitchell, John Moale, Gouverneur Morris, Newark, N.J., committee of safety, William Palfrey, Samuel Patterson, Nathaniel Pendleton, Andrew Peters, Charles Pettit, William Phillips, Timothy Pickering, Richard Platt, Enoch Poor, James Potter, Augustine Prevost, James Mark Prevost, Israel Putnam, Jonathan Reed, Joseph Reed, Rochambeau, Gurdon Saltonstall, Alexander Scammell, David Scott, James Searle, Adam Shaply, Meriwether Smith, Thomas Storm, Samuel Stringer, William Thompson, John Tunno, Anthony Wayne, James Wilkinson, William Williams, Andrew Williamson, Henry Wynkoop, and Richard Young.

NICHOLAS VAN DYKE PAPERS
1 vol., 1780–93.

1096   Van Dyke (1738–89): New Castle, Del., lawyer and landholder; member, New Castle committee of safety, 1776, Continental Congress, 1777–82; pres., Delaware, 1783–86.

Correspondence to Van Dyke discussing financial problems in the State and Nation. Includes several letters of members of Congress. Two unpublished letters of Eleazar McComb describe a mutiny by Continental troops and the flight of Congress from Philadelphia in 1781. Several letters of Samuel Patterson concern land sales and speculation.

Principal correspondents: Thomas Barclay, Samuel Hardy, George Latimer, Robert R. Livingston, Thomas McKean, Thomas Mifflin, Robert Morris, and Charles Nixon.

Peter Van Schaack Papers
1 box, 1776–1841.

1097   Van Schaack (1747–1832): New York lawyer and loyalist; member, New York committee of correspondence and Kinderhook committee of safety; emigrated to London, 1778, returned to Kinderhook, 1785.

     Contains reports on conditions in New Brunswick, requests for legal aid to secure pensions from the British Government, and petitions to regain forfeited land in New York. Most of the material concerns Van Schaack's law practice in Albany County, N. Y., after 1785.

     Principal correspondents: Ann Colden, Edmund Fanning, George D. Ludlow, and Philip Skene.

Varnum and Stark Papers
1 vol., 1777–80.

1098   James Varnum (1748–89): Massachusetts, Rhode Island; brig. gen., Continental Army, 1777–79; John Stark (1728–1822): New Hampshire; brig. gen., Continental Army, 1777–83.

     Returns for the brigades of Gen. James Varnum and Gen. John Stark, Peekskill and Valley Forge, Aug. 1777—Mar. 1779, and Providence, R. I., and vicinity, May 1779—Nov. 1780.

Vermont, Board of War
1 folio, 1779–81.   Force transcripts.

1099   Includes minutes of the Board of War as well as miscellaneous letters to the board from Jonas Fay and Ira Allen.

     Published in John A. Williams, ed., *State Papers of Vermont*, vol. 17 (Montpelier, Vt., 1969). Originals in Vermont State Archives.

Vermont, Council of Safety
1 folio, 1777–82.   Force transcripts.

1100   Concerns Vermont's participation in the war, the internal politics of the self-proclaimed republic, and its relations with the Continental Congress, New York, New Hampshire, and British authorities in Canada.

     Published in part in John A. Williams, ed., *State Papers of Vermont*, vol. 17 (Montpelier, Vt., 1969). Originals in Vermont State Archives.

Vermont, Council of Safety, Letters
1 folio, 1777–85.   Force transcripts.

1101   Resolves, proclamations, and letters pertaining to Vermont's independence from New York and New Hampshire.

     Principal correspondents: Ethan Allen, Ira Allen, Jacob Bayley, Timothy Bedell, Benjamin Bellows, Thomas Chittenden, George Clinton, Roger Enos, Jonas Fay, Enoch Hale, Moses Hazen, Samuel Livermore, Elisha Payne, Nathaniel Peabody, Philip Schuyler, John Stark, and Washington.

     Originals in Vermont State Archives.

Vermont, Governor
1 folio, 1779–91.   Force transcripts.

1102   A collection of proclamations of Gov. Thomas Chittenden.

     Published in John A. Williams, ed., *State Papers of Vermont*, vol. 17 (Montpelier, Vt., 1969).

     Originals in Vermont State Archives.

VERMONT PAPERS
36 vols., 1762–1824.   Photostats.

1103   Series one (11 volumes) contains a few letters from Ethan Allen to British officials at Quebec concerning trade between Canada and Vermont and the possibility of Vermont's allegiance to England; letters of Ira Allen and others concerning land sales, cattle raising, and lumbering in Vermont; and miscellaneous receipts, petitions, addresses, and debentures. Also letters concerning Ethan Allen's role in the Susquehanna Company, 1785–86, and copies of the records of conventions held in the New Hampshire Grants to chart a course of action against New York, 1776–77. Documents in series two (25 volumes) include letters, deeds, and accounts of the Allen brothers—Herman, Ethan, and Ira; routine letters and accounts of both Isaac Tichnor, assistant commissary general of purchase for northern accounts, and Jonathan Child, assistant commissary general of purchase for the Northern Department; court records for Cumberland County, N. Y., 1769–70, and New London, Conn., 1762–74; and miscellaneous legal papers.

Principal correspondents: Remember Baker, Thomas Butterfield, Thomas Chittenden, Jacob Cuyler, Ebenezer Judd, Levi Shepard, Jonathan Warner, and James Whitelaw.

Originals in Vermont Historical Society and New York State Library.

VERNON–WAGER COLLECTION
17 vols., 1654–1773).   Force manuscripts.

1104   Edward Vernon (1684–1757) and Sir Charles Wager (1666–1743): British admirals.
Contains one letter, Mar. 1773, from Lord Dartmouth to Lord Dunmore communicating the King's allowance of colonial laws pertaining to slaves, stock, and taxes and recommending that no action be taken on election of members to the house of Burgesses.

VIRGINIA, MISCELLANY
1 box, 1773–89.   Part photostats.

1105   Includes personal correspondence, executive orders in council, account books, resolutions, land grants, lists of workmen, and militia returns. Also a reproduction of the first draft of the Virginia Declaration of Rights, 1776, a list of State naval vessels "fit for duty," an expense account kept by Joseph Jones, 1780, the Berkeley County rent book, 1780, and resolutions of the directors of the Hospital for the Insane at Williamsburg.

Principal correspondents: Richard Caswell, Dudley Digges, William Grayson, Nathanael Greene, Benjamin Harrison, Patrick Henry, Richard Henry Lee, James McClurg, William Moore, Edmund Pendleton, Beverley Randolph, Edmund Randolph, Meriwether Smith, and William Woodford.

VIRGINIA, RATIFICATION OF CONSTITUTION
1 vol., 1788.   Force manuscripts.

1106   Records of the proceedings of the Virginia Convention for consideration of the U.S. Constitution, July 25–27. 1788, signed by Edmund Pendleton. Includes lists of the Declaration of Rights, 20 recommended amendments to the Constitution, and committee appointments and votes.

VIRGINIA PAPERS
14 vols., 1758–1890.   Draper Mss., series ZZ, WHi. Microfilm, 3 reels.

1107   Miscellaneous original documents, transcripts, notes, and memoranda pertaining to frontier defense and campaigns against the Indians. Original materials include military accounts, muster rolls, returns, survey books, journals, and correspondence. Contains three journals of Dr. William Fleming—one of the Point Pleasant campaign, Sept. 5—

Nov. 22, 1774; and two of his journeys into Kentucky as commissioner of Virginia to settle accounts, Nov. 6, 1779—Apr. 28, 1780, and Jan. 4—Apr. 22, 1783. Also Capt. Joseph Martin's orderly book from the Cherokee campaign, Sept. 5—Oct. 20, 1776; and James Newell's journal of the campaign of 1774, published in the *Virginia Magazine of History and Biography*, vol. 9 (Jan. 1904), p. 242–53.

Principal correspondents: Matthew Arbuckle, Anthony Bledsoe, William Christian, John Cook, William Fleming, James Henderson, William McClanahan, John Madison, William Preston, William Russell, Isaac Shelby, John Stewart, John Vanbibber, and Francis Walker.

The papers are calendared in *The Preston and Virginia Papers of the Draper Collection of Manuscripts* (Madison, Wis., 1915). See also Thwaites, *Descriptive List of Manuscript Collections*, p. 91–98.

James Wadsworth Collection
2 boxes, 1775–1818.   Photostats.

1108   Jeremiah Wadsworth (1743–1804): Connecticut sea captain; commissary of Connecticut forces, 1775; deputy commissary general of purchases, 1777; commissary general, 1778–79; commissary for Rochambeau's army, 1780–83.

Chiefly correspondence from Joseph Trumbull (1738–78) to Jeremiah Wadsworth concerning the supply of the American and French Armies. Contains some information of troop movements and battle plans in New York, New Jersey, and Pennsylvania. The Constitution is discussed in a Gouverneur Morris letter of 1787.

Principal correspondents: Benedict Arnold, Aaron Burr, Oliver Ellsworth, David Humphreys, Ebenezer Huntington, Jedediah Huntington, Samuel Huntington, Henry Knox, Lafayette, Samuel H. Parsons, Israel Putnam, Rochambeau, and Joseph Trumbull.

Richard Waldron Papers
1 vol., 1726–70.   Force manuscripts.

1109   Waldron (1694–1753): Secretary to Gov. Jonathan Belcher (1681–1757) of Massachusetts; member, New Hampshire Assembly.

Chiefly drafts of letters from Waldron to Belcher, but includes drafts of two letters from William Wentworth to Gov. Benning Wentworth concerning political affairs in Massachusetts and New Hampshire, 1770.

Joseph B. Walker Collection
14 items, 1774–79.   Force transcripts.

1110   Personal correspondence from Benjamin Thompson, later Count Rumford, a Massachusetts loyalist, to Rev. Timothy Walker of Concord, Mass., Dec. 1774—Aug. 1775. Also contains the verses to several Revolutionary War songs.

Artemas Ward Papers
5 reels microfilm, 1684–1880.   *NUCMC* 69–1649

1111   Ward (1727–1800): Col., Massachusetts Militia, 1775; maj. gen., Continental Army, 1775–77; commander in chief, Eastern Department, 1776–77; member, Continental Congress, 1780–81.

Documents pertaining to Ward's service during the Revolution include letters, dispatches, and miscellaneous military papers relating to the siege of Boston, 1775–76; copies of letters from Ward to General Washington and other officers; two orderly books, April 20, 1775—April 3, 1776, and July 13, 1775—Mar. 20, 1777, containing general orders issued from Cambridge headquarters and orders issued by Ward at the Roxbury camp; and drafts of letters written by Ward during his service in Congress, 1780. Also includes personal accounts and receipts, 1778–87; family correspondence; deeds, bills of sale, surveys, and muster rolls; and official papers concerning Ward's position as Shrewsbury's representative in the Massachusetts General Court, 1766.

Principal correspondents: John Avery, Jr., William Bartlett, James Bowdoin, Benjamin Church, Samuel Flagg, John Frazer, Horatio Gates, Jonathan Glover, John Hancock, Robert H. Harrison, William Heath, John Langdon, Benjamin Lincoln, Thomas Mifflin, Stephen Moylan, John Nixon, Hannah Pierpont, Rufus Putnam, Joseph Reed, Philip Schuyler, William Story, Jonathan Trumbull, Joseph Ward, Thomas Ward, and Joseph Warren.

Originals in Massachusetts Historical Society.

MERCY OTIS WARREN PAPERS
3 boxes, 1790–1814.

1112   Warren (1728–1814): Writer of patriotic plays, poetry, and history; sister of James Otis, wife of James Warren.

Contains the original manuscript copy of Mercy Otis Warren's *History of the Rise, Progress, and Termination of the American Revolution* (Boston, 1805), with the author's pre-publication corrections. Also two additional copies in the hand of her son, James, and one copy with notes for a revised edition.

MERCY OTIS WARREN PAPERS
2 reels microfilm, 1709–1841.

1113   Warren (1728–1814): See entry no. 1112.

Contains correspondence of Mercy Otis Warren with leaders of the Revolution in Massachusetts and spokesmen for the American cause in England. A 500-page letter-book, 1770–1800, describes events of the Revolutionary period. The letters focus on Massachusetts politics, but remarks to Mrs. Catherine Macaulay touch on issues and events in all of the Colonies. Also includes miscellaneous poems and dramatic works of Mrs. Warren.

Principal correspondents: Abigail Adams, John Adams, Elbridge Gerry, Nathaniel Gorham, John Hancock, Samuel Holten, Rufus King, Benjamin Lincoln, James Otis, James Warren, Winslow Warren, and Martha Washington.

Originals in Massachusetts Historical Society.

BUSHROD WASHINGTON PAPERS
1 reel microfilm, 1669–1829.

1114   Washington (1762–1829): Nephew of General Washington; Virginia lawyer and statesman; associate justice, U.S. Supreme Court, 1798–1829.

Contains letters from Bushrod Washington's father and mother, John A. and Hannah, 1780–83, primarily concerning business matters. Also includes three business letters from George Wythe, 1785–87.

Originals in the possession of Nat W. Washington, Ephrata, Wash.

GEORGE WASHINGTON PAPERS
77,000 items, 1592–1937.   Microfilm available.

1115   Washington (1732–99): Col., Virginia Militia; member, Virginia House of Burgesses, 1759–74, Continental Congress, 1774–75; commander in chief, American forces, 1775–83; President of the U.S.

Material from the Revolutionary era chiefly concerns military and political affairs during the active years of the war. Includes official correspondence with militia and Continental officers, Governors and officials in the various States, members of Congress, British officers, and private citizens concerning virtually every aspect of the war—supply, maneuvers, peace negotiations, prisoner exchanges, rank disputes, naval affairs, etc. Also includes returns for troops and supplies, intelligence reports, general orders, proceedings of courts-martial and councils of war, battle plans and maps, petitions, proclamations, and addresses. Documents from the prewar period primarily relate to Washington's surveying activities, service in the Virginia Militia, plantation affairs, provincial politics, and personal and family matters. Postwar documents cover subjects ranging from personal and business affairs to the Constitutional struggle.

See John C. Fitzpatrick, ed., *The Writings of George Washington from the Original Manuscript Sources, 1745–1799,* 39 vols. (Washington, D.C., 1964), which contains a complete description of the collection and a manual for use of the 124-reel microfilm edition. A comprehensive new edition of the Washington papers is in preparation at the University of Virginia.

NEHEMIAH WATERMAN, JR., PAPERS
1 folio, 1733–1801.

1116   Waterman (1736–1801): New London County, Conn., justice of the peace.

Contains Waterman's casebook as justice of the peace, 1788–89; marriage records for Norwich, Conn., 1781–1801; and genealogical records of the Waterman family from 1733.

WILLIAM WATSON
1 vol., 1782.

1117   Watson: Lt. and capt., 9th Massachusetts Regiment, 1777–82.

Roll of the men in Capt. Watson's company listing age, size, color, trade, hometown, and term of enlistment.

MESHECH WEARE PAPERS
7 folios, 1777–80.   Force transcripts.

1118   Weare (1713–86): New York statesman; pres., Council of New Hampshire, 1776–84; chairman, committee of safety, 1776–84; pres., New Hampshire, 1784–85.

Weare's official correspondence as president of the State Council of New Hampshire with delegates in Congress, political leaders throughout New England, Continental officers, and officials at the Treasury Office and the Board of War. Also personal and family correspondence, military returns, memorials, extracts from newspapers, resolutions of Congress, and a list of towns and counties in Connecticut showing population figures for 1777 and 1779. Subjects discussed in the official correspondence include Continental and State finance, the Convention Army, the conduct of the war, military supply, the organization of the Army, and the Vermont boundary controversy.

Principal correspondents: Samuel Adams, Ira Allen, Josiah Bartlett, John Burgoyne, Horatio Gates, William Greene, Lyman Hall, Patrick Henry, Silas Hedges, William Howe, John Jay, Richard Henry Lee, Samuel Livermore, Joseph Otis, Nathaniel Peabody, Jeremiah Powell, Alexander Scammell, Roger Sherman, Baron von Steuben, John Sullivan, Jonathan Trumbull, Jeremiah Wadsworth, Washington, and William Whipple.

Originals in Massachusetts Historical Society.

GIDEON WELLES PAPERS
109 units, 1777–1911.   *NUCMC* 78–2085

1119   Welles (1802–98): Journalist; public official; secretary of the navy, 1862–69.

Volume 1 contains five items from the period of the Revolution: a letter from Gen. William Maxwell to Gen. James Potter concerning charges lodged against Maxwell for his conduct at the battle of Germantown, 1777; a Joseph Reed letter, 1779, concerning frontier defenses, bounty lands, and troop morale; an Elias Boudinot letter dealing with personal and business matters, 1782; a sailing permit, 1786, for the port of New York; and a 1787 promissory note.

WEST FLORIDA PAPERS
15 vols., 2 boxes, 1565–1827.

1120   "Secretary of State's Letter Book," containing correspondence between Gov. Peter Chester and Secretaries Hillsborough, and Dartmouth, Apr. 1770—Sept. 1774; record of land patents issued by Governor Chester, June 1771—Jan. 1776; "Conveyances of Land" indentures, June 1771—Aug. 1772, Apr. 1774—Dec. 1777 (3 vols.); record of patents, commissions, and other papers, 1764–81; minutes of the assembly, Nov. 1766—Jan. 1767, Feb. 1767—June 1769; minutes of the council, Feb. 1767—July 1769, Dec. 1769—May 1772; and entry books of fees for warrants, bonds, licenses, surveys, etc., Secretary's Office, Pensacola, June 1774—May 1777.

WEST INDIES, BAHAMAS
1 box, 1785–86.

1121   Accounts of provisions sent by William Moss and others to loyalists arriving from East Florida, 1785. Also an issue of the London *Gazette*, Mar. 1786, and a circular letter from Whitehall concerning trade regulations between the United States and British colonies in America, 1786.

GEORGE WHITEFIELD PAPERS
2 vols., 1736–70.

1122   Whitefield (1714–70): British evangelist; founder of Calvinistic Methodists.
    Material from the period of the Revolution includes about 35 letters to Whitefield from ministers, friends, and admirers in England and America; one sermon; and three engravings, two of Whitefield and one of the Whitefield Tabernacle. The letters are primarily invitations to preach, requests for aid in securing a minister, and accounts of personal religious experiences. Several letters written from Georgia pertain to Whitefield's Bethesda Orphanage at Savannah.
    Principal correspondents: Matthew Bagshaw, William Bean, William Darke, Anne Dutton, Sarah Gill, John Graves, Mathew Graves, James Ingram, Robert Parsons, Abraham Thorn, and James Waddell.

WILLIAM WHITING COLLECTION
5 boxes, 1731–1952.   Finding aid available.   *NUCMC* 70–988

1123   Whiting (1843–1925): U.S. naval officer, 1863–1905.
    Items from the Revolutionary era include bills of sale, receipts, and notes of Gertgen and Conrat Scharp [Coenraed Sharp] of Albany, N.Y., primarily concerning slaves and sloops.
    In Naval Historical Foundation Collection.

WILDER FAMILY PAPERS
1 folio, 1776–1838.   Photostats.

1124   Wilder: Winchendon, Mass., farming family.
    Contains Mrs. Anna Wilder's plea for her husband to return home from the Army, Apr. 1776.

HENRY A. WILLARD II COLLECTION
1 box, 1777–1881.   *NUCMC* 71–1429

1125   Willard (b. 1902): Autograph collector.
    Contains miscellaneous accounts, receipts, and legal items, 1770–89, chiefly from Boston, Mass.

SAMUEL WILLIAMS PAPERS
1 folio, 1774.

1126   Williams: Vermont minister.

Sermon on peace and the danger of factions, delivered at Bradford, Vt., Nov. 6, 1774, before a church meeting concerning a complaint of A. Day, Jr., against J. Day, Jr.

WILLIAM WILLIAMS PAPERS
1 folio, 1740–80.   Force transcripts.

1127   Williams (1731–1811): Connecticut statesman; member, Continental Congress, 1776–77.

Contains a letter of Timothy Green concerning the printing of the Congressional resolves and proceedings, 1774; a Washington letter describing the battle for Philadelphia, Oct. 1777; an Eliphalet Dyer letter on the decaying economic and military situation in America, Feb. 1778; and an Oct. 1780 letter apparently to John Trumbull, the painter, discussing the surrender of Charleston, the defeat at Camden, the role of the French Army in America, and personal matters. Also a letter of Joseph Trumbull concerning mercantile conditions in London in 1764.

WILLIAMSBURG, VIRGINIA, MASONIC LODGE
1 box, 1773–79.   Photostats.

1128   Minutes of the Williamsburg, Va., Masonic Lodge, June 1773—Apr. 1779, recording names of members attending meetings, new members, and membership transfers.

JAMES WILSON PAPERS
1 box, 1787.   Photostats.

1129   Wilson (1742–98): Pennsylvania lawyer, political leader, essayist, jurist; member, Continental Congress, 1776–77, Philadelphia Convention, 1787; professor of law, College of Philadelphia; justice, U.S. Supreme Court, 1789.

Documents pertaining to the work of the committee of detail of the Philadelphia Convention, 1787.

Published in Max Farrand, ed., *The Records of the Federal Convention of 1787* (New Haven, Conn., 1934), vol. 2, p. 129–37, 152–75. Originals in Historical Society of Pennsylvania.

JAMES A. WILSON LETTERBOOK
1 vol., 1777–78.

1130   Wilson (d. 1783): Capt., 6th Pennsylvania Battalion, 1776–77; maj., Carlisle garrison, Oct. 1777—June 1778.

Correspondence with the Board of War and the quartermaster department of the Continental Army concerning military supplies. Also includes miscellaneous orders and receipts.

Principal correspondents: John Carothers, Benjamin Flower, Charles Lukens, James Mease, Joseph Nourse, Richard Peters, and Timothy Pickering.

WINDHAM, CONNECTICUT
1 folio, 1768–83.   Force transcripts.

1131   Extracts from the records of Windham town meetings include debates, resolves, and votes on issues such as nonimportation, the Intolerable Acts, Continental Association, salt distribution, Articles of Confederation, Army supplies, enlistments, taxation, and the loyalists' return.

JOHN WINTHROP PAPERS
1 box, 2 folios, 1744–79.

1132   Winthrop (1714–79): Massachusetts scientist and professor of mathematics at Harvard College.

Contains 16 letters from the 1760's and 1770's discussing Winthrop's scientific studies and his viewing of Venus and the aurora borealis.

JOHN WITHERSPOON PAPERS
1 vol., 1 box, 1758–83.

1133   Witherspoon (1723–94): Pres., College of New Jersey; member, New Jersey Provincial Congress, 1776, Continental Congress, 1776–82.

Chiefly notes and drafts of miscellaneous sermons, newspaper articles, speeches, and letters of instruction. Contains nine undated sermons in two small notebooks, two letters to Lord Marchmont soliciting his aid in securing charters for Presbyterian churches, and Witherspoon's essay on the need for common sense. Also Witherspoon's draft of Congressional instructions to the American Ministers in Paris, 1781, and the report of the committee on the Saratoga Convention.

JOHN D. WOELPPER PAPERS
1 box, 1763–1810.

1134   Woelpper: Farmer; surveyor; lt. in one of Virginia's additional companies attached to British Army in 1760; 1st lt., capt., Continental Army, 1776; served in German Battalion, 1776–78, and Corps of Invalids, 1778–83.

Consists primarily of letters, legal documents, and surveying records concerning claims of the Woelpper estate to Ohio River lands under proclamations of 1754 and 1763. Includes Woelpper's account of a 1773 surveying expedition from Philadelphia to Pittsburgh, Pa., down the Ohio River, and back to Philadelphia via Williamsburg, Va. Also contains a speech of Thomas Bullitt, Virginia surveyor for the Ohio District, to the Shawnee and their reply, 1773.

Principal correspondents: Jonathan Harris and Washington.

LEVI WOODBURY FAMILY PAPERS
60 vols., 45 boxes, 1638–1899.

1135   Levi Woodbury (1789–1851): New Hampshire lawyer and politician.

Box 45 contains the Blair-Woodbury family autograph collection, 1638–1839, 12 items of which are from the period of the Revolution. They include part of a letter concerning the dispute between John Paul Jones and Capt. Pierre Landais over the action between the *Serapis* and the *Bonhomme Richard*; a letter from Gen. John Sullivan to Joseph Reed concerning discord in the Army, 1781; a letter from Edmund Quincy to Miss Katherine Quincy concerning religion and politics, 1775; and a letter from John Hancock to his wife regarding the occupation of Philadelphia, 1777. Also includes photostats of letters of Mordecai Gist, 1779, and Arthur Lee, 1780.

WOOLSEY & SALMON LETTERBOOK
1 vol., 1774–84.   Force manuscripts.

1136   Woolsey & Salmon: Baltimore, Md., partnership.

Correspondence between Woolsey & Salmon and John Pringle of Philadelphia, a partner in the firm until Dec. 1780, concerning business operations. Includes information on the Irish servant and convict trade, 1774–78, and the impact of French entry into the war, 1778. Includes instructions to Irish correspondents concerning the evasion of British patrol ships along the American coast.

Principal correspondents: Robert Allison, John Armstrong, William Bryan, John Cox, James Cumming, Waddell Cunningham, George Darley, David Gaussan, Thomas Greg, Thomas McCabe, George Moore, Philip Moore, Stephen Steward, Benjamin Titcomb, William Van Wyck, and the firms Delap & McCrury, Norton & Beall, Robinson & Sandwith, and William Wilcocks & Co.

Extracts of selected letters published in William Clark Bell, ed., *Naval Documents of the American Revolution* (Washington, D.C., 1964–70), vols. 1–5.

NATHANIEL WRIGHT FAMILY PAPERS
77 boxes, 1787–1917.   Finding aid available.

1137   Wright (1789–1875): Teacher, lawyer, and director of Ohio railroads.

Contains a promotional tract by John C. Symmes for the sale of Ohio land at the mouth of the Miami River, 1787, and two land agreements of Benjamin Stiles of New Jersey, 1788.

RICHARD YOUNG PAPERS
1 folio, 1780–82.

1138   Young: Assistant deputy quartermaster at Fredericksburg, Va., 1780–82.

Correspondence, receipts, requisitions, and accounts concerning military supplies received and issued at Fredericksburg. Includes four letters from Young to Maj. Richard Claiborne, Capt. Charles Russell, and John Pierce, 1781–82. Letters to Young are from William Davies, Thomas H. Drew, William Finnie, James Hendricks, Miles Hunter, George Rice, Oliver Towles, and Henry Young.

Foreign Reproductions

Austria

Vienna, *Haus-, Hof-, und Staatsarchiv*

STAATSKANZLEI

GROSS BRITANNIEN
18 boxes, 1768–1844.　　　Photostats.

1139　　Contains diplomatic correspondence and papers relating to America. Documents from the period of the Revolution concern the developing dispute between England and her American Colonies, French emissaries to America, the appointments of Sir William Howe, Sir Henry Clinton, and Sir Guy Carleton over British forces in America, the Comte d'Estaing expedition, Prussian mediation, and decisions in the British Parliament.

FRANKREICH
7 boxes, 1768–1824.　　　Photostats.

1140　　Diplomatic correspondence and reports relating to America. Pertinent documents concern military supplies shipped across the Atlantic, the Spanish attitude toward England and America, French involvement in the war, Lafayette's secret voyage to America (1777), and the arrival of Jefferson at the Court of France.

NIEDERLANDE
3 boxes, 1767–1806.　　　Photostats.

1141　　Contains a few papers concerning troops sent to America, the shipment of goods and supplies, contraband trade, commerce, and the dispute between Spain and Holland over colonial possessions.

SPANIEN
5 boxes, 1770–1823.　　　Photostats.

1142　　Diplomatic correspondence. Material relating to the Revolution concerns the organization of new governments in America, Spanish rejection of American agents, inquiries from England over the treatment of American insurgents, trade with America, and the general progress of the war.

Canada

Ottawa, *Public Archives of Canada*

RECORD GROUP (RG) 8. SERIES C. MILITARY PAPERS. LOYALIST REGIMENT MUSTER ROLLS
18 vols., 1777–83.　　　　Photostats, oversize.

1143　　Muster rolls of loyalist corps which made up the Provincial Service of the British Army during the war. Units represented are as follows:

American Legion, Oct. 1780—Aug. 1783 (vols. 1871–72); British Legion, Jan. 1778—Apr. 1783 (vols. 1883–85); Carolina King's Rangers, Apr.—June 1783 (vol. 1892), Nov. 1779—June 1782 (vol. 1898); Carolina Light Dragoons, Jan.—June, 1781 (vol. 1899); Connolly's Loyal Foresters, June 1781—Mar. 1782 (vol. 1892); DeLancey's Brigade, 2d Bn., Aug. 1777—Nov. 1779, Feb. 1781—Oct. 1783 (vols. 1876, 1878), 1st Bn., Apr. 1782—Oct. 1783 (vol. 1877), 3d Bn., Aug. 1777—Aug. 1782 (includes random rolls of the 2d Bn.) (vols. 1879–80, 1882), 3d Bn., Apr.—June 1781 (vol. 1900); Emmerick's Chasseurs, Apr. 1778—Aug. 1779 (vol. 1891); Guides and Pioneers, Oct. 1778—Oct. 1783 (vols. 1888–89); King's Dragoons, Jan. 1782—Apr. 1783 (vol. 1901); King's American Regiment, Feb. 1779—Dec. 1781 (vol. 1902), Apr. 1782—June 1783 (vol. 1903); King's Orange Rangers, Aug. 1777—Aug. 1778 (vol. 1908); Loyal American Regiment, Sept. 1777—Oct. 1782 (vols. 1867–69); Loyal New Englanders, Feb. 1779—Oct. 1780 (vol. 1892); Maryland Loyalists, Nov. 1777—Oct. 1783 (vols. 1904–5).

Nassau Blues, June—Oct. 1779 (vol. 1894); New Jersey Volunteers, 1st Bn., Apr. 1777—Oct. 1783 (vols. 1851–53), 2d Bn., Nov. 1777—Oct. 1783 (vols. 1854–55), 3d Bn., Nov. 1777—Aug. 1783 (vols. 1856–57), 4th Bn., Nov. 1777—Oct. 1781 (includes random rolls of the 3d Bn.) (vols. 1858–59), 5th and 6th Bns., Aug. 1777—Mar. 1778 (vol. 1860), 1st, 2d, and 4th Bns., Feb.—Apr. 1781 (vol. 1900); New York Volunteers, Aug. 1777—Oct. 1783 (vols. 1874–75); Pennsylvania Loyalists, Nov. 1777—Oct. 1783 (includes some returns of the United Pennsylvania and Maryland Loyalists (vols. 1906–7); Philadelphia Light Dragoons, Dec. 1777—July 1778 (vol. 1894); Prince of Wales American Regiment, Dec. 1778—Apr. 1779 (vol. 1894), Oct. 1777—Oct. 1783 (vols. 1895–97), Apr.—June, 1783 (vol. 1900); Queen's Rangers, Aug. 1777—June 1783 (vols. 1861–66); Roman Catholic Volunteers, Nov. 1777—Sept. 1778 (vol. 1900); Royal American Reformees, June, Sept., 1778 (vol. 1894); Royal Fencible Americans, Dec. 1775—Dec. 1777 (vol. 1893); South Carolina Rangers, June 1780—Dec. 1781 (vol. 1899); South Carolina Royalists, Feb. 1781—Aug. 1783 (vol. 1902), Dec. 1779—June 1782 (vol. 1890); Volunteers of Ireland, Dec. 1778—June 1782 (vols. 1886–87); Volunteers of New England, Dec. 1781—June 1782 (vol. 1893); Wentworth's Volunteers, Oct. 1777—Apr. 1781 (vol. 1893).

SERIES M, DANIEL CLAUS PAPERS (VOLS. 104–5)
2 vols., 1716–80.

1144　　The papers of Lt. Col. Daniel Claus, deputy superintendent and commissary for Indian trade at Montreal, 1768–75, and superintendent of Indian affairs for the Northern District, Quebec, ca. 1775–80, concern British support for Indians and loyalists along the

New York–Canadian border, 1760–80. The collection also provides information on the relations of the Six Nations with Great Britain and the American Colonies, missionary activities among the Canadian tribes, white men living with Huron Indians, relations between the Hurons and the Six Nations, and Indian trade. Also contains accounts of Alexander McKee, deputy superintendent for the Western District of the Northern Department, Mar.—June 1774 and Mar.—Sept. 1776, concerning goods delivered at Fort Pitt for the Indians, as well as Claus' anecdotes about Joseph Brant.

Principal correspondents: John Blackburn, Mary Brant, Guy Carleton, Frederick Haldimand, Henry Hamilton, John Johnson, William Johnson, and R. Matthews.

Miscellaneous Collections
RESERVED PAPERS. INDIAN AFFAIRS. MINUTES (VOLS. 6–8, 10–12)
5 boxes, 1761–80.   Photostats.
1145   Consists of entry books of documents relating to Indian affairs on the northern frontier during the superintendencies of Sir William Johnson and Guy Johnson. Includes minutes of councils with the Indians, transcripts of speeches, intelligence reports, orders, and correspondence of the superintendents with military officers, governors, and various colonial officials.

France

Avignon, *Musee Calvet*

MANUSCRITS (VOLS. 1330, 2750)
1 box, 1778–79.   Photostats.

1146   An anonymous journal of the vessel *Le Marseillais*, from the Toulon Fleet, off the coast of France, 1778–79. Also miscellaneous records of the Toulon Fleet.

Lorient, *Archives Municipales de Lorient*

5me REGISTRE DES DÉLIBERATIONS DE LA VILLE ET COMMUNAUTÉ DE LORIENT
1 reel microfilm, 1775–81.

1147   Contains a brief proposal on Lorient as a free port for ships and goods from the United States, a committee report on the proposal, and the records of the assembled leaders of the city to study the possibilities of operating the free port.

Archives du Port de Lorient

LETTRES DU MINISTÈRE

SERIES I, E4 (VOLS. 71, 77–111, 114–15, 118, 121, 123–25, 135–36, 138)
4 reels microfilm, 1775–93.

1148   Select correspondence of Sartine and Castries to officials at Lorient on issues such as strengthening the French Navy, handling American privateers and their prizes, the shipment of goods to America, arming American ships, the sale of ships to America, and supplying French and American ships. Also the embarkation and return of French troops, the postwar settlement of accounts, particularly with John Paul Jones, the joint Franco–American ventures of the Lorient–New York packet service, and the whaling industry at Dunkerque and Lorient.

SERIES IP240b, 2P50, 2P69
3 reels microfilm, 1775–90.

1149   Letters, documents, accounts, and bills chiefly concerning disputes arising from the settlement of accounts for prize vessels taken by John Paul Jones during expeditions off the English coast, 1778–79. Also includes material on supply shipments, warship armaments, crews of American ships in Lorient, and the Lorient–New York packet service, 1784–85.

Paris, *Archives Nationales*

ARCHIVES DES AFFAIRES ÉTRANGÈRES

SERIES BI. CORRESPONDANCE CONSULAIRE (CARTONS 209–10, 372, 909–10, 927, 945–46, 1183)
9 reels microfilm, 1779–92.

1150   Correspondence of French consuls in America. Letters of Joseph Chevalier de Valnais, French consul at Boston, 1779–81; Jean Toscan, vice consul at Boston, 1779–83; and Philip-André-Joseph de Létombe, consul for New Hampshire, Massachusetts, Rhode Island, and Connecticut, 1781–92, with Castries concerning the supply and service of the French Army and Navy in America, privateers, French prisoners of war, finance, commerce, the slave trade, the Confederation government, and the Constitutional Convention. Correspondence of Antoine-René-Charles Mathurin de la Forest, vice consul at Savannah, 1783, and Charleston, 1783–85, and consul general and Chargé d'Affaires to Congress, 1785–92; Ignatius Romain Chevalier D'Avistry de Chateaufort, consul at Charleston, 1785–86; Jean-Baptiste Petry, vice consul at Wilmington, N. C., 1783–86, and consul, Charleston, 1786–92, concerning contraband trade, Carolina debts to France, Indian-Spanish intrigue, the Constitutional Convention, and commerce. Correspondence of De la Forest and Saint John de Crèvecoeur, 1783–92, consuls at New York, concerning Spanish seizures on the Mississippi, border claims, the exploits and claims of John Paul Jones, the French in New York, debts, the Robert Morris tobacco contract, Shays' Rebellion, and the ratification of the Constitution. Includes several tables of commerce and navigation. Correspondence of Martin Oster, vice consul at Philadelphia, 1781–83, and Norfolk, 1784–92, with consuls at Williamsburg and Norfolk concerning commerce, seizures, debts, Virginia politics, prices, Morris' tobacco contract, paper money, the Constitutional Convention, and personal matters. Correspondence and accounts of Jean Holker relating to Holker's commercial and financial activities, supplies for the French Army and Navy, commerce with France, the Continental Congress, paper money, the seat of the United States Government, the Western States, American politics, and the Constitution. Also correspondence of François Barbé-Marbois, consul general, 1781–85, and Chargé d'Affaires, 1780–85, and La Luzerne, Minister Plenipotentiary to the United States, 1779–87.

    Materials in these cartons are cataloged in Abraham P. Nasatir and Gary E. Monell, *French Consuls in the United States: A Calendar of Their Correspondence in the Archives Nationales* (Washington, D. C., 1967).

    See Holker Papers, entry no. 339.

SERIES BIII. AFFAIRES COMMERCIALES (CARTONS 439–49, 457)
11 reels microfilm, 1648–1892.

1151   Consular correspondence, with official reports, chiefly relating to commerce. The reports provide an expert view of American trade and finance in the postwar period, including details on the Robert Morris tobacco contract, lists of ship arrivals and departures from the principal American ports, and numerous lists and tables containing data on exports and imports. Also contains applications for consular posts, with supporting documents, and royal instructions and ordinances relating to the establishment of the American consular system.

    Cataloged in Nasatir and Monell, *French Consuls*, p. 201-326.

ARCHIVES DES COLONIES

SERIES A. ACTES DU POUVOIR SOVERAIN (VOLS. A8–9, 12, 22)
2 reels microfilm, 1 box transcripts, 1712–68.

1152   Contains three items pertaining to North America during the Revolutionary era:

the King's instructions to colonial officials following peace in 1763; the King's instructions to Jesuits in the colonies, 1768; and a Spanish passport for entrance to Louisiana, 1767.

SERIES B. CORRESPONDANCE ENVOYÉE (VOLS. B 119, 121–23, 125–27, 129, 131–32, 149, 158)
6 reels microfilm, 2 boxes transcripts, 1764–76.

1153   Chiefly correspondence of the Minister of Marine with French officials in Louisiana concerning the withdrawal of French troops, the rights and restrictions of French citizens, Jesuit missionary activities, and problems related to Spanish assumption of power in Louisiana. Also includes a few Jesuit instructions for missionaries in Louisiana and petitions for pensions from former missionaries.

Series C. Correspondance Générale. Lettres Reçues
SUB-SERIES C9A. SAINT–DOMINGUE, I (VOLS. 124–62)
33 boxes, 1764–89.   Transcripts.

1154   Correspondence of French colonial Governors of St. Domingue, Reynaud, and Bellecombe with the French Ministry, chiefly concerning peacetime commerce and routine colonial administration. Includes a few letters relating to French trade and naval warfare during the American Revolution.

SUB-SERIES C13A. LOUISIANE, I (VOLS. 1, 44–50)
9 boxes, 1764–88.   Transcripts.

1155   Contains letters and documents of French officials in Louisiana and France pertaining to the cession of Louisiana. Topics discussed include Indian unrest, administrative and financial chaos, 1765–68, Gov. Antonio de Ulloa's refusal to assume control for Spain, revolt against Ulloa in New Orleans, assumption of power by Gov. Alexander O'Reilly, commerce during the American Revolution, and the large numbers of Americans on the Mississippi River after the war. Also includes inventories of French supplies and military equipment.

SUB-SERIES C13B. LOUISIANE, II. LETTRES ENVOYÉES (VOL. 1)
1 box, 1699–1803.   Transcripts.

1156   Includes a few reports on French fears of an Anglo-American conflict, the progress of the War of American Independence, and attacks on English installations west of the Appalachians.

Series D. Troupes des Colonies
SUB-SERIES D2C. MATRICULES ET REVUES (VOLS. 52, 54, 59, 222)
2 boxes, 1624–1780.   Transcripts.

1157   Contains lists of officers, civil officials, and enlisted men stationed in North America, particularly in Louisiana.

SUB-SERIES D2D. PERSONNEL MILITAIRE ET CIVIL; LISTES GENERALES (VOL. 10)
1 box, 1716–68.   Photostats.

1158   A mixed collection of personal records of services in Louisiana, assembled after the colony was ceded to Spain. Includes lists of military and civilian officers, with their commissions and accounts of their salaries, and lists of Jesuit and Ursuline missionaries.

Series F
SUB-SERIES F2B. COMMERCE AUX COLONIES (VOL. 9)
3 boxes, 1780–84.   Photostats.

1159   A detailed account of French commerce with the United States and French colonies in the West Indies, 1780–84.

SUB-SERIES F3A. COLLECTION MOREAU DE SAINT-MÉRY (VOLS. 24, 84)
3 boxes, 1765–1806.   Photostats and transcripts.

1160   Chiefly documents and letters relating to the French revolt against the Spanish Governor of Louisiana, Antonio de Ulloa, and reports and petitions from French officials and merchants concerning colonial commerce, 1765–90.

SUB-SERIES F5A. MISSIONS RELIGIEUSES (VOL. 2)
1 box, 1639–1775.   Photostats.

1161   A report on French missionaries in Canada, 1639–1775.

ARCHIVES DE LA MARINE

Series B. Service Général
SUB-SERIES B^1. DÉCISIONS. II. TRAVAIL DU ROI, TRAVAIL DU MINISTRE (VOLS. 85–87, 89–94, 96–102)
2 boxes, 1778–89.   Photostats.

1162   Select documents concerning naval preparations made at the following French ports during the American Revolution: Brest, Lorient, Rochefort, La Rochelle, Dunkerque, Calais, Boulogne, Le Havre, Nantes, Bordeaux, Bayonne, Toulon, and Marseille. The documents bear notations indicating the approval and disposition of various proposals, petitions, and plans submitted to the Ministry of Marine for the formation of squadrons, the outfitting of ships, the acquisition of armaments and provisions, and the preparation of convoys. Several postwar documents pertain to the settlement of accounts for supplies shipped during the war.

SUB-SERIES B^2. CORRESPONDANCE AU DÉPART (VOLS. 413–15 417, 420, 422, 424, 426–27, 429, 431–32)
2 boxes, 1778–86.   Photostats.

1163   Select orders and dispatches to officers commanding ships or squadrons involved in naval operations of the American Revolution. Includes orders to port commanders at Brest, Toulon, Rochefort, Bordeaux, Le Havre, Nantes, and La Rochelle, and to such officers as De Grasse, De Guichen, Lapérouse, D'Orvilliers, Ternay, and Turpin. A few documents relate to Lafayette's postwar proposals for a contract to supply the French Navy from American sources; French plans to maintain packet service with the United States; L'Enfant's voyage to America, Mar. 1784; and Josiah Harmar's voyage to Paris in Apr. 1784 to exchange the ratified treaty of peace.

SUB-SERIES B^4. CAMPAGNES. (VOLS. 106–30, 132, 134–264, 266–68, 270–79, 284–88, 311–15, 318–20)
200 boxes photostats, 28 reels microfilm, 1763–89.

1164   Contains material concerning French naval operations in North America, the West Indies, the Mediterranean, and off the coasts of Spain, England, and France.

Includes letters and documents concerning the planned Franco-Spanish invasion of England in 1779 and their efforts to recapture Gibraltar; plans for the defense of French colonies in the West Indies; captains' journals, private accounts, correspondence, and reports on naval operations in West Indian waters; letters, journals, instructions, and other documents relating to French naval activity in North American waters; and material pertaining to troops, supplies, and ships sent to the United States and French colonies in America, American privateer operations, the French fleet off North America, the French military campaigns of 1778–83, application of the Treaty of Versailles to the Newfoundland fisheries, and American commerce in the French West Indies after the war.

Also letters, documents, instructions relating to the French seaports and home fleets at Brest and Toulon; attempts by France to counter British naval strength in the English Channel; ship assignments for 1780–83; records of troops and ships sent to America; the supply of French forces in the West Indies and the United States; and material on the buildup of ships, men, and supplies for American operations, fleet maneuvers, naval ships, and officer rosters.

For additional information see D. Neuville, *État sommaire des Archives de la Marine antérieures à la Révolution* (Paris, 1898).

SUB-SERIES B⁷. PAYS ÉTRANGERS, COMMERCE ET CONSULATS. LETTRES RECUES, MÉMOIRES ET DOCUMENTS DIVERS. AMÉRIQUE. ÉTATS-UNIS (VOLS. 458–61)
2 boxes, 1664–1812.   Photostats.

1165   Memoranda and reports on Franco-American commerce. Includes Martin Oster's report on Virginia trade, Comte de Moustier's report on Massachusetts commerce, and letters of Admiral d'Argout and Adm. James Young on American trade in the West Indies during the early years of the war. Also letters of John Adams, Franklin, John Paul Jones, and Arthur Lee to Sartine concerning the activities of American warships and privateers off the coasts of England and France, and a report on the progress of the Revolution, June 1775, from "Flaherty" to Sartine.

MM851. JOURNAL OF JOHN PAUL JONES
1 reel microfilm, 1775–86.

1166   An autobiographical account of Jones' career in the American Revolution and its aftermath, written after the fact to enhance his reputation with the King of France, from whom he hoped to obtain a naval commission. This copy was presented to Louis XVI. The Library has Jones' manuscript copy, which contains additional letters of dignitaries as supporting testimony of his exploits.

See John Paul Jones Papers, entry no. 364.

INVENTAIRE

418 reels microfilm, 1257–1936.

1167   The Library of Congress has on microfilm about 200 unpublished inventories of material in the Archives Nationales. For documents in the series with particular emphasis on the American Revolution see 3JJ, Scientific and Hydrographic Documents, 17th–20th centuries; 393, Répertoire Chronologique des Ordonnances Royales Enregistrées au Parlement de Paris du XIV Siècle à 1784; Fonds Marine, Marine C¹ 160–92, Table Alphabétique des états de service, avec le détail des embarquements, des officiers militaires de marine de 1660 à 1792.

Many other inventories deal with collections of documents of the French internal government in this period. The microfilm of this ongoing project is located in the Library's Microfilm Reading Room. Finding aids are available in the Manuscript Division and the Microfilm Reading Room. For a complete listing of holdings up to 1969 see *News from the Center*, no. 6 (Fall, 1969), p. 12–39.

Bibliothèque de l'Arsenal

MANUSCRITS
1 box, 9 folios, 1738–1812.   Photostats.

1168   Vol. 4565. Plan for war against Great Britain, prepared in 1763–66 by Comte de Broglie and revised in 1778. The plan analyzes the possibilities of attack and defense in a dual war with Spain and England or a war with England with Spain as an ally and outlines enterprises against Gibraltar, Jamaica, and England, with particular emphasis on an invasion of England.

Vol. 4789. Contains extracts from an anonymous history of the American Revolution, 1763–79.

Vol. 6402. Papers of Pierre Lucien Joseph Dreux, secretary to Vergennes. Includes notes on a geography of North America and the West Indies and poems on America, 1775–81.

Vol. 6880. Papers of Paul P. Gudin de la Brenellerie, 1738–1812. Contains notes for a political history of France and the United States, with a summary history of the American Revolution.

Vol. 7054. Autograph collection of Victor Luzarche. Contains a presidential cover letter of John Jay, Jan. 1779.

Vols. 7586–7688. Anonymous notes and memoranda on American colonial history and the American Revolution.

Vol. 7593. Notes of Mirabeau on the American Revolution.

Vol. 9039. Correspondence of Capt. John Collet with the British Treasury Office in 1786 concerning his claims for reimbursement of funds expended at Fort Johnson, Cape Fear, N.C., 1773–75.

ARCHIVES DE LA BASTILLE
1 folio, 1777.   Photostats.

1169   Fol. 12478. Orders for imprisonment, Aug. 1777, and release, Sept. 1777, of William Hodge, Philadelphia merchant in Paris

Bibliothèque Historique de la Marine

LETTRES AU CHEVALIER D'OLIVARI
1 reel microfilm, 1777–82.

1170   Anonymous letters to D'Olivari, the mayor of Aix-en-Provence, informing him of events related to the American Revolution and their ramifications in court politics and for France. The letters, written from Paris, often contain court news and rumors.

SERIES CC 1247. DOSSIERS PERSONNELS. JOHN PAUL JONES
1 reel microfilm, 1779–93.

1171   Contains letters by Jones, Castries, Franklin, and Sartine and miscellaneous documents relating to the settlement of accounts on prizes taken during the voyage of the *Bonhomme Richard*.

Bibliothèque Mazarine

MANUSCRITS
1 folio, 1775   Photostats.

1172   Fol. 3749. Two reports on English and Spanish military preparedness in Europe and their colonies, July 1775, analyzing the revolt of the American Colonies. One report, "Observations sur l'Armement de l'Espagne," advises against Spanish aid to the insurgents.

Bibliothèque Nationale

DÉPARTEMENT DES MANUSCRITS

MANUSCRITS AMÉRICAINS (VOLS. 1, 16, 17)
1 box, 18th century.   Photostats.
1173   Items numbered 16 and 17 consist of a dictionary of the Iroquois language, in French.

MANUSCRITS ANGLAIS (VOL. 68)
1 folio, 1776–82.   Photostats.
1174   A list of signals for the British ships in New York harbor.

MANUSCRITS FRANCAIS
69 boxes and folios, 1763–89.   Photostats.

1175   Manuscrits Français comprise a closed series (nos. 1–33, 264) of material acquired before 1862.

Fol. 4586. Record of destruction of paper money from Canada in conformity with decrees of June 1764 and Jan. 1766.

Fol. 5682. Report on French foreign commerce written shortly after the treaty of peace, 1783, to suggest means of restoring finances and trade.

Fol. 6198. Balance sheet of products and their value, trade between France and the rest of the world, and the revenue derived by the French Government, 1788.

Fols. 6233–6256. Letters and documents relating to settlement of Cayenne, or French Guiana, 1763–75.

Fol. 6349. Includes a 1782 report by Pierre Charles Lemonnier on Rigobert Bonne's memoir concerning the longitude and latitude of Boston and New Cambridge, Mass.

Fol. 6431. Reports on commerce from the papers of Abbé Guillaume Thomas Raynal, which include prices of goods in Canada, the West Indies, and Africa, 1725–71, and extracts from a 1774 report to Lord Dartmouth on America.

Fols. 6682–6684. Journal kept by Simeon Prosper Hardy, a Paris bookseller, constituting a daily record of events in Paris. Includes frequent reports of news concerning the American Revolution.

Fols. 10764–10770. Papers of Beliardi, 1768–70, French Chargé d'Affaires at Madrid, 1758–71. Includes reports on English trade with the American Colonies and with Spain, American commerce with Spain and her colonies, the transfer of Louisiana, and Franco-Hispanic relations.

Fol. 11344. Journal of Lapérouse, French naval commander in American waters, Oct. 1779—Apr. 1780. Covers the conclusion of his campaign with De Rions and the start of his campaign with De Ternay.

Fol. 11907. Address of John Adams to Louis XVI on the presentation of his credentials as U. S. Minister and the response of the King.

Fols. 12081–12085. Reports on the administration of the French colonies in America and related legislative proposals formulated by Emilien Petit, author of two books on the colonies published in 1772 and 1778.

Fol. 12099. Report on Santo Domingo. Includes remarks on trade with the United States after 1783.

Fol. 12305. Letter of recommendation by Franklin for an American doctor, Foulke, Oct. 1780.

Fols. 12763, 12768. Autograph letters. Includes letters from Franklin to Mme. Helvetius concerning his return trip to America, July and Oct. 1785, and his desire to escape public life, Apr. 1788; and letters from Samuel Huntington, John Adams, and Washington to Barbé-Marbois concerning commerce, the need for American youth to be educated in or about France, and French naval actions, 1779–81.

Fol. 13090. Lists of vessels passing through the Oresund, 1780–1802. Includes American ships.

Fol. 13357. Legislative and administrative documents concerning the control of Negroes, mulattoes, and other colored persons in France and her colonies, 1776–78.

Fols. 13359, 13362. Manuscript work on world geography written in 1773. Contains sections relating to the British American Colonies.

Fol. 13418. Miscellaneous papers of Abbé Beliardi. Includes Franklin's remedy for a cold; tables on the French Navy for 1761–66 and 1770; and Abbé de Mably's comments on the U.S. Constitution.

Fol. 13862. Pamphlets on the Yorktown victory printed at Paris and Boston, 1781.

Fols. 14611–14612. Reports of Chevalier de Ricard, infantry colonel, to the French Ministry of Foreign Affairs, 1776–77, on the commercial and military opportunities in North America and the West Indies.

Fol. 14695. Detailed, perceptive account about American citizens, manners, institutions, customs, etc., by a French civilian traveling along coastal United States between South Carolina and Massachusetts, 1777.

Fol. 15449. Notes on the geography of North America in the 18th century.

Fols. 21813–22060. Archives of the Chambre Syndicale de la Librairie et Imprimerie de Paris. Contains censorship reports on books relating to America, 1767–88, including *Response à la Déclaration du Congress Américain* (1777), and Abbé Gabriel Bonnet de Mably's *Observations sur le gouvernement et les loix des États de l'Amérique*. Also a translation of a calendar for Boston, Mass., with daily precepts for 1777.

Fols. 22061–22193. Collection Anisson-Duperron. Composed of the archives of the service of inspection of books and printing. Correspondence of Joseph d'Hemery, inspecteur de la librairie, and Etienne Anisson-Duperron, directeur de l'Imprimerie Royale, concerning censorship and laws of defamation and slander. Items relating to America, 1763–89, can be found in volumes 22073, 22096, 22098, 22102, 22154, 22179, 22180.

For detailed descriptions of this material see Leland, *Guide*, vol. 1, p. 2–73; *Catalogue des Manuscrits Français, Ancien Fonds*, 5 vols. (1868–1902) and H. Ormont, et al., *Catalogue Général des Manuscrits Français*, 9 vols. (1895–   ). Many of the items in the collection are cataloged in Benjamin F. Stevens, "Catalogue Index of Manuscripts in the Archives of England, France, Holland & Spain Relating to America, 1763–1783," in the Library's Manuscript Division; and reproductions of select documents appear in Stevens, *Facsimiles* and Doniol, *Histoire*.

MANUSCRITS FRANCAIS, NOUVELLES ACQUISITIONS
36 boxes and folios, 1763–89.   Photostats.

1176   1479. Contains a table of changes in the French and British Navies in 1779, with a list of West Indian islands conquered or lost, and a comparative table of the French and English Navies as of Jan. 1780. Also a list of officers serving in the colonies.

Fols. 2571–2583. Documents relating to the history of French Guiana. Includes a "Histoire des colonies françaises de la Guiane," 1633–1777, by Artur, a doctor at Cayenne.

Fol. 2721. Documents and reports on French commerce in the 1780's.

Fol. 3012. One-act play, "Les Vaches Américaines," written in 1772.

Fol. 3173. Summary of the maps for the Americas in the Colonial Department.

Fol. 5214. Contains three letters from Antonio de Ulloa, Governor of Louisiana, to Bory, July 1766, Apr. and Dec. 1767, concerning relations with England and frontier defenses, and a letter from Franklin to Anisson, Nov. 1787, concerning a shipment of new printing type.

Fol. 5398. Documents relating to the French colonies in the 18th century. Includes an anonymous memoir of events in America in 1777.

Fols. 5944–5964. Registres de la Régie Générale des Vivres et Subsistances Militaires, 1778–90, and accounts of the French expeditionary force to America led by Comte de Rochambeau, 1779–83.

Fol. 6577. Correspondence of Mme Dupont de la Motte. Includes verses on Franklin and American independence.

Fols. 21076–21090. Dr. Corre Collection. Contains a letter by Fr. Dieudonné protesting Spanish detention of nine missionaries in Louisiana, 1770; and a letter of Louis XVI explaining France's motives for war against England, Apr. 1779.

Fol. 21510. B. Fillon Collection. Contains six letters of Vicomte de Tressan from Newport, R.I., complaining of profiteering, personal expenses, and the like, Oct. 1780—Jan. 1781.

Fol. 21516. Letters and documents relating to Santo Domingo. Includes a letter of J. F. Billon discussing paper money in Boston, 1786, and a letter of Antoine Terrasson of Charleston, concerning a lumber contract in France, 1786.

Fol. 22085. Includes a list of decrees, edicts, and ordinances relating to the French colonies, 1782–86.

Fol. 22736. Engraved portrait of Franklin. Designed in 1777 by C. N. Cochin and engraved by Augustin de St. Aubin.

Fol. 22737. Engraving of John Paul Jones by Carl Guttenberg.

Fol. 22738. Two engraved portraits of Lafayette and a letter from Lafayette to Louis XVI explaining why he espoused the American cause, Feb. 1779.

Fol. 22817. Letter of Franklin to M. Le Roy, Sept. 1768, commenting on Dickinson's "Letters from a Farmer in Pennsylvania . . ."

LETTERS TO SAINT JEAN DE CRÈVECOEUR
1 reel microfilm, 1786–90.

1177 Contains 81 letters chiefly relating to Crèvecoeur's efforts to collect information on the history and natural science of the United States and written works of the same nature. Also includes several William Short and Thomas Jefferson letters to Crèvecoeur reporting on developments in France, 1788–89.

  Principal correspondents: James Bowdoin, Franklin, Jefferson, John Paul Jones, Lafayette, James Madison, Daniel Wadsworth, and Washington.

  See also Crèvecoeur Papers, entry no. 222.

COLLECTION JOLY DE FLEURY (VOLS. 503, 1727, 2118, 2437)
4 folios, 1778–87.　　　Photostats.

1178　　Contains correspondence of Joly de Fleury, Sartine, and Chardon, May—June 1778, on regulations of privateers, prizes, and neutral vessels, along with printed copies of the alliance between France and the United States. Also notes and reports concerning the establishment of packet service between France and the United States, 1787, and an edict of the King establishing a record center at Versailles for the colonies, along with a 1779 essay on the motives behind France's support of America.

Bibliothèque Sainte-Geneviève

MANUSCRITS (VOLS. 530–533, 1806–1809, 2088, 2342, 2551)
5 boxes, 1 folio, 1771–72.　　　Photostats.

1179　　Includes journals, logbooks, maps, and the like compiled during the scientific expedition of the *Flore* in waters off Canada, the West Indies, and South America, 1771–72. Also an anonymous missionary's memoirs, 1777, concerning experiences in Canada after 1754 and speculating on the course French Canadians will follow in the revolt of the American Colonies.

Bibliothèque du Service Historique de l'Armée

SERIES A. ARCHIVES ANTÉRIEURES À. 1789

SUB-SERIES A1. CORRESPONDANCE (VOLS. 3704, 3726, 3728, 3731–36)
12 boxes, 1775–86.　　　Photostats.

1180　　Select letters and documents pertaining largely to French military operations in the United States under Rochambeau, 1780–83. Includes correspondence of Castries, La Luzerne, Rochambeau, Ségur, and Washington concerning Franco-American military plans and cooperation; numerous reports by Rochambeau and La Luzerne, with their instructions from the French Minister of War; and extracts from American and British newspapers. Also reports on the sessions of the British House of Commons, 1775–86, assessments of the strength of British, French, and Spanish naval forces; and maps, plans, memorials, and plans for the defense of the French possessions in the West Indies, 1778–82.

SUB-SERIES A4. CORRESPONDANCE SUPPLÉMENTAIRE (VOLS. 45–57, 88)
13 boxes, 1777–83.　　　Photostats.

1181　　Chiefly intelligence reports and comparability studies of the English Fleet. Includes information on the French and Spanish Fleets for the Revolutionary era; correspondence of Prince de Montbarey, Minister of War, concerning supply plans and problems of Rochambeau's expedition, 1780; letters, reports, and documents related to Rochambeau's Yorktown campaign, and reports to De Montbarey on plans for an invasion of England, a defense of French colonies, operations in America, and worldwide troop movements.

CORPS DES TROUPES

SERIES Xb. INFANTERIE (VOLS. 11, 13–16, 18–19, 22, 24–30, 32, 34, 36–38, 40–42, 45–46, 48, 53, 55, 57, 60–61, 63–64, 68, 70, 72–73, 75–77, 79–81, 83–85, 87–89, 91–95, 97–100, 104)
SERIES Xd. ARTILLERIE (VOLS. 7, 11, 24, 29, 79)
SERIES Xe. CAVALERIE (VOLS. 57, 60, 78–79, 83, 87, 89)
42 boxes, 1762–92.   Photostats.

1182   Select muster rolls, pension lists, and other military records and official correspondence of the regiments listed below. Asterisk indicates service with French land forces in the United States, 1780–83.

Infanterie: d'Agénois, 1777–84; d'Angoumois, 1762–67, 1781–88; d'Aquitaine, 1761–79, 1782; d'Armagnac, 1776–90; d'Artois, 1755–91; d'Auvergne, 1776–89; *de Royal Auvergne, 1779–82; d'Auxerrois, 1776–90; de Barrois, 1776–90; de Bassigny, 1781–89; de Beaujolais, 1781–88; de Berwick, 1775–90; de Blaissois, 1780–87; de Boulonnais, 1762–89; *de Bourbonnais, 1781–86; de Bresse, 1780–87; de Brie, 1777–89; Cambrésis, 1777–88; de Champagne, 1780–92; de Chartres, 1780–89; de Dauphin, 1779–88; de Dillon, 1780–88; d'Enghien, 1780–90; *de Foix, 1762–66, 1775–90; de Forez, 1763–67, 1779–89; *de Gatinais, 1776–81; *de Hainault, 1778–85; de Langueduc, 1776–89; de La Reine, 1771, 1776–88; de La Sarre, 1777–92; de Limousin, 1780–86; de Lorraine, 1786; de Lyonnais, 1779–89; du Maine, 1781–92; de Medoc, 1770, 1773–87; de Monsieur, 1781–89; de Neustrie, 1779–83; d'Orleans, 1780–87; de Penthievre, 1780–86; de Picardie, 1780–83; de Piémont, 1780–83; Poitou, 1779–83; Infanterie Provence, 1780–82; de Rohan-Soubise, 1780–88; d'Infanterie de Rourgue, 1782–84; de Royal Comtois, 1780–89; *de Royal-Deux-Ponts, 1781–89; Royal Italien, 1781–87; Royal Roussillon, 1756–90; *de Saintonge, 1765–89; *de Soissonnais, 1781–99; *de Touraine, 1779–89; de Vermandois, 1767–86; de Vexin, 1765–90; de Viennois, 1776–90; de Vivarais, 1780–85; *de Walsh-Serrant, 1779–87; Volontaires Étrangers de la Marine, 1778.

Artillerie: *Artillerie, Colonies, 1776–90; Compagnie, d'ouvriers de Neyremand, 1782–90; d'Auxonne, 1780–84; de Besançon, 1781–85; *de Metz, 1779–87; de Toul, 1785.

Cavalerie: Chasseurs à cheval, Ardennes, 1778–82; *Hussards, Lauzun, 1780–99; de Chasseurs des Vosges, 1777–87; de Belzunce, 1777–80; de Condé, 1778.

MÉMOIRES HISTORIQUES ET RECONNAISSANCES

MÉMOIRES HISTORIQUES (VOLS. 241, 248)
3 boxes, 1777–83.   Photostats.

1183   Contains largely anonymous reports on the campaigns in the West Indies, 1777–80. Also includes a memoir of Preudhomme de Borre, concerning his experiences as commander of an American brigade, 1777–78; an account by M. de Fugan, major and aide-de-camp to Governor de Bouille of Martinique, of a trip to New York, Aug.—Oct. 1777, to negotiate the release of French sailors held captive by the British; a French intelligence report on the State of Vermont, 1778; and a 400-page report on the administration of French colonies and Navy, 1783.

RECONNAISSANCES MILITAIRES (VOLS. 1105, 1669, 1681)
5 boxes, 1720–1804.   Photostats.

1184   Memoranda and reports on the defense of French outposts in the West Indies. Includes plans for Martinique, 1764, 1766, 1785; St. Lucia, 1764; Guadaloupe, 1775; Tobago, 1785; Cuba, 1767, 1786; Louisiana and West Florida, 1768, 1782. Also an anonymous plan for the seizure of Jamaica, 1780, and a report recommending the building of a canal linking the Atlantic and Pacific Oceans.

PAPIERS DU COMTE GUIBERT (VOLS. 1791–92, 1794)
3 boxes, 1776–85.   Photostats.

1185   Anonymous reports to the Minister at War concerning the American Revolution, with suggestions on how France can best exploit the situation, 1776–80. Also includes a secret report on comparative military strength of France and Great Britain, 1776, and a postwar report on military preparedness in the French colonies.

DONATION PERRET (VOL. 1797)
1 folio, 1778–82.   Photostats.

1186   Includes a report on the French "attack" on New York, 1778, and an anonymous plan for peace, 1782.

FONDS PREVAL (VOLS. 1891–92)
2 boxes, 1762–84.   Photostats.

1187   Contains copies of printed ordinances of the French King and lists of recompense for French soldiers in Rochambeau's expedition, 1780.

ARCHIVES ADMINISTRATIVES

TRAVAIL DU ROI (VOLS. 1758–59, 1778, 1780)
3 boxes, 1756–82.   Photostats.

1188   Citations, awards of pensions, promotions, and related documents pertaining chiefly to wartime activities during the years 1756–63 and 1778–82.

Bibliothèque de l'Institute de France

PAPERS OF ABBÉ P. L. LEFEBVRE DE LA ROCHE (VOL. 222)
1 folio, 1774–84.   Photostats.

1189   Benjamin Franklin's notes on the earth as a globe and the theory of light, 1782–84, with a biographical sketch of Franklin. Also contains a photostat of an engraved map of America, 1774.

Archives du Ministère des Affaires Etrangères

CORRESPONDANCE POLITIQUE

ANGLETERRE (VOLS. 508–45)
56 boxes, 1775–83.   Photostats and transcripts.

1190   Diplomatic correspondence, with enclosures, between Vergennes, Minister of Foreign Affairs, and French ambassadors and agents in London. Among the enclosures are reports on parliamentary debates, ship departures and arrivals, military activities in America, and the proceedings of the Continental Congress. Also includes correspondence between the Office of Foreign Affairs and other departments of the French Government concerning aid to the United States, the approaching confrontation with England, 1775–78, the wartime activities and concerns of the Ministry, 1778–82, American agents in France, and negotiations for peace, 1782–83.
The Library has reproductions of approximately half of the material contained in the original volumes and unpublished transcripts by Benjamin F. Stevens of 110 letters and

documents in volumes 539–45.

Principal correspondents: Adhémar, Beaumarchais, Thomas Gage, Garnier, Germain, De Guines, Adm. Richard Howe, Maurepas, Moustier, Noailles, Rochford, Sartine, Stormont, Turgot, and Villère.

Many letters from the collection are published in Henri Doniol, *Histoire de la participation de la France à l'éstablissement des États-Unis d'Amérique*, 6 vols. (Paris, 1886–1900), and B. F. Stevens, *Facsimiles*. For additional information see Waldo G. Leland, ed., *Guide*, vol. 2, p. 169–235.

ESPAGNE (VOLS. 606–9)
2 boxes, 1782.   Transcripts.

1191   Contains Benjamin F. Stevens' transcripts of Vergennes' correspondence with Montmorin, French Ambassador to Madrid, and Aranda, Spanish Ambassador to Paris, concerning negotiations. Among the issues discussed are territorial settlements, the North American fisheries, Spanish recognition of American independence, and the status of Gibraltar. Also contains information on the attitude of Vergennes toward John Jay's attempts to secure recognition of American independence before the negotiations of a general peace, and the reaction of the French Foreign Minister to Spanish efforts to delay or withhold recognition of American independence.

ÉTATS-UNIS (VOLS. 1–34)
20 reels microfilm, 1774–89.

1192   Chiefly correspondence and documents of American commissioners to France, the Office of Foreign Affairs and its agents, French ministers to America, and the Continental Congress. Topics discussed include activities of American agents in Paris, political and military affairs in America, the French alliance, pro-American sympathy in France, prizes brought into French ports, French naval operations, Spanish policy toward America, French aid to America and postwar commerce.

Principal correspondents: Edward Bancroft, Beaumarchais, Broglie, Silas Deane, d'Estaing, Franklin, Garnier, Gérard, Jean Holker, John Jay, Lafayette, La Luzerne, Arthur Lee, William Lee, Le Ray de Chaumont, Maurepas, Joseph Reed, Sartine, and Vergennes.

See also Leland, *Guide*, vol. 2, p. 560–618. Selections published in Doniol, *Histoire* and in Stevens, *Facsimiles*.

États-Unis Supplement
SERIES I (VOLS. 1, 3–4, 11)
6 boxes, 1776–89.   Photostats.

1193   Letters and documents from French consuls in America to Vergennes, Sartine, Borda, and d'Estaing concerning military affairs, establishment of the French consular system in the United States, American politics, military supplies, peace, and the Rhode Island campaign. Topics discussed during the postwar period include western expansion, politics, commerce, paper money, Shays' Rebellion, and the new government. Also contains drafts and minutes of ministerial correspondence concerning consular affairs such as appointments, instructions, and circulars to consuls. Miscellaneous items include a journal of events in New Hampshire, July—Sept. 1787, W. Sargent's map of Indian cession in the Ohio River Valley, and memoranda.

Principal correspondents: d'Annemours, Chateaufort, Crèvecoeur, Silas Deane, Ducher, Gérard, Jean Holker, John Jay, La Forest, Létombe, Gouverneur Morris, Oster, William Paca, Thomas Paine, Petry, Joseph Reed, John Sullivan, Toscan, and Washington.

See Leland, *Guide*, vol. 2, p. 837–47.

SERIES II (VOLS. 12–20, 29–30)
13 boxes, 1772–94.

1194   Military Operations, 1778–85. Miscellaneous documents concerning the French military effort in America. Includes accounts of land and naval engagements; notes on French officers in the American service; memoranda and letters on combined Franco-American military operations; and naval lists for France, Great Britain, Holland, and Spain. Also journals of the siege of Savannah, Sept.—Oct. 1779, and other French military operations, July—Aug. 1781.

    Principal correspondents: d'Annemours, Comte de Barras, Boichon, Carleton, Cornwallis, Duportail, d'Estaing, Fleury, Franklin, Gérard, Greene, Guichen, De Grasse, Heath, Huntington, Lafayette, La Luzerne, Henry Laurens, Lincoln, Marbois, Peters, Rochambeau, Ségur, Steuben, De Ternay, Trumbull, Vaudreuil, and Washington.

Exchange of Prisoners, 1775–85. Correspondence of British commanders Burton, Guy Carleton, Henry Clinton, and French Minister La Luzerne concerning the execution of cartels, principally regarding prisoners confined in New York and on prison ships. Several letters of Miralles and Rendon discuss Spanish prisoners.

Intendant of the Army, 1780–84. Correspondence of Corny, Tarlé, LaPanneterie, Chesnal, and D'Aure concerning the supply of French forces in America, army hospitals, American finances, and State loans to the commissariat of the French Army.

Finance, 1781–87. Mostly correspondence of Robert Morris with French representatives in Philadelphia, 1781–84, concerning Franco-American financial relations. In several letters Morris defends U.S. financial operations. Also accounts of the U.S. debt.

Memoirs, 1772–94. Memoranda by French consuls and agents in the United States concerning politics, commerce, the war, Indians, western expansion, the State of Franklin, population, and finance. Also memoranda on the English colonies, 1776, on the State of Virginia, 1779–80, and on the U.S. Constitution, 1788.

War and Marine, 1778–84. Chiefly correspondence concerning provisioning of the French colonies, Navy, and Army in North America and the West Indies; the importation of English goods from French ports into the United States; the conduct of French officers in America; and the conduct of Jean Holker.

    Principal correspondents: Castries, Gérard, La Luzerne, Marbois, Necker, David Ramsay, John Rutledge, Sartine, Ségur, and Vergennes.

Marine and Colonies, 1778–94. Correspondence of Marbois, Rochambeau, and Sartine concerning French consular representation in the United States; the provisioning of the French colonies and military forces; and French commercial activities in the United States.

MÉMOIRES ET DOCUMENTS

AMÉRIQUE (VOLS. 10–14, 16–17, 20–21)
15 boxes, 1666–1823.   Photostats.

1195   Most material in these volumes pertains to French Canada and Louisiana. Items relating to the American Revolution include D'Ennery's reports to Vergennes on Revolutionary prospects in New England and New York, 1775–76; a memorandum on the state of war with England, 1780; and reports on Franco-American trade.

    See also Leland, *Guide*, vol. 2, p. 869–927.

ANGLETERRE (VOL. 55)
1 box, 1779.   Photostats.
1196   Edward Bancroft's "Relation" to Vergennes of his voyage to Ireland in 1779, to evaluate prospects for a planned invasion by Lafayette.

ÉTATS-UNIS (VOLS. 1–10, 14–15, 17–18)
18 boxes, 1766–1829.   Photostats.
1197   Miscellaneous letters, memoranda, and other documents relating to the American Revolution and its aftermath, with particular emphasis on its effects on France. Most of the material for the postwar period concerns Franco-American commerce.
        An item catalog is provided in Leland, *Guide*, vol. 2, p. 953–84.

FRANCE (VOLS. 446, 463, 518, 530–31, 565–66, 582, 584, 586–87, 1385–87, 1389, 1888, 1969, 2005–6, 2010, 2012–13, 2016, 2020, 2026–27, 2034–36)
16 boxes, 1648–1852.   Photostats.
1198   Selected memoranda, edicts, reports, and letters concerning Franco-American relations, economic and political affairs in Canada, Louisiana, and the West Indies, and finance and politics in the United States. Supplements material in the two section of Mémoires et Documents entitled "Amérique" and "États-Unis."
        American items are cataloged in Leland, *Guide*, vol. 2, p. 985–1037.

SERVICE GÉOGRAPHIQUE

CARTES
2 reels microfilm, 1778–82.
1199   A French map of Army dispositions, two French maps of the British defenses of New York, and an account of the American defeat at Camden, S.C., Aug. 16, 1780.

Bibliothèque du Museum National d'Histoire Naturelle

MANUSCRITS
1 box, 1784–88.   Photostats.

1200   Vol. 1935. Lists of American flora sent to French royal and noble gardens during the 1780's. Includes an extract from a catalog of John Bartram, Philadelphia.

Bibliothèque du Service Central Hydrographique de la Marine

SERVICE HYDROGRAPHIQUE. ARCHIVES (VOLS. 2, 4, 5, 12–13, 62, 64, 65, 69, 91, 109, 176, 186, 221, 230, 274, 5576)
30 boxes, 1741–1802.   Photostats.
1201   Selected documents consisting chiefly of reports on navigation in North American and West Indian waters. Includes reports on longitudinal and latitudinal observations by the Marquis de Chabert during the French naval campaigns and a 1778 report on the longitude and latitude of cities, capes, harbors, forts, and the like along the east coast of the United States. Also includes lists of vessels and officers in the French Navy in 1779; a "Liste Générale des Officiers de la Marine Suivant Leur Rang," 1764–79 and 1764–82; a list of French ships stationed in America, 1777–78; Laperouse's report on his expedition

to Hudson Bay, 1782; reports concerning colonial administration in the French West Indies, 1780 and 1785; a historical diary of navigation off California, 1768; and an anonymous memoir focusing on California, 1770.

CARTES ET PLANS (VOLS. 66–67, 105, 110–11, 119, 7263A, 7228B)
8 boxes, 1581–1856.   Transcripts.

1202   Selected reports, plans, correspondence, and journals chiefly relating to French naval activity. Includes a journal of the siege of Savannah, 1779, by O'Conor, containing additions by D'Estaing and an anonymous journal kept by a marine serving under D'Estaing, Apr. 1778—Dec. 1779. Also a report on military, economic, and political conditions in the United States in 1777; a copy of Crèvecoeur's memoir of the Ohio Valley, 1785; reports from America on commerce between the United States and France, 1781 and 1782; records of an interview with William Bingham, U.S. agent in the French West Indies, concerning trade with the United States, 1777; and letters of Sartine, Castries, and Marquis de Chabert, director of the marine depot, concerning the supply of French and American ships in France, 1779–90.

Toulon, *Archives du Port Toulon*

SERIES 1A. LETTRES ÉCRITS AU MINISTÈRE
1 reel microfilm, 1776–78.

1203   Letterbook of out-letters of the naval commander at Toulon to Sartine concerning preparations for the expedition of D'Estaing, 1778. Also material relating to the supply of ships at Toulon, the building and refitting of ships, the administration of the naval base, and American privateers and prizes.

Private Collection of Dr. and Mrs. Pierre Perruchio

PAPERS OF JOSEPH-JACQUES-FRANÇOIS DE MARTELLI CHAUTARD: WAR OF INDEPENDENCE
1 reel microfilm, 1778–83.

1204   Martelli-Chautard (1734–1810), a French naval officer, served in American waters as captain of *la Pléiade*, *l'Expériment*, and *le Palmier*. Included here are orders to Martelli concerning operations around Yorktown and in the Chesapeake Bay during the siege of Yorktown, 1781. Also letters from Sartine to the naval commander at Toulon, Marquis de Saint-Aignan, which were forwarded to Martelli, concerning the probability of war with England and French recognition of American independence.

Principal correspondents: Comte de Barras, Castries, Marquis de Chastellux, Comte de Custine, Marquis St. Simon, Sartine, and Marquis de Vaudreuil.

Vendôme, *Château de Rochambeau*

ROCHAMBEAU-WASHINGTON CORRESPONDENCE
1 box, 1781.   Photostats.

1205   Includes a memorandum from Rochambeau to Washington, May 1781, regarding the coming campaign and several related letters of Washington.

Germany

Ansbach

HISTORISCHER VEREIN FUR MITTELFRANKEN
2 reels microfilm, 1776–84.

1206   Ms. 485. Copy of a diary of an Ansbach soldier describing his experiences in America, Mar. 1777—Oct. 1781. Includes a plan of Philadelphia and battle plans of the British Army in New York, Oct.—Nov. 1776.

Ms. 485a. Contains several texts of songs sung at the departure of Ansbach-Bayreuth troops for America, 1777.

Ms. 487. Contains numerous petitions for financial relief from relatives of soldiers serving in America, 1779–84.

Baden (Karlsruhe)

GENERAL–LANDESARCHIV
4 reels microfilm, 3 boxes photostats, 1754–1809.

1207   Durlach. Papers relating to emigration, chiefly to Cleves and to Pennsylvania, 1770–71.

Generalia. Decrees against efforts of agents to induce subjects to emigrate to foreign colonies. Prescribes death penalty for such agents and fixes high rewards for informers, 1766.

Pforzheim. Papers relating to emigration to Pennsylvania, 1769–87.

   Boxed materials include decrees, petitions, official reports, and memoranda relating to emigration from Baden, 1769–71, and from the Palatinate, 1754–1809.
   See also Learned, *Guide*, p. 229–37.

Bamberg

BAYERISCHES KREISARCHIV
3 reels microfilm, 1763–89.

1208   Miscellaneous papers relating to regiments from the principality of Ansbach-Bayreuth that served in America. Includes poems eulogizing and lamenting the dispatching of troops to America, extracts from German newspapers, subsidy contracts, reports, decrees, and diaries. Also includes a treatise by Dr. Johann F. Eisenhard regarding the legal rights of the princes of the Empire to lend troops to foreign powers, 1760; an extract from the *Hamburger Zeitung* concerning a riot by soldiers ordered to America, 1777; a letter from Lt. N. F. Hoffmann, Philadelphia, Jan. 1778, describing a voyage to New York and his initial military experiences in America; a decree of Dec. 21, 1781, prohibiting idle and derogatory talk by citizens regarding the capture and imprisonment of Bavarian troops in America; and a copy of an article in the *Bayreuther Neue Zeitungs Calendar*, 1778, giving an official account of the reasons for sending Ansbach-Bayreuth troops to America.

See also Learned, *Guide*, p. 204–5.

Bayreuth

HISTORISCHER VEREIN FUR OBERFRANKEN
1 reel microfilm, 1777–83.

1209   Ms. 85. Diary of Stephan Popp, a corporal, later lieutenant, in the Bayreuth Regiment von Seybothen, 1777–83. Most of the diary consists of a rather sparse record of military operations in America, but there is a full description of the battle of Yorktown and a description of living conditions for German soldiers held captive in Virginia and Maryland towns. Includes plans of Philadelphia, Fort Montgomery, and the battle of Brandywine.

Berlin, *Preussisches Geheimes Staatsarchiv (Berlin-Dahlem)*

KONIGLICH GEHEIMES MINISTERIAL ARCHIV. TIT. LVIII No. 7
2 boxes, 1776–1801.   Photostats.

1210   Volumes 1–2 contain official correspondence, in French and German, of American commissioners in Europe with the government of Frederick the Great, and ministerial memoranda and notes concerning the recognition of American independence and commercial ties with the United States. Marginal notes on letters from the American commissioners, in the hand of the King, reflect Frederick's views on the American Revolution. Also included are a report on an interview with William Carmichael regarding trade with Prussia, Nov. 1776; an extract from a letter describing the battle of Trenton, Jan. 1777; Schulenburg's memorandum to the King regarding a proposal by Stephen Sayre for a joint whaling enterprise based in Emden, 1777; and memoranda and letters concerning the purchase of arms and provisions, and recruitment for the British Army in Germany, Russia, and Denmark, 1777.

Principal correspondents: William Carmichael, Silas Deane, Benjamin Franklin, Arthur Lee, William Lee, and Stephen Sayre.

Selected documents from the collection are printed in Jared Sparks, ed., *The Diplomatic Correspondence of the American Revolution*, 12 vols. (Boston, 1829–30), and Francis Wharton, ed., *The Revolutionary Diplomatic Correspondence of the United States*, 6 vols. (Washington, 1889). There also are extracts in Friedrich Kapp, *Friedrich der Grosse und die Vereinigten Staaten* (Leipzig, 1871); and B. Rosenmuller, *Shulenburg-Kehnert unter Friedrich dem Grossen* (Berlin, 1914).

REP. 11, 21 a. CONV. 1. AMERIKA
2 boxes, 1778–1817.   Photostats.

1211   Bundle 1. Copy of a letter, in French, from Prussian Minister Schulenburg to Arthur Lee, Jan. 1778. Original in Harvard University Library.

Bundle 2. Various documents concerning the inheritance claims of a Brandenburg farmer, Friedrich Kuhn. Relates to certain properties in the parish of Raleigh, Va., 1780–1817.

Bundle 3. Contains brief documents, in French and German, concerning relations between Prussia and America and involving Steuben.

Bundle 5. Documents, in French and German, concerning negotiations for the treaty of friendship and commerce between Prussia and the United States and the appointment of consuls in both countries. Includes a copy of a letter from Thulemeier, Prussian Ambassador at The Hague, to John Adams outlining the main articles of exchange in a future trade, Mar. 1784; a draft treaty of commerce, in English and French; credentials issued by Congress to Ministers Plenipotentiary Adams, Franklin, and Jefferson, May 1784.

Bundle 6. Documents relating to the inheritance of the heirs of Christian Ravenshorst in Ebenezer, Ga., 1784.

Bundle 7. Miscellaneous papers, in German and French, concerning inheritances, 1785.

Kabinetts Ministerium

REP. 96. FRANKREICH
15 boxes, 1775–83.   Photostats.

1212   Diplomatic correspondence, partly in cipher but with French transcriptions, between Frederick the Great and his Minister in Paris, Goltz, 1775–83. The rough drafts for Frederick's instructions, in German script and often scribbled on the diplomatic dispatches themselves, are practically illegible. The documents contain numerous references to events in America, the struggle for independence, and the war between Britain and France. During the War of the Bavarian Succession, 1778–79, the subject of America recedes to the background. Box 2037 contains an "Exposé des motifs de conduite de Sa Majesté Très Chrétienne, relativement à la l'Angleterre," dated Madrid, 1779, which is a kind of Franco-Spanish yellow book setting forth and justifying the policies of France and Spain toward England and the American Colonies.

Goltz's instructions from the King are published in *Die Politische Correspondenz Friedrich's des Grossen*, vols. 36–46, along with summaries and extracts of dispatches from Paris.

REP. 96. GROSSBRITANNIEN
14 boxes, 1774–85.   Photostats.

1213   Diplomatic correspondence, largely in cipher but with French transcriptions, between Frederick the Great and his Ministers in London, Maltzan, 1774–81, and Lusi, 1781–85. Most of the material concerns Britain's struggle with the American Colonies and with France and Spain. Also includes "Memoire Justificatif pour servir de Réponse etc. de la Cour de France," explaining and justifying Britain's actions in the war, 1779.

For official instructions from the King, 1774–79, which have not been copied by the Library, see *Politische Correspondenz Friedrich's des Grossen* (Berlin, 1789–1928), vols. 35–42.

See also Learned, *Guide*, p. 39.

REP. 96. NIEDERLANDE
13 boxes, 1774–85.   Photostats.

1214   Diplomatic correspondence, partly in cipher but with French transcriptions, of Frederick the Great and his Ambassador at The Hague, Thulemeier. The correspondence is complete from Jan. 1779–Dec. 1783. For the years 1784–85 only documents which refer to the negotiations for a treaty of commerce and friendship of 1785 between the United States and Prussia have been copied.

For instructions from the King, 1774–79, see *Politische Correspondenz Friedrich's des Grossen*, vols. 35–43. See also Learned, *Guide*, p. 39.

REP. 96. SPANIEN
1 box, 1781–84. Photostats.
1215 Contains the entire diplomatic correspondence, mostly in cipher with French transcriptions, between Frederick the Great and his Ambassador in Madrid, Nostiz. Contains few references to American affairs.

REP. 96. POLITICA
1 box, 1776–77. Photostats.
1216 Miscellaneous items chiefly relating to Austria and Bavaria. Includes a brief report on the battle of Yorktown by Colonel Arendt, Dec. 1781.
  See Learned, *Guide*, p. 37.

REP. 96. 224A
1 box, 1786–97. Photostats.
1217 Miscellaneous documents chiefly concerning Prussian trade and finance. Includes a memorandum, in German script, from Minister Schulenburg to the King, Aug. 1786, concerning prospects for profitable trade with America.
  See Learned, *Guide*, p. 38.

REP. 96. 224B. VOL. 1
1 box, 1787–94. Photostats.
1218 Miscellaneous papers dealing exlusively with Prussian corn trade.

Dresden

SACHSISCHES HAUPTSTAATSARCHIV
5 reels microfilm, 1764–85.

1219 Loc. 2420. Papers relating to negotiations for a commercial treaty between Saxony and the United States, 1783–85. Includes an extract from a report from the Saxon Minister in Paris, Schönfeld, Jan. 15, 1784, concerning negotiations with Benjamin Franklin; letters and reports, in French, on trade possibilities in America, Apr.–Oct. 1784, by Philip Thieriot, the Saxon commissioner in Philadelphia; and a letter, in French, signed by Franklin, John Adams, and Jefferson, proposing negotiations with a Saxon plenipotentiary, Sept. 28, 1784.

  See Learned, *Guide*, p. 296–301.

Loc. 2610. Vol. 1. Papers, in French and German, relating to efforts to establish commercial relations, 1778–83.
  See Learned, *Guide*, p. 297–98.

Loc. 2610. Vol. 2. Correspondence, in French, between the Saxon Foreign Minister and Thieriot relating to trade and commerce, 1783–85. Also contains observations on American institutions and economic and social conditions; lists of Saxon manufactures for possible export; instructions to Thieriot upon appointment as commercial commissioner in Philadelphia, June 30, 1783, and a table of ciphers used in correspondence.

Loc. 5291. Documents, in French and German, relating to proposals for direct trade with American Colonies via the Danish isle of St. Thomas, 1768–70.

Loc. 5366. Papers relating to commerce with North America, 1778–84. Contains references to profitable French trade with America. Also includes lists of Saxon wares for export; a report by Schönfeld, Saxon Ambassador in Paris, on exploratory talks in Paris with Jay, John Adams, and Franklin, 1783.

Düsseldorf, *Preussisches Staatsarchiv*

HERZOGTUM BERG: LANDESDIREKTION, I. No. 6
1 reel microfilm, 1764–68.

1220   Contains decrees, memoranda, and related papers concerning measures to be taken against unauthorized emigration and the high-pressure tactics of foreign agents, 1764–68. Only of marginal interest to America.
    See Learned, Supplement I.

Halle

MISSIONSBIBLIOTHEK DES WAISENHAUSES
1 reel microfilm, 1779–81, 31 boxes photostats, 1733–1809.

1221   Diary of Pastor Heinrich Melchior Muhlenberg, Oct. 1779—Oct. 1781, chiefly concerning religious and ecclesiastical matters in Pennsylvania. Also reports, journals, and miscellaneous material dealing with three Evangelical Lutheran parishes in Pennsylvania, 1733–69; correspondence with ministers teaching in Pennsylvania, 1745–89; and Pennsylvania church accounts, 1767–76, 1787–88.
    The above portion of Muhlenberg's diary is published in *The Journals of Henry Melchior Muhlenberg*, translated by Theodore G. Tappert and John W. Doberstein (Philadelphia, 1958), vol. 3.

Hamburg, *Staatsarchiv*

RITZEBUTTEL
3 reels microfilm, 1775–89.

1222   VII. Papers relating to the transit and embarkation of Hannoverian troops in 1775 and of Brunswick and Hessian troops in 1776 for service in the British Army. Papers concerning the transit of returning Hannoverian, Brunswick, and Hessian troops from America, 1780, 1782, and 1783.

Cl. VIII. Nos. 108–11. Lists of ships arriving with merchandise from foreign countries, including America, 1778–80, and lists of merchandise from foreign ports, 1787–89.
    See Learned, *Guide*, p. 273.

Hanau

GESCHICHTSVEREIN
1 box, 1776–85.   Photostats.

1223   Miscellaneous papers, in German, concerning Hessian troops, their march to ports of embarkation in Germany, overseas passage, and military experiences in America. Includes a proclamation granting tax relief to families of Hessian soldiers sent to America, Sept. 1776; seven letters by a Hessian soldier, Paul Wilhelm Schaeffer, to his family in Hanau, describing his voyage to America and camp life in Canada; and a journal of the passage of the Hanau regiment from Germany to Quebec by "F. G.," Mar.—June 1776. Also the journal of Johannes Reuber of Simmershausen, a soldier of Col. Johann Rall's regiment, 1775–1806. The Reuber journal contains a detailed description of the ocean passage to New York and brief accounts of military campaigns, 1776–83, with numerous sketches of ships, harbors, and forts.

Hannover, *Preussisches Staatsarchiv*

MIN. D. AUSW. ANGELEGENHEIT
2 reels microfilm, 1755–90.

1224   Ha. Des. 9. Werbungen. No. 16. Vol. 2. Papers relating to British recruitment of troops in Germany, 1766–82. Includes printed instructions to recruiting officers, and miscellaneous papers.

GENERAL COMMANDO
7 reels microfilm, 1766–84.

1225   Des. 41. V. Nos. 1–33 and 41. Papers concerning the recruitment, transit, and embarkation of German auxiliary troops, mostly Brunswick and Hessian, for service in America, 1776–83. Includes regimental lists and budget instructions for recruiting, quartering, and requisitioning of troops; reports by army officers on routes of march; and reports on the conduct of recruits. Numbers 30–31 concern troops from Anhalt-Zerbst, Ansbach, Hanau, and Waldeck in transit through Hannoverian lands, 1778. Numbers 32–33 include documents relating to the return of German auxiliary troops from America.
    Erroneously described in Learned, *Guide*, p. 102–5, under Des. 41 E.

Herrnhut

ARCHIV DER BRUDER-UNITAT
36 boxes, 1735–1853.   Photostats.

1226   Reports, diaries, correspondence, memoranda, and financial papers, mostly in German script, relating to Moravian communities in Pennsylvania, North Carolina, and Georgia. Included are a copy of a printed pamphlet entitled, "Historical report on the recent massacre in Lancaster County perpetuated by unknown persons on a number of Indians who were friends of this province," 1764; a petition of the deputies of the Unitas Fratrum to King George III on behalf of the Moravian brethren in America, Jan. 1763, with regard to continued exemption from swearing oaths and performing military service; miscellaneous letters and memoranda concerning the administration of fraternal communities and churches, 1763–67, and the establishment of a Society for the Furtherance of the Gospels among the Heathen, 1787; and a "Short Report relating to the disturbances in America and the conduct of the brethren," 1764–81, by John Ettwein.
    Also a letter of Ettwein to editor Towne, protesting, on religious grounds, against the proposed constitution of Pennsylvania, Sept. 1776; a petition of the United Brethren to the General Assembly of Pennsylvania regarding their religious rights, Oct. 1776; miscellaneous papers and letters of Ettwein, 1771–88, concerning the proper conduct of brethren during the difficult times of war and revolution; miscellaneous papers relating to the Christiansbrunn community, 1783–88; and a report on the origins and progress of the Moravian settlement at Wachovia, N.C., 1752–72.

Kassel

LANDESBIBLIOTHEK
2 boxes, 1776–85.   Photostats.

1227   Ms. Hass. 40. Journals and diaries of Hessian soldiers serving in America: Ernst Philip Theobald, chaplain of the Hereditary Prince's Regiment, Mar.—Aug. 1776; Carl von Butzingsloewen, of the Mirbach Regiment, Mar. 1776—Dec. 1777; Lieutenant Schotten,

Mirbach Regiment, Aug.—Oct. 1776; August Schmidt, quartermaster, Lossberg Regiment, Mar. 1776—May 1784; and Lieutenant Colonel von Dincklage, grenadier, Linsing Battalion, Jan. 1776—May 1784. Also G. Langenschwarz's account of the voyages to and from America, the campaigns in New York, Pennsylvania, Delaware, and others, 1776–85, and an account of his experiences in campaigns chiefly in New York and Nova Scotia. In addition to descriptions of military operations, the Von Dincklage journal contains numerous observations regarding life and manners in America, flora and fauna, and interesting facts about Philadelphia, New York, and other cities.

Mrs. Hass. 20. No. 247. Miscellaneous papers relating to the Mirbach brigade, chiefly letters, instructions, and military orders from Landgrave Friedrich II of Hesse-Cassel to Major General von Mirbach concerning the organization, equipment, and provisioning of Hessian troops and their march to the port of embarkation. Includes a brief journal, 1776, by Mirbachs' adjutant, Lieutenant Schotten, and several military lists and charts.

Kiel, *Preussisches Staatsarchiv*

DANISCHES KANZLERIARCHIV
1 reel microfilm, 1772–1805.

1228   Abt. 11. Req. VI. Schiffahrt, Commercium. Nos. 50, 199. Miscellaneous papers and decrees relating to Danish commerce with the Danish West Indies.

SCHLESWIGSCHE STADTE
1 reel microfilm, 1719–1849.

1229   C. XIX.1. No. 50. Includes a document authorizing a Danish company to engage in the slave trade, 1765.

Koblenz

PREUSSISCHES STAATSARCHIV
2 boxes, 1764–85.   Photostats.

1230   Abt. 22 (Nassau-Saarbrucken). Contains two bundles concerning decrees against the "craze of emigration to the new country" and the debts owed by emigrants from Carlbrunn (Eberhard and Kramer).

Abt. 33 (County of Sponheim). Contains papers dealing with the confiscation of property of the brothers Alberthal of Sohren who emigrated to New England without manumission, 1771. Other papers concern the properties of deceased or unknown emigrants, 1777–82.

Lübeck, *Staatsarchiv*

SENATAKTEN. HANDELS-UND SCHIFFAHRTS-BEZIEHUNGEN
1 reel microfilm, 1782–84.

1231   Vol. A. Bundle 1. Papers relating to proposals to negotiate a commercial treaty between Lübeck (and other Hanseatic cities) and the United States, 1782–84.
        See Learned, *Guide*, p. 279.

Mannheim

STAATSARCHIV
1 box, 1709–1800.   Photostats.

1232   Rubr. V. 3, 1. Contains one bundle of papers relating to emigration.
        See Learned, *Guide*, p. 319.

Marburg, *Preussisches Staatsarchiv*

O.W.S. 1247. BUNDLE A, MILITARIA
1 box, 1777–83.   Photostats.

1233   Correspondence between Landgrave Friedrich II of Hesse and various Hessian officers
        on duty in America and reports on military matters, including personnel lists from the
        following: Colonel Woellwarth, Lieutenant Colonel Matthaeus, Lt. Col. Johann Wilhelm
        Endemann, Col. Johann Christian Koehler, Col. Friedrich von Corbeck, and Capt. Jakob
        Boedicker. Part II contains papers relating to deserters, 1782–83, including a proclamation
        by the Governor of Georgia promising land and livestock to would-be deserters.
        See Learned, Supplement I.

REP. 15 A, KAP. XXXIV
5 boxes, 1776–80.   Photostats.

1234   No. 382. Diary of an anonymous officer of the Prince Frederick Regiment of the ocean
        voyage to America, Mar. 1776—Jan. 1779, with detailed and skillfully executed illustra-
        tions of soldiers, ship interiors, and the like.

        No. 851. Journal of the 1st Brunswick division under Major General von Riedesel, Feb.
        1776—Aug. 1777. Contains a letter of Riedesel to the Duke of Brunswick, dated Jan.
        25, 1778, giving a detailed description of the defeat at Saratoga.

        No. 852. Journal of Colonel von Specht, commander of the 2d Brunswick division, Feb.
        1776—Nov. 1777.

        No. 853. Diary of Army Chaplain Melsheimer of the voyage of the 1st Brunswick
        division to America, Feb.—June 1776; letters of Captain Cleve (also in Peter Force
        Collection), Lieutenant Gerlach, Lieutenant Schroeder, Major von Hille, and Captain
        Tunderfeld, Feb. 1776—Jan. 1779; and the journal of Captain Cleve, with comments on
        prison life in Boston, Nov. 1777—Jan. 1779.

        No. 854. Letters from Captain Bauermeister and Captain von Münchhausen, Feb. 1776—
        May 1778, and a detailed diary of Capt. Friedrich von Münchhausen, May 1777—May
        1778, relating to campaigns in New York, New Jersey, Maryland, Pennsylvania, among
        others.

        No. 855. Contains two brief journals on the campaign against Charleston, S.C., under
        General Clinton, Dec. 1779—Aug. 1780, with maps and charts. Also a few papers
        regarding the construction of flat-bottomed boats and field ovens and the baking of
        bread.

O.W.S. 1247. PARTS I–VI
3 boxes, 1776–82.   Photostats.

1235   Letters, reports, investigations, and protocols relating to the surprise attack on the
        Rall Brigade and capture of Hessian troops at Trenton, Dec. 1776.
        See Learned, *Guide*, p. 112–13.

O.W.S. 1248. Vols. I–V
13 boxes, 1776–84.   Photostats.

1236   Papers relating to Generals von Heister, von Knyphausen, von Lossberg, and others, and their military operations in America. Includes the journal of Heister's corps, Feb. 1776—June 1777, lists of troops, casualty returns, lists of deserters, and numerous reports and letters from commanding officers to the Landgrave of Hesse. General Lossberg's reports for the year 1783 contain references to the problems of desertion and of soldiers seeking legal discharge in order to remain in America.

O.W.S. 1268. Tom. I–X; Vol. XI; CXXVII
13 boxes, 1776–84.   Photostats.

1237   Journals, diaries, military orders, and reports. Also correspondence between Hessian officers in America and the Landgrave of Hesse. Includes "Ordre-Buch Berthier," containing miscellaneous military orders, regulations, and the like, chiefly from General Riedesel's Canadian headquarters, Oct. 1776–Oct. 1777; correspondence of Colonel von Janecke with the Landgrave, 1781–83, giving details on the hardships of camp life on Long Island and vicinity, and including a "Conduiten Liste" of officers of the Hesse-Hanau "Freycorps," Jan. 1783, showing records of military service, family status, and personal qualities. Also memoranda on English military requisitions with observations by Generals Burgoyne, Carleton, and others; correspondence with British officers, 1777–80; several order books kept during the Canadian campaign and at Saratoga, N.Y., Cambridge, Mass., and Reading, Pa.; muster rolls of all Hesse-Hanau troops in America, Mar. 1776— July 1783, containing names of officers and men arranged according to regiment and rank; and military reports on operations in America from various Hessian officers chiefly to Lieutenant General von Ditfurth, 1776–82.

O.W.S. 1386
15 boxes, 1776–84.   Photostats.

1238   Journals, diaries, correspondence, and miscellaneous military papers relating to Hessian regiments in America.
     See Learned, *Guide*, p. 121–26.

O.W.S. 1387
1 box, 1782–83.   Photostats.

1239   Contains the diary of Capt. Friedrich von der Malsburg, with detailed descriptions of the ocean voyage to America, Feb.—Dec. 1776.
     See Learned, *Guide*, p. 125 under item I.Ba. 18 1/2.
     See also entry no. 420.

Rep. 15A. Kriegsministerium (formerly Heeresarchiv)
26 boxes, ca. 1775–1783.   Photostats.

1240   Military orders, rank lists, reports, financial documents, and official and private correspondence relating to Hessian troops in America.
     Detailed listing in Learned, *Guide*, Supplement I, p. 28–35.

O.W.S. 1433. Rep. D
1 box, 1776–84.   Photostats.

1241   Miscellaneous documents relating to English subsidy payments to Hessian troops.
     See Learned, *Guide*, p. 126–27.

O.W.S. 1513–18.
9 boxes, 1763–84.   Photostats.

1242   Contains rank lists and reports of individual Hessian regiments.
     See Learned, *Guide*, p. 127–31.

WALDECK DOCUMENTS (FURSTLICH WALDECKISCHES KABINETT)
16 boxes, 1776–84.   Photostats.

1243   Miscellaneous papers, muster rolls, fiscal statements, and the like concerning the 3d English-Waldeck Regiment.
See Learned, *Guide*, p. 144–49.

Mecklenburg-Neustrelitz, *Hauptarchiv*

BRIEFE DER SOPHIE CHARLOTTE
1 reel microfilm, 1775–85.

1244   Letters, in French, of Sophie Charlotte, Queen-Consort of George III, to her brother, Karl Ludwig Friedrich, concerning events in America during the Revolution. References to "this diabolical war," "the obstinacy of those people," and hopes for a large number of German mercenaries, including some from her home state of Mecklenburg, reflect Sophie Charlotte's intense patriotic interest in the struggle and, occasionally, the King's views about military developments in America.

Munich, *Bayerisches Geheimes Staatsarchiv*

KASTEN SCHWARZ. 321/5, 7; 444/14; 457/20; 502/1–9
11 reels microfilm, 1765–70, 1777–88.

1245   Correspondence, in French, of Count Haslang, Bavarian Minister Plenipotentiary at London, concerning political and diplomatic developments in Great Britain before, during, and after the war of the American Revolution. Most of the letters are addressed to Haslang's Minister in Munich. References to America are few during the early years except in letters of July and Aug. 1770, which discuss American opposition to new taxes. Correspondence from 1777 forward contains frequent and detailed reports on royal and parliamentary policies toward America. Also contains papers concerning the imperial edict of 1768 prohibiting illicit emigration.
See Learned, *Guide*, p. 179–84.

Hauptstaatsarchiv

ABT. KREISARCHIV MUNCHEN. 405/1
1 reel microfilm, 1764–90.

1246   Papers relating to emigration. Contains occasional references to America.
See Learned, *Guide*, p. 192.

Münster, *Preussisches Staatsarchiv*

PADERBORN. GEN. RAT. I.B. No. 71
1 reel microfilm, 1777–99.

1247   Official correspondence between Paderborn and the governments of Hesse-Cassel, Hannover, and Anhalt concerning free transit through Paderborn territory of Hannoverian, Hessian, Ansbach, Anhalt, and Waldeck troops enlisted for service in America, 1777–83. Includes lists of troops.

Neuwied, *Fürstliches Archiv zu Neuwied*

SCHRANK 2. GEFACH 13
1 box, 1757–82.   Photostats.
1248   Correspondence between the reigning Count of Neuwied and his nephew, Count of Schwerin, who served with the French Army in America, 1779–82. In French and German, the letters chiefly concern personal matters. Also papers dealing with a land concession in Maine to the Count of Neuwied by Samuel Waldo, on condition of furnishing 1,000 Protestant families as settlers, 1757–74.

Nürnberg, *Bayerisches Staatsarchiv*

VERTRAGE MIT GROSSBRITANNIEN
1 box, 1776.   Photostats.
1249   Includes a copy of a treaty between England and Margrave Alexander of Brandenburg-Ansbach, negotiated by Colonel Fawcett, for furnishing 1,200 troops for service in America.
          See Learned, *Guide*, Supplement I.

ANSBACHER OBERAMTSAKT
3 reels microfilm, 1777–81.

1250   No. 1551. Papers relating to the departure of Ansbach-Beyreuth troops destined for service in America, their transport, provisioning, and quartering in Ansbach territory, and similar matters.

Oldenburg

LANDESARCHIV
3 reels microfilm, 1777–89.
1251   Aa. Herrschaft Jever. Abt. A. Tit. XXXIII.

Nos. 17a-b. Papers dealing with the recruitment, payment, provisioning, and transport of auxiliary troops of Anhalt-Zerbst (to which the district of Jever belonged at that time) for service in America. Includes almost day to day reports of councillors and orders of the reigning prince, Friedrich August. Also a few reports from officers in America and several drawings of artillery pieces.

No. 18. Documents concerning negotiations for the consignment of Anhalt-Zerbst troops returning from America to service under the German Emperor, 1783–85.

Speyer

KONIGLICH BAYERISCHES KREISARCHIV DER PFALZ
1 box, 1685–1779.   Photostats.
1252   Documents relating to illegal emigration.
          See Learned, *Guide*, p. 214.

Stettin

KONIGLICH PREUSSISCHES STAATSARCHIV FUR DIE PROVINZ POMMERN
1 box, 1777.　　　　　Photostats.
1253　　Documents concerning the possible effects of the American Revolution on commerce with England and Holland.
　　　See Learned, *Guide*, p. 165.

Wiesbaden, *Königliches Staatsarchiv*

BESTAND VII. NASSAU-DILLENBURG
1254　　R. 206. Vols. I–VIII. Decrees, reports, and miscellaneous papers dealing with illegal emigration, 1750–91. Includes a minute account of the Waldo colony in Maine.
　　　See Learned, *Guide*, p. 169–70.

BESTAND IX. KURMAINZ
1 box, 1723–84.　　　　　Photostats.
1255　　5. Oberant Hochst. 11/12. Tit. I. Nos. 3–4. Papers concerning emigration.

BESTAND XII. NASSAU-KATZENELNBOGEN
1 box, 1697–1805.　　　　　Photostats.
1256　　Generalia XIV C. Nos. 1–2. Papers concerning emigration.

Wolfenbüttel, *Landeshauptarchiv*

ACTA MILITARIA
15 reels microfilm, 1775–85.
1257　　Nos. 231–32. Contains a treaty between the Duke of Brunswick and Great Britain, Jan. 1776, providing for a specified number of auxiliary troops for service in America; lists of personnel of individual regiments, 1775–85; papers relating to recruitment, including official instructions to recruiting officers; letters of Riedesel and other officers in Canada, 1776–77; Riedesel's orders from British headquarters in Quebec, 1776; financial data, 1776–82; and muster rolls of the Convention Troops, 1777–83. Also papers relating to supplies lost at Yorktown from the flagship *Riedesel*, with detailed self-justificatory report from Captain Gerlach to Colonel von Mengen, Dec. 28, 1781; official reports; and an alphabetical list of all officers and men who were killed and of those who deserted or otherwise stayed in America, 1783.

HISTORISCHE HANDSCHRIFT
3 reels microfilm, 1776–83.
1258　　VI. 11,248, vol. 2. Comprises a journal of the 1st division of Brunswickers in America, 1776–83, maintained by Julius Friedrich Wasmus, regimental surgeon, and lists of officers, 1776.

RIEDESEL PAPERS
57 reels microfilm, 1761–85.
1259　　Correspondence of Baron Friedrich Adolph von Riedesel, commander of Brunswick Troops in America, with German and British officers and officials, 1776–83; letters and communications from residents in America relating to personal and local matters, 1776–82; papers concerning subsidy agreements between Brunswick and Britain, including

copies of treaties, soldiers' oaths of loyalty; a letter of appointment as commander of German troops in America, Jan. 10, 1776; and keys for ciphers, scouting marks, paroles, and various charts and maps. Also an official diary of Brunswick troops under Riedesel's command, Feb. 1776—Jan. 1779; documents relating to the capitulation at Saratoga and the exchange of captive officers, including a report from Riedesel justifying his conduct at Saratoga; miscellaneous orders and instructions, 1776–83; two order books of the Brunswick corps, 1776–83; and lists of soldiers and officers, financial statements, expense accounts, and related data, 1776–83.

See also entry nos. 1001 and 1002.

Würzburg

BAYERISCHES STAATSARCHIV
6 reels microfilm, ca. 1764–82.

1260   Includes documents dealing chiefly with the problem of illegal emigration and unauthorized recruitment and papers relating to the free passage of Ansbach troops through Würzberg territory on their way to America, 1777–82.

See Learned, *Guide*, p. 217–20; Learned, Supplement II.

Italy

Florence, *Archivio di Stato*

AFFARI ESTERI (VOLS. 69, 76, 930, 2332, and 2335–36)
5 reels microfilm, 1776–85.

1261   Chiefly dispatches and notes of the Tuscan Ambassadors in Paris, Abbate Niccoli and Francesco Favi, and the Chargé d'Affaires to the Grand Duke, concerning the American Revolution. Includes information on political affairs in England and France, war news, recruitment of German troops, the movement of supplies and troops, the Franco-American alliance, and peace negotiations. Also material relating to the first diplomatic rapprochement between the United States and Tuscany, including official letters from Jefferson, Franklin, and Adams to Ambassador Favi notifying him of their power to enter into negotiations with the Grand Duke for a treaty of amity and commerce, 1784–85, and drafts of the proposed treaty.

Naples, *Archivio de Stato*

AFFARI ESTERI (BUNDLE 2410)
1 reel microfilm, 1783.

1262   Notes and correspondence between U.S. agents and the Neapolitan Government concerning attempts to establish a commercial treaty.

Turin, *Archivio di Stato*

CORTI STRANIERE. INGHILTERRA
5 reels microfilm, 18th century.

1263   Contains copies of various documents by Sardinian Ministers in London relating to trade, as well as American propositions to the King of Sardinia for a treaty of amity and commerce, 1784.

LETTERE MINISTRI

1264   FRANCIA (BUNDLES 219–29)
17 reels microfilm, 1775–83.
    Diplomatic correspondence between the Kingdom of Sardinia and its envoys in Paris, Viry, Scarnafigi, and others. Includes instructions from the King.

INGHILTERRA. (BUNDLES 80–86)
14 reels microfilm, 1774–84.

1265   Dispatches, with enclosures, of Gordon, Sardinian Envoy in London, to his home government. Includes instructions from the King.

SPAGNA (BUNDLES 89–92)
6 reels microfilm, 1778–83.

1266   Correspondence and dispatches of the Sardinian Court with its envoy in Madrid, Maisin. Includes instructions from the King.

Venice, *Archivio di Stato*

CORTE (VOLS. 151–61, 164)
2 reels microfilm, 1774–87.

1267   Official copies (registers) of letters and dispatches to ambassadors and other representatives of the Venetian Republic.

DISPACCI AL SENATO

INGHILTERRA. SERIES 126
7 reels microfilm, 1773–84.

1268   Correspondence of Venetian ambassadors in London to their home government. Contains extensive reports on events in England and America from the beginning of the American rebellion to the final treaty of peace.

SPAGNA. SERIES 179–80
1 reel microfilm, 1776–81.

1269   Correspondence of Venetian ambassadors in Spain to their home government, chiefly on the American War of Independence.

Mexico

Mexico City, *Archivo General de la Nación*

MARINA
44 boxes, 1706–1810.   Photostats and transcripts.

1270   Contains a few documents relating to Florida, Louisiana, and the United States. Includes royal *cédulas* and correspondence concerning relief for New Orleans and Havana during the Revolution, 1779–83; troops sent to New Orleans; naval patrols along the gulf coast; commerce; the construction of ships at Philadelphia, 1786–87; and rights of deposit and passage at the port of New Orleans.

See vols. (*tomo*) 3, 12, 16, 21, 27, 31, 33, 56, 71, 75, and 76.

The Netherlands

The Hague, *Algemeen Rijksarchief*

ADMIRALITEITS COLLEGES
6 reels microfilm, 1735–92.

1271 XXXI. No. 239. Reports and recommendations on emigration to America, July 6, 1764—Dec. 24, 1771.

XXXI. Nos. 250–253. Verrameling Bisdom. Extracts of States-General resolves, and information concerning Dutch-French trade relations; reports on the seizure of Dutch vessels by England, 1778–80, and extracts of States-General resolves concerning efforts to exchange prisoners, 1782. Also a letter of Nov. 23, 1783, regarding the definitive peace treaty between Britain and the United Provinces, and extracts of States-General resolves on the negotiations of the magistrate of Amsterdam with the Continental Congress, 1780–81.

XXXVII. Nos. 484–85. Verrameling van der Heim. Various documents related to relations with European powers, 1777–79. No. 485 covers reports on the League of Armed Neutrality, secret discussions with English shipowners, and the naval battle at Doggersbank, 1781.

XXXVII. Nos. 486–87. Contains diplomatic correspondence and resolutions of the States-General concerning Dutch trade with the United States; a British request for auxiliary naval aid and naval stores; the conduct of Dutch commandant at St. Eustatius in firing upon the American ships *Baltimore Hero* and *Andrew Doria*; a bill of lading for the seized ship *Two Brothers*; Sir Joseph Yorke's protest over John Paul Jones' anchorage in Texel Roads, 1779; Jones' own account of the incident; and extracts from treaties relating to rights of belligerent vessels in neutral ports.

LEGATIE ARCHIEVEN
2 reels microfilm, 1777–89.

1272 872. Includes English protests over De Graaf's conduct at St. Eustatius, 1777; complaints against British privateers and replies by Suffolk and Weymouth, 1778–79; George III's 1780 proclamation on Dutch shipping; and a copy of Privy Council order on the same subject, Dec. 22, 1780.

1161. Reports by P. J. van Berckel, Dutch Resident Minister in Philadelphia and New York, June 4, 1783—Feb. 27, 1789, on the wandering course of Congress, the British evacuation of New York, and other political events.

STATEN-GENERAL
8 reels microfilm, 2 boxes photostats, 1775–95.

1273 Nos. 737–48. Printed resolutions of States-General, 1775–83, relating to munitions shipments from the Netherlands to the United States, shipping losses, and protests against

British privateers. Includes some official letters from Duc de la Vauguyon and Sir Joseph Yorke.

Nos. 2421, 2423–28. Register of secret resolutions of States-General and provincial legislatures, 1776, 1778–83, and diplomatic correspondence from Dutch Ministers in major European capitals. Reel no. 2 covers the period of negotiations, 1782–83.

No. 4441. Copies of dispatches from the Dutch consuls at Charleston (J. Boonen Graves), New York (P. J. van Berckel), and Philadelphia (Jan Hendrik Heineken), Oct. 1788— Nov. 1789. Includes references to George Clinton, Diego de Gardoqui, John Jay, Jefferson, and Rufus King.

Nos. 4580–81, 4584–88. Secret dispatches from Dutch Ministers in major European capitals, 1775–76, 1779–83. Includes reports from J. W. van Welderen (London), De Swart (St. Petersburg), and dispatches from L. van Berkenrode (Paris) to Vergennes.

No. 7130

Part I. Photostats of Van Berckel's reports, Aug. 8, 1783—Oct. 4, 1785. Includes several memoranda from C. W. F. Dumas; reports on congressional sessions at Princeton, Trenton, and Annapolis; and several requests for passports signed by John Adams.

Part II. Consular reports, Apr. 30, 1785—Apr. 23, 1786, by Heineken (Philadelphia), Herman LeRoy (New York), Van Berckel (New York), Boonen Graves (Charleston), and A. Valck (Baltimore). Includes a report on the state of the U.S. foreign debt, and reports on shipping activities in larger port cities.

Part III. Numbered diplomatic correspondence of Van Berckel, 1787–88, mainly concerning political affairs, and reports of the Dutch consul at Boston. Also copies of letters and a memorial from John Adams to the secretary of the States-General, Oct. 1787.

Part IV. Numbered diplomatic correspondence, Jan. 2—Apr. 7, 1788. Includes extracts from the journals of the Continental Congress; letters from John Adams, Cyrus Griffin, and Charles Thomson to States-General; Van Berckel's correspondence with John Jay; and reports on the New York ratifying convention. Enlargement prints.

No. 7131. Parts I–II. Dispatches of Van Berckel and Heineken, 1788–91, with notes between John Adams and William Short and the States-General. Also enclosures of American treaties, published correspondence of Government officials, and acts and resolutions of Congress.

No. 7370. Reports from Dutch diplomats in the United States, 1788–94. Includes a letter from Charles May to Heineken, Nov. 10, 1788, explaining the decline of Dutch American trade since 1784.

Secrete Resolutiën. Printed resolutions of the Dutch legislatures, 1782–96. Includes mention of John Adams and the 1782 Dutch-American treaty of commerce and amity, and Van Berckel's appointment as Minister Plenipotentiary, Dec. 30, 1788.

GEMENGD

ARCHIEF C. W. F. DUMAS
3 reels microfilm, 1775–95.

1274   Inventories I. Lettres et Mémoires pour servir à l'Historic des Etats Unis D'Amérique, in French, 1768–[76?]. Includes relation of events, ciphers, codes, and code names. Letters in Dutch, English, and French to or from John Adams, William Carmichael, Silas Deane, Benjamin Franklin, John Jay, Thomas Johnson, John Paul Jones, Henry Laurens,

James Lovell, Arthur Lee, William Lee, Robert R. Livingston, Philip Mazzei, Jean de Neufville & Sons, secret committee of Congress, Van Berckel, and Duc de la Vauguyon.

Inventories II. Diplomatic messages and letters, Feb. 1783—Nov. 1795, of John Adams, Francis Dana, Lafayette, Henry Laurens, Benjamin Lincoln, John Rutledge, Jr., William Short, Nicholas van Staphorst, Vergennes, Washington, and W. & J. Willink.

Inventories III. Printed memorials of Yorke regarding the *Baltimore Hero* at St. Eustatius, Feb. 21, 1777; copies of diplomatic correspondence with British and French Ministers concerning the League of Armed Neutrality; preliminary peace treaty between Great Britain and the United Provinces; protests over John Paul Jones' presence in Texel Roads; copies of captured letters from Henry Clinton to Germain, 1780; commercial agreement between United Provinces and the United States, 1778; documents relating to the Dutch-American treaty of friendship, 1782; and details of a Dutch loan for three million guilders, 1782, and the "liquidated debt" loan of 1786.

ARCHIEF CAPELLEN
1 reel microfilm, 1768–84.

1275   Papers of Jean Derk, Baron van der Capellen van der Pol, a leader of the patriot party in the United Provinces and an unofficial adviser to John Adams. Includes letters of Jonathan Trumbull to Dartmouth and Hillsborough, 1768–77; Thomas Cushing's account of the expenses and exertions of Massachusetts Bay Colony since 1620; consular reports from America, 1777–78; correspondence by John Adams, Horatio Gates, John Paul Jones, Rawlins Lowndes, and Richard Price; and a catalog of Dutch merchants "with their reputed political characters."

ARCHIEF L. P. VAN DE SPIEGEL (No. 495)
1 reel microfilm, 1782–83.

1276   Brief memorandum, written in 1782, analyzing the political and mercantile interests of the United States, and secret instructions of States-General to Van Berckel, May 27, 1783.

AC. 9462
1 box, 1625–1869.   Photostats.

1277   Selected photostats of Dutch-American documents exhibited in Philadelphia in 1950. Includes correspondence of Col. J. G. Diriks with Governors Livingston and Trumbull, 1780; unsigned memoranda on financial arrangements and the need for regulation of commerce by Continental Congress, May 5, 1784; and Jefferson's letters to G. K. van Hogendorp.

VERZAMELING G. K. VAN HOGENDORP (Nos. 12, 36, 50, 54)
4 reels microfilm, 1783–86.

1278   Letters of Charles van Hogendorp to his mother on American politics, manners, customs, social attitudes, women's dress and habits, and the like which he observed during a year of travel in the United States and residence in Boston and Philadelphia. Also includes fragments from Van Hogendorp's diary, 1783–84, and miscellaneous related documents.

Spain

Seville, *Archivo General de Indias*

AUDIENCIAS. SANTO DOMINGO
200 boxes, 1530–1822.   Photostats and transcripts. Finding aid available.

1279   Most documents in the collection pertain to internal affairs in Florida and Louisiana. They include records of official appointments, retirements, and the like, official correspondence between the intendants and Governors of Florida and Louisiana: legal briefs and pleas; census returns; treasury reports; and documents concerning routine administrative matters and religious affairs. Also documents concerning relations with France, England, and America: instructions on commerce with the United States, records of land grants; letters and documents concerning the tobacco industry; military warrants and commissions; papers relating to fortifications, munitions, and troop subsidies; and miscellaneous items.
     See bundles (*legajos*) 2529, 2531–39, 2541–72, 2574–83, 2585–90, 2594–97, 2602, 2604, 2606–8, 2633–34, 2638–41, 2642, 2645–51, 2654, 2661, 2673–79, 2681, 2684–89, and 2691.

PAPELES DE ESTADO
30 boxes, ca. 1700–1836.   Photostats and transcripts.

1280   Bundle 86 contains a report on Spanish expeditions to America, 1764; scattered letters concerning exploration and trade in America, 1764–76; and instructions to Governors and officials regarding contraband trade and other matters.

MINISTERIO DE ULTRAMAR
1 box, 1771–97.   Transcripts.

1281   Contains a few letters relating to Louisiana and Florida by José Alvarez and Diego José Navarro.

PAPELES PROCEDENTES DE CUBA
450 boxes, 23 vols., photostats and transcripts; 26 reels microfilm, 1580–1872.

1282   Originally part of the Archivo General de Cuba; the Papeles de Cuba were transferred to Spain in 1888–89. They consist chiefly of official correspondence between the Ministry of the Indes; captains-general at Havana; and Governors, intendants, and subordinate officials in Cuba, Louisiana, the Floridas, and various other districts in the viceroyalty of New Spain. The collection comprises about 2,400 bundles arranged in 23 series. About 950 bundles contain material relating to the territory of the present United States. The Library of Congress has copies of all or parts of 233 bundles, 18 on microfilm and the remainder in the form of photostats and typescripts.
     Materials from the Revolutionary era (106 bundles) include royal orders, decrees, warrants, commissions, and instructions; papers concerning the government of New Orleans, Mobile, Pensacola, and St. Augustine; court proceedings; and routine correspondence of the Ministry of the Indies, and various bishops and ecclesiastics. Also correspondence of Spanish commissioners in the United States, captains-general at Havana, Governors and intendants in Louisiana and the Floridas, commandants at Natchez, Baton Rouge, St.

Louis, Mobile, St. Marks, and other outposts. Correspondence concerns Indian affairs, commerce, agriculture, colonization, navigation of the Mississippi River, American encroachments in Louisiana and the Floridas, relations with Great Britain, military organization and supply, expeditions against British garrisons at Mobile and Pensacola, the general progress of the war, contraband trade, slavery, the treaty of peace, the Acadians, and the Georgia commissioners.

Principal correspondents: Francisco Bouligny, Antonio María de Bucareli, Domingo Cabello, Juan Manuel de Cagigal, Francisco Cruzat, Conde de Floridablanca, Bernardo de Gálvez, José de Gálvez, Diego de Gardoqui, Carlos Grand Pré, Alexander McGillivray, Juan de Miralles, Estevan Miro, Athanase De Mizieres, Diego José Navarro, Martin Navarro, Alejandro O'Reilly, William Panton, Antonio Portlier, Francisco de Rendon, Bernardo Troncoso, Antonio de Ulloa, Luis de Unzaga y Amezaga, and Antonio Valdes. Also in the collection are original letters and extracts of letters by John Barry, William Bowles, Archibald Campbell, John Campbell, John Dickinson, Benjamin Franklin, Alexander Gillon, Nathanael Greene, Lyman Hall, John Hancock, Patrick Henry, Samuel Huntington, Thomas Jefferson, La Luzerne, Henry Laurens, Thomas Sim Lee, Benjamin Lincoln, Robert Loundes, George Morgan, Robert Morris, Abner Nash, Oliver Pollock, John Rutledge, Baron von Steuben, Washington, and James Wilkinson.

See bundles 1–2, 4, 11, 36–38, 40, 70, 102, 104A–B, 107, 149–51A, 167A–69, 171A–B, 174–77, 180–82, 187A–88, 192, 200, 203, 267A–B, 270–71, 274, 538B, 569, 584A, 593–95, 633, 671, 683, 685, 697, 1051, 5054–55, 1109, 1137, 1145–47, 1227, 1232–33, 1281–83, 1290–91, 1301, 1304, 1309, 1318–19, 1330, 1335–36, 1354–55, 1368, 1375–76, 1393–95, 1409, 1425, 1432, 2317, 2343, 2351–52, 2357–61, 2370, 2373.

For additional information see Roscoe R. Hill, *Descriptive Catalogue of Documents Relating to the History of the United States in the Papeles Procedentes de Cuba . . .* (Washington, D.C., 1916).

Simancas, *Archivo General de Simancas*

PAPELES DE ESTADO

INGLATERRA
34 boxes, 1562–1823.   Photostats and transcripts.
1283   Pertinent materials comprise chiefly the official and private correspondence of Spanish Ambassadors to England the Prince of Masserano and the Marqués de Almodovar and Chargé d'Affaires Francisco Escarano with the Marqués de Grimaldi and Floridablanca, as well as notes exchanged between Lord Grantham, British Ambassador to Spain, and Floridablanca, with related papers. The letters concern the establishment of English government in Florida, 1763–64; British trade in the Gulf of Mexico, 1763–68; military affairs, i.e., troops and supplies sent to the area, and the construction of forts in Florida; the revolt of English Colonies in North America; Spanish attempts to mediate differences between England and France; and Spanish entrance into the war. Also secret intelligence on affairs in England, the Franco-American alliance, the Carlisle Commisson, activities of American privateers, and news on events in America and the West Indies.

See bundles 6960–61, 6964–65, 6968–69, 6972–73, 6976–77, 6985–86, 6988–91, 6997–7005, 7016 (modern nos. 2352, 2354–57, 2359–61, 2363–64). See also William R. Shepherd, *Guide to the Materials for the History of the United States in Spanish Archives* (Washington, D.C., 1907), p. 21–22.

FRANCIA
14 boxes, 1761–83.   Photostats and transcripts.
1284   Correspondence of Conde de Aranda, Spanish Ambassador to France, and Marquis

d'Ossun, French Ambassador to Spain, with Secretaries of State Grimaldi and Florida-blanca concerning the proposed Franco-Spanish alliance against England, 1775–78; a rumored Russo-English alliance; British recruitment in Germany; and Spanish relations with England. Also British naval operations and home defenses; the Franco-American alliance; the progress of the war; aid to America through New Orleans and Havana; French financial problems; and West Indian trade. Includes letters of José de Gálvez, Shelburne, Vergennes, Guichen, and others.

See bundles 4598–4600, 4602–6, 4608–12, 4614, 4616–18, 4620, 4622, 4624, 4630 (modern nos. 1734–40, 1742).

Described in part in Shepherd, *Guide to Materials in Spanish Archives*, p. 24.

HOLANDA
4 boxes, 1776–82.   Photostats.

1285   Correspondence of Vizconde de Herreria and Sebastian de Llano, Spanish Ministers at The Hague, with Secretaries of State Grimaldi and Floridablanca concerning Russo-Dutch relations, the British capture of Henry Laurens, the League of Armed Neutrality, and American attempts to secure a loan from the Dutch. Also letters concerning the movements of American envoys in Germany and Sweden, British protests of Dutch contra-band trade and the activities of American privateers, efforts by the British to buy up all available gunpowder in Holland, Dutch relations with France and England, the Hessian troops, John Paul Jones, Holland's refusal to convoy French ships, and peace negotiations.

See bundles 6368–75 (modern nos. 2177–80).

SECRETARÍA DE GUERRA

LAS FLORIDAS Y LOUISIANA
41 boxes, 1781–1801.   Photostats and transcripts.

1286   Political and military correspondence and papers of officers and officials in Florida and Louisiana. Subjects discussed include the capture of English posts along the Mississippi River; the capture of Pensacola by Bernardo de Gálvez, 1781; the construction of Fort San Marcos de Apalache; the unsuccessful expedition from Cádiz to the West Indies in 1780, and aid from Mexico. Also plans for campaigns, cooperation with the French, mili-tary dispositions in Florida, and related matters. Includes letters of Bernardo de Gálvez, José de Gálvez, Victorio de Navia, first commander of the army, and Juan Manuel Cagigal, his successor, and Conde de O'Reilly.

See bundles 6913–16, 7303.

SECRETARÍA DE MARINA

LAS INDIAS (OCCIDENTALES)
14 boxes, 1780–83.   Photostats.

1287   Contains correspondence and papers relating to naval operations in the West Indies. Includes letters between Marqués Gonzales de Castejon, Ministry of the Navy, Don José Solano, commander of the fleet bound for America, 1780, Comte de Guichen, and Don Juan Bonet, naval commander at Havana. Subjects discussed include military organiza-tion and supply, movements of the French and English Fleets, naval engagements, prizes and prisoners taken, and the naval aspects of the Pensacola expedition, 1781. Includes reports from commanders stationed all over the Spanish Empire, and reports from the Minister of the Navy to the Secretary of State.

See bundles 420–24.

Sweden

Stockholm, *Riksarkivet*

AMERICANA. A1–A4
3 boxes, 1783–1818.   Photostats.
1288   Contains a few letters and papers of Swedish consuls relating to early diplomatic negotiations between Sweden and the United States.

Union of Soviet Socialist Republics

Leningrad

ARCHIVE OF THE STATE
4 boxes, 1724–1789.   Photostats.

1289   Contains a report by Polkovnik Plenisner concerning general historical and commercial relations between Asia and America, 1765.

MINISTRY OF FOREIGN AFFAIRS
4 boxes, 1783–1800.   Photostats.

1290   Includes reports, in French, submitted to Catherine II about 1784 on the North American states and their relations with Russia and on Anglo-American relations. Also a 250–page memoir of the religious and business activities of Larinovich Golikov and Grigor Shelikov in Alaska, 1783–96.

UNITED KINGDOM

England

BERKSHIRE, Holyport, *Gays House*

FAIRFAX OF CAMERON PAPERS
1 reel microfilm, 1758–99.

1291   Selected items from the Revolutionary era include four Washington letters to Bryan Fairfax, Sept. 25, 1777, June 15, 1783, and Jan. 10, 1786; and to Robert Cary, July 12, 1773. Also two letters to Washington from Lord Drummond, Nov. 14, 1778, and from George William Fairfax, Dec. 9, 1783; and a 1771 deed signed by Thomas, 6th Lord Fairfax granting Washington 20 1/2 acres of land.

Published in *Virginia Magazine of History and Biography*, vol. 77 (Oct. 1969), p. 441–63.

Windsor Castle

JAY PAPERS
1 reel microfilm, 1776–94.

1292   Autograph collection of John Jay correspondence, primarily letters to Jay, 1776–94. The letters relate to many aspects of the American Revolution and bear on much of Jay's career during the era, particularly his foreign activities, 1780–84.

Principal correspondents: John Adams, George Clinton, James Duane, D'Estaing, Floridablanca, Franklin, James Gardoqui, Gérard, Alexander Hamilton, David Hartley, Samuel Huntington, Jefferson, John Paul Jones, Lafayette, Henry Laurens, Robert R. Livingston, William Livingston, Montmorin, Gouverneur Morris, Robert Morris, Richard Oswald, Philip Schuyler, Charles Thomson, Vergennes, and Washington.

Photostats of this correspondence are in the John Jay Papers, entry no. 356.

CUMBERLAND, Whitehaven, *Whitehaven Public Library*

JOHN BRAGG PAPERS
1 folio, 1774–88.   Enlargement prints.

1293   Consists primarily of five letters from the family of John Hadwen, merchant of Newport, R.I., to his sister's family, the John Bragg's of Whitehaven, England. The correspondence is largely personal in nature, but contains information on the experiences of a Quaker family of loyalist sentiments during the Revolutionary era.

GLOUCESTERSHIRE, Bristol, *University of Bristol Library*

BRICKDALE NOTES
2 reels microfilm, 1 box photostats, 1770–74.

1294   Notes of debates in the House of Commons, Nov. 1770—Mar. 1774, kept by Matthew Brickdale (1735–1831), M.P. for Bristol. There are 11 notebooks, each of which contains an index by Brickdale.

KENT, Dover, *Waldershare Rectory*

VERNON SMITH MANUSCRIPTS
1 reel microfilm, 1753–1806.

1295   Primarily the papers of Joseph Smith, secretary to William Pitt the younger, about a dozen of which pertain to Pitt's affairs during the 1780's. Includes a few letters to Smith from Pitt, one each from Pitt to Cornwallis, Shelburne, and Mr. Cotton, and two letters from Adm. George Rodney to an unidentified friend, Mar. and Apr. 1782. Also contains a document on Jamaica sugar plantations, with detailed "Remarks on the Births, Deaths, and Diminution of Slaves," covering the years 1779–85.
    See Born, *British Manuscripts Project*, p. 83.

Sevenoaks, *Knole*

SACKVILLE PAPERS. DORSET CORRESPONDENCE AND MISCELLANEA
5 reels microfilm, 1740–1803.

1296   Correspondence of John Frederick Sackville, 3d Duke of Dorset (1745–99), primarily with Carmarthen, the foreign secretary, concerning Dorset's position as Ambassador to France, 1783–89. Also contains several letters, 1782–85, from Dorset's uncle Viscount Sackville, previously Lord George Germain, and from Thomas Jenkins and George Grenville.
    Principal correspondents: Robert Ainslie, James Callander, William Eden, David Hartley, Lord Hawkesbury, William Pitt, Rutland, and Edward Thurlow.
    See Born, *British Manuscripts Project*, p. 134–35.

LANCASHIRE, Manchester, *John Rylands Library*

ENGLISH Ms. 517
3 items, 1744–87.   Photostats.

1297   Consists of a tabular account of 43 slaving voyages, 1744–74, designating ship names, where slaved, where sold, value, number of slaves sold, deaths, net sales, average price per slave, and year. The cargoes were sold mainly in the West Indies, but five ships went to Maryland and the Carolinas. Also contains an account of a single voyage, 1781–83, a list of voyages, 1776–85, and capsule summaries of 11 voyages, 1781–87.

LONDON, *British Museum*

EGERTON MANUSCRIPTS

1298   1941. Letter from "Eugenius," Philadelphia, to Dr. William Lewis, Kingston on Thames [Oct. 1767?], discussing various scientific subjects. Transcripts.

2134. Miscellaneous political and other papers, 1618–1817. Includes an address by New York merchants to Maj. Gen. John Vaughan upon his departure for England, 1779, and instructions from the King to Adm. George Rodney and Vaughan concerning disposal of property captured in the Dutch islands of St. Eustatius, St. Martin, and Saba, 1781. Transcripts.

2135. Original letters and papers concerning military and naval operations in North America and the West Indies, 1762–95. Includes military journals, Mar.—Dec. 1776 and Oct. 1777; assessments of the military situation in New York, Georgia, and New England, 1775–79; plans for campaigns, 1778 and undated; reports on naval operations in the West Indies; a memorial by Sir James Wright concerning a royal pension, 1785; and a memorandum on tropical medicines. Transcripts.

2136. Letters from British officers in the West Indies; also comments of George Jackson on political affairs in England during the summer of 1782. Transcripts.

2423. Journal of Janet Schaw describing a trip from Scotland to the West Indies and North Carolina, 1774–76.
　　Published in Evangeline W. Andrews, ed., in collaboration with Charles M. Andrews, *A Journal of a Lady of Quality* . . . (New Haven, 1939).

2591. Journal of Captain Cook's third voyage to the South Sea, 1776–78, kept by David Samwell, surgeon on the *Discovery*. Photostats.

2659–60, 2669, 2671–74. Hutchinson Family Papers. Principal correspondents: Thomas Hutchinson Francis Bernard, Andrew Oliver, Robert Auchmuty, and Lord Loudoun.
　　Portions published in P. O. Hutchinson, ed., *Diary and Letters of Thomas Hutchinson,* 2 vols. (London, 1884–88).

　　2659. Correspondence, 1741–83. Photostats.

　　2660. Printed abstract of the case of uncompensated American loyalists. Photostats.

　　2669. Diary kept by Elisha Hutchinson, 1774–75, 1777–88. Photostats.

　　2671. "Origin and Progress of the Rebellion in America to 1776," by Peter Oliver (1713–91), written or completed in 1781. Transcripts.
　　　　Published in Peter Oliver, *Origin and Progress of the Rebellion in America: A Tory View*. Edited by John Schutz and Douglas Adair (Stanford, Calif., 1961).

　　2672–73. Journal kept by Peter Oliver on a voyage from America to England, and other trips, 1776–80. Photostats.

　　2674. Memoir of Dr. Peter Oliver (1741–1821), son of Chief Justice Peter Oliver, covering the years 1756–1820. Photostats.

2697. Memorial of Dennys De Berdt and Stephen Sayre to Secretary of State Conway in behalf of Alexander McDougall, merchant of New York [1768]. Transcript.

HARGRAVE MANUSCRIPTS

1299　494. Attorney general's report to the King on the petition of Norborne Berkeley concerning the Barony of Botetourt, Oct. 1763. Photostats.

KING'S MANUSCRIPTS

1300　202. Letters from Gov. Thomas Pownall to Dr. Samuel Cooper, 1769–74, concerning parliamentary action on American matters. Includes Pownall's explanation of certain votes and party strategy. Transcripts.

203. Letters from Dr. Samuel Cooper to Gov. Thomas Pownall, 1769–75, explaining Boston patriots' attitude toward Britain, reasons for patriot resistance, and the hardships imposed by parliamentary measures. Transcripts.
Published in *American Historical Review*, vol. 8 (Jan. 1903), p. 301–30.

205. Part I contains the replies of Gov. Francis Bernard to queries by the Board of Trade, Sept. 1763. Part II comprises answers of Gov. Francis Fauquier and Gov. Arthur Dobbs to Board of Trade inquiries, 1766. Transcripts.

206. Replies of colonial Governors to a circular from the Board of Trade, Aug. 1766, regarding manufacturing, land disposition, quit rents, and the like. There are no reports from Rhode Island, Delaware, and East and West Florida. Also contains a list of legal fees allowed in each Colony, with statements by Governor Bernard and Governor Fauquier. Transcripts.

208. "A General Description of the Province of Nova Scotia, by Lt. Col. Morse, Chief Engineer in America," 1783–84, written pursuant to orders issued by Sir Guy Carleton, July 1783. Photostats.

210–11. Report of a general survey in "the Southern District of North America" by William Gerard de Brahm, surveyor general, based on information gathered between 1751 and 1771. Includes a general description of South Carolina, with a map of Charleston; a compendium of the Cherokee language, with an English translation; a description of Georgia, with maps of Salzburger Ebenezer and Bethanian settlements; a list of inhabitants of East Florida showing occupations and the number of white males, indentured servants, and Negroes. Also De Brahm's map of East Florida with a table of the general survey of the region. Photostats.
Published in Louis De Vorsey, Jr., ed., *DeBrahm's Report of the General Survey in the Southern District of North America* (Columbia, S.C., 1971).

213. Journal kept by Lord Adam Gordon during his service in the British West Indies, Florida, and northward to New York, 1764–65. Contains observations on diet, health, politics, and society. Transcripts.
Published in Newton D. Mereness, ed., *Travels in the American Colonies* (New York, 1916).

214. A description of Jamaica with a general plan of defense, 1782. Prepared by Maj. Gen. Archibald Campbell, Governor of the island. Includes maps and sketches. Photostats.

Lansdowne Manuscripts

1301   1219. Selections in the Library concern American capture of British vessels, Feb.—June 1777, including routine interrogation of captured seamen, letters and other papers of Andrew Turnbull, and complaints to Shelburne and Germain regarding the New Smyrna settlement in East Florida, 1780. Also a petition from American prisoners in Mill Prison, Plymouth, to Shelburne, Sept. 1782; an undated memorandum on the use of Irish troops in America; minutes of Parliament regarding repeal of the Prohibitory Act, 1774; and an accounting of West Indian imports (sugar, rum, and cotton) at Liverpool, Mar. 1776–Mar. 1777. Transcripts.

Stowe Manuscripts

1302   119. Contains a list of committee members named in 1777 "to consider . . . the establishment of Episcopacy in America." Transcripts.

142. Stamp Act. A stamp of the variety intended for use in the American Colonies, 1765. Photostat.

261. Phelps Correspondence. Selection in the Library consists of a letter of J. C. Roberts, secretary to the province of East Florida, concerning his salary, 1768. Transcript.

921. Abstracts of British West Indies trade and navigation, 1773–1805, containing information on commodity prices, population, point of origin of slaves imported from Africa, statistical information on slaves reexported, chiefly 1788 and forward. Includes copies of maps of the British West Indies, showing distances and passage times between the islands and England. Transcripts.

ADDITIONAL MANUSCRIPTS

1303 5829. Memorandum on "American Scholes, 1769." A caustic account of a fund raising effort for the Indian Charity School at Lebanon, Conn., by members of the New England clergy. Transcript.

1304 5847. Portion of an undated letter of Gen. John Burgoyne on the battle of Bunker Hill. Transcript.

1305 6058. "A Short Account of the Bahama Islands," by [William Wylly], barrister of Gray's Inn, Apr. 1788. Contains an attack on Lord Dunmore's administration as Governor of the Bahamas, 1787–88, and a brief allusion to the American naval expedition of Feb.—Mar. 1776, under Esek Hopkins. Also mentions the dissatisfaction of American loyalists who settled in the Bahamas and anxieties of the inhabitants over a possible slave insurrection. Transcripts.

1306 8133B. Anonymous "Observations on the Alien's Duty, the American Drawbacks" and effects of other provisions of the English navigation acts. Includes tables showing products and the value of drawbacks for the years 1771–75, 1779–81. Transcripts.

1307 8133C. Various papers on trade with the American Colonies and the application of the acts of trade and navigation, 1761–82. Transcripts.
    See Andrews and Davenport, *Guide to the Manuscript Materials*, p. 77–78.

1308 9344. Letters to George Jackson, Deputy Secretary of the Admiralty, from Lord Chatham, Adm. George Rodney, Capt. John Jervis, and Lord Sandwich, 1774, 1776–82. Contains information on British naval action in Chesapeake Bay, American privateersmen, and other naval matters. Transcripts.

1309 9345. Contains sketches made on Captain Cook's first voyage, 1768–71. Photostats.

1310 9828. Chiefly letters to Sir John Eardley Wilmot, Lord Chief Justice of the Common Pleas, 1746–78. Includes several letters not directly related to Wilmot, including three Washington letters, 1777–86, one of Henry Laurens, 1777, and five from Benjamin Franklin to his son William, 1774–84. Principal correspondents: 2d Earl Bathurst, Gov. Francis Bernard, Earl of Camden, Lord North, John Pownall, Rockingham, Shelburne, and Baron Edward Thurlow. In British Manuscripts Project. Microfilm, 1 reel.

1311 11663B. Contains Washington holographs on agriculture, soil textures, crops, plowing, and planting times. Photostats.

1312 12099. Consists of two Washington letters, one to Mrs. [Patricia] Wright, Jan. 1785, and the other to the Earl of Buchan, Apr. 1793. Photostats.

1313   12438. Historical essays by Edward Long, Governor of Jamaica, on the origins of the Board of Trade and English plantations in the West Indies, including estimates on the size of the white population and militia strength in 1773. Transcripts.

1314   12440. Official letters to Gov. Henry Moore of New York, 1763–69, concerning enforcement of the navigation acts, the Stamp Act crisis, Indian affairs, the New York rent riots, boundary disputes between the Colonies, and customs boards. Principal correspondents: 2d Earl Egremont, Gov. Francis Fauquier, Hillsborough, 3d Duke Richmond, Shelburne, and Benning Wentworth. Transcripts.

1315   13879. West Indian reports on Grenada, Guadeloupe, Dominica, and St. Vincent, 1753–65, with descriptions of towns, harbors, and military installations. Photostats.

1316   13974. Inventory, in Spanish, of troop strength, armaments, and weapons on New Providence, Bahama Islands, when captured by the Spanish, May 1782. Transcripts.

1317   14034. Board of Trade papers on America, West Indies, Africa, and the Canary Islands, 1696–1786. Includes material concerning Indian affairs, commerce, munitions shipments, manumission of slaves in the West Indies, and Board of Trade expenses for 1775–81. Transcripts.

1318   14035. Board of Trade correspondence and petitions from the American colonies, mainly Canada and the West Indies, concerning fisheries, lumber, indigo, and rice. Includes statistics on South Carolina trade, 1781, and a note on direct trade between Danish and British possessions. Transcripts.

1319   14038–39. Contains "The Conduct of Vice Admiral Samuel Graves in North America in 1774, 1775, and January 1776," in two volumes. Includes a list of vessels under Graves' command in American waters, July 1, 1774; a brief account of Ethan Allen's capture at Montreal, 1775; details of Graves' conduct upon his receiving orders for his recall, Dec. 1775; the disposition of the British Fleet in American waters, Jan. 1776; and an account of American vessels seized by the British, June–Dec. 1775. Transcripts.

1320   15485. Extensive statistical record of exports and imports between the American Colonies, England, and Ireland, Jan. 1761–Jan. 1769. Transcripts.

1321   15489. Contains appeals to the King in Council for settlement of a Rhode Island land dispute; a 1772 petition of Peter Wikoff and Joseph Reed regarding a dispute over a lottery ticket; correspondence between Gov. Horatio Sharpe of Maryland and various residents of the Colony, 1771–73; and correspondence concerning the secretaryship of New York, 1771–73. Transcripts.

1322   15491. Various papers pertaining to Canada, including petitions of Montreal, Quebec, and London merchants to the King on Canadian trade. Also Eleazar Levy's appeal to the Privy Council, 1771. Transcripts.

1323   15492. Observations on the Newfoundland fisheries and arguments for colonization of the island, by Dr. Gardner, "late of Boston," undated. Transcripts.

1324   15743. Drawings by William Hodges made during the second voyage of Captain Cook, 1772–74. Photostats.

1325   15945. Contains a memorandum regarding an incident at the court of Louis XVI reported by Franklin, May 1777. Transcript.

1326   16603. Primarily letters to and from Pierce Butler (1744–1822) of South Carolina to his son, Thomas, and to Rev. Weeden Butler of Chelsea, England, 1784–99, concerning political, social, and family matters. Photostats.

1327   18272. Remarks by ship captains and others on slavery, recorded in 1788. Includes descriptions of the Gold Coast and Sierra Leone, 1769–77, with statistics on the number of slaves leaving African ports, fatalities en route to America, and average age of slaves sold in Africa. Photostats.

1328   18274. Document by Edward Long, 1784, intended as a review of trade policies between the United States and the British West Indies, with emphasis on lumber and provisions. Long concluded that fears and suspicions concerning a limited intercourse between the United States and the British West Indies were unfounded. Transcripts.

1329   18738. Letter by George III commenting on Gen. John Burgoyne's campaign southward from Canada, 1776. Contains three pages of remarks on proposals for use of the British Fleet and for troop dispositions. Photostats.

1330   18959. Contains commentaries on conditions in the British West Indies, including a defense of slavery, a treatise on yellow fever, letters to and from Edward Long concerning commerce, 1775–96, and a memorandum on the defense of Jamaica against d'Estaing's French Fleet, 1779. Photostats.

1331   18960. Contains "Observations on the Carolina trade," undated, a 1776 plan for "a party of Rangers in Jamaica," and several letters to Gov. Henry Moore of New York from a Jamaica, L.I., resident, 1764–67. Photostats.

1332   19071. Includes a petition to William Pitt from "the Loyalists of the Church of Scotland," Sept. 1788, in Nova Scotia recounting the sufferings of Tories who left America during the Revolutionary War. Also material concerning the defense of Manhattan Island and Staten Island and the building of permanent forts. Photostats.

1333   19073. Documents primarily concerning Nova Scotia, but includes a copy of Lt. Frederick de Diemar's "Dispositions of France towards America" and letters concerning munitions shipped to America by Beaumarchais, vessels built in France for the American Navy, court policy, and European diplomacy. Photostats.

1334   19074. Meteorological records kept at Halifax, Nova Scotia, Jan. 1776—Oct. 1794. Also includes information on temperature, winds, and ship sailings and arrivals. Photostats.

1335   20733. Contains a Dec. 1776 letter from Dr. Hugh Williamson, of Philadelphia, to John Almon, a pro-American London printer, concerning Franklin's interrogation by the House of Commons regarding the Stamp Act. Another letter of Nov. 1781 from [John?] Pownall to Almon discusses the rumored resignation of Germain. Transcripts.

1336   20926. Spanish naval records, 1740–82. Includes a map of movements by Spanish vessels, 1779, a list of ships of the line, Apr. 1780, and an "impartial" account of the conduct of Adm. George Rodney. Photostats.

1337   21254–55. Minutes of the London Committee for the Abolition of the Slave Trade, May 1787—July 1790. Contains allusions to the loss of the American Colonies, the possibility of replacing the American colonial trade with agricultural produce from Africa, statements concerning the damaging effect of slavery on a nation, and a communication with Benjamin Rush of the Pennsylvania Abolitionist Society, July 1787. Photostats.

1338   21631–60. Bouquet Papers. Letters and documents relating to Brig. Gen. Henry Bouquet (1719–65) and his career in America, 1757–65. In volumes 21634, 21636–39, 21642, 21649–58, and 21660 are letters, Indian council reports, plans for troop reductions, and orders for provisions, 1763–65, when Bouquet commanded the Southern Department. Principal correspondents: Sir Jeffery Amherst, Gov. Francis Fauquier, Franklin, Gov. James Hamilton, Thomas Hutchins, Sir William Johnson, Andrew Lewis, Edward Shippen, Adam Stephen, and William Trent. Photostats.

The papers are calendared in Douglas Brymner, *Report on the Canadian Archives* (Ottawa, 1889).

1339   21661–21881. Haldimand Papers. Sir Frederick Haldimand (1718–91), a native of Switzerland, was a professional soldier with wide experience in Continental warfare. From 1758 to 1775 he served in America as a lieutenant colonel in the 62d Royal American Regiment. Following a trip to England in 1775, ostensibly to report on colonial conditions, he succeeded Sir Guy Carleton as Governor of Canada, 1778–84. Much of Haldimand's correspondence is in French.

His papers are calendared in Brymner, *Reports on Canadian Archives* (1884–89). The calendar forms but a part of each appendix for the year of issue, but a continuous pagination has been adopted.

21666. Correspondence with Gov. James Murray of Quebec, and Col. James Robertson, Jan. 1762—Mar. 1775. Includes scattered letters from Murray to Gen. Thomas Gage. Photostats.

21670. Correspondence primarily with Sir William Johnson, 1760–74. Includes scattered letters from Chief Justice Frederick Smyth of New Jersey, Samuel Cleaveland, and others in New Jersey. Photostats.

21671–72. Correspondence, chiefly with Brig. Gen. William Taylor, commander of British forces in Florida, and Indian superintendent John Stuart, 1765–74. Also correspondence between Haldimand and Gov. Peter Chester of West Florida, Lord Dartmouth, John Moultrie, and Sir James Wright. Topics include Indian problems, Spanish plans in the Mississippi Valley, and trade at Mobile. Photostats.

21673. Correspondence with Governors in North America chiefly concerning treaties with the Creek Indians, the difficulties in provisioning troops, and other military matters. Principal correspondents: Montfort Browne, William Franklin, James Grant, Horatio Sharpe, William Tryon, and Sir James Wright. Photostats.

21674–75, 21677–78. Haldimand's letterbook, Aug. 1768—Feb. 1770. Includes 78 letters, chiefly to officers in Florida, regarding routine troop movements and supply operations. Also two items dealing with ordnance in Florida, 1765–73, and general orders, letters, and instructions for the Niagara garrison, 1759–78. Principal correspondents: Sir Jeffery Amherst, Sir Guy Carleton, Thomas Gage, Sir William Johnson, and Richard Maitland. Photostats.

21680. Letters of Maj. Francis Hutcheson, from duty stations at Boston, Halifax, Staten Island, and elsewhere, 1766–78, concerning camp life, pay, and rumors from American lines. Photostats.

21683. Orders and instructions from Gen. Thomas Gage's headquarters, 1763–75. Pertains to the quartering of troops, changes in command, and payments to civilians for goods and services. Photostats.

21686. Part II contains Thomas Hutchins' journal and map of a trip through the Ohio Valley to Vincennes, 1768; the journal of Sargeant Wright kept on an expedition from Pensacola, Fla., to the Upper Creeks and back, 1771; a list of the Indian tribes along the Mississippi River between New Orleans and the Red River, 1773; and a journal of a trip from Quebec to Falmouth at Casco Bay 1773. Also the journal kept by Hugh Finlay during travels from the Chaudière settlement to the Kennebec River, 1773; notes on the Mississippi and New Iberville Rivers; instructions from Congress to privateers cruising in the St. Lawrence gulf; a map of eastern Massachusetts, Lake Erie, and Lake Sandersby; and an undated plan of Fort Pitt. Photostats.

21687. Fragment from the Haldimand group containing a letter from Benjamin Harrison to Washington, July 21, 1775, and several letters of Gen. Thomas Gage, 1766–71. Photostats.

21693. Correspondence between Haldimand and field officers at Crown Point, Philadelphia, Pensacola, and various other stations, June 1773—Sept. 1774. Contains routine orders, documents relating to British posts in the Illinois country, and materials concerning relations between the military and the civilian population. Principal correspondents: Daniel Dulany, Jr., Thomas Gage, and John Montresor. Photostats.

21695. Haldimand's correspondence with Lord Dartmouth and others, Jan. 1773—Apr. 1775. Includes reports on Indian warfare, fortifications, and views on the disturbance in America. Principal correspondents: Lord Dunmore and John Montresor. Photostats.

21696. Correspondence with Viscount Barrington, Sept. 1764—Sept. 1777. Topics range from the sicknesses at Pensacola to the Boston Tea Party. Photostats.

21697. Official correspondence between Ministers in England and British commanders in America, 1760–78, concerning Indian affairs, troop reinforcements, and the enforcement of customs regulations in 1763. Principal correspondents: Sir Jeffery Amherst, Sir Guy Carleton, and Thomas Gage.

21698, 21701, 21703. Official correspondence between Haldimand, Ministers in England, and officers in America, 1776–79. Subjects include approval for Indian raiding parties under Col. Henry Hamilton, and plans for an attack on New Orleans. Principal correspondents: John Burgoyne, Germain, John Robinson, and Thomas Townshend. Photostats.

21704. Official correspondence, Mar. 1780—Jan. 1782. Primarily letters from Germain to Haldimand on a variety of subjects, including loyalists in Virginia and intercepted Washington-Lafayette letters. Photostats.

21705. Official correspondence, June 1781—June 1784, containing instructions sent to Haldimand as Governor of Quebec. Subjects include Indian problems, military hospitals, trade regulations with the United States, and the evacuation of forts in the Northwest Territory. Principal correspondents: Sir Guy Carleton, Germain, Lord North, and Shelburne. Photostats.

21710, 21714–16, 21726. Official correspondence between Haldimand and Germain, 1777–84. Also includes letters from Haldimand to Shelburne and Thomas Townshend concerning his duties in Quebec, Pensacola, and New York, and the Treaty of Paris. Principal correspondents: Sir Guy Carleton, Thomas Gage, and Thomas Willing. Photostats.

21728. Correspondence with officers and officials, 1757–68, concerning military matters, particularly Indian affairs and the health of British troops. Many letters are in

French. Principal correspondents: William Byrd, J. F. N. DesBarres, James Grant, Sir Basil Keith, and Thomas Willing. Photostats.

21729. Correspondence with officers and officials, 1769–72, containing routine reports, information on duty stations, the disposition of Spanish forces, and military supply. Principal correspondents: William Byrd, James Grant, Thomas Hutchins, and Oliver Pollock.

21735. Letter from Andrew Turnbull to Haldimand, Nov. 2, 1783, introducing Col. Francisco de Miranda. Transcript.

21756. Haldimand's correspondence with commandants at Michilimackinac and Niagara, 1777–83. Topics include mercantile affairs at Detroit, the use of Indians in General Burgoyne's campaign, and the application of the terms of peace. Principal correspondents: Sir Guy Carleton, Arent DePeyster, and Patrick Sinclair. Photostats.

21759. Papers concerning the posts in upper Canada, 1771–82, including reports, letters, troop returns, memorials, and reports of difficulties at Niagara and Detroit. Photostats.

21760–64. Correspondence between British staff officers and commandants at posts on the western frontier, 1777–84. Includes the reports of Brig. Gen. Allan MacLean from Niagara complaining of effrontery and impudence of Virginians sent as emissaries to the Indians. Principal correspondents: Arent DePeyster and A. Dundas. Photostats.

21765. Correspondence with Maj. Robert Mathews, Haldimand's secretary, and Maj. John Butte, commandant of the Ranger corps, mainly concerning Fort Niagara, 1777–84. Pertains to attempts to mobilize the Rangers, exchange prisoners, and employ Indians on the frontier. Principal correspondents: Sir Guy Carleton and Sir Henry Clinton. Photostats.

21767. Correspondence with Col. Guy Johnson, Superintendent of Indian Affairs in the Northern District. Concerns the difficulties of giving presents to Indian allies, 1778–83. Photostats.

21774. Correspondence between Haldimand and Lt. Col. Daniel Claus, 1778–84, pertaining to the Indians of the Six Nations—their methods of warfare, treatment of prisoners, and use as spies. Photostats.

21776. Sir John Johnson's commissions and instructions from the British Government, 1782–83. Johnson was urged to govern "by persuasion and address" and to prevent traders from cheating the Indians. Photostats.

21779, 21783. Material pertaining to Indian affairs, including correspondence, speeches, memorials, and treaties, 1778–84. Contains an Indian report that their former patron, the French King, was helping the Bostonians by sending aid to the rebels. Also contains documents concerning Indian difficulties requiring the attention of the Detroit commandant, 1772–84, including the American attack under Gen. John Sullivan. Principal correspondents: Sir Guy Carleton, George Rogers Clark, Simon Girty, Henry Hamilton, Thomas Hartley, and Philippe Rocheblave. Photostats.

21780. Haldimand correspondence with the commandants of Oswegatchie, 1778–84. Contains reports of warfare between pro-British tribes and Indians favorable to the United States, routine military matters, and raiding parties sent to capture prisoners. Photostats.

21782–83. Correspondence with commandants at Detroit, 1778–84. Concerns Indian allies, military affairs in the Ohio Valley, American troops in the Illinois country, and routine matters. Principal correspondents: Henry Hamilton, John Montgomery, and Philippe Rocheblave. Photostats.

21785. Correspondence with commandants at Oswego, 1782–83, concerning fears of an American attack on Canada, preparedness, Mohawk treachery, rumors of a peace faction in the United States, and threats against Oswego. Photostats.

21786. Correspondence with Maj. John Ross and others at Cataragui, 1783–86. Topics include loyalist settlements, anxieties about the treaty of peace, and reports of American mistreatment of loyalists after the signing of the treaty. Photostats.

21787–88. Correspondence with commandants at Carleton Island, 1778–84, concerning Indian allies, the killing of prisoners, suspicions of Iroquois sincerity, and rumors of an imminent American attack. Photostats.

21792–95. Correspondence with the commandants at Isle aux Noix, 1778–83, and Fort St. John's, 1778–84. Concerns reports on American armies, American prisoners of war, rumors of a military force in Vermont, loyalist claims, desertion, threats by the New York Militia, and the enormous cost of the war. Photostats.

21806–8. Correspondence with Sir Guy Carleton and others, 1777–83. Contains records of troop movements, reinforcements, American activities around Lake Champlain, and the evacuation of New York. Principal correspondents: John André, Marriot Arbuthnot, Sir Henry Clinton, Germain, Sir William Howe, Baron Wilhelm Knyphausen, Baron Friedrich Riedesel, and James Robertson. Photostats.

21818–20. Correspondence with officers in the Royal American Regiment in New York, 1776–83, and the Royal Rangers in Canada, 1779–80. Subjects treated include Indian allies, Canadian recruits, enlistment of deserters from the American Army, espionage, and the recruiting of loyalists. Principal correspondents: John Burgoyne, Sir Guy Carleton, James Rogers, and Robert Rogers. Photostats.

21834. Correspondence, 1778, concerning prisoners of war, particularly the Convention Army, and problems resulting from the Saratoga defeat. Principal correspondents: Sir Guy Carleton, William Heath, William Phillips, and Baron von Riedesel. Photostats.

21835–40. Correspondence concerning an exchange of prisoners, the situation in Vermont, 1777–84, General Burgoyne's surrender, the Convention Army, and George Rogers Clark's expedition into the Illinois country. Also letters and documents concerning the treatment of prisoners, espionage, options open to loyalists, and undercover efforts in Vermont. Principal correspondents: Ethan Allen, Thomas Chittenden, George Clinton, John Hancock, Jefferson, Sir John Johnson, La Luzerne, Philip Schuyler, Baron von Steuben, and Washington. Photostats.

21841–42. Documents related to espionage activities and American prisoners of war, 1775–82. Includes information on the Illinois country before the Clark expedition, battles, troop dispositions above Manhattan Island, prisoners, loyalists, and Indian sentiments toward the Crown. Principal correspondents: George Rogers Clark, George Clinton, Sir Henry Clinton, Sir John Johnson, Joseph Reed, Mathew Visscher, and Anthony Wayne. Photostats.

21844–45. Intelligence reports on affairs in the colonies and on disaffected persons in Canada, 1775–84. Many of the documents are French translations of reports from loyalists concerning Quebec and inhabitants there friendly to the American cause. Includes maps of Ohio country. Principal correspondents: George Rogers Clark, Silas Deane, Franklin, Henry Hamilton, Patrick Henry, and John Todd. Photostats.

21846. Journal kept by Col. Augustin Mottin de la Balme, a French volunteer and inspector general of cavalry in the Continental Army, on a trip to Machias, Maine, May—Sept. 1779. The trip coincided with the Penobscot expedition, and its unfortunate timing resulted in La Balme's capture by the British. Photostats.

21881. Correspondence with Brig. Gen. Barry St. Leger and Henry Hamilton, Nov. 1784, concerning relationships of church and state in Quebec, the duties of authorities toward loyalists, the conduct of Indian allies, and the western posts. Photostats.

1340   22129. A register of civil officials in the colonies, listing their salaries, ca.1780. Transcript.

1341   22130. Letter from Washington to Col. François Menonville, May 9, 1781. Transcript.

1342   22676. Miscellaneous papers pertaining to Jamaica, 1662–1765, including "A Summary Account of the Proceedings between the Governor and Assembly of Jamaica, 1764 & 1765." Photostats.

1343   22677. Contains letters of planters, merchants, and officials in Jamaica concerning the affairs of the island, including several letters of Edward Long, judge of the vice-admiralty court in Jamaica, regarding French and Spanish vessels captured by British privateers, 1779. Also miscellaneous letters from New Bern, N.C., and Charleston, S.C., 1772–73. Photostats.

1344   22678. Correspondence between Thomas Dancer, Jamaica physician and botanist, Edward Long, and Samuel More, secretary of the Society of Arts in London, 1787–91, concerning science. Photostats.

1345   22679. Papers concerning public affairs in New York, 1764–68. Principal correspondents: Francis Bernard, Samuel Holland, Jared Ingersoll, and Sir William Johnson. Transcripts.

1346   22680. Includes notes on shipping, trade, the territorial extent of America, and various European states, 1769–72. Transcripts.

1347   23651. Gen. Charles Rainsford's correspondence, in French, German, and English, regarding the Hessian troops employed by George III, 1776–78. Concerns the collection of Hanau and Ansbach troops and their transport to America. Includes muster rolls. Principal correspondents: Earl of Suffolk and Sir Joseph Yorke. Transcripts.

1348   24131–38. Abstracts of state papers collected by Shelburne, 1763–89, containing entries with succinct digests of letters. Dates of letters and names of correspondents are often missing. Topics cover the entire range of British politics and policy for the Revolutionary era. Photostats.

1349   24320. Papers, Feb. 1779, concerning the surrender of Fort Sackville (Vincennes). Principal correspondents: George Rogers Clark and Henry Hamilton. Transcripts.

1350   24322. Correspondence and papers pertaining to American affairs, particularly the conduct of the war in the Southern Department. Principal correspondents: Peter Chester, Sir Henry Clinton, Lord Cornwallis, Silas Deane, William de Brahm, Thomas Gage, Germain, Elbridge Gerry, Earl Percy, Augustine Prevost, Susanna Riddell, Baron von Steuben, and Patrick Tonyn. Transcripts.

1351   24323. Correspondence, 1770–80, of John Blackburn, a London merchant, with Sir William Johnson, Sir John Johnson, and Col. Guy Johnson. Most of the letters relate to Canada. Transcripts.

1352   25490. Fragments of anonymous observations of the attack on Fort Sullivan, S.C., June 28, 1776. Includes a description of the fort and the surrounding terrain. Transcripts.

1353   25494–25543. Contains the "Minutes of the Court of Directors of the Governor and Company of Merchants of Great Britain trading to the South Seas and other Parts of America and for Encouraging the Fishery," Sept. 1711—Apr. 1856. For documents from the period of the Revolution see nos. 25516–22. Photostats.

1354   25568–74. Official copies of minutes of the Committee of Directors of the South Sea Company, July 1721—Aug. 1845. For documents from the period of the Revolution see nos. 25571–72. Photostats.

1355   25575–78. "Register of all Instruments to which the Common Seal of the Corporation of the Govr and Company of Merchants of Great Britain Trading to the South Seas and other parts of America and for Encouraging the Fishery hath been Affixed," Dec. 1711—Mar. 1856. For documents from the period of the Revolution see no. 25578. Photostats.

1356   25583. Official copies of minutes of South Sea Company committee meetings, Oct. 1737—Nov. 1784. Photostats.

1357   25893–95. Manuscript notes concerning the sea battles between the *Serapis* and *Bonhomme Richard* and other naval engagements, including copies of newspaper extracts, 1779–80. Photostats.

1358   26052. Report of the King's Advocate General on a code of civil and criminal law in Quebec, 1772. Transcript.

1359   27578. Extracts from the correspondence of Rev. Weeden Butler pertaining to local religious matters in Maryland, 1768–69. Transcripts.

1360   27621. Correspondence and an essay by James Ramsay on the treatment of Negroes in the British West Indies, 1784. Includes extracts from a review of Thomas Jefferson's *Notes on the State of Virginia*. Photostats.

1361   27891. Contains sailing directions for the east coast of the United States, 1772–78. Transcripts.

1362   27916. Contains Francis Osborne's essay, "A short Hint to both Sides of the Atlantic," ca. 1777, pertaining to differences between Great Britain and the Colonies. Transcript.

1363   27918. Political memoranda of Francis Osborne, M.P., 1774–96, Lord Chamberlain, 1777, Foreign Secretary of State, 1783, and Home Secretary, 1784. Photostats.

1364   28103. Letter from Adm. George Rodney concerning the French in the West Indies, June 1781. Transcript.

1365   28605. Journal kept by John Lees of Quebec, 1768, while traveling from London to Boston and overland to Quebec. Includes comments on conditions in the Colonies. Transcript.

1366   28727. Contains the correspondence of Peter Collinson, the naturalist, and others, 1725–90. Transcripts.

1367   28851. Diplomatic correspondence and papers of Richard Cumberland, 1780–91, including a record of secret negotiations with Spain, 1780–81. Transcripts.
      See also F. O. 72, entry no. 1565.

1368   29256–59. British monthly troop returns, Nov. 1768—Sept. 1775. Photostats.

1369   29600. Includes letters, 1772–73, and accounts, 1769, 1772, 1776, pertaining to the Principio Iron Works in Maryland. Most of the letters are from Thomas Russell in Maryland to various partners in the company. Transcripts.

1370   30094. Extract from the papers of Benjamin Wilson, 1778, concerning an incident in the Royal Society in which Franklin was involved. Photostat.

1371   30262. Autograph collection containing an exchange of letters between Gen. Benedict Arnold and Col. Beverley Robinson, Sept. 1780. Transcripts. See also Born, *British Manuscripts Project*, p. 7.

1372   30306. Fairfax family correspondence. Contains several letters written by Bryan Fairfax to relatives in England, 1769–83. Photostats.

1373   30868–75. John Wilkes' correspondence, 1764–85, concerning his political activities. For letters pertaining to America see nos. 30870–71. No. 30875 contains many undated items, including a letter from Arthur Lee, ca. 1780. Principal correspondents: John Adams, Samuel Adams, John Almon, and Joseph Warren. Photostats.

1374   32413. Contains the diary of Lt. William Digby, Apr. 1776—Oct. 1777, including the campaign under Gen. John Burgoyne. Transcript.
      Published under the title, *The British Invasion of the North*; . . . , Da Capo Press reprint series (New York, 1970).

1375   32627. Memoirs of Alexander Chesney, 1755–1821, a South Carolina loyalist. Transcript.
      Published in Ohio State University *Bulletin*, vol. 24 (1921), No. 4.

1376   32686–33057. Newcastle Papers. Official correspondence of Thomas Pelham Holles, Duke of Newcastle, 1697–1768.

        32947–70. Letters and documents, 1763–65, concerning the Treaty of Paris, 1763, plans for postwar garrisons in the American Colonies, Britain's national debt, and the elder Pitt's opinions on public questions. Principal correspondents: Duke of Albermarle, Charles Townshend, and Thomas Walpole. Transcripts.

        32971–80. Includes letters and memoranda, 1765–67, concerning American affairs and parliamentary support for the Rockingham ministry. Also petitions from Massachusetts and New York. Principal correspondents: Archbishop of Canterbury, Lord Dartmouth, Grantham, and Rockingham. Photostats and transcripts.

        32981–87, 32990–92. Documents, 1767–68, concerning parliamentary reaction to American colonial legislation pardoning rioters in Massachusetts, the debate over the Quartering Act, and the opposition to George Grenville. Principal correspondents: Duke of Albermarle, Bedford, Bishop of Durham, Richmond, and Rockingham. Photostats and transcripts.

        33030. Miscellaneous items include Gov. Francis Bernard's comments on "outrages" caused by resistance to the Stamp Act; questions and answers regarding enforcement of the Stamp Act; a resolution of London merchants in the American trade, 1766;

"Observations on the Trade of Great Britain to her American Colonies . . . " ca. 1766; "Considerations on the Laws made for the increase of Navigation . . . so far as they relate to the Bullion trade"; and a copy of a letter by Sir Henry Clinton, 1782. Transcripts.

33048. Contains pay records and notes on taxation and indebtedness gathered to show the cost of maintaining British armed forces, 1760–73. Some of the material bears Charles Townshend's endorsement. The originals may have been used to support Townshend's taxation programs. Also includes a "Proposal for raising a Corps of German Deserters" who would be assigned to "the most fertile parts of our Conquest in America," records of troop reductions, and a list of regiments disbanded in 1763. Transcripts.

33056. Includes the royal commissions of Govs. William Tryon of North Carolina and Henry Moore of New York, 1765–66, and an undated petition from the manufacturers of beaver and felt hats. Transcripts.

1377   33131. Chiefly letters of Queen Charlotte, in French, to Lady Holdernesse, 1774–1808. Includes two letters of George III to Lady Holdernesse, 1778–79, pertaining to the death and estate of her husband. In British Manuscripts Project. Microfilm, 1 reel.

1378   33132. Includes several personal letters of members of the royal family, 1774–1836. British Manuscripts Project. Microfilm, 1 reel.

1379   33741. An account of naval appropriations by Parliament, 1775–1807, including the navy debt at the end of each year. Photostat.

1380   34079. Adm. Samuel Hood's account of damage done to Halifax harbor by a gale, Apr. 1768. Transcript.

1381   34187. Letters to George Jackson, Admiralty Office, from America, 1776–86, concerning Admiral Howe's rendezvous at Halifax, 1776, the number of loyalists in America, and the difficulties of settling prize claims following the capture of St. Eustatius. Transcripts.

1382   34412–19, 34428. Auckland Papers, 1775–85. The Library's holdings concerning the personal and political affairs of William Eden, 1st Baron Auckland, consist of Stevens' facsimiles. See Griffin, *Guide to Manuscripts*, p. 152–54.

Documents in no. 34428 consist of a printed pamphlet, *Convention Between His Britannick Majesty and the King of Spain, Signed at London, the 14th of July, 1786* (London, 1786), and a letter estimating Spanish depredations in the Bay of Honduras, mainly the capture of slaves from the British, 1763–79.

1383   34756. Extracts from Madrid newspapers, Mar.—May 1776, regarding a Spanish expedition into northern California, the condition of Indian tribes in the area, and claims made to the territory in 1769, 1770, and 1774. Transcripts.

1384   34813. A lengthy letter from Yorktown, Va., to London, Aug. 1775, disavowing aspirations of independence, and a spurious news story concerning a slave uprising. Transcript.

1385   35155. Papers pertaining to the West Indies, Grenada, Dominica, and St. Vincent, 1764–74. Photostats.

1386   35192. Bridport Papers. Includes letters from Lord Chatham, 1773–74, one of which contains critical remarks on the "Short-sighted and Tyrannical Administration" and expresses the hope that "America will not be their Dupes." Transcripts.

1387   35349–36278. Hardwicke Papers, 1772–79. Contains letters of the first four earls of Hardwicke and members of the Yorke family.

35395. Letter of Joseph Sydney Yorke to his uncle, 2d Earl of Hardwicke, Apr. 1782, at sea on HMS *Formidable* near Jamaica, reporting Adm. George Rodney's recent naval victory. In British Manuscripts Project. Microfilm, 1 reel.

35427. Extensive correspondence between Thomas Hutchinson and Lord Hardwicke, 1774–79. Transcripts.

35433. Copies of resolutions and memorials of the Dutch States General and provincial assemblies, in French and English, 1775–78, concerning the loan of troops to Britain, and American munitions shipments from Dutch ports. Transcripts.

35444. Papers and correspondence concerning diplomacy and the embassy at The Hague, 1756–72, under Sir Joseph Yorke. Includes a letter from the Prince of Orange to the States General pertaining to trade on the Guiana coast, 1772. Transcripts.

35509, 35511, 35513. Correspondence of Robert M. Keith, Ambassador to Austria, Mar. 1775—Apr. 1778. Selections in the Library of Congress include letters from War Office personnel, chiefly Anthony Chamier, concerning political trends, news from America, and troop movements, Apr.–Dec. 1775. Also letters of George Cressner, Count Metternich, and others pertaining to the detention of Hessian troops at Coblenz, 1777, and a declaration of France regarding a treaty with America, 1778. Transcripts.

35525. Contains letters of Robert M. Keith, Mar.—June 1782, including a letter from Sir Charles Douglas, Apr. 1782, describing Adm. George Rodney's victory over Comte de Grasse in the West Indies. Also a report with comments on the relative strength of the English and French Fleets during the battle. Transcripts.

35609. Contains a letter from Thomas Yorke, Apr. 1771, requesting financial assistance and a customs service appointment. Transcript.

35613–14. Letters from Robert Auchmuty, late judge of admiralty in Massachusetts, Apr. 1777—July 1778, regarding General Howe's campaign around New York, Washington's army, General Burgoyne's army, and various events in America. A letter of July 23, 1777, describes an encounter between HMS *Fox* and an American privateer off Newfoundland. Transcripts.

35616. Extracts from a letter of Edward Hay, Governor of Barbados, July 1779, pertaining to the British Fleet in the West Indies. Transcripts.

35520–21. Additional letters from Robert Auchmuty, Oct. 1782—Dec. 1783, regarding his reduced financial situation. Also an extract of a letter by a loyalist describing conditions in America, undated. Transcripts.

35639. Contains the correspondence of Charles Yorke, 1769–70. Transcripts.

35655. Letters of Walter Pollard, of Cambridge University, and members of his family in the British West Indies, 1775–77. Primarily concerns family matters, with occasional references to the war. A letter of Nov. 1788 contains a discussion of slavery. Transcripts.

35898. Contains a letter from a customs collector, July 1772, concerning "the Outrage committed on His Majesty's Schooner *Gaspée*," a deposition on the *Gaspée* affair, a list of British ships carrying ordnance to America, 1775–76, and a list of ships commanded by Lord Howe, Oct. 1776. Transcripts.

35910. Contains papers pertaining to American plantations, including a letter from Sir William Johnson to the Board of Trade, Sept. 1763; a Council order on the Georgia boundary, Oct. 1763; a detailed list of proposed stamp duties on American papers and legal documents, along with the Massachusetts Bay Stamp Act of 1754 and New York Stamp Act of 1757; Henry McCullohs' draft of the Stamp Act bill; and miscellaneous items on Indian and political affairs, 1763–64. Transcripts.

35911–12. Papers principally concerned with Admiralty Court jurisdictions, the enforcement of the Navigation and Stamp Acts, the reaction of Colonies to the Stamp Act, and Benjamin Franklin's letter to William Shirley, Dec. 1754, regarding a "Grand Council" of colonial representatives to levy taxes rather than by parliamentary statutes. Also contains proposals for suspension of the Stamp Act, Thomas Hutchinson's commentaries on the resistance movement, 1773, extracts of private letters from Boston, 1773–74, and New York, 1778, 1783, and "Lord Rocheford's plan to plan an end to the war," ca. 1777, in French. Principal correspondents: Francis Bernard, Thomas Gage, Soame Jenyns, John Pownall, and Rockingham. Transcripts.

35914–15. Papers concerning Quebec and Newfoundland, chiefly official reports, memorials to the Board of Trade, and related items, 1762–73. Transcripts.

35916. Primarily concerns West Indian affairs, 1736–65, but also includes documents on the continued Franco-British tension in the Caribbean and threats of slave insurrections. Principal correspondents: Sir William Burnaby, Dartmouth, Leyborne, and Rochford. Transcripts.

36133. Royal warrants for Gov. James Murray of Quebec, Oct. 7, 1763, Gov. George Johnstone of West Florida, Oct. 7, 1763, Gov. Charles Montague of South Carolina, Feb. 15, 1766, and Gov. John Wentworth of New Hampshire, July 31, 1766. Transcripts.

36194. Contains briefs of Judge Charles Yorke on chancery cases, 1767–68, including a law suit of Tench Francis of Philadelphia, 1767. See no. 36225. Transcripts.

36218–20. Privy Council Appeals, 1759–69. Mainly cases appealed from Jamaica, but includes material concerning decisions on the prize ship *Providence*, 1765, and litigation on entailed estates in Virginia, the "Parsons Cause," 1763, Camm *vs.* Hansford and Moss, 1765–66, and the Pennsylvania Land Company *vs.* Stover, 1766. Transcripts.

36225–26. Contains legal opinions of Judge Charles Yorke, 1762–69, including a report on the court-martial of Daniel McDonald, Martinique, 1763, and the case of Tench Francis of Philadelphia, 1767. See no. 36194. Other items include a "Scheme for an American Stamp Bill," 1763, and minutes of a conference with Mr. McCulloh on "A Scheme for an American Stamp Law," 1763. Transcripts.

1388   36596. Whitefoord Papers. Caleb Whitefoord served as secretary to the British peace commission at Paris. Includes a copy of the preliminary articles of peace, 1783, and notes on the negotiations. Transcripts.

1389   36806. Memos on Barbary pirates and invalid passes for American ships "as the ill consequences of their separation from us" and "Reduction of the Island of Trinidad" with observations on adjacent provinces. Other items deal with Honduras trade and a charitable appeal for dependents of British Honduran captives taken by the Spanish for 1779. Transcripts.

1390   37067. Contains an index to names of testators of Barbadian wills, 1776–1800. Compiled by Edwin Fitzpatrick. Photostats.

1391   37528. Journal of the South Sea voyage "by His Majesty's Ships *Resolution* and *Discovery* . . . kept by Thomas Edgar, Master," 1776–78, containing an account of Capt. Cook's last voyage. Photostats.

1392   37833–35. Correspondence of John Robinson with George III, 1772–84. Robinson served as secretary to the Treasury, 1770–82, and was often the king's intermediary on confidential matters. A note from Windsor Castle, Sept. 24, 1776, indicates the king's tacit approval of the use of Indian allies in efforts to suppress the American rebellion. Photostats.

1393   38389–92. Liverpool Papers, vols. 200–3, 1786–90. "Minutes, etc., of the Privy Council Committee of Trade." Contains proceedings of the committee, its reports to the Privy Council, testimony of various persons examined, and statistics and reports on American economic affairs. Photostats.

    See also P.R.O./B.T.5, entry no. 1413.

Dr. Williams's Library

DR. JOSEPH PRIESTLEY'S LETTERS
1 reel microfilm, 1766–1803.

1394   Consists of 60 letters, dated 1766–89, to the Rev. Theophilus Lindsey primarily concerning Priestley's intellectual interests. His comments about dissenting politics became more numerous in the late 1780's.

    Available from Micro Methods, Ltd.

General Post Office

PAPERS
2 boxes, 1737–85.   Transcripts.

1395   Consists of selections pertaining to postal activities in America from several groups of records retained at the General Post Office:

    1. Treasury letterbooks. Vols. 8–10, 1760–83. Entry books of Treasury Board correspondence, including proposals for new packet routes to America, accounts of expenses, memorials of merchants, and orders. After 1763 the documents reflect the board's increasing concern for better communications with new colonies in Florida and the West Indies.

    2. Order books, 1737–74. Contains order appointing new deputy postmasters and commanders of packets in North America and the West Indies.

    3. Commission books, 1759–83. Entry book of commissions issued to newly appointed deputy postmasters and commanders of packets.

    4. Instructions, 1763–83. Instructions issued to newly appointed officials.

    5. Accounts, 1764–85. Statements of annual expenses of American stations.

    6. American letterbook, 1773–83. Contains letters, chiefly from Secretary Anthony Todd, to postmasters in North America and the West Indies.

    See Andrews and Davenport, *Guide to Manuscript Materials*, p. 273–76.

House of Lords Record Office

COMMITTEE BOOKS, VOLS. 1–78
32 boxes, 1661–1829.   Photostats.

1396   The House of Lords Record Office is the main repository of parliamentary records. There is no parallel for the House of Commons. Documents from the Revolutionary era include committee books containing rough minutes of the proceedings of the various committees of the Lords, chiefly notes of debates, evidence, petitions, and opinions of judges and legal assistants.

For comprehensive lists of these manuscripts see Andrews and Davenport, *Guide to Manuscripts*, p. 192–272, and Paullin and Paxson, *Guide to the Materials in London Archives*, p. 329–60.

Lambeth Palace Library

ARCHIVES OF THE BISHOP OF LONDON
13 reels microfilm, 1626–1822.

1397   Correspondence between the colonial clergy and the Bishop of London, with testimonials and other documents. Does not include regular reports of parochial activity, but contains material on colonial society, politics, and economics, and provides information on problems confronting the established church in America.

Calendared in William Wilson Manross, *The Fulham Papers in the Lambeth Palace Library* (Oxford, 1965).

MANUSCRIPTS OF THE ARCHBISHOP OF CANTERBURY
9 reels microfilm, 1763–89.

1398   Letters to the Archbishop concerning the training, appointment, ordination, and conduct of the American clergy, affairs at King's College and the College of Philadelphia, problems with dissenters, theological disputes, and missions among Indians and remote white settlers. Also letters by Anthony Benezet concerning slavery and the slave trade. Seven of the nine reels contain "Calendars of Allegations for Marriage Licenses," 1632–1864.

Principal correspondents: Thomas Caner, Edmund Chester, Jacob Duché, Samuel Johnson, and Richard Peters.

Public Record Office

ADMIRALTY

Accounting Departments

MISCELLANEA. VARIOUS

ADM. 49. VOLS. 1–9.
3 reels microfilm, 1756–94.

1399   Vol. 1. Documents prepared in 1767 for the House of Commons concerning the total expense of maintaining the navy in North America and the West Indies, 1756–66.

Vol. 2. Material on transports, provisioners, and tenders employed in America, 1775–84; on ships taken into His Majesty's service by colonial Governors; and on the value of ships and stores employed during the evacuation of America, 1782–83.

Vol. 3–6. Musters of Transports, 1775–82. Fifteen musters taken at various times and places in North America and the West Indies, listing the complement of each ship and indexed by name of ship.

Vol. 7. Correspondence of William Fowler, naval storekeeper at New York, 1776–83, containing the record of his disbursements in America during the war.

Vol. 8. Papers relating to surveys in British North America, 1783–93, chiefly those of Sir John Wentworth, surveyor of the woods. Includes papers on appointment of deputy surveyors; Wentworth's "diary of travel performed," Oct. 1783—Dec. 1784, and correspondence, 1783–90; and two maps indicating crown reserves in the Stewiac and Lahave River regions.

Vol. 9. An "account of the expenses that have attended the transport and maintenance of American loyalists who removed from different parts of Nova Scotia, Quebec, Jamaica, Dominica, and the Bahama Islands" prepared for the Treasury, 1786, along with numerous supporting documents. Includes a 14-page table of all transport vessels employed in the relocation of loyalists, Jan. 1783—Jan. 1786, showing origin, destination, and dates of embarkation and disembarkation. Also a return of transports employed in the evacuation of East Florida, Apr. 1784—Nov. 1785.

Admiralty and Secretariat

PAPERS

ADM. 1. VOLS. 310, 482–91. ADMIRALS' DISPATCHES
18 boxes, 1763–89.   Transcripts and photostats. Microfilm available for vols. 482–89.

1100   Contains dispatches to Secretary of the Admiralty Philip Stephens, 1763–95, from commanders in chief of the North American station, letters from junior officers and colonial officials, and numerous enclosures and intercepted documents. Records for the prewar period contain material on the collection of customs duties, illicit trade, rivalry between customs officials and naval officers, the Stamp Act crisis, seizure of the sloop *Liberty*, the shipment of troops to Boston, the burning of the *Gaspée*, and the Boston Tea Party. Documents for the war years include reports concerning the expeditions to North Carolina, Rhode Island, Georgia, Charleston, S.C., and the Chesapeake area; records of operations of the main fleet; inventories of ships captured; accounts of preparations for the evacuation of American ports, 1782–83; and reports of naval engagements. Postwar documents concern loyalists, commercial relations with the U.S., and the northern fisheries.

Organization of the collection is not strictly chronological. Dates in parentheses show the period covered by letters written while commanders were actually in American waters.

Vol. 310. Selections. Mar.—Apr. 1778. Vice Adm. James Young, Antigua.

Vol. 482. Dispatches, 1759–66. Lord Colville's command in America (1763–66).

Vol. 483. Commodores Samuel Hood (July 1767—Oct. 1770) and Jamies Gambier (Oct. 1770—Aug. 1771).

Vol. 484. John Montagu (Aug. 1771—July 1774) and Molyneux Shuldham (Jan. 1776—Jan. 1777).

Vol. 485. Samuel Graves (June 1774—Jan. 1776).

Vol. 486. Commodore Peter Parker's correspondence on the expedition to the Carolinas (chiefly Jan.—July 1776). John Byron (Aug.—Oct. 1778) and Mariot Arbuthnot (Aug. 1779—July 1781).

Vol. 487–88. Lord Howe (July 1776—Sept. 1778).

Vol. 489. James Gambier (May 1778—Apr. 1779) and Thomas Graves (Aug. 1780—July 1782).

Vol. 490. Robert Digby (Sept. 1781—Dec. 1783).

Vol. 491. Commodores Sir Charles Douglas (Dec. 1783—Aug. 1785), Edmund Affleck (July 1781—May 1782), and Herbert Sawyer (May 1785—Aug. 1788).

ADM. 1. VOLS. 1435–2733. CAPTAINS' DISPATCHES
10 boxes, 1763–83.　　　　Transcripts.

1401　Correspondence concerning enforcement of the acts of trade, naval manpower, American privateers and ships of war, and military operations against the rebels. The most extensive collection of captain's dispatches are those of Archibald Kennedy, who took vigorous action to prevent evasion of the Stamp Act in New York, 1765–66. Similar though less extensive reports of other events are scattered throughout the papers.

The collection is arranged alphabetically. However, unless the researcher can determine which captains were assigned to specific stations at particular times, he must examine all 10 boxes to cover the period. Captains' dispatches can be located by volume according to surname as follows:

A. 1443–47; B. 1497–1504; C. 1609–15; D. 1704–10; E. 1761–62; F. 1790–91; G. 1836–40; H. 1899–1907; I. and J. 1986–88; K. 2012–15; L. 2052–57; M. 2116–24; N. 2221–22; O. 2247–50; P. 2300–07; R. 2388–94; S. 2479–86; T. 2590–93; V. 2627–28; W. 2669–76; Y. 2733.

ADM. 1. VOLS. 3678–81. LETTERS RELATING TO THE SOLICITOR'S DEPARTMENT
9 boxes, 1760–83.　　　　Photostats.

1402　Contains letters, usually of a routine nature, from the Solicitor's office to Philip Stephens, Secretary of the Admiralty, concerning legal affairs under Admiralty jurisdiction. Topics include murders at sea, piracies, thefts, salvage rights, and the status of seamen and naval personnel held in custody. Includes a few items relating to North America.

See Andrews, *Guide to Manuscripts*, vol. 2, p. 18.

ADM. 1. VOLS. 3819–20. LETTERS FROM THE GOVERNORS OF PLANTATIONS
1 box, 1759–90.　　　　Transcripts.

1403　Letters concerning routine matters such as requests for Mediterranean passes for American merchants, transportation of troops and officials to various Colonies, and relations with vice-admiralty courts. Contains reports of John Wentworth, surveyor general of the woods, and Adolphus Benzel on the availability of timber and naval stores in the Carolinas and New England, 1767, 1773. A few letters deal with American challenges to royal authority before 1775. Letters from the period of the war concern privateering and issuance of letters of marque and reprisal, but after 1776 most of the correspondence is from Governors in the West Indies. Also includes extensive lists of American, French, and Dutch ships captured and taken into Jamaica before Apr. 1783.

Principal correspondents: Jeffery Amherst, William Bull, William Campbell, Francis Fauquier, William Franklin, Thomas Gage, James Grant, Thomas Hutchinson, George Johnstone, William Nelson, Andrew Oliver, John Penn, Richard Penn, and Charles Williams.

ADM. 1. Vols. 3883–87. Letters From the Officials of Doctors Commons
5 boxes, 1753–82.   Photostats.

1404   Contains documents concerning the creation, jurisdiction, and operation of vice-admiralty courts in America. Letters from Doctors Commons—seat of College of Advocates and law office of the Admiralty—which were frequently signed by Procurator General George Gostling, often enclose opinions on cases for possible prosecution and commissions of appointees to the vice-admiralty courts. Mentioned in volume 3884, 1768–77 are Judges Jonathan Sewall (Halifax district), Robert Auchmuty (Boston), John Andrews (Newport), Robert Bayard (New York), and Augustus Johnston (Charleston), and advocates Richard Starke and Benjamin Waller (Virginia). Documents in volumes 3885–87, 1777–82, primarily concern seizures and condemnations in the West Indies during the war, including instructions for proceedings against captured vessels, Aug. 1778, lists of captures, and tables of division of prize money.

ADM. 1. Vols. 5307–11, 5314–16, 5318–19. Reports of Courts–Martial
3 boxes, 1775–81.   Photostats.

1405   Reports and minutes of courts-martial sent to the Admiralty office. Contains information concerning events and engagements resulting in the loss of British ships during the war. Includes cases involving 36 vessels. The hearing on the most famous of these ships, the *Serapis* and the *Countess of Scarborough*, which had engaged John Paul Jones' *Bonhomme Richard*, was perfunctory, as the conduct of their officers had previously been aired in public. The collection is organized chronologically and by name of ship within year.

OUT-LETTERS

ADM. 2. Vols. 1057–61. Letters Relating to Admiralty and Vice-Admiralty Courts
11 boxes, 1762–83.   Photostats.

1406   Entry books of letters sent by the Secretary to officers within the Admiralty pertaining to the legal operations of the office. Includes letters to Governors, vice-admiralty and other colonial officials containing directives ordering investigations, apprehensions, prosecutions or defenses, payments, and issuance of letters patent to appointees. Each volume contains an excellent summary of letters sent.

ADM. 2. Vols. 1333–41. Secret Orders and Letters
9 boxes, 1770–82.   Photostats.

1407   Secret dispatches indicating plans to prevent the Americans from obtaining arms abroad, as early as Oct. 1774; to meet the challenge of French aid to the rebels; and to prosecute the war. The orders provide information on assumptions which governed British command decisions, the numerous revisions of orders that were necessitated by constantly changing conditions, and difficulties encountered by the Admiralty in meeting challenges from colonial rebellion and naval warfare with France, Spain, and the Dutch Republic.
          Volume 1333, Aug. 1770—Dec. 1779, consists of Secretary Philip Stephens' letterbook. The remaining eight volumes form a separate and complete series covering the period Oct. 1776—Dec. 1782.
          See Andrews, *Guide*, vol. 2., p. 43–45.

REGISTERS, RETURNS, AND CERTIFICATES. MISCELLANEA

ADM. 7. Vols. 299–300. Law Officers' Opinions
2 boxes, 1756–83.   Photostats.

1408   Opinions solicited by the Secretary from the advocate of the Admiralty, the Attorney

General, and the Solicitor General concerning the limits of Admiralty jurisdiction, courts-martial, prize cases, salvage rights, and seamen's claims. The American crisis raised new issues such as the application of the Prohibitory Act, the authority of the vice-admiralty judge at New York during military occupation, the rights of French merchant ships, and the application of preliminary peace articles.

See Andrews, *Guide*, vol. 2, p. 48–50.

LOG BOOKS, ETC.

ADM. 51. VOLS. 23–1100. CAPTAINS' LOGS. SELECTIONS
10 reels microfilm, 1763–85.

1409   Ships represented saw patrol duty in North American or West Indian waters during the Revolutionary era. Their logs contain accounts of encounters with privateers, seizure of ships running supplies to the Americans, and routine naval data. Most vessels are sloops and schooners; none of the largest classes of warships are represented.

Vol. 23. *Albany*, Oct. 1776—Oct. 1782. North America. *Astrea*, July 1782—Feb. 1784. North America.

Vol. 51. *Antelope*, Sept. 1777—May 1778, Apr.—July 1784. West Indies. *Alert*, July 1777—Apr. 1783. West Indies.

Vol. 60. *Ariadne*, Dec. 1776—Nov. 1784. Cape Finistere-Gibraltar, West Indies.

Vol. 118. *Blonde*, Dec. 1775—Sept. 1781. St. Lawrence, Carolina, New York.

Vol. 156. *Camel*, Jan. 1777—Aug. 1782. North America, West Indies. *Chameleon*, Mar. 1777—Mar. 1783. West Indies.

Vol. 157. *Camilla*, Aug. 1776—May 1780, Apr. 1783—Apr. 1785. North America, West Indies.

Vol. 293. *Eagle,* Feb. 1776—Feb. 1784. North America, Africa, India. *Essex*, Jan. 1764—May 1766. West Indies.

Vol. 331. *Experiment*, July 1775—Oct. 1778, July 1781—Oct. 1784. North America, West Indies.

Vol. 360. *Flora*, Dec. 1775—Apr. 1785. North America, West Indies.

Vol. 420. *Greyhound*, July 1764—Feb. 1768, Nov. 1775—July 1781. West Indies, North America.

Vol. 548. *Liverpool*, Mar. 1767—Mar. 1772, July 1775—May 1778. St. Lawrence, Mediterranean, North America.

Vol. 607. *Milford*, Apr. 1763—Nov. 1766, Jan. 1777—Nov. 1780. West Indies, North America.

Vol. 630. *Nautilus*, Sept. 1776—June 1780, May 1763—Mar. 1768. West Indies, North America.

Vol. 675. *Pearl*, June 1777—July 1782. North America, West Indies. *Perseverance*, Mar. 1781—Sept. 1783. North America.

Vol. 749. *Quebec*, June 1769—Aug. 1772, June 1781—Sept. 1783. West Indies, North America.

Vol. 762. *Rainbow*, Dec. 1776—Mar. 1783. North America. *Raleigh*, Dec. 1778—Oct. 1780. North America.

Vol. 875. *Sibyl*, Oct. 1778—July 1783. West Indies, North America.

Vol. 895. *Shark*, Mar. 1776—Aug. 1778, Feb. 1780—May 1785. West Indies, Gibraltar, North America.

Vol. 906. *Snake*, May 1777—Aug. 1780. West Indies. *Somerset*, Jan. 1771—Feb. 1778. North America.

Vol. 931. *Star*, Dec. 1778—May 1783. North America, West Indies. *Strombolo*, Apr. 1776—Apr. 1780. North America.

Vol. 1017. *Ulysses*, July 1779—May 1783. West Indies. *Unicorn*, Mar. 1776—Aug. 1779, July 1781—Dec. 1784. North America, West Indies.

Vol. 1044. *Vulture*, Aug.—Nov. 1780. New York.

Vol. 1091. *Yarmouth*, Apr. 1777—Aug. 1779. West Indies.

Vol. 1100. *Zebra*, May 1777—Dec. 1784. North America, West Indies.

Vol. 4141. *Ceres*, Mar. 1777—Mar. 1778. West Indies. *Charlestown*, Aug. 1781—July 1782. North America.

Vol. 4172. *Druid*, Sept. 1776—Sept. 1777. West Indies.

ADM. 52. VOL. 1865. MASTERS' LOGS
2 boxes, 1775–78.   Photostats.

1410 HMS *Milford* log books, kept by Joseph Sowell, master, Oct. 1775—Jan. 1778, during which time the ship was patrolling North American waters from Cape Cod to Halifax.

Greenwich Hospital

MISCELLANEA. VARIOUS

ADM. 80. VOLS. 131–32
1 reel microfilm, 1768–83.

1411 Vol. 131 consists of an entry book of letters, June 1768—Jan. 1777, from Henry Hulton, principal deputy receiver of the sixpence duty due to the Royal Hospital at Greenwich at all ports under management of the American Board of Customs Commissioners. Contains information on enforcement activities of the American Board, statistical data such as Hulton's quarterly returns of duties collected for the hospital, and letters to Hulton from collectors at various American ports. Vol. 132 comprises an entry book of letters to Hulton from the Receivers Office for Greenwich Hospital, Nov. 1768—Oct. 1783. It also contains accounts of monies received and lists of receivers employed at various American ports.

BOARD OF CUSTOMS AND EXCISE

Ledgers of Imports and Exports

CUSTOMS 16. AMERICA. 1768–73
1 vol., 1768–73.   Photostats.

1412 Annual accounts based on reports sent home by the American Board of Customs Commissioners, covering 52 ports from Bermuda to Newfoundland. Contains detailed records of ships entering, by port of origin; ships clearing; goods imported and exported,

with destination; amount of duty on designated items; and foreign goods imported.
See Andrews, *Guide*, vol. 2, p. 111–17, and *Guide to the Public Record Office*, vol. 2, p. 105–7.

BOARD OF TRADE

Papers of the "modern" Board of Trade, which pertain to the United States during the years 1783–89, are located in classes 5 and 6. Following abolition of the "old" Board of Trade in 1782 (papers make up C.O.5, vols. 388–90), business previously conducted by the Board fell successively to three committees of the Privy Council (1782–84; 1784–86; 1786–). The third of these, the "Lords of the Committee of Council appointed for the Consideration of all Matters relating to Trade and Foreign Plantations," became known commonly as the Board of Trade. Papers microfilmed for LC falling within the Revolutionary era include minutes of these various committees and 11 volumes of miscellaneous material.

See Paullin and Paxson, *Guide*, p. 442–43, and Andrews, *Guide*, vol. 1, p. 100–3.

General

MINUTES

B. T. 5. Vols. 1–5.
3 reels microfilm, 1784–89.

1413   These minutes reflect the Government's commercial concerns, special pleading of several interest groups, and steps taken to formulate trade policies with the newly independent United States. They contain reports and testimony of persons examined by the committee and its own reports and recommendations for future legislation and orders in council. The volumes are indexed and often contain appendixes consisting of statistical tables and reports. Volume 1 includes a 75-page report of May 1784 on American trade.

The Library owns a contemporary copy of the first three of these volumes. See entry no. 310. Another copy of the minutes, Apr. 1786–1792, is in the Liverpool Papers. See entry no. 1393.

MISCELLANEA

B.T. 6 Vols. 20–22, 80–81, 83–87, 187. America
4 reels microfilm, 1784–91.

1414   Vol. 20. Contains papers received by the Board pertaining to trade with the United States, 1784–91, including records of State legislation affecting British trade, the collection of debts, and prices current in the United States. Also includes summaries of the trade of each State, lists of duties imposed on British goods; issues of several American newspapers containing commercial data; and material on West India trade and the Newfoundland fisheries.

Corresponds to vol. 28 described in Paullin and Paxson, *Guide*, p. 463.

Vols. 21–22. Papers of Phineas Bond, 1786–91, British consul at Philadelphia. Chiefly papers on American trade and manufactures forwarded by Bond to the Board. Corresponds to vols. 29–30 described in Paullin and Paxson, *Guide*, p. 463–64.

Vol. 80. Includes abstracts of legislation empowering the King to regulate trade with

America, orders in council, and several petitions of merchants seeking to influence the development of British trade policies, 1783–84.

Corresponds to vol. 20 described in Paullin and Paxson, *Guide*, p. 462.

Vol. 81. Legislation and orders in council on American trade, rough minutes of the Board's proceedings, and testimony of witnesses examined, such as George Chalmers, 1783–86.

Corresponds to vol. 21 described in Paullin and Paxson, *Guide*, p. 462.

Vols. 83–84. Minutes, testimony and reports on American trade, memorials, newspapers and other documents laid before the Board, 1784–86.

Corresponds to vols. 24–25 described in Paullin and Paxson, *Guide*, p. 463.

Vol. 85. Contains material, 1784–86, similar to that in vols. 80–81.

Corresponds to vol. 22 described in Paullin and Paxson, *Guide*, p. 463.

Vol. 86. Contains accounts of American ships entering and clearing British ports, 1783–84, including manifests of cargoes and ship registry.

Corresponds to vol. 23 described in Paullin and Paxson, *Guide*, p. 463.

Vol. 87. Papers concerning the response of the Privy Council to memorials of merchants seeking to limit U.S. trade with Newfoundland and Nova Scotia.

Corresponds to vol. 27 described in Paullin and Paxson, *Guide*, p. 463.

Vol. 187. A list of American ships cleared from the Port of London, 1783–85, showing destination. Also includes the manifests of their cargoes.

Corresponds to vol. 177 described in Paullin and Paxson, *Guide*, p. 464 65.

COLONIAL OFFICE

America and West Indies (C.O. 5)

VOLS. 2, 7–8. PLANTATIONS GENERAL
5 reels microfilm, 1762–1805.

1415   Miscellaneous material, including dispatches from the Secretaries of State to officers in America; representations from the Board of Trade to the King; annual estimates for the cost of a general survey in North America, 1764–76; estimates of the value of goods shipped to America, 1768–74; a précis of operations on the Canadian frontier, 1774–76; and "treasonable" correspondence of James Peisley, Thomas Burdy, Thomas Hutchins, and Samuel Wharton, 1779. Also contains military accounts, returns, lists, plans, reports, and correspondence; papers and correspondence concerning peace negotiations and instances in which Americans violated the treaty, 1782–84; documents pertaining to the recruitment of provincial troops; and memorials and petitions from loyalists and British merchants. Additional documents concern the supply and employment of Indians on the southern frontier; the testimony of Enoch Story on the state of America, 1783; and activities of slaves owned by the patriots.

VOLS. 38–39. COPLEY–PELHAM CORRESPONDENCE
1 reel microfilm, 1739–79.

1416   Personal and business correspondence of Henry Pelham (1748–1806), painter, engraver and cartographer of Boston, and his stepbrother John Singleton Copley (1738–1815), the American artist. Includes several letters from Pelham to his brother Charles Pelham, 1774–75; letters by Benjamin West, Myles Cooper, John Small, John Morgan, Susanna Copley, and Charles Pelham; and mercantile letters of the Philadelphia firm of Willing and Morris.

Vol. 40. Intercepted Letters
1 reel microfilm, 1774–82.

1417   In addition to the letters listed individually in Andrews, *Guide*, vol. 1, p. 120–22, the volume contains several unidentified letters, 1775–77, and intercepted correspondence between Versailles and Philadelphia, Feb. 1780—Apr. 1782. Includes letters of Vergennes, La Luzerne, Marbois, Castries, and Montmorin.

Vol. 43. Miscellaneous Papers
1 reel microfilm, 1743–83.

1418   Material concerning the seizure of English ships by the Spanish, 1769; French and Spanish intrigues in America, 1768; prewar debts to British merchants; a plan of accommodation with England, 1777; loyalist claims; a treaty of commerce with Holland; and the arrest and confinement of Henry Laurens, 1780.

Most of these documents are listed in Andrews, *Guide*, vol. 1, p. 122–24.

Vol. 63. Military Correspondence
2 reels microfilm, 1763.

1419   Includes papers relating to Lt. Col. Henry Bouquet's defeat of the Indians at Bushy Run during Pontiac's Rebellion, Aug. 1763; correspondence from Gen. Jeffery Amherst to Secretary Egremont on the disposition of troops, Indian affairs, and land claims; and papers delivered by Amherst to Gen. Thomas Gage upon giving up his command in America. Also includes letters and documents relating to the transfer of Florida to England, with a plan of the fort at St. Augustine, and a copy of a memorial signed by George Washington, Adam Stephen, and Andrew Lewis, 1763, requesting that they be given grants of land pursuant to a 1754 proclamation by Lt. Gov. Robert Dinwiddie.

Vols. 65–82. Plantations General
11 reels microfilm, 1760–84.

1420   Material primarily concerning Indian affairs. Includes correspondence of John Stuart, Shelburne, Hillsborough, Dartmouth, and Germain, and scattered letters of Sir William Johnson, Guy Johnson, deputy superintendents and Indian traders throughout the frontier, and Govs. Thomas Boone, Peter Chester, Arthur Dobbs, Lord Dunmore, Francis Fauquier, Patrick Tonyn, and James Wright. Documents include proceedings of Indian congresses at Augusta, 1763, Detroit, 1766, and Fort Stanwix, 1768; proclamations and acts regulating trade with the Indians and the purchase of Indian lands; talks, addresses, and treaties with the Indians; reports on treaty violations; returns of supplies and presents furnished allied tribes; and plans for the deployment of the southern Indians against patriot outposts. Also contains the journal of William Croghan, describing an expedition into the Illinois country, 1765, and the journal of David Taitt, describing a visit to the Lower and Upper Creeks, 1772. Miscellaneous items pertain to the work of surveyors Samuel Holland and William de Brahm, chiefly reports, maps, plans, and surveys; the Willing raid along the lower Mississippi, 1778; Spanish attacks at Mobile, 1780, and Pensacola, 1781; and the Associated Loyalists, 1780–82.

See also Vol. 225, entry no. 1450.

Vols. 83–111. Military Correspondence
13 reels microfilm, 1763–84.

1421   Consists of the correspondence, with enclosures, of Gens. Thomas Gage, vols. 83–92, William Howe, vols. 93–96, Henry Clinton, vols. 96–105, and Guy Carleton, vols. 106–111, with the Secretaries of State and various officials in England. Also contains a few letters of Gen. Frederick Haldimand written while he was in command at New York, 1773–75.

Documents in the collection written before 1775 primarily concern Indian congresses and treaties, encroachments by white settlers on Indian lands, disputes between the military and civil authority over requisitions for supplies and the quartering of troops, inventories and reports on military supplies and weapons acquired during the Seven Years War, and disorders stemming from the Stamp Act and the Townshend Acts. Also includes military accounts and returns; maps and plans of forts, harbors, and cities; correspondence with the Spanish Governors of Louisiana; and the journal of Capt. Harry Jordon describing a trip along the Ohio and Mississippi Rivers, 1766. Material for the years 1775–84 includes reports from officers to the commander in chief in America, and official reports from British headquarters in America on the progress of the war. Among the enclosures are scattered newspapers, broadsides, and proclamations; letters from loyalist Governors and officials; captured correspondence, intelligence, and returns on troops and supplies; exchanges with Continental officers on the treatment of prisoners; the articles of capitulation for Charleston, Mobile, and British posts along the Mississippi; and a printed copy of *A Remonstrance, of the Council of the State of Vermont, Against the Resolutions of Congress of the 5th of December* [1782].

Vols. 112–13. Estimates of Annual Expenses of Colonial Governments
2 reels microfilm, 1767–68.

1422 Prefacing each of these volumes is a copy of Shelburne's circular letter to the American Governors requesting estimates on the cost of government in each Colony, an account of the manner of granting lands and imposing quit rents, and a schedule of established fees. The remaining documents comprise the responses of the Governors, including those of Guy Carleton for Canada and James Grant and Montfort Browne for the Floridas— chiefly auditors' reports, lists of fees, salaries estimates, lists of patents granted, and related items.

Vols. 114–17. Petitions
2 reels microfilm, 1768–81.

1423 Memorials and petitions to the King, the Secretary of State, the Lords Commissioners of the Treasury, the Committee of the Privy Council for Plantation Affairs, and the Secretary at War concerning requests for relief and compensation for losses resulting from the war. Also includes protests from merchants in England and the West Indies against fees, taxes, and seizures.

 For a nearly complete list of these documents, see Andrews, *Guide*, vol. 1, p. 127–29.

Vols. 119–32. Secretary of State: In- and Out-Letters
4 reels microfilm, 1771–81.

1424 Entry books containing selected correspondence between the Secretary of State for the Colonies and the Lords of the Admiralty primarily concerning the West Indies before the Revolution and focusing on North America after 1774. Includes letters and reports of naval officers, merchants, intelligence agents, and military commanders concerning problems of naval support and supply, military campaigns, the coastal blockade, commerce, the arming of loyalists, the Continental Congress, and the evacuation of Philadelphia. Specific items include records of troop transports, 1774–75; Montfort Browne's description of the New Providence raid; a report on the Boston Tea Party; and a list of ships and crews under Adm. Richard Howe at New York, 1778.

Vol. 133, Council Office, East India Company
1 reel microfilm, 1771–74.

1425 Consists chiefly of Lord Dartmouth's correspondence with the council, but includes letters and documents concerning the reception of East India tea in Boston, New York, and Philadelphia. Also contains letters of ship captains Richard Rotch, Richard Clarke, and Jonathan Musso, New Hampshire land grants, and material pertaining to the Peter Livius Affair.

VOLS. 134–37. SECRETARY OF STATE: IN- AND OUT-LETTERS
3 reels microfilm, 1771–80.

1426   Primarily concerns post office operations in North America, particularly at Quebec, New York, Charleston, Jamaica, and Falmouth, England. Letters of Thomas Wharton, Hugh Finlay, John Wentworth, James Tilghman, and Benjamin Franklin pertain to the progress of the war, and a Franklin letter, Oct. 1775, discusses the prospects for a peaceful settlement with Great Britain. Also includes captured ships journals from American privateers.

VOLS. 138–44. SECRETARY OF STATE: CORRESPONDENCE WITH OTHER SECRETARIES
4 reels microfilm, 1771–82.

1427   Chiefly correspondence concerning the recruitment and use of German mercenaries. Includes letters, with enclosures, from Under Secretaries John Pownall, William Knox, Benjamin Thompson, and William Eden, reports from Joseph Yorke, English Ambassador at The Hague, on ships sailing to America, and similar reports from Ireland, Scotland, and England. Also material pertaining to American privateers, the African trade, St. Eustatius, and the war effort in North America, and a 12-page report by J. Banister on the state of America and the futility of the English war effort, July 1775.

VOLS. 145–53. SECRETARY OF STATE: CORRESPONDENCE WITH THE TREASURY AND CUSTOM HOUSE
6 reels microfilm, 1770–81.

1428   Letters concerning the collection of customs duties and enforcement of trade regulations in British North America and the West Indies, 1770–74. After the outbreak of war the focus shifts to intelligence regarding ships sailing for the United States or the Dutch West Indies, including information on cargoes, destination, owners, and whether seized or released. Also contains returns of provisions for British troops and dependents at New York and Philadelphia, 1778; lists of ships cleared from Senegal, with ports of origin and destination, 1767–77; instructions for the provisioning of prisoners in America, 1780; petitions of loyalists in England; and documents concerning courts in Quebec, quit rents in Florida, and Indian affairs.

VOLS. 154–58. MISCELLANEOUS AND PRIVATE LETTERS
4 reels microfilm, 1771–81.

1429   Chiefly letters and dispatches to and from Hillsborough, Dartmouth, and Germain concerning military efforts, provincial troops, French involvement, commerce and customs, loyalists, and Indian affairs. Includes a census of Detroit, Sept. 23, 1773; a report on prisoners at Mill and Forton prisons, 1780; a return of supplies by Cornwallis' commissary general; accounts of Hessian hospitals, 1776–80; and an intelligence report on Vermont, New York, and Massachusetts, 1781.

    Principal correspondents: Gen. Jeffery Amherst, William de Brahm, Brig. Gen. Oliver de Lancey, Lord Dunmore, Arthur Lee, and Chief Justice Peter Oliver of Massachusetts.

    See Andrews, *Guide*, vol. 1, p. 134–36.

VOLS. 159–60. SECRETARY OF STATE: CORRESPONDENCE WITH THE ATTORNEY GENERAL AND SOLICITOR GENERAL
1 reel microfilm, 1772–81.

1430   Opinions of law officers on issues such as the Governor's right to pardon in murder cases, Catholic troops in Canada, letters of marque, and trading with the enemy. Includes a 67-page report on the Boston Tea Party and court closing in Massachusetts.

VOLS. 161–66. SECRETARY OF STATE: CORRESPONDENCE WITH THE ORDNANCE OFFICE
3 reels microfilm, 1772–81.

1431   Copies of reports and accounts of engineers and ordnance officers on ordnance shipped to America. Includes reports for Quebec, West Florida, New York, Crown Point, Detroit, Halifax, and Ticonderoga, 1774–75. Letters and related documents trace annual shipments of ordnance from the estimate of requirements through the delivery of arms, ammunition, and artillery supplies.

Vols. 167–73. Secretary of State: Correspondence with the Secretary at War
3 reels microfilm, 1772–82.

1432   Correspondence of Hillsborough, Dartmouth, and Germain for the Office of the Secretary of State, and Lord Barrington and Charles Jenkinson for the Office of the Secretary at War containing information on official policy during the Revolution. Additional correspondence to the Secretary at War includes letters with enclosures from Gens. Thomas Gage, Frederick Haldimand, Alexander Leslie, William Maxwell, and John Dalling concerning appointments and promotions; the arrival, state, and disposition of troops; civil disturbances; and the recruitment of American prisoners of war for service in the West Indies. Enclosures include medical reports on the effect of the climate on newly arrived troops; military accounts and returns; and a petition by Philip Skene, former Lieutenant Governor of Crown Point and Ticonderoga, outlining his career in America, 1780.

Vol. 174. Secretary of State: Correspondence with the Commander in Chief
1 reel microfilm, 1778–82.

1433   Consists chiefly of the correspondence of Sir Jeffery Amherst with Germain and Under Secretaries William Knox and Thomas de Gray concerning routine military affairs, i.e., appointments, promotions, organization, and the embarkation and disposition of troops. Among the enclosures are a memorial by Thomas Shirley, 1778; embarkation returns; and a report on fortifications on the island of Dominica, 1778.

Vols. 175–76. Secretary of State: Correspondence with Civil Officers in America
2 reels microfilm, 1774–83.

1434   Contains reports on the progress of the war from Gov. William Wentworth of New Hampshire, 1776–78; from Gov. Josiah Martin of North Carolina to Germain, Ellis, and Shelburne concerning the southern campaign; and from Maj. Gen. James Robertson and Lt. Gov. Andrew Elliot concerning civil affairs, customs, problems in the American Army, and the Huddy-Asgill affair, 1781–82. Also letters of Lt. Gov. William Bull, Sir Egerton Leigh, Chief Justice Gordon, and various officers and merchants in South Carolina, 1778–83; correspondence of Gov. James Wright concerning the defenseless state of Georgia, 1780–82; routine letters of Gov. Thomas Hutchinson and Chief Justice Peter Oliver of Massachusetts, and a single letter from Benjamin Hallowell describing disturbances in Boston, 1774–80. Includes a plan of Lord Dunmore, Governor of Virginia, for use of loyalists in the war effort, 1782.
See Andrews, *Guide*, vol. 1, p. 139.

Vols. 177–78. Peace Commissions
2 reels microfilm, 1776–78, 1779–82.

1435   Volume 177 contains material pertaining to the first peace commission under Adm. Richard Howe and Sir William Howe. Includes a copy of the Royal Order creating the commission, correspondence between the Howes and Germain showing the nature and progress of early negotiations, a proclamation offering pardon to persons returning their allegiance to the Crown, Lord Howe's circular letter to the American Governors, petitions from American loyalists, letters to Congress, an exchange of letters between Washington and Henry Laurens concerning the transmission of information on the Carlisle peace commission, 1778, and a letter from Andrew Elliot to Lord Howe concerning the shipment of prize goods to England, 1778.
Volume 178 primarily contains the correspondence of Germain with commissioners

who were subsequently appointed: Sir Henry Clinton, Vice Adm. Marriot Arbuthnot, Rear Adm. Robert Digby, and Sir Guy Carleton. Also includes a précis of correspondence in the American Department, 1779; letters to Germain from James Simpson, secretary to the commission, on economic, political, and military affairs in South Carolina; petitions for pardon signed by Charles Pinckney, Daniel Horry, Rawlins Loundes, and Henry Middleton, 1780; and Shelburne's account of negotiations with Franklin, 1779–82.

See also Vol. 264, entry no. 1465 and Andrews, *Guide*, vol. 1, p. 140–41.

VOL. 179. BURGOYNE–HEATH CORRESPONDENCE
1 reel microfilm, 1777–78.

1436   Chiefly copies of correspondence between Maj. Gen. William Heath and Burgoyne concerning the treatment of the Convention Troops after their arrival at Cambridge, Mass., particularly with regard to paroles, quarters, supplies, and various infringements of the terms of the Convention. Also a list of collateral correspondence relative to the Convention Troops, Jan.—Mar. 1778.

Principal correspondents: Horatio Gates, William Howe, and Washington.

See Andrews, *Guide*, vol. 1, p. 141.

VOLS. 180–81. PEACE COMMISSION OF 1778
1 reel microfilm, 1778.

1437   Records of the Carlisle peace commission—the Earl of Carlisle, William Eden, George Johnstone, and later Sir Henry Clinton, 1778—including official orders and instructions; correspondence of the commissioners with Congress, Washington, and Germain; newspapers and proclamations; petitions; a list of prices current in New York in 1778; and a pamphlet entitled "Letters and other Papers relating to the Proceedings of his Majesty's Commissioners" (55 p.).

See Andrews, *Guide*, vol. 1, p. 141–42.

VOLS. 182–84. MISCELLANEOUS MILITARY CORRESPONDENCE
2 reels microfilm, 1778–84.

1438   Miscellaneous collection of letters and documents chiefly relating to the progress of the war in the southern Colonies, with dispatches from Germain to Burgoyne, Cornwallis, Augustine Prevost, Archibald Campbell, and others. Among the enclosures are returns of ordnance, stores, and casualties; muster rolls for foreign troops; general returns of provincial and regular forces in the Southern District; proclamations; reports from Alexander McGillivray and Alexander Cameron on Indian affairs; correspondence on the exchange of the Convention Troops; and letters of Henry Laurens, Aug. 1778, and Benjamin Rush, Aug. 1778.

VOL. 185. MISCELLANEOUS IN-LETTERS
1 reel microfilm, 1779–94.

1439   Papers concerning Canada and the West Indies, chiefly after 1783. Includes military accounts; correspondence pertaining to the capture of Martinique, St. Vincent, Grenada, and the Grenadines; a list of Germans captured en route to Port au Prince, 1779; and two letters from Franklin to William Hodgson on the exchange of prisoners, 1781–82.

VOL. 186. NAVAL DISPATCHES: ADMIRAL DIGBY
2 reels microfilm, 1782–84.

1440   Adm. Robert Digby's reports to Shelburne and North from his station off New York, concerning rebel privateers, the disloyalty of British sailors, and the evacuation of New York. Among the enclosures are letters by Sir Andrew Hammond, Adm. Hugh Pigot, Rear Adm. Joseph Rowley, Archibald Campbell, and others pertaining to American attacks on Nova Scotia, defensive operations in the West Indies, particularly for the protection of Jamaica, the evacuation of Charleston, and abuse of British prisoners of war.

Vols. 201–3. Plantation Entry Books
3 reels microfilm, 1763–71.

1441   Part of a series of entry books containing copies of commissions, instructions, circulars, letters, warrants, and the like for Governors, Lieutenant Governors, councillors, clerks, registers, and other officials in North America and the West Indies.

Vol. 204. Patents
1 reel microfilm, 1770–79.

1442   Consists of the commissions of Walter Pattison, receiver general and collector of the revenues on the island of St. John, 1770; Joseph Wanton, Governor of Rhode Island, to hold an inquiry into the case of the *Gaspée*, 1772; Samuel Holland, surveyor general of Quebec, 1776; and Jonathan Clarlee and Isaac Winston Clarke, assistant commissaries of the army in Canada, 1776. Also a commission for the trial of pirates in Grenada, and commissions of Adm. Richard Howe, Sir William Howe, and Sir Henry Clinton to make peace and grant pardons, 1776.

Vols. 205–8. Plantations Entry Books
2 reels microfilm, 1771–84.

1443   Similar to Vols. 201–3, entry 1441, but relating chiefly to Canada and the West Indies. Also contains miscellaneous instructions to officers and officials in Pennsylvania, New York, Massachusetts, South Carolina, and Florida, some being drafts with space for names of recipients.

Vol. 216. Miscellaneous Papers
1 reel microfilm, 1761–69.

1444   Includes acts of Parliament, orders in council, representations from the Treasury Board to George III, figures on annual expenses of the civil establishment in America, and a plan for vice-admiralty court districts.

Vol. 218. Précis of Correspondence with Governors in America
1 reel microfilm, 1765–67.

1445   Abstracts of letters and dispatches from Governors in East and West Florida, Georgia, South Carolina, and the West Indies.

Vol. 220. Secretary of State: Dispatches to the Commander in Chief in America
1 reel microfilm, 1766–68.

1446   Correspondence and papers from Secretary Shelburne to Maj. Gen. Thomas Gage concerning American trade, Indian affairs, the western boundaries of Virginia, North Carolina, and South Carolina, the disposition of troops, and an "American Fund" for defraying the cost of government in the Colonies.

Vol. 222. Secretary of State: Dispatches to Governors in America and the West Indies
1 reel microfilm, 1766–67.

1447   Chiefly instructions to Sir Henry Moore, Governor of New York, concerning Indian lands, the Wentworth grants, billeting of troops, and an insurrection in Dutchess County. Also includes circular letters to Governors in America and the West Indies containing instructions on commerce, the manner of granting land, and imposing quit rents, and a request for estimates on the annual expense of the civil establishment.

Vol. 223. Secretary of State: Out-Letters
1 reel microfilm, 1766–68.

1448   Chiefly instructions from Secretary Shelburne to the Board of Trade concerning appointments, Indian affairs, agricultural bounties, commerce, and slaves. Also includes recommendations on petitions and memorials, scattered entries of Privy Council minutes, and lists of documents.

VOL. 224. SECRETARY OF STATE: OUT-LETTERS
1 reel microfilm, 1766–68.

1449   Orders and instructions from Secretary Shelburne to the Treasury on sundry matters involving the American Colonies—expenses incurred in transporting a group of Indians to England, compensation for officials who suffered losses in the colonial disturbances, and the like. Also includes a list of papers laid before Parliament relating to America, and a list of King's Attorneys in America.

VOL. 225. SECRETARY OF STATE: OUT-LETTERS
1 box, 1766–68.   Photostats and transcripts.

1450   Instructions to Superintendents of Indian Affairs John Stuart and William Johnson and to William de Brahm, surveyor general for the Southern District, concerning encroachments on Indian lands and deceptive practices of white traders.
    See also Vols. 65–82, entry no. 1420.

VOLS. 227–31. SECRETARY OF STATE: IN-LETTERS
1 reel microfilm, 6 boxes photostats, 1768–82.

1451   Chiefly correspondence of Superintendents of Indian Affairs William Johnson and John Stuart and their assistants, John Thomas, Thomas Browne, Charles Stuart, David Taitt, Charles Shaw, Guy Johnson, and Alexander Cameron. Documents dating before 1775 concern Indian trade and disturbances along the frontier. The remaining documents relate intelligence on the movements of Spanish and American forces in the South and the supply and deployment of Indian tribes. Also includes letters and reports from surveyors Samuel Holland, William de Brahm, Wentworth, Frederick Mulcaster, and Thomas Wright; miscellaneous correspondence relating to the peace commissions of Generals Howe and Clinton; and letters to the Secretary of State from James Simpson, superintendent of police at Charleston, S. C., 1780–81, describing the movements of British and American forces and the economic and political situation in South Carolina.

VOL. 232. SECRETARY OF STATE: PRÉCIS OF DOCUMENTS RELATING TO THE REVOLUTION
1 reel microfilm, 1768–75.

1452   Includes a report on fortifications in America and the West Indies, with related correspondence between Secretary Hillsborough and the Office of Ordnance; complaints from customs officers in Massachusetts regarding their being taxed by local assessors; propositions for the establishment of a colony upon land ceded to the Crown in the Treaty of Fort Stanwix, ca. 1772; and a printed pamphlet, "Narrative of Facts Relative to American Affairs," concerning disorders in Massachusetts between 1764 and 1774.
    See also Vol. 253, entry no. 1458.

VOL. 236. SECRETARY OF STATE: IN-LETTERS
1 box, 1776–79.   Photostats.

1453   Entry book of letters from Gens. William Howe and Henry Clinton on the progress of the war, and from Muster Master General George Osborne, William Porter, and others on the state of the German troops. Also includes scattered letters by Generals Burgoyne, Cornwallis, James Grant, Augustine Prevost, Knyphausen, and Riedesel.

VOLS. 241–45. SECRETARY OF STATE: OUT-LETTERS
3 reels microfilm, 1768–90.

1454   Letters to Governors, officers, and officials in America and the West Indies, many of which are repeated elsewhere in the C.O.5 series. Includes circular letters to the Governors about Indian affairs, correspondence with surveyors, instructions to the commanding officers in America before and during the war, and lists of papers laid before both houses of Parliament.

VOL. 246. SECRETARY OF STATE: IN- AND OUT-LETTERS
1 reel microfilm, 1771–77.

1455   Private correspondence of Governors and officials in America and the West Indies with the Secretaries of State, including about 10 letters from Gov. Thomas Hutchinson on disturbances in Massachusetts Bay, 1771–73. Also represented are Andrew Oliver, William Bull, James Wright, Hugh Finlay, and Lord Dunmore.

VOLS. 247–49. SECRETARY OF STATE: IN-LETTERS
1 reel microfilm, 1771–82.

1456   Routine correspondence to the Secretary of State from various departments of government.
    See Vols. 250–52, entry no. 1457.

VOLS. 250–52. SECRETARY OF STATE: OUT-LETTERS
2 reels microfilm, 1776–82.

1457   Chiefly correspondence of the Secretary of State for the Colonies to other departments and officials in England, but includes letters to officers and officials in America and the West Indies. Letters relating to America include responses to requests for relief, leave to travel to America or to return home, and instructions to agents in the West Indies.

VOL. 253. SECRETARY OF STATE: PRÉCIS OF DOCUMENTS RELATING TO THE REVOLUTION
1 reel microfilm, 1774–77.

1458   Abstracts of documents concerning military operations on the Canadian frontier and the campaigns of Gens. William Howe and Henry Clinton. This volume should follow Vol. 232 entry no. 1452.
    See Andrews, Guide, vol. 1, p. 118.

VOLS. 254–55. SECRETARY OF STATE: OUT-LETTERS
1 reel microfilm, 1775–82.

1459   Instructions of Secretaries Germain and Shelburne to the Lords of the Admiralty concerning the shipment of munitions, ordnance, supplies, Indian presents, and the like to America; passage for officials and civilians traveling to and from North America; the protection of vessels trading in the West Indies; and the powers of provincial Governors. Most of the correspondence is signed by under secretaries and officials in the Office of the Secretary.

VOLS. 256–67. SECRETARY OF STATE: IN-LETTERS
1 reel microfilm, 1775–82.

1460   Correspondence from the War Office and Ordnance Board concerning the shipment of ordnance, military stores, and troops to America, and military organization, appointments, and promotions.

VOL. 258. SECRETARY OF STATE: IN-LETTERS
1 reel microfilm, 1776–81.

1461   Correspondence from the Treasury regarding the shipment of troops and supplies, requests for relief, and payment of bills, vouchers, and accounts from America.

VOLS. 259–60. SECRETARY OF STATE: IN-LETTERS
1 reel microfilm, 1775–82.

1462   Routine correspondence from the Lords of the Admiralty regarding the shipment of troops and supplies to America, and reports on the arrival, departure, and location of vessels, including lists of enclosures.

VOLS. 261–62. SECRETARY OF STATE: OUT-LETTERS
2 reels microfilm.
1463   Routine correspondence to the War Office and Ordnance Board concerning the administration of the army, appointments and promotions, and the shipment of troops, ordnance, and supplies to America.

VOL. 263. SECRETARY OF STATE: OUT-LETTERS
1 reel microfilm, 1778–82.
1464   Secret correspondence of Secretaries Germain and Shelburne to officers and officials in America including Henry Clinton, James Grant, John Dalling, John Vaughan, Robert Prescott, Archibald Campbell, Frederick Haldimand, and Vice Admiral Montagu. Letters contain intelligence on the movements of British ships, instructions on the disposition of troops, reports on the progress of the war in the West Indies, and information on German troops being sent to New York. A letter from Shelburne to Haldimand, Apr. 1782, expresses distrust of Ethan Allen.

VOL. 264. MINUTE BOOK: PEACE COMMISSION
1 reel microfilm, 1779–83.
1465   Minutes of the meetings of Commissioners Henry Clinton, Guy Carleton, Adm. Marriot Arbuthnot, and Adm. Robert Digby. Includes transcripts of letters of Gov. James Wright, Germain, Clinton, and Digby, and sundry proclamations and declarations of the commission.
    Supplemental to Vol. 178, entry no. 1435.

VOL. 265. PARDON BLANKS
1 reel microfilm, 1781.
1466   A book of printed forms intended for the use of the peace commissioners in granting pardons. Twenty have been completed.

VOL. 266. SECRETARY OF STATE: OUT-LETTERS
1 reel microfilm, 1784–88.
1467   Correspondence of Secretary Townshend to the president of the Privy Council regarding bishoprics in the West Indies, Roman Catholics, loyalists, trials of pirates, trade with the United States, and acts of the assemblies in the Canadian and West Indian provinces.

VOL. 284. MISCELLANEOUS DOCUMENTS
1 reel microfilm, 1756–65.
1468   Two documents for the year 1765—one a letter of Sir William Johnson concerning means of redressing frauds committed against Indians—are the only items from the Revolutionary era.

North Carolina

VOLS. 299–304. BOARD OF TRADE: IN-LETTERS
3 reels microfilm, 1760–75.
1469   Letters, with enclosures, from Govs. Arthur Dobbs, William Tryon, and Josiah Martin. Subjects discussed include trade, Indian affairs, western land, the North Carolina-South Carolina boundary, quit rents, agriculture, and care of lunatics and idiots. Also acts of assembly; emission of paper bills; customs fees; the Stamp Act; seizure and condemnation of merchant vessels; various civil disorders, particularly those involving the

Regulators, and measures taken to suppress them; the importation of Negroes; religious matters; and military supplies. Among the numerous enclosures are public accounts, lists of taxables, reports on acts passed by the assembly, various legal papers, land grants, surveys, petitions, proclamations, and John Randolph's observations on a method for fixing the payment of quit rents in North Carolina.

See Born, *British Manuscripts Project*, p. 51.

Vol. 305. Board of Trade: Out-Letters
1 reel microfilm, 1765–75.

1470   Correspondence from the Board of Trade to George III, with recommendations to the Privy Council on petitions for land. Also recommendations of the Board on acts passed by the North Carolina Assembly and instructions to Gov. William Tryon.

See Born, *British Manuscripts Project*, p. 51.

Vol. 307. Secretary of State: Miscellaneous In-Letters
1 reel microfilm, 1749–83.

1471   Includes a letter from Gov. Josiah Martin to the Treasury recommending relief for a loyalist merchant in North Carolina, 1779; three letters from Benjamin Hawkins, merchant at New Bern, N.C., and three from John Hollaway to Messrs. Curson & Gouverneur of St. Eustatius concerning trade, May—Nov. 1780; correspondence pertaining to American prisoners in Charleston, 1781; and letters from Gov. John Mathews and Gen. Alexander Leslie concerning the British evacuation of Charleston and release of captured Negroes, 1782.

See Born, *British Manuscripts Project*, p. 51.

Vols. 310–18. Secretary of State: In-Letters
4 reels microfilm, 1761–77.

1472   Letters with enclosures from Govs. Arthur Dobbs, William Tryon, and Josiah Martin, many of which duplicate items appearing in other collections of the Public Record Office. Contains letters from Tryon to Alexander Cameron, deputy agent for the Cherokees, concerning Indian affairs, and letters from Martin to Germain written from aboard ship off Charleston and at New York, 1776. Other documents include a plan for the governor's house at New Bern, N.C., land patents, select issues of the North Carolina *Gazette*, public accounts, petitions, council minutes, and a printed address of Governor Tryon to the assembly. Also proclamations; orders issued by the Governor to the militia for quelling insurrections; military returns; accounts of sedition, with names of leading rebels, June— July 1775; a printed journal of the proceedings of the Provincial Congress of North Carolina, Aug. 1775; and loyalist applications for relief.

See Born, *British Manuscripts Project*, p. 51.

Vols. 320–22. Grants of Land
1 reel microfilm, 1765–75.

1473   Records of land patents granted by the court of claims at Wilmington, 1765–70, and of patents granted in 1774 and 1775. Includes patent number, name of patentee, number of acres, county, date, and location.

See Born, *British Manuscripts Project*, p. 51.

Vols. 325–26. Board of Trade: Entry Books
1 reel microfilm, 1760–75.

1474   Contains copies of letters, instructions, commissions, warrants, patents, and the like, 1760–70, 1771–75.

See Born, *British Manuscripts Project*, p. 51.

Vols. 328–31. Secretary of State: Entry Book of In-Letters
1 reel microfilm, 1766–82.

1475   Précis of letters received concerning instructions, patents, warrants, and commissions. Topics include land grants, Indian affairs, colonial administration, trade, the vice-admiralty, boundary disputes, local industry such as the iron works and pitch collection, defense, and religion.
See Born, *British Manuscripts Project*, p. 51.

Vol. 332. Secretary of State: Entry Book of Out-Letters
1 reel microfilm, 1768–82.

1476   Précis of letters sent, of the same nature as Vols. 328–31, entry no. 1475.
See Born, *British Manuscripts Project*, p. 51.

Vols. 337–41, 350–57. Acts of Assembly, Legislative Journals, Council Minutes, and Sessional Papers
6 reels microfilm, 1760–74.

1477   Contains minutes of Virginia Assembly, Mar.—Apr. 1768.
See Born, *British Manuscripts Project*, p. 51.

South Carolina

Vols. 377–80. Board of Trade: In-Letters
2 reels microfilm, 1760–75.

1478   Original papers and letters, with enclosures, from Govs. Thomas Boone and William Bull addressed chiefly to the Board of Trade and the Secretary of State. Topics include legal matters, Indian affairs, land grants, surveys, public fees, agriculture, acts of assembly, official appointments, and the settlement of French and German Protestants. Also illicit trade, nonimportation, discontent in the back country, opposition to the Stamp Act, importation of Negroes, fortifications, and military supplies. Enclosures include memorials and petitions requesting relaxation of trade restrictions, proclamations, council minutes, acts of assembly, legal papers, lists of exports from the port of Charleston, a plan for civilizing and instructing Indian youths, and a copy of Christopher Gadsden's account of the dispute between the Governor and the assembly published in the *South Carolina Gazette*, Feb. 5, 1763.
See Born, *British Manuscripts Project*, p. 51.

Vol. 381. Board of Trade: Out-Letters
1 reel microfilm, 1722–74.

1479   Contains instructions from the Board to colonial Governors, representations to the King, and miscellaneous papers.
See Born, *British Manuscripts Project*, p. 51.

Vol. 386. Miscellaneous Correspondence
1 reel microfilm, 1754–76.

1480   Includes a letter from George Roupell, a Crown-appointed official at Charleston, to Anthony Todd, Aug. 1775, complaining of harrassment of the friends of government; a list of commercial and revenue bills passed in South Carolina, 1776–77; and several undated items.
See Born, *British Manuscripts Project*, p. 51.

Vols. 390–97. Letters from the Governors, with Enclosures
3 reels microfilm, 1762–84.

1481   Contains material also in Vols. 377–80, entry no. 1478. Additional items include information on the arts and sciences, legislation concerning Negroes, complaints from judges regarding the obstruction of justice in the province and exchanges between Gov. William Campbell and the Provincial Congress of South Carolina, 1775. Also reports of Governor Campbell on the progress of the rebellion in South Carolina, correspondence of Govs. Patrick Tonyn and Peter Chester, Bernardo de Gálvez, Elias Durnford, Sir Henry Clinton, and others concerning political and military affairs in Louisiana and East and West Florida, and returns of troops captured at posts along the Mississippi River. Also includes papers concerning the exchange of the Convention Troops; memorials and representations from South Carolina loyalists and merchants; correspondence between Gens. Benjamin Lincoln and Henry Clinton on the surrender of Charleston, 1780; military returns; and letters between Clinton, Lord Cornwallis, and Banastre Tarleton on the Southern campaign; and scattered letters of Alexander Innes, William Henry Drayton, Gov. Josiah Martin, and Adms. Peter Parker and Samuel Graves.

See Born, *British Manuscripts Project*, p. 51.

VOLS. 398–99. ABSTRACTS OF SOUTH CAROLINA LAND GRANTS
1 reel microfilm, 1674–1773.
1482   Abstracts of the records of grants of land made in South Carolina. Includes names of grantees, dates granted, acres, quit rents, and locations of land.

See Born, *British Manuscripts Project*, p. 51.

VOLS. 404–5. BOARD OF TRADE: ENTRY BOOKS
2 reels microfilm, 1760–75.
1483   Contains drafts of instructions to the Colonies for the regulation of trade and navigation.

See Born, *British Manuscripts Project*, p. 51.

VOLS. 407–10. SECRETARY OF STATE: ENTRY BOOK OF IN-LETTERS AND OUT-LETTERS
1 reel microfilm, 1766–82.
1484   Copies of letters from Gov. Charles Montagu, Lt. Gov. William Bull and Secretaries Dartmouth, Germain, Shelburne, and Hillsborough concerning trade and navigation, political events, defense, Indian affairs, official appointments, and the like.

See Born, *British Manuscripts Project*, p. 51.

VOLS. 422–24. ACTS OF ASSEMBLY
1 reel microfilm, 1761–75.
1485   See Born, *British Manuscripts Project*, p. 52.

VOLS. 477–478, 481–507. LEGISLATIVE JOURNALS
9 reels microfilm, 1760–73.
1486   Minutes of Council, Assembly, and Council in Assembly.

See Born, *British Manuscripts Project*, p. 52.

VOLS. 510–11. SHIPPING RETURNS
1 reel microfilm, 1763–67.
1487   Records of the port of Charleston contain the name and date of ships entering, master and owner, type of ship including number of tons, guns and men, when and where bond given, where from, and cargo, including the number of Negroes.

See Born, *British Manuscripts Project*, p. 52.

VOLS. 513–26. ENTRY BOOK AND JOURNAL OF THE PROCEEDINGS OF THE BOARD OF POLICE
1 reel microfilm, 1777–82.
1488   Contains records primarily concerning the maintenance of order during the British occupation of Charleston, 1780–82.

See Born, *British Manuscripts Project*, p. 52.

Vols. 527–34. Oaths of Allegiance
1 reel microfilm, 1780.

1489   Printed forms, most of them blank.
    See Born, *British Manuscripts Project*, p. 52.

Vol. 535. Demands Brought Against Sequestered Estates
1 reel microfilm, 1781.

1490   Records of debts include name of estate, nature of debt, date of bond, date executed, amount, and name of creditor.
    See Born, *British Manuscripts Project*, p. 52.

East Florida

Vols. 540–47. Board of Trade: In-Letters
3 reels microfilm, 1763–83.

1491   Correspondence of Govs. James Grant and Patrick Tonyn to the Board of Trade concerning conditions in Florida at the time the territory was acquired from Spain; methods for peopling the new province; Indian affairs; military matters; agriculture; the work of naturalist John Bartram; civil appointments; Dr. Andrew Turnbull's settlement of Greeks at New Smyrna; land grants; complaints against William de Brahm, surveyor for Florida; and a dispute between Governor Tonyn and Chief Justice William Drayton. Among the enclosures are surveys and survey reports, correspondence with the Society for the Propagation of the Gospel, letters concerning the removal of settlers from Bermuda to Florida; military returns, lists of fees, applications for land, a schedule of estates purchased, memorials, petitions, legal opinions, depositions, accounts of exports, addresses by the Governors to the assembly, and council minutes.
    See also Vols. 548–61, entry no. 1492.

Vols. 548-61. Secretary of State: In-Letters
6 reels microfilm, 1763–86.

1492   Letters from the Governors, many of which duplicate letters in Vols. 540–47, entry no. 1491. Subjects not previously discussed include the rebel invasion of East Florida led by Maj. Gen. Robert Howe, the exchange of prisoners with the Spanish, and the transfer of Florida back to Spain, 1784. Among the enclosures are loyalist petitions, public accounts, council minutes, surveys, lists of vessels entering and departing at St. Augustine, 1769–73, with records of cargoes, military returns and accounts, select issues of South Carolina and Georgia newspapers, proclamations, addresses to the Indians, intelligence reports on skirmishes near Cumberland and Amelia islands, paroles, and miscellaneous legal papers. Captured letters in the collection include one each from Franklin, John Lewis Gervais, Robert Howe, and John Rutledge, all dated between Mar. and Nov. 1777.

Vols. 563–64. Board of Trade: Entry Book
1 box, 1756–80.   Transcripts.

1493   Selected letters and documents from the Board of Trade to Govs. James Grant and Patrick Tonyn and various departments of government. Includes commissions, instructions, recommendations on petitions, and estimates on the expense of the civil establishment. A letter from the Board to Governor Tonyn, Feb. 1782, concerns trials for slaves.

Vols. 565–66. Secretary of State: Entry Books
1 box transcripts, 1766–83.   Transcripts.

1494   Selected circulars and instructions to Governors in America.

VOLS. 570–72. MINUTES OF THE COUNCIL AND ASSEMBLY OF EAST FLORIDA

1495   4 boxes, 1764–81.   Photostats.

        See also entry no. 1561.

VOL. 573. SHIPPING RETURNS

1 vol., 1765–69.   Photostats.

1496   Lists of ships and vessels entering and clearing the port of St. Augustine.

West Florida

VOLS. 574–81. BOARD OF TRADE: IN-LETTERS

4 vols., 4 boxes, 1763–82.   Photostats.

1497   Official correspondence of Govs. George Johnstone and Peter Chester, and Lt. Gov. Montfort Browne with the Earl of Hillsborough, president of the Board of Trade; Gen. Thomas Gage; John Ellis, agent for West Florida; and various officers and officials in and around Pensacola, including William Clifton, Elias Durnford, Frederick Haldimand, Edward Maxwell, John Stuart, William Taylor, John Thomas, and Edmund Rush Wegg. Also contains a few letters between Governors of West Florida and French and Spanish Governors of Louisiana Philip Aubry, Antonio de Ulloa, Alejandro O'Reilly, and Luis de Unzaga. The correspondence of Governor Johnstone primarily concerns disputes between the civil and military authority and between the Governor and his council. Letters and documents from the administrations of Browne and Chester touch upon a greater variety of topics such as religious matters, trade with the Spanish, new settlements, Indian affairs, military concerns, boundaries, and cooperation with Spanish officials in Louisiana in the apprehension of deserters and runaway slaves. Enclosures include petitions, memorials, surveys, accounts, military returns, legal papers, council minutes, communications between the Governors and the assembly, and a report on the state of West Florida, 1768.

VOLS. 582–98. SECRETARY OF STATE: IN-LETTERS

7 vols., 11 boxes, 1763–81.   Photostats.

1498   Letters and documents from the Governors, many of which duplicate Vols. 574–78, entry no. 1497. Also includes correspondence of Gen. John Campbell, Gov. John Dalling, Maj. Robert Farmar, Henry Hamilton, Anthony Hutchings, Joseph Munn, David Taitt, and James Willing concerning military affairs in the interior and along the Louisiana border; plans of forts and defense works in West Florida and maps of the lower Mississippi River; the journal of Edward Mease kept on a trip through the Choctaw country, Nov. 1770—Apr. 1771; lists of civil officials, new French settlers; land grants; and "A Description of West Florida with the State of Its Settlements," Jan. 1774, by Lt. Elias Durnford.

VOLS. 599–600. BOARD OF TRADE: ENTRY BOOKS

3 boxes, 1763–82.   Photostats.

1499   Contains correspondence of the Board of Trade with Gov. George Johnstone; a draft of Johnstone's commission, with orders and instructions; and reports of the Board to the King.

VOLS. 601–17. GOVERNORS' ENTRY BOOKS

8 vols., 8 boxes, 1764–80.   Photostats.

1500   Miscellaneous indentures, bonds, certificates, proclamations, warrants, and grants. Vols. 603–4 contain a ledger of Surveyor General Elias Durnford, 1765–68, apparently written by David Taitt, an assistant surveyor. Vols. 606–11 are entry books of land grants, 1767–80.

Vols. 618–22. Secretary of State: Entry Books
2 vols., 2 boxes, 1766–81.   Photostats.

1501   Entry books of in- and out-letters, primarily containing abstracts of letters and documents in Vols. 582–98, entry no. 1498.

Vol. 623. Acts of Assembly
1 vol., 1766–71.   Photostats.

1502

Vol. 624. Acts of the Assembly of East Florida
1 vol., 1781–83.   Photostats.

1503

Vols. 625–31. Minutes of the Council and General Assembly
7 vols., 1 box, 1764–78.   Photostats.

1504

Vols. 632–35. Entry Books of Minutes of the Council
4 vols., 1 box, 1764–80.   Photostats.

1505

Georgia

Vols. 648–52. Board of Trade: In-Letters
2 reels microfilm, 1760–82.

1506   Chiefly correspondence of Gov. James Wright on such subjects as Indian affairs, commerce, agriculture, emigrants, a dispute with Governor Boone of South Carolina over land south of the Altamaha River, the Stamp Act controversy, quit rents, and land grants. The bulk of the material consists of enclosures—petitions, acts of assembly, minutes and proceedings of the council, abstracts of land grants, extracts from the journals of the assembly, and accounts of customs receipts for the port of Sunbury, 1763–64. Also contains a few letters from James Habersham, president of the council, to Hillsborough, written during the absence of Governor Wright, 1771–73, concerning a dispute with the assembly, Indian affairs, and routine administrative matters.

See also Georgia, Colonial Records, entry no. 289.

Vol. 657. Miscellaneous
1 reel microfilm, 1733–83.

1507   The bulk of the documents in this volume dates before 1763. Most items relating to the Revolution are listed in Andrews, *Guide*, vol. 1, p. 163–64. Those not listed include a sketch of the siege of Savannah, 1779; a letter from Gen. Augustine Prevost to Henry Clinton informing the latter he is under siege at Savannah, Sept. 1779; a letter from Admiral d'Estaing to Prevost calling for the surrender of Savannah, Sept. 1779; Gov. James Wright's representation of the sufferings of the loyalists of Georgia on the evacuation of that province, Sept. 1782; and loyalist petitions.

See also Georgia, Colonial Records, entry no. 289.

Vols. 658–65. Secretary of State and Board of Trade: In-Letters
3 reels microfilm, 1761–80.

1508   Letters from Gov. James Wright largely duplicate Vols. 648–52, entry no. 1506. Additional material includes letters by Admiral Arbuthnot, Sir Henry Clinton, Germain, and Gen. James Paterson, chiefly concerning the southern campaign, 1779–80; a letter from Lt. Gov. Francis Fauquier to Governor Wright concerning Indian affairs, 1763; and scattered issues of South Carolina, Georgia, and Pennsylvania newspapers.

See also Georgia, Colonial Records, entry no. 289.

VOL. 674. BOARD OF TRADE: ENTRY BOOK
1 reel microfilm, 1761–82.
1509   Letters from Gov. James Wright of Georgia to the Board of Trade. Includes estimates on the expense of the civil establishment.

VOL. 675. ABSTRACTS OF GRANTS OF LAND
1 reel microfilm, 176–, 1768.
1510   See Georgia, Colonial Records, entry no. 289.

VOLS. 676–80. SECRETARY OF STATE: ENTRY BOOKS
2 reels microfilm, 1766–81.
1511   Includes correspondence of Secretaries Shelburne, Hillsborough, Dartmouth, and Germain with Governor Wright, chiefly concerning instructions and routine administrative matters, and copies and abstracts of correspondence from Wright and President James Habersham.
    See also Vols. 648–52, entry no. 1506, and Georgia, Colonial Records, entry no. 289.

VOLS. 683–85. ACTS OF ASSEMBLY
2 reels microfilm, 1768–81.
1512   See Georgia, Colonial Records, entry no. 289, and Born, *British Manuscripts Project*, p. 52.

VOLS. 698, 703, 705, 707. MINUTES OF THE PROCEEDINGS OF THE GOVERNOR IN COUNCIL
3 reels microfilm, 1760–73.
1513   See Born, *British Manuscripts Project*, p. 52.

VOLS. 699–700, 702, 706, 708. LEGISLATIVE JOURNALS
4 reels microfilm, 1761–80.
1514   See Born, *British Manuscripts Project*, p. 52.

1515   VOL. 701. MINUTES OF THE PROCEEDINGS OF THE GOVERNOR IN COUNCIL
1 reel microfilm, 1766–67.

1516   VOL. 704. COUNCIL MINUTES
1 reel microfilm, 1768–73.

VOLS. 709–10. SHIPPING RETURNS
1 reel microfilm, 1752–67.
1517   Includes lists of ships and vessels entered and cleared at the ports of Sunbury and Savannah, 1762–63, 1765, and 1766–67.

Maryland

VOL. 721. SECRETARY OF STATE: MISCELLANEOUS
1 box, 1704–80.   Photostats.
1518   Contains six documents from the period of the American Revolution: a "copy of an Association by Hugh Kelly," affirming allegiance to the King, 1775; a letter of Luke Mathewman describing an encounter with rebel privateers, June 1780; and four commercial letters from Baltimore merchants Jonathan Hudson, N. R. Morre, William McCreery, and William Patterson to traders in France and the West Indies, 1779–80.

VOL. 722. SECRETARY OF STATE: IN-LETTERS
1 box, 1777.   Photostats.
1519   Selections consisting of three documents: a proclamation by the General Assembly against Tories in Somerset and Worcester Counties, Feb. 1777; a list of prices of items for sale at Annapolis and Baltimore, Mar. and June 1777; and an extract of a letter from William Eddis to Gov. Robert Eden, July 1777, concerning the political situation in Maryland, the persecution of loyalists, and defenses at Annapolis and Baltimore.

VOL. 738. ACTS OF ASSEMBLY
1 reel microfilm, 1769–71.
1520   See Born, *British Manuscripts Project*, p. 53.

Massachusetts

VOLS. 759, 761. SECRETARY OF STATE: IN-LETTERS
4 boxes, 1769–72.   Photostats.
1521   Letter from Gov. Thomas Hutchinson includes an account of the Boston Massacre, with lengthy depositions from witnesses, particularly British soldiers. Also a 70-page report on events in Massachusetts, 1766–70; an inventory of stores and ordnance at Castle William, Boston, 1770; and a statement of Massachusetts' claims to lands between the Kennebec and St. Croix Rivers, 1772.

VOLS. 778–84. ACTS OF ASSEMBLY
2 reels microfilm, 1760–74.
1522   See Born, *British Manuscripts Project*, p. 53.

VOLS. 825–33. SESSIONAL PAPERS: COUNCIL AND COUNCIL-IN-ASSEMBLY
5 reels microfilm, 1762–74.
1523   See Born, *British Manuscripts Project*, p. 53.

VOLS. 842–47. SESSIONAL PAPERS: ASSEMBLY
2 reels microfilm, 1761–74.
1524   See Born, *British Manuscripts Project*, p. 53.

VOL. 854. MISCELLANEOUS: TREASURERS' ACCOUNTS
1 reel microfilm, 1760–69.
1525   See Born, *British Manuscripts Project*, p. 53.

New Jersey

VOLS. 1012–14, 1017–18. ACTS OF ASSEMBLY
3 reels microfilm, 1754–75.
1526   See Born, *British Manuscripts Project*, p. 54.

VOLS. 1026–28, 1033–34. LEGISLATIVE JOURNALS
3 reels microfilm, 1761–75.
1527   See Born, *British Manuscripts Project*, p. 54.

VOL. 1036. SHIPPING RETURNS
1 reel microfilm, 1743–64.
1528   Information for the port of Perth Amboy includes date; name of vessel and owner; master's name; type of ship; number of tons, guns and men; when and where built, registered, and bond given, and cargo imported.
       See Born, *British Manuscripts Project*, p. 54.

New York

VOLS. 1070–78. BOARD OF TRADE: IN-LETTERS
4 reels microfilm, 1760–79.

1529 Correspondence, with enclosures, from Governors, officers, and officials, chiefly in New York. Includes letters of Cadwallader Colden, William Johnson, Robert Monckton, Matthew Lamb, Philip Skene, Henry Moore, Benning Wentworth, Jeffery Amherst, William Tryon, and Richard Jackson. Among the enclosures are legal papers, newspapers, reports on proceedings and acts of the assembly, petitions, memorials, surveys, a list of persons naturalized in the province, and lists of persons in New York City, 1777, and on Long Island, 1778, who took the oath of allegiance to the Crown.

VOLS. 1088–90. SECRETARY OF STATE: MISCELLANEOUS CORRESPONDENCE
2 reels microfilm, 1784.

1530 Contains Gen. Augustine Prevost's report on the Franco-American attack on Savannah; loyalist petitions to the British Government, 1779–84; a Joseph Galloway report on loyalist forces in New York, 1782; Galloway's 1782 plan for winning the war; and letters and documents related to the evacuation of New York. Also contains material concerning land speculation in Ohio, 1768–72.

VOLS. 1097–1110. SECRETARY OF STATE: IN-LETTERS
12 reels microfilm, 1762–80.

1531 Letters to the Secretary of State from Govs. Cadwallader Colden, Robert Monckton, Sir Henry Moore, Lord Dunmore, and William Tryon. Also contains copies of contemporary maps of New York's boundaries on Quebec and Massachusetts and of New Hampshire; land grant surveys; letters concerning enforcement of the trade acts; a list of letters of marque issued by Governor Tryon; and a list of prizes taken into New York, 1777–79. Also British intelligence concerning the American military plans, 1780; reports of Congressional activities and fortifications at New York and Philadelphia; and lists of persons who took the oath of allegiance to the Crown, 1777–78.

VOLS. 1114–32. BOARD OF TRADE: ENTRY BOOKS
3 boxes, transcripts, 2 reels microfilm, 1692–1779.

1532 Correspondence of the Board of Trade with New York Govs. Robert Monckton, Cadwallader Colden, Lord Dunmore, and William Tryon concerning the New York boundary dispute with Massachusetts in 1764; Indian relations, land grants, the Stamp Act, Townshend Acts, nonimportation, and the outbreak of hostilities. Includes orders and instructions for James Robertson as Governor of New York, 1779.

VOL. 1141. SECRETARY OF STATE: ENTRY BOOK OF OUT-LETTERS
1 folio, 1768–82.   Transcripts.

1533 Several letters relate to the appointment of William Tryon as Governor of New York, but there are other miscellaneous items, such as Richard Morris' salary petition, appointment of Sampson Salter Blowers as solicitor general of New York, and loyalist claims.

VOL. 1201. SESSIONAL PAPERS: COUNCIL
1 reel microfilm, 1757–75.

1534 Contains papers of the council, Apr. 1774—July 1775; council in assembly, Jan. 1773—Apr. 1775; and assembly, Dec. 1757—Mar. 1773.
  See Born, *British Manuscripts Project*, p. 54.

VOLS. 1203–11. SESSIONAL PAPERS: COUNCIL AND COUNCIL IN ASSEMBLY
3 reels microfilm, 1760–75.

1535 See Born, *British Manuscripts Project*, p. 54.

Vols. 1217–20. Sessional Papers: Assembly
1 reel microfilm, 1760–75.
1536   See Born, *British Manuscripts Project*, p. 54.

Vol. 1221. Miscellaneous
1 reel microfilm, 1765–66.
1537   Includes several copies of each of the following: *New York Gazette*; "His Excellency's Speech," Massachusetts, Jan. 1766; the assembly's answer to the same, Jan. 1766; and a pamphlet concerning Andrew Oliver and the Sons of Liberty, Dec. 1765.
     See Born, *British Manuscripts Project*, p. 54.

Pennsylvania

Vols. 1249–54. Acts of Assembly
3 reels microfilm, 1762–74.
1538   See Born, *British Manuscripts Project*, p. 55.

Proprietary Colonies

Vols. 1280–86. Secretary of State: In-letters
3 reels microfilm, 1762–76.
1539   Correspondence, with enclosures, from Governors and officials in Connecticut, Rhode Island, Pennsylvania, and Maryland, chiefly concerning disturbances in the wake of the Stamp Act, illicit trade, land disputes, political activities of American radicals, the controversy in Pennsylvania between the proprietor and the inhabitants, and miscellaneous administrative matters. Includes letters of Govs. Thomas Fitch, William Pitkin, Jonathan Trumbull (Connecticut), Samuel Ward, Stephen Hopkins, Josias Lyndon, Joseph Wanton (Rhode Island), John Penn (Pennsylvania), Horatio Sharpe, Robert Eden (Maryland), and of Metcalf Bowler, Thomas Moffatt, Charles Garth, Franklin, and Joseph Shippen, Jr. Among the enclosures are copies of colonial newspapers, petitions, and depositions, printed copies of the rules and articles of the First Continental Congress and the Continental Army, and acts and proceedings of the assemblies. Also includes copies of letters and instructions from Secretaries Conway, Shelburne, Egremont, Hillsborough, Germain, and Dartmouth.

Vols. 1296–97. Board of Trade: Entry Books
2 reels microfilm, 1761–76.
1540   Contains reports to the Lords of the Committee of the Privy Council for Plantation Affairs, with drafts of instructions to Governors in Pennsylvania and Connecticut. Also a representation to the King concerning complaints by Delaware Indians against the proprietors of Pennsylvania.

Virginia

Vols. 1308–34. Board of Trade: In-letters
18 boxes, 1691–1781.   Transcripts and photostats.
1541   Correspondence of Virginia Governors to the Board of Trade. Includes accounts of the King's revenue from tobacco for the entire period and scattered accounts on quit rents. For the Revolutionary era the material includes land grant records and related letters; Fauquier's reports on the reception of the Stamp Act in Virginia, and trans-Appalachian settlement; and letters discussing Negroes, Indians, the scarcity of salt, boundaries, the courts, civil government, and routine matters. Also includes legislative acts sent to England for allowance.

VOL. 1344. MISCELLANEOUS
1 box, 1776–83.   Transcripts.

1542   Includes a petition from London merchants trading in Virginia and Maryland to the Secretary of State, 1776; captured letters from Virginia merchants to Messrs. Curson and Gouverneur at St. Eustatius, 1779–80; the memorial of Katherine Sproule, formerly of Gosport, to Thomas Townshend concerning reinstatement on the pension list, 1782; and two letters by Ralph Wormeley, Jr., of Rosegill, requesting the return of slaves taken to New York in June 1781.

VOLS. 1345–53. SECRETARY OF STATE: IN-LETTERS
1 box, 1762–76.   Transcripts and photostats.

1543   Correspondence of Govs. Francis Fauquier, John Blair, Lord Botetourt, William Nelson, and Lord Dunmore. Topics include frontier defense, reaction to the Stamp Act and the Townshend duties, and John Robinson's misuse of treasury funds. Also contains Dunmore's report on the present state of Virginia, 1774; accounts of revenue from customs and quit rents; letters and documents relating to the northern and western boundaries of Virginia; extracts from council minutes; petitions on various grievances; a list of patents granted by Lord Dunmore; and Dunmore's reports on the rebellion in Virginia, 1775–76.

VOLS. 1368–69. BOARD OF TRADE: ENTRY BOOKS
1 box, 1760–70.   Transcripts.

1544   Chiefly correspondence of the Board of Trade with the King, the Secretaries of State, and Govs. Francis Fauquier, Sir Jeffery Amherst, Lord Botetourt, William Nelson, and Lord Dunmore concerning Indian affairs, western land, and the disallowance of acts passed in Virginia.

VOLS. 1374–75. SECRETARY OF STATE: ENTRY BOOKS
1 box, 1767–76.   Transcripts.

1545   Chiefly instructions of Secretaries Dartmouth and Hillsborough to Governors Botetourt and Dunmore concerning commerce, patents, revenue, and the disallowance of acts of assembly.

Barbados (C.O. 28)

VOLS. 50–61. SECRETARY OF STATE: IN-LETTERS
13 boxes, 4 vols., 1761–88.   Photostats.

1546   Contains letters from Govs. Charles Pinfold, William Spry, Edward Hay, James Cunningham, and David Parry concerning the economy, society, and politics of Barbados. Also includes material pertaining to British and French naval operations and American privateers in West Indian waters, preparations for war on the French island of Martinique, British defenses on Barbados, and prisoners of war. Among the enclosures are letters by Gens. John Vaughan and Gabriel Christie, Adms. George Rodney and James Young, and the Marquis de Bouillé, Governor of Martinique; military returns; statistics on births and deaths among the civilian population; figures on Negroes brought into the Colony, 1768–69 and 1772–73; and council minutes, proceedings of the assembly, depositions, petitions, and various official papers.
       See also Herbert Bell, David Parker, et. al., *Guide to British West Indian Archive Materials in London and in the Islands, for the History of the United States* (Washington, 1926).

Canada (C.O. 42)

VOLS. 37–38. SECRETARY OF STATE: IN-LETTERS
1 box, 1787–88.   Photostats.

1547   Selections from the correspondence of Canadian Governors include a report by Gother Mann, captain and commanding engineer at Quebec, to Brigadier General Hope relative to laying out a new town at Sorel and building fortifications for its protection, 1787; Lord Dorchester's instructions to Capt. Gother Mann concerning a survey and report on the conditions of fortifications at Forts Ontario, Niagara, Erie, Detroit, and Michilimackinac, 1788; and Mann's report, Dec. 1788.

Dominica (C.O. 71)

VOLS. 2, 5–10, 14. SECRETARY OF STATE: IN-LETTERS
7 boxes, 2 vols., 1730–1801.   Photostats.

1548   Volume 2 contains a single letter from Capt. John Hanson, Aug. 1773, offering to obtain French maps of the Ohio, Mississippi, and Missouri Rivers from Versailles.

Volumes 5–10 contain letters from Govs. Thomas Shirley and John Orde, 1774–88, concerning financial matters, disputes with the council and assembly, supplies and provisions, French assistance to the revolting Colonies, privateering, the 1778 expedition against St. Lucia, and the capture of Dominica by the French, 1778. Among the enclosures are documents on the cession of Dominica to the French, military returns, reports on the island's defenses, council minutes, assembly journals, and customs office records.

Volume 14 contains accounts of Negroes brought into the colony, 1784–88; rough census figures that divide the inhabitants as to race and color, 1772, 1780, and 1788; shipping accounts; and answers to queries on the management of slaves, 1788.

See also Bell and Parker, *Guide to British West Indian Archives*, p. 124–28.

Grenada (C.O. 101)

VOLS. 21–23. SECRETARY OF STATE: IN-LETTERS
4 boxes, 1777–78.   Photostats.

1549   Official letters, with enclosures, from Gov. George Macartney to Germain. Topics include the capture and disposal of rebel vessels captured in the West Indies, the treatment of prisoners, activities of the French at Martinique, and defense. Among the enclosures are a report on the defenses at Tobago, with returns of ordnance, military stores, and troops; select issues of newspapers published at Martinique and Antigua; and copies of correspondence between Governor Macartney, Admiral Barrington, Gen. James Grant, and the Governor of Trinidad. Miscellaneous captured correspondence includes a letter from C. Lownes to John Lownes of Philadelphia, London, May 1777, commenting on political affairs in England and the treatment of American prisoners.

See also Bell and Parker, *Guide to British West Indian Archives*, p. 151–53.

Jamaica (C.O. 137)

VOLS. 61–83. SECRETARY OF STATE: IN-LETTERS
34 boxes, 1761–83.   Photostats.

1550   Letters to Secretary Egremont from Gov. William Lyttleton, with enclosures on trade regulations, military affairs, disputes between the Governor and the assembly arising at the time of the Stamp Act, and relations with the Spanish, 1761–67. Correspondence between Gov. William Trelawney and Secretary Hillsborough includes enclosures concerning political affairs, currency, problems with the Spanish, military affairs, and conditions on the Mosquito Coast, 1769–73. Correspondence, with enclosures from Gov. John Dalling to Dartmouth and Germain, pertains to the disallowance of acts of assembly, trade, smuggling, defense, and a variety of other subjects, 1773–81. Material dated 1779–81 concerns military operations in the West Indies, and recruiting among prisoners and loyalists in North America. Letters from Gov. Archibald Campbell, 1781–83, describe operations against the Spanish, illegal trade with the enemy, and the arrival of loyalists and rebel volunteers from America. Other correspondents include Lt. Gov. Richard Elletson, Stephen Fuller, Sir Basil Keith, Charles Lord Montagu, and Col. William Odell.

See also Bell and Parker, *Guide to British West Indian Archives*, p. 188–97.

St. Vincent (C.O. 260)

VOLS. 4–5, 7. SECRETARY OF STATE: IN-LETTERS
1 vol., 1776–86.   Photostats.

1551   Volumes 4 and 5 primarily contain letters from Gov. Valentine Morris concerning the desperate need for provisions and military supplies, operations of British and American privateers, French and Spanish assistance to the Americans, and difficulties with runaway slaves and Carib Indians. Volume 7 contains a letter from Gov. Edmund Lincoln, 1786, appealing the release by a local court of an American schooner seized for violation of the Acts of Navigation.

West Indies (C.O. 318)

VOLS. 1–2. BOARD OF TRADE: ORIGINAL CORRESPONDENCE
5 boxes, 1624–1808.   Photostats.

1552   Chiefly commercial papers, 1763–87. Includes tables of vessels clearing British ports for England and North America; accounts of exports, imports, and revenues, 1763–87; lists of prices; and figures on the population of St. Domingo and Barbados, 1783–87. Also figures on Negroes brought into various French ports at St. Domingo, and answers to queries from the Secretary on the state of Tobago, 1773.

See Bell and Parker, *Guide to British West Indian Archives*, p. 313–14.

Colonies General (C.O. 323-324)

C. O. 323. VOLS. 17–21, 24. BOARD OF TRADE: IN-LETTERS
2 boxes, 1763–68.   Photostats.

1553   Letters of John Stuart, Superintendent of Indian Affairs in the Southern District, to the Board of Trade, and Stuart's observations on a plan for the management of Indian affairs, Dec. 1764, make up the bulk of the selections from these volumes. Volume 19 consists chiefly of correspondence and documents concerning colonial currency. Also includes accounts of bills of credit issued in several provinces, plus rates of exchange.

See Andrews, *Guide*, vol. 1, p. 325–26.

C. O. 324. Vols. 17–19, 21, 39–43, 49, 51–54, 58, 60. Board of Trade: Entry Books of In- and Out-letters
7 boxes, 1759–82.　　　　Transcripts.

1554　　Includes representations to the King, drafts of bills, reports from the solicitor general on acts passed in America, circulars to the Governors, petitions, proclamations, and warrants. Also contains lists of Indian tribes and a plan for the management of Indians; information on the transport of new settlers; surveys and abstracts of land grants in Nova Scotia, Quebec, East Florida, and North Carolina; and correspondence with surveyors Samuel Holland and William de Brahm.

Maps and Plans (C.O. 700)

Maps
2 folios, 1764, 1778.　　　　Photostats.

1555　　Contains a report of William Spry, commanding engineer, to Major General Massey, concerning the defenses of Halifax, Sept. 1778. Includes maps. Also a map of a temporary boundary line between the provinces of North Carolina and South Carolina, agreeable to Gov. Arthur Dobbs of North Carolina and Lt. Gov. William Bull of South Carolina, Sept. 1764.

EXCHEQUER AND AUDIT DEPARTMENT

Declared Accounts

A. O. 1. Bundle 818, Roll 1067–Bundle 829, Roll 1087. Customs: Receivers General and Cashiers
12 reels microfilm, 3 boxes transcripts, 1763–88.

1556　　Reports of duties and fines collected in England and America for each auditing period, and the salaries and allowances of customs officials. The transcripts constitute a virtual index of the material on microfilm.

A. O. 1. Bundle 1261, Rolls 147–51. Governor, Agents, etc.: West Florida
5 volumes, 1763–86. Photostats.

1557　　Declared accounts of the following East Florida officials: Lt. Gov. John Moultrie, 1772–75, roll 147; Gov. Patrick Tonyn, 1773–85, roll 148; agent William Knox, 1763–75, rolls 149–50; and acting agent John Cowan, 1782–86, roll 151.

A. O. 1. Bundle 1261, Rolls 152–54. Governor, Agents, etc.: East Florida
2 volumes, 1764–70.　　　　Photostats.

1558　　Declared accounts of Gov. George Johnstone, 1764–67, rolls 152–53, and Gov. James Grant, 1769–70, roll 154. Grant's accounts include funds expended for relief of distressed Greek immigrants at New Smyrna, East Florida.

Claims, American Loyalists

A. O. 12. Series I. Vols. 1–146.
30 reels microfilm, 1776–1831.　　　　Finding aid available.

1559　　Records of the American Loyalist Claims Commission. Volumes 1–56 contain evidence submitted to the Claims Commission. The material, which is organized by residence of claimant, includes memorials, schedules of losses, sworn testimony of witnesses, and proof of loyalty such as service during the war. Volumes 57–77 record the commissioners' decisions on each claim. The remaining volumes include minute books of the commission's proceedings, requests for temporary support while claims were being investigated, withdrawn claims, documents submitted by State governments to enable the commission to ascertain what legal actions had been taken against proscribed claimants, reports on debts due loyalists, and miscellaneous information.

See also A.O.13, entry no. 1560; F.O.4, entry no. 1562; T.79, entry no. 1590; and Proceedings of the Loyalist Claims Commissioners, entry no. 497.

A. O. 13. SERIES II. BUNDLES 1–135
140 reels microfilm, 1780–1835.
1560   Papers of the American Loyalist Claims Commission. The papers were originally collected into 140 bundles; numbers 66, 77–78, 89, and 101 are missing. The information was transcribed into the volumes which make up A.O.12. Reel 1 contains an index and a copy of B. F. Stevens' 244-page index of names.

Bundles 1–10 (A.O.12 vols. 71–77) contain "examinations" concerning supplies furnished to the army and navy. The following bundles consist of "Claims" and "New Claims": New York, 11–16, 52–53; New Jersey, 17–20; New Brunswick, 21–22; New Hampshire, 23, 59; Nova Scotia, 24–26; Virginia, 27–33, 58, 134; Georgia, 34–38, 134, 136; Maryland, 39–40; Connecticut, 41–42, 76; Massachusetts, 43–49, 50 51; Pennsylvania, 47, 70A–72; Rhode Island, 68–69, 79; North Carolina, 117–24; South Carolina, 125–36; Bahamas and Vermont, 59; Canada, 81; "Various," 82–85; "Received too late," 80 (chiefly South Carolina).

Papers relating to temporary assistance are in the following bundles: New York, 54–56, 63–65, 67, 113–16; Maryland, 60–62; Rhode Island, 68–69; Massachusetts, 73 75; New Jersey, 108–12. The remaining bundles consist of papers designated "various," "letters and schedules," and "miscellaneous."

See also F.O.4, entry no. 1562; T.79, entry no. 1590; and Proceedings of the Loyalists Commissioners, entry no. 497.

Miscellanea

A. O. 16. VOL. 43. MINUTES OF THE PROCEEDINGS OF THE EAST FLORIDA COUNCIL
2 boxes, 1764–76.   Photostats.
1561   Consists primarily of petitions for land, recommendations of the East Florida council, and final decisions of the King in Council. Includes correspondence concerning pacification of Indians, availability of troops, and fraudulent attempts to purchase Indian lands during the administrations of Govs. James Grant and Patrick Tonyn. Entries for the years 1775–76 relate largely to the suspensions of Councillor Arthur Gordon, Chief Justice William Drayton, and Secretary Andrew Turnbull.

Duplicates material in C.O.5, Vols. 570–71, entry no. 1495, but is more detailed.

FOREIGN OFFICE

General Correspondence

AMERICA, UNITED STATES OF

F. O. 4. SERIES I. VOLS. 1–7
4 reels microfilm, 6 boxes photostats, 1776–94.
1562   Miscellaneous correspondence and intelligence collected during the period before

England's establishment of diplomatic relations with the United States. Volume 1 consists of claims of American loyalists, 1782–94, primarily those of prominent men who had special claims or direct access to important officials, though many were merely submitted before the creation of the Loyalist Claims Commission. Includes memorials, supporting letters, and affidavits recounting past services to the Crown.

The remaining volumes contain material concerning trade, tariffs, debts, loyalists, fisheries, Indians, boundaries, western lands, and forts. Includes correspondence of David Hartley, appointed to negotiate with American commissioners in Paris; Sir John Temple, consul general at New York; Phineas Bond, consul at Philadelphia; George Miller, consul in South Carolina and Georgia; John Hamilton, consul in Virginia; John Adams and other U.S. national and State officials; and Secretary Carmarthen, Under Secretary William Fraser, and other British officials. Intelligence reports on American affairs were written by Edward Bancroft and P. Allaire, the latter's letters being comprehensive and complete for Aug. 1786—Mar. 1791.

See also A.O. 12, entry no. 1559, A.O. 13, entry no. 1560, and Paullin and Paxson, *Guide*, p. 12–15.

FRANCE

F. O. 27. Vols. 2–3, 5–9
11 boxes, 1782–83.   Photostats and transcripts.
1563   Letters and papers relating to peace negotiations with France and America, 1782–83. Includes correspondence and papers of Richard Oswald, Thomas Grenville, Thomas Walpole, and Alleyne Fitzherbert from Paris, and of Charles James Fox and Lords Shelburne and Grantham from London. Includes draft instructions; minutes of conversations; Franklin's correspondence with Oswald; and letters of the Duke of Manchester, Vergennes, Castries, D'Aranda, and Henry Strachey.
See also F.O. 97, entry no. 1566.

HOLLAND AND NETHERLANDS

F. O. 37. Vol. 4
1 box, 1782.   Transcripts.
1564   Selected documents comprise intelligence reports, in French, sent from The Hague, Apr.—Oct. 1782, a letter of Sir Joseph Yorke to Under Secretary William Fraser, May 1782, on apparent French and Dutch indifference to immediate negotiations. The reports contain information concerning naval preparations, movements of the Texel Fleet, Dutch trade, the disposition of the States-General toward opening peace negotiations, and contacts with the Russian Minister to invoke support of the League of Armed Neutrality.

SPAIN

F. O. 72. Vol. 1
1 box, 1781.   Photostats.
1565   Selected letters, with enclosures, to Secretary Hillsborough from Richard Cumberland and Thomas Hussey, Jan.—Feb. 1781, concerning their secret peace mission to Spain.
See also British Museum, Add. Mss., 28851, entry no. 1367.

SUPPLEMENT TO GENERAL CORRESPONDENCE

F. O. 97. VOL. 157. FRANCE, SUPPLEMENTAL
2 boxes, 1782–83.   Photostats.

1566   A letterbook primarily containing the correspondence of Richard Oswald and Secretaries Shelburne and Townshend. Contains material concerning the peace negotiations in Paris, including letters from the American commissioners forwarded to London, minutes of conversations, and proposed articles and letters of Henry Strachey, Benjamin Vaughan, and Alleyne Fitzherbert. Duplicates much of the material in F.O. 27, vol. 2, entry no. 1563.

Miscellaneous

MISCELLANEA

F. O. 95. SERIES I. VOLS. 2, 356
4 items, 1780.   Facsimiles and photostats.

1567   Transcripts of two intercepted letters to Benjamin Franklin from Thomas Digges, but bearing the signatures William Singleton Church, Oct. 17, 1780, and William Fitzpatrick, Oct. 27, 1780. Stevens, *Facsimiles*, nos. 952 and 953. Also photostats of two letters from Lord Stormont, Jan. 1780, concerning charts of the northwest coast of America to be supplied to the Empress of Russia.

HIGH COURT OF ADMIRALTY

Instance and Prize Courts

LIBELS, ETC.

H. C. A. 24. BUNDLE 149. "ALLEGATIONS"
7 boxes, 1778–83.   Photostats.

1568   A bundle from the original files of the court containing allegations against vessels captured and taken into English ports. Made in behalf of the captain and crew of the ship making the capture, they state the name, registry, and captain of the condemned ship, plus date of capture and port where entered. Includes French, Dutch, Spanish, and American ships captured chiefly during the years 1780–82.

PRIZE PAPERS

H. C. A. 32. BUNDLES 491, 493. NEW YORK COURT OF VICE-ADMIRALTY
6 boxes, 1 vol., 1776–83.   Photostats.

1569   Bundle 491. Consists of claims, rejoinders, and depositions filed with Vice-Admiralty Judge Robert Bayard concerning the following captured American ships: *Wanton, Warren, Warrior, Washington, Wasp, Welcome, Wexford, Whim, Whipperwill, William, William & John, Willing Lass, Willing Maid, Willis, Willy & Menta, Wolfe, Wonder,* and *Wren.* Captured papers include ship logs and correspondence between North American West Indian and French merchants. Also includes material on wartime commerce and practices adapted to curb American trade.

See Andrews, *Guide*, vol. 2, p. 333–40.

Bundle 493. Contains miscellaneous captured correspondence, more than half of which is in French and Spanish. Includes letters from John Bondfield of Bordeaux to Robert Morris, Richard Henry Lee, and Thomas Wharton; also letters from Samuel Tucker of Bordeaux to the Navy Board of the Eastern Department in Boston.

Vice-Admiralty Courts

PROCEEDINGS

H. C. A. 49. BUNDLES 91–93. NEW YORK COURT OF VICE-ADMIRALTY
9 boxes, 4 vols., 1775–82.   Photostats.

1570 Bundle 91. Consists of papers "called up" from the New York Vice-Admiralty Court and forwarded on appeal to the High Court of Admiralty. Includes cases of the ships *LaLemire*, *L'Amité*, *Yorick*, *Young Cromwell*, *Young Benjamin*, and *Zephyr*.

Bundle 92. Contains assignation books of the New York Vice-Admiralty Court, Dec. 1777—Dec. 1782, consisting of a calendar of libels and motions filed before Judge Robert Bayard.

Bundle 93. Minutes of the proceedings of the court, Sept. 1777—Feb. 1778.

HOME OFFICE

Correspondence and Papers, Departmental

LAW OFFICERS, LETTERBOOKS

H. O. 49. VOLS. 1—2
4 boxes, 1762–96.   Photostats.

1571 Two entry books, one consisting of queries submitted by the Secretaries of State to the attorney general and solicitor general, with replies; the other of letters to the law officers from the Secretary of State or Under Secretary William Fraser. Although volume 1 contains no entries for the period Mar. 1776—June 1782, several letters concern the operation of the English Government and trials of John Wilkes and "Junius."

See Andrews, *Guide*, vol. 1, p. 72–3.

Correspondence and Papers, Domestic and General

GEORGE III, CORRESPONDENCE

H. O. 42. VOLS. 1–3
1 box, 1782–83.   Transcripts.

1572 Transcripts of selected items submitted to the King pertaining to American affairs. Topics include abolition of the American Department and the Board of Trade, including accounts of the American Office's expenses, 1776–82, and lists of employees whose positions were abolished; Henry Laurens' stay in England after his release from prison; and claims for prize money. Also contains petitions from loyalists and officers of provincial corps; a few items concerning merchants formerly trading with America; Franklin's scheme to assist artificers in migrating to America; and a plan submitted by George Duff, May 1782, proposing "to reinstate the British Empire by a general war."

Formerly State Papers Domestic, George III, vols. 98–100. See Andrews, *Guide*, vol. 1, p. 71–2.

Entry Books

H. O. 43. VOLS. 1–2. OUT-LETTERS
2 reels microfilm, 1782–89.

1573 Consists primarily of letters from the Home Secretaries to other departments concerning domestic matters, though a few letters pertain to American affairs, Mar. 1782—Feb. 1789. Includes copies of enclosures and a few in-letters, 1782–84, including a letter to Secretary Fox from Edward Bancroft, Aug. 1783.

In British Manuscripts Project.

PRIVY COUNCIL OFFICE

Papers, Mainly Unbound

P. C. 1
1 box, 1766–74.   Photostats and transcripts.

1574 Selections consist of the petition of Denys Rolle regarding a settlement in East Florida, Oct. 1766, and two petitions of Thomas Walpole and associates for a grant of land (Vandalia), July 1769, Aug. 1774. Includes report of the attorney and solicitor general on Walpole's petition, July 1773, and a Privy Council order of Oct. 1773 on the Walpole grant.

See *Acts of the Privy Council of England* (London, 1912), Colonial Series, vol. 6, "The Unbound Papers," items 729, 822, 911, and 930.

Registers

P. C. 2. VOLS. 129–33
5 vols., 1784–89.   Photostats.

1575 Selections from Privy Council minutes concerning American issues brought before the Council, Jan. 1784—Apr. 1789. Trade with the United States, often discussed in context of petitions from protesting British merchants or West Indies planters, is the chief subject of these selections.

PUBLIC RECORD OFFICE

Documents Acquired by Gift, Deposit, or Purchase

CARLETON PAPERS

P. R. O. 30/55
30 reels microfilm, 1747–83.

1576 Headquarters papers of the British Army in America. Consists chiefly of official correspondence and papers of Sir Guy Carleton (1724–1808), commander in chief of British forces in America, 1782–83. Major concerns include the exchange of prisoners;

disbanding provincial corps; evacuation of Charleston and New York; and establishing asylums for homeless loyalists in East Florida, the West Indies, Canada, and Nova Scotia. Also contains numerous letters from inspectors of loyalist claims for temporary support and from William Franklin, who presided over the Board of Associated Loyalists.

Documents relating to Carleton's predecessors, Gens. Thomas Gage, William Howe, and Sir Henry Clinton include Howe's orderly book, June 1775—May 1776, accounts, returns, intelligence, requests for reinforcements and supplies, and reports on the general progress of the war. Also letters from Gen. Augustine Prevost during the expedition against Savannah in cooperation with Col. Archibald Campbell and Capt. Hyde Parker, 1778–79; from Clinton and Admiral Arbuthnot during the siege of Charleston, 1779–80; from Lord Cornwallis and officers under his command in the southern campaign, 1780–81; from officers in West Florida concerning the defense of Pensacola and Mobile; from Gov. Patrick Tonyn on the defense of East Florida; and from officers and officials at Halifax and St. John's Island concerning military operations, fortifications, and supplies. Documents in the collection not duplicated elsewhere comprise instructions from Carleton to subordinate officers, largely in the Southern Department.

The arrangement of the collection no longer coincides with the calendar in the Historical Manuscripts Commission *Report on American Manuscripts in the Royal Institution of Great Britain*, 4 vols. (1904–9). Reels 1–2 contain a keyed copy of the calendar. Principal correspondents are best determined through the index to the calendar which appears at the end of each volume. Microfilm was made from photostats of the collection at Colonial Williamsburg, Inc.

CORNWALLIS PAPERS

P. R. O. 30/11
80 reels microfilm, 1614–1854.

1577   Lt. Gen. Cornwallis (1738–1805) served under Gen. William Howe in the northern Colonies, 1776–78, and commanded British forces in the southern Colonies from 1780 until his capture at Yorktown in Oct. 1781. The material here consists primarily of his official correspondence as commander in chief in the Southern Department, 1780–81. Included are instructions from Germain and Sir Henry Clinton on military and civil policy in Georgia, Virginia, and the Carolinas; Cornwallis' reports to Clinton and Germain on maneuvers, battles, skirmishes, Indian affairs, recruitment of loyalists, and the progress of pacification; and reports from officers at various posts in the department: Nesbit Balfour, Charleston; Lord Rawdon, Camden, and elsewhere; Maj. James Wemyss, Georgetown; John Cruger, Ninety-six; Thomas Brown, Augusta; Alured Clarke, Savannah; John Campbell, Pensacola; and others. Also letters from Govs. John Dalling, Patrick Tonyn, William Maxwell, and James Wright; correspondence from American officers on the treatment and exchange of prisoners; reports from Gens. Benedict Arnold, Alexander Leslie, and William Phillips on the invasions of Virginia; and returns of troop casualties and stores. Represented in intercepted correspondence are Nathanael Greene, Joseph Jones, William Langborn, Lafayette, Isaac Motte, Griffith Rutherford, William Sharpe, William Smallwood, Washington, and George Weedon.

The present collection of Cornwallis papers consists of 291 boxes and bundles. The Library has microfilm of 283 bundles. Papers relating to America described above, bundles 1–7, 58, 60–100, 270, 275, and 277 (14 reels), are calendared in George H. Reese, *The Cornwallis Papers: Abstracts of Americana* (Charlottesville, Va., 1970). Some of the American papers are printed in full or in part in Charles Ross, ed., *The Correspondence of Charles, First Marquis Cornwallis*, 3 vols. (London, 1859). See also *Eighth Report of the Royal Commission on Historical Manuscripts* (London, 1881).

EGREMONT PAPERS

P. R. O. 30/47. Vols. 14, 22, 24
1 reel microfilm, 1733–63.

1578   Selections concern American affairs, especially during the Earl of Egremont's tenure as Secretary of State for the Southern Department. Contains information on the disposition of the British Army in America, 1761–63, and on the consequences of peace in 1763; a 15-page list, Nov. 1761, of officials in America "in the recommendation of" the southern secretary; "Hints respecting the settlement of Florida"; and a few letters regarding policies being formulated on the eve of the Treaty of Paris.

    Principal correspondents: Gen. Jeffery Amherst, Gov. Francis Fauquier, Charles Garth, Gov. George Johnstone, Benjamin Martyn, and John Pownall.

Transcripts

VENETIAN ARCHIVES

P. R. O. 31/14. Vol. 158
1 reel microfilm, 1776–87.

1579   Consists of transcripts of material from Venetian state papers selected by Rawdon Brown in 1868, chiefly letters from Venetian ambassadors to their government discussing Benjamin Franklin's activities in Paris and the American war. Includes a Dec. 1784 letter from Adams, Franklin, and Jefferson to Venetian Ambassador Delfino. The transcripts are in Italian, but numerous notes, in English, appear in the margins.

STATE PAPER OFFICE

Domestic

STATE PAPERS DOMESTIC, GEORGE III

S. P. 37. Vols. 2–15. Letters and Papers
1 box, 1763–82.   Transcripts.

1580   Miscellaneous documents to the Secretary of State from nearly every department of government, including petitions; papers on colonial trade, Indian relations, the Spanish in North America, and royal Governors; materials concerning the *Gaspée* incident, the quartering of troops in the Colonies, the Quebec Act, and the escalation of the Revolutionary crisis; and documents containing information on the conduct of the war.

    For a more complete list see Andrews, *Guide*, vol. 1, p. 45–50. Several of the more important letters were reproduced in Stevens, *Facsimiles*, though a few significant items such as a letter from Samuel Wharton to Edward Bancroft, London, July 1777, were unnoted by both Stevens and Andrews.

NAVAL

S. P. 42. Vol. 138. Law Reports and Papers
5 boxes, 1704–81.   Photostats.

1581   Papers relating to maritime law, chiefly letters from the College of Advocates, Doctors Commons, to the Secretary of State for the Southern Department rendering opinions on prize cases and neutral rights. Most of the correspondence is dated 1776–81; the cases involve American, French, Dutch, Spanish, Swedish, and Portuguese ships.

Foreign

FRANCE

S. P. 78. Vols. 296–306
3 boxes, 1775–78.   Stevens' facsimiles.
1582   Selected correspondence of Lord Stormont, Ambassador to France, and Horace St. Paul, Chargé d'Affaires at Paris, chiefly with Lord Weymouth, the Secretary of State for the Southern Department.

HOLLAND

S. P. 84. Vol. 572
1 folio, 1780.   Transcripts.
1583   Selections consist of correspondence of Sir Joseph Yorke, Ambassador to Holland, Oct. 1780.
    See Stevens, *Facsimiles*, nos. 948, 950, and 951.

PRUSSIA

S. P. 90. Vol. 101
1 box, 1777.   Transcripts.
1584   Selected correspondence of Hugh Elliot, Minister to Prussia, May—Oct. 1777.
    See Stevens, *Facsimiles*, nos. 1452–59, 1466, 1470, 1475–80, 1482.

SPAIN

S. P. 94. Vols. 209, 254
4 boxes, 1780–81.

1585   Vol. 209. Papers collected in the Southern Department on the Richard Cumberland–Thomas Hussey mission to Spain, Mar. 1780—May 1781. Includes Cumberland's and Hussey's correspondence with Lord Hillsborough, Hillsborough-Floridablanca correspondence, letters of Henry O'Neil, and several issues of a newspaper, June—Aug. 1780.

    Vol. 254. Two selections consisting of Cumberland's draft instructions for a treaty with Spain, ca. Apr. 1780, and a précis of Cumberland–Hussey correspondence summarize events of the mission from Hussey's first contact with Hillsborough in Apr. 1780 to his return to London, Oct. 1780.

TREASURY

In-letters and Files

TREASURY BOARD PAPERS

T. 1 BUNDLES 338–39, 423–26, 429–31, 433–43, 445–55, 463, 465–68, 471–72, 475, 479–80, 485–86, 491–92, 501, 521
46 boxes, 1763–83.   Transcripts and photostats.

1586   A variety of papers, for the most part chronologically arranged, including official materials concerning civil and military colonial expenses, duties and quit rents, trade, enforcement measures, and Indian affairs. Also merchant petitions and private reports on economic activities in the Colonies, correspondence from other Government departments, reports of American customs officials, proposals and plans for raising revenues, and accounts of colonial opposition to enforcement efforts. Bundles 463, 465–68, 471–72, 475, 479–80, 485–86, and 521 are complete.

Out-letters

VARIOUS

T. 28. VOLS. 1–2
4 boxes, 1763–83.   Photostats.

1587   Primarily commissions, instructions, and warrants for Crown-appointed colonial officials—Governors, judges, surveyors, naval officers, attorneys general, postmasters general, and various special appointees. The warrants concern contracts, salaries, allowances for civil establishments and for property seized or damaged, expenses of surveys, and distribution of prize money. During the war years letters directed to New York Vice-Admiralty Judge Robert Bayard and to military commanders pertain to ship captures and civil expenses in areas under British control. The photostats are complete through vol. 2, fol. 185.

Minutes

MINUTE BOOKS

T. 29. VOLS. 37–54
8 reels microfilm, 1765–84.

1588   Entry books of minutes of the Treasury Board recording the daily work of the Lords Commissioners of the Treasury, May 1765—Jan. 1784. The minutes contain a digest of business brought before the Board, in the form of memorials, reports, and letters from other departments of government and colonial officials, and a statement of action taken on each proposal or request.
See also Andrews, *Guide*, vol. 2, p. 211–12.

Miscellanea

VARIOUS

T. 64. VOLS. 45, 106–14, 116–20, 188, 276
3 reels microfilm, 3 boxes photostats, 1740–84.

1589   Vol. 45. Lists of fees collected by customs officers at more than 40 American ports from Newfoundland to Bermuda, 1764–71.
     See Andrews, *Guide*, vol. 2, p. 238.

Vols. 106–7. Entry books of letters from the Treasury to Generals Gage, Howe, Clinton, and Carleton, June 1774—Nov. 1783, and miscellaneous documents such as paymasters receipts, accounts of the military chests, and abstracts of provisions shipped.

Vols. 108–13. Entry books of letters received from Generals Howe, Clinton and Carleton, Nov. 1775—Jan. 1784, with numerous enclosures, including correspondence of American commanders with their supply officers, various accounts, returns and estimates, and detailed lists of "Warrants Issued for Extraordinaries."

Vol. 114. Letters of Commissary General Daniel Wier to the Treasury, Jan. 1778—Dec. 1779, with enclosures.
     See Andrews, *Guide*, vol. 2, p. 245.

Vols. 116–20. Correspondence of the Treasury with various commissaries regarding supplies for the army in America, including a register of letters received at the Treasury, 1778–82; out-letters to Anthony Merry, merchant of London, concerning the shipment of livestock to General Howe, Jan.—May 1776, and copies of correspondence with Commissaries Daniel Chamier, Daniel Wier, Peter Paumier, and Brook Watson, Apr. 1776—June 1783.
     See Andrews, *Guide*, vol. 2, p. 246.

Vol. 188. Law Officers' Opinions, 1763–83. Entry book of letters to the Lords Commissioners of the Treasury chiefly from the attorneys general and solicitors general: Yorke, Norton, De Grey, Willes, Dunning, Wedderburn, Wallace, Kenyon, Lee, and Arden. Opinions rendered on questions pertaining to America cover such issues as application of the acts of trade and navigation, collection of customs revenues, allowance of drawbacks, and imposition of duties at New York on prize goods during the war. The opinions often provide information on general problems of enforcement and colonial administration, including an affirmative opinion, Feb. 1770, on the legality of a Massachusetts tax on customs officers' fees. The volume contains a detailed index.
     See Andrews, *Guide*, vol. 2, p. 247.

Vol. 276. Detailed customs accounts of exports and imports to and from the Colonies drawn up as reports or statements pursuant to orders of the Treasury, 1740–79.
     See Andrews, *Guide*, vol. 2, p. 252–53.

Expired Commissions, etc.

AMERICAN LOYALIST CLAIMS COMMISSION

T. 79. 151 VOLUMES AND BUNDLES
30 reels, microfilm, 1777–1832.

1590   Consists of material concerning three commissions: the Loyalists Claims Commission of the 1780's; the commission appointed to settle debts covered by the 4th article of the 1783 Treaty of Paris and the 6th article of Jay's Treaty; and the commission appointed pursuant to the 1st article of the Anglo-American Convention of 1802. The papers of the first commission were utilized by the later commissions in their work during the 1790's and the first decade of the 19th century. As a result the records of the three commissions are not clearly designated.

See also A.O. 12, entry no. 1559; A.O. 13, entry no. 1560; and Proceedings of the Loyalist Claims Commissioners, entry no. 497.

TREASURY SOLICITOR AND H.M. PROCURATOR GENERAL

Treasury Solicitor and King's (Queen's) Proctor

PAPERS

T. S. 11. Bundle 3662. East Florida Claims
3 boxes, 1780–1820.   Photostats.

1591   Notes concerning loyalist claims in East Florida, chiefly depositions taken by the Commissioners on East Florida Claims, 1786–89. Miscellaneous items include a printed copy of the "Convention between His Britannick Majesty and the King of Spain," July 1786, a copy of the *South Carolina and American General Gazette*, Apr. 2, 1778, and an annotated "List of East Florida claimants who emigrated to the Revolted American States."

See Andrews, *Guide*, vol. 2, p. 268–69. See also A.O. 13, entry no. 1560.

Miscellaneous

WEST NEW JERSEY SOCIETY RECORDS

T. S. 12. Vols. 1–100
13 reels microfilm, 1675–1921.

1592   In-letters, entry books, and drafts of out-letters; minute books of meetings of the proprietors of the West New Jersey Society and of the society's "Committee"; maps, plans, charters, deeds, ledgers, and accounts; registers of transfer of shares; Joseph Payne's history of the society; and miscellaneous papers. Correspondence from the society's agents in America include letters from Lewis Johnston and John Smyth, 1760's, John Hunt, 1769–78, and Robert Morris of New Jersey (1745–1815), 1784–95. Material relating to the society's activities and interests during the Revolutionary era is located in volumes 1–2, 6–7, 17, 22–23, 25, 39, 51, 54–55, 57, 59–68, 73, 75–77, 82, 87.

WAR OFFICE

Correspondence

IN-LETTERS

W. O. 1, Vols. 1–14, 49, 683–84
11 boxes photostats, 4 reels microfilm, 1755–92.

1593   Vols. 1–14. Letters, with enclosures, from officers and officials in America to the Secretary at War concerning the management and condition of troops in America, i.e., rank disputes, discipline, vacancies, appointments, promotions, requests for leave, the disposition of troops, supply, housing, and internal disorders. The most frequently represented correspondents are Gen. John Burgoyne, Gov. Arthur Dobbs, Gen. Alexander Leslie, Lt. Col. Allan Maclean, Lt. Col. Henry Monckton, Gen. James Murray, Gen. James Paterson, Lord Rawdon, Colonel Pigot, and Gen. James Robertson. Also contains scattered letters from Generals Gage, Howe, Carleton, Clinton, and Haldimand regarding military engagements, Indian affairs, and the general state of affairs in the Colonies. Among the enclosures are returns of troops, casualties, and stores; lists of officers; pay abstracts; orders, memorials and petitions; accounts; warrants; and related items.

Vol. 49. Papers relating to the cession of West Florida, 1763–64. Includes material concerning the Spanish evacuation of Mobile, Oct. 1763—Feb. 1764; lists of inhabitants; embarkation returns; returns of ordnance; lists of Indian villages; communications with the Governor of Louisiana; and reports on forts in the province.

Vols. 683–84. Letters from the Secretaries of State and their under secretaries to the Secretary at War concerning military affairs in America, particularly the organization and disposition of troops during and after the Revolution. Enclosures include returns on troops and supplies, estimates on expenses, and pay abstracts.

OUT-LETTERS

W. O. 4. VOLS. 92–123, 273–75, 987–88
62 boxes, 1763–84.   Photostats.

1594   Vols. 92–123. Letters to officers in America concerning military appointments, vacancies, discharges, pay, and the shipment of troops, arms, and stores. Enclosures include lists of officers, a list of the Irish battalions, lists of arms needed, and estimates of the cost for augmentation of particular corps.

Vols. 273–75. Secretary Barrington's dispatches to Generals Gage, Howe, Clinton, Carleton, and Haldimand, and lesser officers concerning promotions, vacancies, transfers, supplies, leaves of absence, warrants for courts-martial, the disposition of troops, and the relocation of troops after the war.

Vols. 987–88. Includes occasional letters from America by Thomas Whately concerning routine military affairs. Supplements vols. 273–75.

Miscellanea

HEADQUARTERS RECORDS

W. O. 28. VOLS. 2–4, 10
5 boxes, 1775–1805.   Photostats.

1595   Vols. 2–3. Letters, with enclosures, from field officers in North America, 1777–83, concerning the state of defenses and condition of troops at various posts in New York, the northwest territory, and Canada; recommendations for promotions; requests for leaves of absence; and discharges, recruitment, and the purchase of officers. Enclosures include copies of speeches delivered to the Six Nations by the Americans, returns of prisoners, court-martial proceedings, and related items. Regiments represented are the 8th, 29th,

31st, 34th, 44th, 53d, and 84th. For a complete list of corresponding officers and regimental stations see Andrews, *Guide*, vol. 2, p. 291–92.

Vol. 4. Letters, officers' commissions, returns, pay bills, lists of officers, accounts, warrants, orders, musters, and papers concerning the recruitment and service of provincial troops. Among the units represented are Butler's Rangers, the Royal Highland Emigrants, Jessup's Loyal Rangers, the King's Loyal Americans, the Loyal Volunteers, Peter's Corps, McAlphine's Volunteers, and the King's Rangers.

Vol. 10. Miscellaneous returns, lists, and letters relating to provincial corps in Canada, 1775–83.

Private Collections

AMHERST PAPERS

W. O. 34. VOLS. 1–260
146 reels microfilm, 1712–84.

1596   Maj. Gen. Sir Jeffery Amherst (1717–97) succeeded Gen. James Abercromby as commander in chief in America, 1758–63. In 1792 he became commander in chief of all English forces, retaining the office until 1795. His papers contain material concerning Indian affairs, the regulation of troops in North America at the close of the French and Indian War, and the organization and maintenance of the army during the Revolution. Includes weekly and monthly troop returns, lists of officers, reports on defenses and battles, plans for campaigns in America and the West Indies, secret orders and instructions, correspondence with Germain and others in the Ministry on military policy and operations, and numerous documents concerning promotions, transfers, and vacancies. Also extracts and copies of letters from officers in America, petitions from merchants and customs officials in the West Indies requesting better protection, and a précis of correspondence from the American Department, 1779.

See Born, *British Manuscripts Project*, p. 59–77.

Royal Artillery Institution, Woolwich

JAMES PATTISON PAPERS
1 reel microfilm, 1777–81.

1597   Maj. Gen. Pattison (ca. 1723–1805), served as commandant of the city and garrison of New York, July 1779—Sept. 1780. His papers include a brigade order book for the Royal Artillery, Sept. 1777—Feb. 1778; general order book, Sept. 1777—Feb. 1778; register of appointments of warrant officers in the artillery in America, 1777–80; and bills of lading for ordnance stores shipped to America. Also a record of commissions, warrants, and appointments granted by Pattison; a daybook of the commandant's office, Oct. 1779—May 1780; orders concerning the government and administration of New York, May 1778—July 1779; and three letterbooks kept by Capt. Stephen Adye, Pattison's aide-de-camp, Oct. 1777—Jan. 1781, two of which have been printed in New York Historical Society *Collections,* vol. 8 (1875).

Available from Micro Methods, Ltd.

Royal Courts of Justice

ADMIRALTY. REGISTRY (MUNIMENT BOOKS). VOL. 10
1 folio, 1768–71.　　　　　Transcripts.
1598　　Contains letters patent granted to Governor Botetourt for the office of Vice Admiral of Virginia, Aug. 1768, and to Governor Dunmore for the same office, Feb. 1771.

Royal Society (Burlington House)

LETTERS AND PAPERS COLLECTION
1 box, 1765–85.　　　　　Photostats.
1599　　Selected items include a brief account of an experiment with electricity by Dr. Joseph Priestley, 1768, and a description of the entrance of the Mississippi River by Lt. John Blankett [or Blake] of His Majesty's Navy, enclosed with a letter from Philip Aubry, June 1765.

Royal Society of Arts

SERIES B. THE AMERICAN CORRESPONDENCE
2 reels microfilm, 1755–1840.
1600　　Correspondence of the society with over 40 Americans interested in the encouragement of arts, manufacture, and commerce, early 1770's. Among the particular topics discussed are the production of important raw materials such as silk, naval stores, potash, vines and indigo. Also proceedings of the society meetings, 1754–57; minutes of committees, 1758–70; "Manuscript transactions," 1770–76; and letters.

Principal correspondents: Francis Bernard, William Bull, Cadwallader Colden, Thomas Cushing, James Duane, Lewis Evans, Francis Fauquier, Benjamin Franklin, Benjamin Gale, Alexander Garden, Charles Garth, Jared Ingersoll, Philip Livingston, Philip Schuyler, Philip Skene, William Tryon, John Wentworth, and Charles Woodmason.

Correspondence available from Micro Methods, Ltd.

United Society for the Propagation of the Gospel

SERIES B. VOLS. 1–25
25 reels microfilm, 1701–1800.
1601　　Consists largely of original letters and documents from missionaries, would-be missionaries, church wardens, and civil officials in British colonies in North America and the West Indies concerning work among Germans, Indians, and Negroes; shortages of equipment; vacancies resulting from deaths and dismissals; breaches of conduct among the clergy; the use of property owned by or willed to the Society; and sundry related matters. Letters of Anglican clergymen in the American Colonies written shortly before and during the war consist primarily of accounts of personal suffering and restrictions placed on clerical activities, petitions for relief or continuance of salaries, and general war news.

SERIES C. BOXES 1–16
1 reel microfilm, 1630–1811.
1602　　Miscellaneous unbound manuscripts relating to the American Colonies, 1630–1811. The Library has selections from box 9, about 80 letters concerning religious affairs in Georgia, 1758–82.

SERIES X. PACKAGES 1–13
25 reels microfilm, 1773–1833.

1603   Packages 1–7 (17 reels) contain letters and documents from the period of the American Revolution, chiefly reports on the progress of missionary work; certificates, testimonials, petitions, and appeals for additional support; accounts, receipts, and bills of exchange; reports of suffering as a result of the war; appeals for continued support from aging missionaries desiring to remain in America; and documents concerning the transfer of S.P.G. property to the Episcopal Church in America during the postwar period. This material has been reorganized since it was filmed. It probably belongs in Series C but should be ordered as American Colonies, Packages 1–7. A volume by volume index showing correspondents, persons mentioned, petitions and signers of petitions, and miscellaneous items is available (1 reel).

JOURNALS AND MINUTES OF THE SOCIETY AND ITS COMMITTEES
76 reels microfilm, 1701–1833.

1604   Includes abstracts of letters received. Volumes 23–25, 1783–92, contain a record of incoming correspondence, decisions on requests from missionaries, and treasury and auditor reports (3 reels). The minutes of the meetings of the standing (executive) committee contain essentially the same information as the journals. The Library has copies of vols. 28–49, 1757–82 (3 reels).

ACCOUNTS AND ACCOUNT BOOKS. PART G
3 boxes, 1745–85.   Photostats.

1605   Contains records of payments to missionaries, many of whom worked in the American Colonies before the war.

MANUSCRIPTS OF DR. BRAY'S ASSOCIATES
5 boxes, 1695–1808.   Photostats.

1606   For a full description of material relating to the Revolution see Andrews and Davenport, *Guide*, p. 334–35.

Archdiocese of Westminster

ARCHIVES
1 folio, 1763–84.   Transcripts.

1607   Selections from the archives of the diocese pertaining to the Catholic church in North America and the West Indies, including documents pertaining to mission activities in territories ceded to Britain in 1763, and lists of missionaries in the West Indies, Maryland, and Pennsylvania. Also an estimate of the number of Roman Catholics in Maryland and Pennsylvania; petitions for assistance to erect a place of worship in Nova Scotia, 1782; a letter of John Thayer of Boston proposing to return to New England to teach the Catholic faith, 1784; and a letter appointing John Carroll as bishop in the United States, 1784. Three of the 10 documents are in Latin.

NORTHUMBERLAND, *Alnwick Castle*

MANUSCRIPTS OF THE DUKES OF NORTHUMBERLAND. VOLS. 34–56
13 reels microfilm, 1763–88.

1608   Volumes 34–48 and 53–56 concern the career of Hugh Smithson Percy, 1st Duke of Northumberland (1715–86). During the early 1760's when he was lord lieutenant of Ireland, Barrington, Bedford, Halifax, Sandwich, and Shelburne were among his correspondents. In the next decade, when he played a more prominent political role, his correspondents included Bute, Camden, Hardwicke, Newcastle, North, Pitt, Rochford, Temple, Weymouth, Thomas Townshend, and Joseph Yorke.

Volumes 49–52 pertain to the activities of Hugh Earl Percy, 2d Duke of Northumberland (1742–1817). In addition to correspondence associated with General Percy's military career at Boston, New York, and Newport, the papers "relating to the American War" include a 75–page British journal of the siege of Quebec, Nov. 1775—May 1776; a 65-page journal of a Connecticut Quaker schoolmaster who was seized by the Americans for suspected Tory activities, Feb.—Mar. 1777; an "Account of the Institution of the Society of, Cincinnati in America, May 10—June 19, 1783"; and Percy's numerous letters home, of which those written from Boston and New York were published in Charles K. Bolton, ed., *Letters of Hugh Earl Percy . . . 1774–1776* (Boston, 1902). Also contains intelligence reports, 1775–77, several maps and sketches, and numerous letters from Sir Henry Clinton, who frequently confided in Percy on the conduct of the war. After Percy returned to England in 1777, he frequently received letters from officers and friends reporting on the progress of the war, notably Henry Barry, William Bayard, John Campbell, J. Ferguson, George Harris, George Hutchinson, Stephen Kemble, John Kinnon, Richard Molesworth, Robert Pigot, Cortlandt Skinner, Lionel Smythe, and F. Thorne.

See Born, *British Manuscripts Project*, p. 83–84.

NOTTINGHAMSHIRE, Nottingham, *University of Nottingham*

PORTLAND MANUSCRIPTS
1 folio, 1767–81.   Photostats.

1609   Consists of letters to William Bentinck, 3d Duke of Portland (1738–1809), discussing political developments in the context of American affairs. Letters from the Marquis of Rockingham are dated Sept. 17, 1767, Jan. 31, 1775, Mar. 4 and Nov. 5, 1777; and a letter from Edmund Burke is dated Nov. 12, 1781.

STAFFORDSHIRE, Stafford, *Sandon Hall*

HARROWBY PAPERS. VOL. 94
1 reel microfilm, 1765–66.

1610   Consists of typewritten transliterations of shorthand notes of parliamentary debates taken by Nathaniel Ryder, 1st Baron Harrowby. The original notes form documents 61–65 preserved by the Harrowby Manuscripts Trust. The transliterations were prepared by Dr. K. L. Perrin for Prof. Lawrence H. Gipson, who permitted the Library to microfilm them.

See Gipson's article, "The Great Debate in the Committee of the Whole House of Commons on the Stamp Act, 1766, as Reported by Nathaniel Ryder," *Pennsylvania Magazine of History and Biography*, vol. 86 (Jan. 1962), p. 10–41.

Scotland

LANARKSHIRE, Glasgow, *University of Glasgow*

HUNTERIAN MANUSCRIPTS
1 box, 1775–89.   Photostats.
1611   Contains a letter of Benjamin Franklin to Dr. Richard Price concerning an edict by the King of France for the establishment of a new sinking fund, 1784; a letter from George Washington to John Marshall, 1789; and a contemporary copy of a journal kept by a soldier on Benedict Arnold's expedition to Quebec, 1775.

MIDLOTHIAN, Dalkeith, *Dalkeith House*

BUCCLEUCH AND QUEENSBERRY MUNIMENTS. TOWNSHEND PAPERS
3 reels microfilm, 1735–67.
1612   Selections primarily concern the work of Charles Townshend as an officeholder, 1765–67, especially during his chancellorship, 1766–67. Consists of letters from the War Office concerning estimates of expenses for the army in America, financial papers relating to excise duties, proposals for regulating trade, observations on American affairs, extracts of papers pertaining to the Stamp Act crisis, and petitions, accounts, and reports containing information on the development of British colonial policy in the 1760's.
        Available from Micro Methods, Ltd. See also Crick and Almon, *Guide to Manuscripts*, p. 502–3.

Edinburgh, *National Library of Scotland*

MS. 119. CHARLES STRACHAN LETTERBOOK
1 reel microfilm, 1763–76.
1613   The correspondence of Strachan, a Scottish merchant trading in America, is almost exclusively commercial in nature and contains information on the activities of Scottish traders in the Floridas, Georgia, and South Carolina. Also contains letters, 1770–76, written from Kinnaber, Strachan's estate in Scotland, concerning his experiences with Indians in the region around Mobile and with Spanish and French traders.
        Principal correspondents: John Beswicke & Co., Dunbar, Young & Simpson, Greenwood & Higginson, Thomas Hardy, David Hodge, Johnson & Wylly, John Owen, Mr. Petit (New Orleans), and William Telfair.

ALEXANDER HOUSTOUN AND COMPANY LETTERBOOKS
3 reels microfilm, 1776–81.
1614   Three letterbooks of the Glasgow firm Alexander Houstoun and Company, which carried on an extensive American trade. Books "E" and "F," Mar. 1776—June 1781, contain letters directed to firms, agents, and ship captains in Antigua, Dominica, Grenada,

Jamaica, Nevis, St. Christopher, St. Croix, St. Vincent, Tobago, and Cork. Book "H" contains letters to merchants and firms in England and Scotland who were engaged in business with the company.

STUART STEVENSON PAPERS. Ms. 5375
1 reel microfilm, 1776–77.
1615   Letters of Maj. Charles Cochrane. Includes two letters to Andrew Stuart, Mar. 1776, Oct. 1777, containing Cochrane's observations on the war in America and four letters which fell into British hands: Robert R. Livingston to Alexander Hamilton, June 6 and Aug. 2, 1777; Hamilton to Livingston, Aug. 7, 1777; and Gouverneur Morris to Hamilton, July 4, 1777.

Scottish Record Office

CUNINGHAME OF THORTON PAPERS. Mss. 489–98
1 reel microfilm, 1771–82.
1616   Primarily documents pertaining to the career of Lt. John Peebles of the 42d Regiment. Includes a few letters to his father, 1771–81, miscellaneous returns and accounts pertaining to Peebles' company, and 13 journals maintained by Peebles from the beginning of his voyage to America in Apr. 1776 to his departure for England in Mar. 1782. The journals, which are continuous except for the period Nov. 1778—Apr. 1779, contain extensive material on the military campaigns of the war.

Yugoslavia

Dubrovnik, *Historijski Arhiv*

FRANCESCO FAVI PAPERS
5 reels microfilm, 1774–99.

1617   Letters and reports of Francesco Favi, diplomatic agent of the Republic of Ragusa (Dubrovnik) in Paris. Favi's letters and reports are in Italian, but copies of letters by Marquis de Castries, 1781, 1785, and Vergennes, 1783, 1786, are in French. During the period of the Revolution (reels 1–3) Favi kept his Government well informed on troops and arms sent to America, the progress of the war, political developments in France and England, and peace negotiations.

Index to Repositories

Subject Index

New York, 1079
Pennsylvania, 148, 964
Rhode Island, 446
South Carolina, 139, 1011
Virginia, 350, 1003
Leach, Thomas, 108
Lear, Susan, **415**
Lear, Tobias, 471, 1039
Lebanon, Conn., 457, 1303
Leckie, Alexander, 202
Le Couteulx & Co., 819
"Lectures on Universal History, 1787-1788," 1076
Ledyard, Isaac, 844
Ledyard, William, 1081
Lee, Arthur, 94, 107, 190, 209, 246, 288, 348, 364, **481**, 483, 485, 532, 680, 971, 1031, 1052, 1076, 1084, 1135, 1165, 1192, 1210, 1274, 1373
Lee, Charles, 198, 286, 312, 317, 482-483, 493, 532, 819, 894, 1054
Lee, Francis Lightfoot, **1031**
Lee, Hanna Ludwell, 681, 683, 693
Lee, Henry, 136, 191, 279, 317, 482, 484-485, 601, 634, 825, 1060, 1095
Lee, John, 1589
Lee, Joseph, 305
Lee, Ludwell, 1031
Lee, Richard, 203, 833
Lee, Richard, Jr., 485
Lee, Richard Bland, 202, **482**
Lee, Richard Henry, 107, 161, 257, 322, 333, 340, 482, 484, 680, 682, 817, 1004, 1031, 1076, 1088, 1094, 1105, 1118, 1569
Lee, Thomas, 202-203, 268, 344, 483
Lee, Thomas Sim, 311, 485, 513, 581, 655, 749, 1282
Lee, William, 94, 107, 288, 333, 482, 683, 826, 1192, 1210, 1274
Lee, William R., **1042**
Lee family, **483-484**
Lee-Palfrey Papers, **486**
Leech, Nathan, 524
Leeds, John, 160
Leeds, Va., 1057
Lees, John, 1365
Legal records
  Connecticut, 88, 205, 1103, 1116
  Georgia, 31, 145, 289, 294
  Kentucky, 466, 499, 1025
  Maryland, 181, 186, 251, 258, 284, 517, 784, 1085
  Massachusetts, 90, 108, 151, 225, 374, 457, 471, 488, 528, 969, 1021, 1068, 1111, 1125
  New Hampshire 140, 463, 969
  New Jersey, 414, 839, 959
  New York, 319, 464, 491-492, 818, 821, 844, 851, 1097, 1103, 1119, 1529
  North Carolina, 865, 969, 978, 1472, 1554
  Pennsylvania, 2, 124, 148, 176, 505, 810, 860, 963-964, 966, 1039
  Rhode Island, 999

  South Carolina, 309, 495, 971, 1478
  Vermont, 1103
  Virginia, 24, 110, 115, 355, 367, 656, 854, 969, 986, 988, 994, 999, 1004, 1025, 1035, 1087, 1104-1105
  miscellaneous mentions, 263, 272
Legal works, 1000
Legislative records
  Early State Records Microfilm Collection, 252
  Peter Force Historical Manuscripts, 272
Legra, J. M. T., 1032
Le Griffon, D., 339
Legros, J. M. P., 190
Le Havre, France, 1162
Leigh, Sir Egerton, 1434
Leitch, Andrew, 355
Leland, John, 183
Leland, Joseph, 202
Le Marseillais, 1146
Lemonnier, Pierre Charles, 1175
L'Enfant, Pierre, 136, **243**
Leonard Town, Md., 44, 303
Le Palmier, 1204
Le Pléiade, 1204
Le Ray de Chaumont. *See* Chaumont
Le Robuste, 379
Le Roy, Herman, **1273**
Le Roy, Jean Baptiste, 275, 1176
Leslie, Alexander, 311, 971, 1432, 1471, 1577, 1593
Leslie, Samuel, 272
"Les Vâches Américaines," 1176
Letombe, Philip-André-Joseph de, 1150, 1193
Letters of marque, 1430, 1531
Lettsom, John C., 1073
Le Veillard, Louis, 275
Leverett, John & Co., 1039
Leveson, Gower, 684
Levy, Andrew, 148
Levy, Eleazar, 1322
Lewis, Andrew, 178, 277, 986, 1004, 1338, 1419
Lewis, Asa, 487
Lewis, Betty, 685
Lewis, Charles, 986
Lewis, Francis, 161, 286, 322, 847-848, 850
Lewis, George, 178
Lewis, John, **487**
Lewis, John Z., 49
Lewis, Mordecai & Co., 494
Lewis, Morgan, 304, 686
Lewis, Robert, 49, 1076
Lewis, Thomas, 988
Lewis, William, 1298
Lexington, 193
Lexington, Ky., 960
L'Experiment, 1204
Leyborne, William L., 1387
L'Hommedieu, Ezra, 197, 343
Liberty, 1400
Lidell, George, 898
Light, John, 73
Lightfoot, Thomas, 202

ADVISORY COMMITTEE
Library of Congress American Revolution Bicentennial Program

JOHN R. ALDEN
James B. Duke Professor of History, Duke University

JULIAN P. BOYD
Editor of The Papers of Thomas Jefferson, *Princeton University*

LYMAN H. BUTTERFIELD
Editor of The Adams Papers, *Massachusetts Historical Society*

JACK P. GREENE
Professor of History, The Johns Hopkins University

MERRILL JENSEN
Vilas Research Professor of History, University of Wisconsin

CECELIA M. KENYON
Charles N. Clark Professor of Government, Smith College

AUBREY C. LAND
Research Professor of History, University of Georgia

EDMUND S. MORGAN
Sterling Professor of History, Yale University

RICHARD B. MORRIS
Gouverneur Morris Professor of History, Emeritus, Columbia University

GEORGE C. ROGERS, JR.
Yates Snowden Professor of American History, University of South Carolina

☆ U.S. GOVERNMENT PRINTING OFFICE: 1975 O——470-503